15. 00

D1084251

ORGANIZED CIVIL SERVANTS

ORGANIZED

UNIVERSITY OF CALIFORNIA PRESS
Berkeley   Los Angeles   London

Public Employer-Employee Relations in California

CIVIL SERVANTS

by WINSTON W. CROUCH

University of California Press
Berkeley and Los Angeles, California

University of California Press, Ltd.
London, England

Copyright © 1978 by The Regents of the University of California
ISBN: 0-520-03626-3
Library of Congress Catalog Card Number: 77-91767

Printed in the United States of America

TO LOIS,
ardent supporter of the conscientious public servant

CONTENTS

PREFACE

Two subjects that have figured prominently in my research and teaching interests over a considerable number of years have been combined in this book. State and local government, in which my interest was whetted by field experience while a graduate student at Claremont Graduate School and the University of California, Berkeley, has been the central subject in my university teaching experience. An interest in public personnel policy and administration, seeded by a graduate seminar, flowered later when I had an opportunity to serve as a member of the Los Angeles County Civil Service Commission. During twelve years on that commission and eight additional years on the Los Angeles Community College District Personnel Commission, I have known many elected officials, personnel administrators, management officers, union and association representatives, and hundreds of civil servants. Participation in professional associations, academic and government-oriented, has broadened my perspectives. Attracted by the growth of public employee organizations and the campaigns by state and local employees to achieve legislation to permit collective bargaining, I have sought to analyze the factors involved in those processes. As an academic political scientist, I have used the analytical tools, concepts, and concerns in vogue in my field. I have not attempted to employ the approaches that specialists in industrial relations or labor law might have used.

Implementation of this research interest has been made possible by a grant from the John Randolph Haynes and Dora Haynes Foundation of Los Angeles, a charitable and educational trust devoted to aiding the study of public affairs affecting California and the Los Angeles region. The trustees of this foundation had no part in formulating the study's research design. They are not responsible for the conclusions or opinions expressed in the book. Similarly, the University of California, through which the grant was administered, bears no responsibility for the opinions expressed herein. The author, though aided by many persons, is responsible.

I appreciate the work of several research assistants, who gave invaluable aid at several stages of the work, particularly Monty Brice, Ann Cowden, H. George Frederickson, Robert Giordano, Richard Harris, Mustafa Rejai, and Alan Saltzstein. All have established careers in government-related fields since aiding this project. Jean Brice and Beverly Stewart, formerly of the Bureau of Government Research, and numerous members of the UCLA central stenographic bureau gave capable assistance in the preparation of the manuscript. Charles Nixon and John Bollens, colleagues in the Political Science Department, gave helpful advice. The former kindly read a draft of chapter four. Robert Zachary and James Kubeck of the University of California Press have been very helpful in preparing the manuscript for publication.

Special gratitude is due my wife, Lois Kimbrough Crouch, a past state president of the League of Women Voters and an officer of the California Federation of Women's Clubs. Without her steadfast support and encouragement, this book could not have been completed. Although busy with her own activities, she noted and clipped information, alerted me to sources, and read and commented on most of the manuscript, all of which benefited me greatly.

Pacific Palisades, California   Winston W. Crouch
December 1977

I

INTRODUCTION: ORGANIZED EMPLOYEES DEMAND TO PARTICIPATE IN POLICY MAKING

A bruising election battle at the 1964 convention of the American Federation of State, County, and Municipal Employees Union symbolizes the dramatic change of attitude that has taken place among a considerable portion of state and local government employees toward employer-employee relations since 1960. The union replaced its founder-president, Arnold Zander of Wisconsin, who had consistently maintained a low public profile, supported merit system policies, and counseled against strikes, with Jerry Wurf, the New York district director, who aggressively advocated that employing governments bargain with their employees on every subject of employment policy and that civil servants strike in support of their demands.

THE NEW MILITANCY

During the decade of the 1960's national attention was drawn to the new, aggressively stated demands by several public employee organizations to participate in employment policy making. The first major occasion was in 1964, when the nation saw New York City residents walk to work while flamboyant Mike Quill, the transit workers' union president, directed striking workers from a city jail cell. Soon after, the teachers' union struck the New York public schools. The union president, Albert Shanker, was sent to jail and the organization was fined for violating a court order. John J. DeLurey and his Uniformed Sanitationmen's Association refused to haul away the city's waste until they received satisfactory terms from the municipal employer, thereby causing extensive disruptions in the life-style of New York metropolitan inhabitants.

1

The events were not confined to one area. Fire fighters' union locals in Atlanta and Kansas City defied their national leadership and staged so-called job actions. A militant element in the International Fire Fighters Association caused that union's 1968 convention to delete the no-strike clause from the forty-nine-year-old union constitution. State teachers' associations in Florida and Utah, affiliates of the independent National Education Association, led mass refusals of teaching contracts until employment policies and salary levels were changed. The NEA previously had opposed work disruptions in schools.

REACTIONS IN SOME STATES

These events exposed a woeful lack of public policy and of administrative technique to cope with problems thrust upon elected and appointed state and local officers by large, aggressive, innovative groups of public employees. Although civil servants in many communities had been organized for as long as fifty years, public attitudes about how such organizations should fit into the political and administrative systems were hazy in the 1960's, and official policies were fragmentary or nonexistent. Demands from organized public employees to participate in making decisions relating to conditions of employment and compensation caused administrators, political leaders, and scholars to reassess sharply the attitudes, concepts, doctrines, and relationships involved in administering public programs. Official reaction was more immediate in some jurisdictions than in others.

Legislation proposed by a New York state commission appointed by Governor Rockefeller set a framework within which a state board began to develop supervision of state and local labor relations.[1] The city of New York was exempt, however, from the jurisdiction of this board and was permitted to establish its own machinery and procedures.

Some other states, notably Michigan, Wisconsin, Connecticut, and Rhode Island, rushed to adopt legislation patterned on the national industrial labor relations legislation established by the Wagner Act of 1935. These states, the first to adopt this type of legislation, were ones in which the two major political parties contested sharply and continuously for control of state and local governments. Executive officers at both the state and local level were elected on partisan lines and a relatively small proportion of the top administrators were career professionals. Organized labor was also strongly influential in making public policy at both local and state levels. Conventional civil service procedures had been adopted by the states of New York, Michigan, and Wisconsin, but were not widely used among local governments. Moreover, several of the other states that first adopted labor relations legislation had relatively little experience with civil service in their public work forces.

REACTIONS IN CALIFORNIA

California developed its policies relative to public employer-employee relations at a different pace, addressing a number of policy concerns not emphasized by those states that rushed to establish the private sector model of collective bargaining in their public employment systems. Although employee organizations are not new phenomena in California politics, their openly aggressive action against public employers is of recent date. For sixty years the organized civil servants have relied heavily on lobbying legislative bodies, executives, and administrative commissions, appealing to the electorate through initiative petitions, and litigating in the courts to enforce rights won through these procedures. Several public employee groups created such institutions as merit employment and retirement systems. Their methods of conducting relationships prior to the 1960's seldom drew the attention of the news media. The confrontation tactics and the advocacy of collective negotiations, appearing during the 1960's in California public employment, as in other states, brought about as traumatic a reassessment of attitudes and relationships within the public employee organizations as it did within the employing institutions.

The California legislature and local governing boards have wrestled extensively with the complex problems of labor relations. Study commissions have been appointed and reported. The judiciary has been presented with a flood of cases concerning the right to organize, the right to strike, rights and procedures in compensation setting, and the rights of employee representatives. Policies have emerged slowly, and an effort will be made in this book to ascertain reasons for California's deliberate pace with respect to public employer-employee relations compared to other populous, urban, high income, and largely industrialized states. Advocacy of such procedures as collective bargaining and arbitration of interest disputes has been nationwide in scope.

This book is an analysis of the development within the California political system of public policies concerning government employer-employee relations. It proposes to examine the major groups and institutions that have been involved in bringing about this development. It is a study of the politics of public administration, concerning itself with matters that affect the employment and compensation of members of the bureaucracy, the allocation of power and responsibility between top appointed administrative officers and elected officials, and the roles performed by managers, supervisors, workers, and political leaders in governmental bureaucracies. Occasional reference will be made to administrative organization theory.[2]

Allocation of public resources among programs, groups, and activities falls within the broader scope of this book, which will examine the development of a public employer-employee relations policy in the context of the political system of a large, populous, relatively wealthy, and complex state. Groups of persons, including public employee unions and associations, taxpayer associations, industrial trade unions, chambers of commerce, other industrial and professional associations, and political parties, communicate their demands on the state's political system through the various avenues provided by the political process. Authoritative institutions, such as the legislature, the governor and his associates in the executive branch, the courts, and the bureaucracy, transform those demands into outputs of public policy embodied in multitudinous statutes, executive orders, and judicial or administrative decisions and rulings.[3]

The analytical concept employed in this book places the local governments within the larger frame of the state political system. The 58 counties, 411 cities, 1394 school districts, and more than 800 special districts might be considered, in one sense, to be separate decision-making entities when they employ work forces to implement their programs, but they are also local governmental subdivisions of the state of California. The state has given them legal life, and the state legislative process constantly places new constraints on their actions. Hence, they are parts of the state political system.

The concept must be pushed still further. In a broad sense, political rather than legal, the state and its local units comprise integral parts of one interrelating system. No unit operates completely independently of the others. Some compensation decisions, particularly those made by the larger employing entities, cause immediate reactions among employees in many other units. Employment policy transactions made within the particular legal and political constraints of one jurisdiction become known to persons in the other agencies and provide either models or warnings for the latter's decisions. The state's political system is, therefore, an important part of the framework within which this book's analysis is pursued.

Students of policies made by state governments have been challenged by a paradox in which the fifty states possess similar formal political institutions but produce policies that vary widely, whether the subject be publicly supported education, taxation, treatment of the poor, or public employment. Some political scientists have sought to explain the differences in state policy output by focusing primarily on the state political parties and the contests between the two major parties to control the institutions of government.[4] More recently, students of state politics have broadened the array of variables they employ to examine state policy output.[5] Some have used population density, personal income, degree of urbanization, and industrialization as their major analytical variables. Others seek, by using statistical data, to compare the states' performances in one or more subject areas.[6] Some confine their comparisons to a few states, testing a set of hypotheses against data drawn from selected samples.[7]

A good bit of the literature about state government and policy output is made up of case studies, however, particularly since the study of states has moved away from the previous, overwhelming reliance on descriptions of institutional structure. Gathering data about the actual operations of numerous governments is an enormous and intricate task that is apt to defy the resources of most individual scholars or small research teams.[8] The remarks of Professor Duane Lockard with respect to case studies gives some perspective to this method:

Case studies serve, however, two significant purposes: they provide sustaining evidence to illustrate generalizations made elsewhere, and they emphasize the importance of the operational as opposed to the formal side of government.[9]

This book is primarily a study of one, albeit the most populous, state in the union. It seeks to examine in some depth the factors that have influenced the development of public employer-employee relations policies in this state, which employs a large number of persons in its administrative agencies. In 1972, the California state government employed 199,914 full-time equivalent employees, and 125 local governments had 1,000 or more persons on their payrolls (see table 1).[10] The state ranked first among the states and the District of Columbia in total state and local employees and in public payrolls.[11] It ranked nineteenth, however, in the number of state and local employees per 10,000 population.

Statistics showing the percentage of state and local employees belonging to unions or associations are difficult to assemble because the basic data is held by a large number of sources, many of which are reluctant to provide accurate data. Most published data on this subject, moreover, is not broken down by states. A very limited estimate of the percentage of California municipal employees belonging to organizations can be drawn from data gathered from 1533 cities by the International City Management Association in a nationwide survey in 1970.[12] The data were categorized by regions rather than by states, but they showed that eight-nine percent of municipal

Table 1

Distribution of Full-Time Equivalent Employees
Among California Local Government Work Forces, 1972

Number in Work Force	Counties		Municipalities		Special Districts		School Districts		Total	
	No.	%	No.	%	No.	%	No.	%	No.	%
Less than 50	1	2	162	40	2,111	95	501	44	2,775	73
50-99	2	3	66	16	43	2	134	12	245	6
100-199	2	3	76	19	33	2	138	12	249	7
200-399	12	21	48	12	10	—	136	12	206	5
400-599	6	11	24	6	13	1	77	7	120	3
600-799	4	7	10	2	3	—	45	4	62	2
800-999	4	7	2	—	4	—	27	2	37	1
1,000 or more	26	46	19	5	6	—	74	7	125	3
Total	57	100	407	100	2,223	100	1,132	100	3,819	100

Source: U.S. Bureau of the Census, *Census of Governments*, vol. 3, no. 2, *Compendium of Employment* (1972).

employees in the Northeast were members of unions or associations, whereas fifty-eight percent of those in the West (including California), fifty-seven percent in the North Central area, and thirty percent of those in the South were members.

A principal theme or generalization, in Lockard's term, which this book seeks to substantiate is that the making of public policy is bound to follow an incremental process when it involves so complex a set of changes as the adoption of collective bargaining in a state and local government employment system previously committed to civil service procedures. Much of legislative action is, of course, incremental in nature. The approach taken in this book, however, reflects to a limited extent the influence of decision theories expounded by Charles A. Lindblom.[13] In an article in the *Public Administration Review*, Lindblom remarks that decision making is ordinarily formalized as a means-ends relationship: means are conceived to be evaluated and chosen in the light of ends selected independently of and prior to the choice of means. Such a means-ends relationship is possible only to the extent that values are agreed upon, are reconcilable, and are stable at the margin. This relationship is absent from any method where means and ends are chosen simultaneously.[14]

In *A Strategy of Decision: Policy Evaluation as a Social Process*, Lindblom and David Braybrooke discuss several strategies of decision making and policy evaluation.[15] One is the synoptic or rational-deductive approach, suited to an analysis of policy decision that takes a stand on fixed principles.[16] Another is the disjointed incremental approach, which proceeds through a sequence of approximations. A policy is directed at a problem; it is tried, altered, tried in its altered form, altered again, and perhaps again. Incremental policies follow one upon the other in the solution of a given problem.[17] The authors contend that the characteristics of the strategy encourage the analyst to identify situations or ills from which to move away rather than goals toward which to move. In the diagram on page 8 they distinguish these two approaches from other forms:[18]

Once California governments had adopted a civil service personnel system rooted in the principles of the merit system, decision making on personnel policy was largely administrative (quadrant 2). It was treated as a series of technical problems to be decided within the framework of principles identified as the merit system.[19] The public was seldom involved and knew little about the decisions made. When organized civil servants began to make demands on the state political system to adopt collective bargaining, arbitration, and related procedures for the public employment, they were met by a policy-making response that resembled disjointed incrementalism (quadrant 3). There has been virtually no agreement concerning

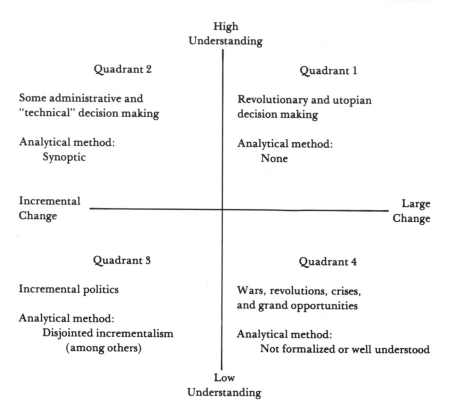

High
Understanding

Quadrant 2

Some administrative and
"technical" decision making

Analytical method:
    Synoptic

Quadrant 1

Revolutionary and utopian
decision making

Analytical method:
    None

Incremental
Change

Large
Change

Quadrant 3

Incremental politics

Analytical method:
    Disjointed incrementalism
        (among others)

Quadrant 4

Wars, revolutions, crises,
and grand opportunities

Analytical method:
    Not formalized or well understood

Low
Understanding

values or goals in the public employment field. The strategists who have
sought to make the changes have not been consistent in their selection of
means to accomplish what they have publicly identified as their goals.
Those who have challenged them can sometimes agree with them on a specific settlement in a particular episode without agreeing with them on the
underlying values involved. The policies the political system has produced
have been directed at a series of problems. They have been tried, altered,
and tried again, then altered again. The consequences of the proposed
changes have not been well understood by the parties involved in deciding
the course of change. Steps taken in the continuum of policy decisions have
seemed to follow the demonstrated consequences. This process has been
called by some observers a learning experience, in which the officials who
perform the key roles as public employers and the leaders and members of
public employee organizations have learned by experience the consequences of the changes that have been advocated. In the same way, groups

outside the bureaucracy have discovered what the consequences of adoption of collective bargaining in public employment are for them, in terms of tax demands and impact on other programs funded from the general tax budgets. Consequently, the policy-making process has become highly political and has involved continuous interaction between an increasingly large number of groups.

In practice, collective bargaining in public employment shows that changes in structure, as well as in procedures and bureaucratic relationships, take place. Some of the changes affect legislative-executive relations, a subject which is undergoing constant analysis and change throughout most governments in the United States. Some involve structural changes within the administrative agencies. Most of the affected governmental structures were created originally in response to demands not related to public employment issues. Proposals to institute collective bargaining, to change these structures to accommodate recent demands in the public employment field, cause additional groups in the political system to become concerned. The problems involved in the public employment policy changes, therefore, have proven to be far more complex than many at first perceived them to be.

On a less lofty level of conceptualization, this book seeks to present evidence about how the state of California has attempted to deal, in practice as well as in formal policy making, with three areas of tension in the public service. Foremost is the matter of the tension between the civil service system and the proponents of the collective bargaining method of determining compensation and working conditions. Questions being debated are: Will collective bargaining displace the civil service as the system in which public employment policies are to be decided? Does each system possess values and satisfy needs to such an extent that both will be retained in modified form, thereby resulting in some new form of public employment policy system?

Associated with this tension area, but possessing its own stratifications, is the tension that exists between those who contend that the state should adopt a single, comprehensive statement of policy applicable to all public employees and those who prefer separate statutes and administrative systems applicable to the public schools, the state universities and colleges, the remainder of the state government, and the local governments. Most states have experienced this tension to some degree. The subject is a major part of the California story.

A third area of tension arises from the struggle to choose a plan that encompasses all government employers and their employees in California, in which the machinery for decision making and dispute settlement is primarily dominated by the state, and in which local government-employers have a considerable degree of freedom to make decisions in conjunction with their organized employees. All states face this state-local tension in a variety of government operations. When they consider the demands of organized public employees to establish collective bargaining and related methods of employment dispute resolution, however, they experience an increased tension. This subject, also, is a major part of the California story.

In chapters two and three, the public employee organizations that aggregate and present the demands of the civil servants are examined. Chapter four seeks to explore both formal and informal aspects of the California state political system that have influenced the development of public policy concerning public employer-employee relations. It also looks at the public employers. In chapter five, changes in public policy concerning the political rights of public employees are examined. First, the limitations enumerated during the period in which the civil service system developed are considered. This is followed by an inquiry into the legislative and judicial actions that removed most of these restrictions and prepared the way for public employees, acting individually and through organizations, to use political action in pursuit of chosen goals, including the adoption of collective bargaining and the exercise of influence over the decisions concerning their compensation and working conditions. Chapter six recounts the series of actions that produced explicit legislative and judicial statements recognizing the right of public employees to organize for the purpose of making demands about wages and working conditions. Chapter seven examines the principal political methods employed by organized civil servants in California, and considers some of the consequences of these actions. Chapter eight traces the history of efforts to obtain an expression of state policy regarding strikes by public employees, and presents some case studies of local government that have dealt with a strike within the framework of the existing state policies. Chapter nine traces the legislative history of proposals to establish a state policy governing public employer-employee relations and draws conclusions from the themes developed throughout the book.

II

PUBLIC EMPLOYEE
ORGANIZATIONS:
THE ASSOCIATIONS

When one visualizes the California state and local governmental employment scene as a stage on which many actors stride, portraying organizations of civil servants, interrelating with each other and with mimes representing the employing governments, one witnesses a drama in which the cast of characters changes costumes as well as postures with bewildering frequency. Moreover, the lines that members of the first group speak to each other change with equal facility. Furthermore, their manner of approach to the opposite group constantly changes, often becoming more shrill and provocative as time goes on. The audience cannot be fully certain which actors are consorting or whether close allies in one scene will be revealed as bitter opponents in the next. Despite the tendency among employee groups, since approximately 1966, to merge and hence to reduce the number of players, new performers—and several old ones, dressed in new garb and speaking new lines—keep coming on stage. The number of organizations continues to be large, and the espoused philosophies and action tactics continue to be diverse.

FROM STABILITY TO UNCERTAINTY

The development of the nonaffiliated employee associations in state, city, county, and school district work forces provides a significant chapter in the story of California public employer-employee relations. The associations' structures, relationships, methods, and vested interests are important factors that help explain the maneuverings that took place in the 1960's and 1970's. This chapter deals first with these associations' original roles in the public employment scene and then with their newer condition, when they were subjected to the strains of competition with the nationally affiliated unions.

Several factors have caused the nonaffiliated associations to change. The drives to achieve collective bargaining for public employees, by unions whose historic home was in the private sector, have changed the strategy choices available to many California civil servants. When such large local employer-governments as the county and city of Los Angeles adopted collective negotiation procedures, based on the recognition of an exclusive bargaining representative in each of several representation units, the impact on the associations was drastic. Adoption of this procedure changed the traditional basis of employer-employee relations, in which each organization spoke for its members and in which public employees often joined more than one organization. The associations' power bases usually lay in the number of members they recruited by offering a variety of services, many of which were unrelated to employer-employee relations. To meet the competition from unions, associations that formerly were placid and slow-moving in identifying and representing members' interests vis-à-vis the employer have become shrill, impatient, and demanding in their public stances. They have been forced, to a considerable extent, to recruit enlarged staffs or to seek mergers with other groups that can supply the expert knowledge, organizing manpower, information, and political strength needed to cope with the staff expertise mobilized by the employer-governments. Whichever choice the associations have made, the result is increased costs to their members, both in dues and in time and energy spent on organization affairs. The traditional characteristics of these organizations are changing rapidly.

Several issues concerning the structure of public employee organizations are not unique to California but have been significant in the life of the associations in this state. A prominent issue has been whether employees should organize and represent their interests in occupational groups, or whether all occupations composing the work force of a particular agency should combine in a single, umbrella organization. The general associations that undertook to speak for all employees of an employer-government have played an outstanding part in the history of public employer-employee relations in this state. A question that has become more prominent as certain forms of collective negotiating have been used is whether supervisory and management personnel should form and join organizations. If so, should they join the same generic organizations elected by the workers they supervise, or should they form totally separate organizations? For many years, the associations included virtually all ranks in their membership. Should workers who identify their occupations as professions turn their professional associations into bargaining agencies? Should the professional and technical personnel join with other classifications in the same work organization to select a bargaining representative, but also maintain their professional societies to meet other needs?

Two other questions, philosophical and tactical, confronted the employee association members when unions began to compete seriously for members. Should public employees form and join organizations composed exclusively of government workers, or should they team with private sector workers in mixed organizations to avail themselves of the bargaining skills and political strength accumulated in industrial labor relations? A second, equally pivotal question existed. Should public employees form associations that seek a variety of employee welfare objectives and that advocate gradual change in employment policies, or should they affiliate with national and international groups that concentrate primarily on wages and benefits and that favor confrontation tactics in employer-employee relations? We will examine some of the efforts to answer these questions.

California governments have had extensive experience with nonaffiliated associations. A survey of county and city employers in 1961 showed that half had employee organizations in their work forces, and well over a third had only independent associations representing their employees. Fourteen percent had both independent associations and unions, whereas a tiny 1.5 percent had only unions.

A survey of 227 city and county employee organizations, also made in 1961, showed 116 to be independent general associations, 27 police associations, and 19 independent firemen's units. An additional 5 associations combined police and firemen. The remainder were union locals.[1]

A study made in 1968 of state, as well as local, employee organizations revealed 260 independent associations in California with a total membership of 500,000. This membership figure was estimated to equal half the state and local employment.[2] The largest number of associations was found in the cities, although school district employees accounted for the largest percentage of the total membership. Persons employed in almost all occupational groups were members of these associations, although the professional, technical, and clerical aggregations contributed the largest percentage in most jurisdictions.

A nationwide survey of council-manager cities in 1966 provides a limited national perspective regarding the distribution of general employee associations. Data supplied by 623 cities possessing 10,000 or more population showed California municipalities with an exceptionally high percentage of work forces with general employee associations. Ninety-one California cities reported associations, whereas Michigan, the second largest, listed only eleven. Florida reported ten cities; several other states had two to four each, and many indicated they had no such organizations.[3]

It is concluded from these data that more California cities and counties had experience with the association type of public employee organization in the 1960's than those in other states. There were also state-wide federations of local associations and associations whose primary purpose was to aggregate public employees who worked in various parts of the state. One example of the latter is the California Teachers Association which was organized in 1863 and became a truly state-wide enterprise in 1910. The California State Employees Association came into being in 1923. Both have become the largest examples of their respective types.

The objectives sought by the associations and the environmental factors that stimulated the creation and growth of this type of organization can best be exhibited by examing the profiles of some of the larger associations. Some are categorized as general associations because their purpose is to represent workers employed in virtually all occupations. Others are grouped with those who have historically sought to represent one occupation or a related cluster of occupations. The organizational problems, goals, and strategies in relations with the government-employers of the two groups tend to differ.

ASSOCIATIONS OF LOCAL EMPLOYEES

The Los Angeles County Employees Association

The Los Angeles County Employees Association (LACEA) is an arch example of the general associations that brought local government employees from many occupations together to achieve a variety of objectives. Its history, over a space of more than sixty-five years, illustrates most of the strains to which this type of organization has been subjected. The LACEA underwent four metamorphoses since its inception in 1911. Initially organized as a social and welfare entity, it came under county management dominance when it sought to concern itself with employer-employee relations in the 1930's. It partially freed itself from this condition when it evolved into an independent, nonaffiliated organization after 1953. By that time, some unions had gained small footholds in the county work force and had begun to challenge the association. When the county board established negotiation procedures by ordinance in 1968, LACEA experienced some setbacks at the hands of AFSCME and SEIU locals, and in 1971 it merged with the SEIU but retained some of its organizational format and staff at first. Three years later, however, it was exhibiting the behavior and organizational characteristics of a union.

The First Period, 1911-1935. An early president of the association recounts that the primary need for organizing the LACEA in 1911 was to provide a mechanism to finance a mutual benefit insurance fund which paid death benefits to families of deceased members.[4] This function became redundant when the county established an officially supported retirement system in 1919. Social activities dominated the organization's agenda for several years thereafter. A monthly bulletin began publication in 1923 and was soon converted into a magazine financed by advertising. This medium stressed group interests in salaries, but it also underlined the need to give the public courteous and efficient service.

The Second Period, 1936-1952. An eight-point credo adopted by the association in 1936 stressed protection of the merit system in county employment. The membership chairman boasted that the LACEA had protected members' pension and civil service rights, put twelve credit unions into operation, carried on an active legislative program, but charged its members less dues than most other associations.[5]

Membership was open to any employee of the county government willing to pay the relatively modest dues. Therefore, department heads, supervisors, professional, and technical employees, as well as clerical, mechanical, and laboring employees found the organization's social and welfare programs attractive. Membership figures for the first thirty years are not available, but by 1944 the LACEA had recruited more than fifty-two percent of the county work force to its ranks. The percentage figure rose annually, with some exceptions, until it reached approximately seventy-five percent in the early 1960's, when the total membership count was 27,000.[6]

The association's activities included nationwide studies of civil service procedures, which it used to lobby county management. It made continuous salary surveys on which to base its demands for wage adjustments for entire classes of workers. It did classification studies that benefited individuals as well as classes and it pressed for employee benefits. The LACEA also organized and offered numerous benefit programs, such as low cost life, health, optical, and medical insurance plans. It offered theater ticket and travel agency services, and provided an extensive series of social and athletic events. Despite the array of services offered, however, it was never able to recruit the total membership of this very large work force which was scattered widely throughout the county in numerous administrative centers, hospitals, warehouses, and field stations.

Member participation in association elections seldom exceeded thirty percent during the period studied, 1944-1963. A ballot on such an impor-

tant matter as an increase in dues brought out less than fifty percent participation, and when a second increase was proposed in 1957, participation
was less than thirty-three percent.

The organization's activities during the early history were carried on
mainly by elected officers and appointed committees. The chief policy determining body was a board of directors whose members were frequently
returned to office year after year; the president was usually elected from
among those who served on the board of directors, and customarily only
one candidate was nominated for each association office. This club-like situation is illustrated by the career of William McKesson, one of the most
influential figures during the 1930-1940 era. He was president in 1933,
member of the board of directors in 1936-1938, chairman of the nominating convention in 1938, and president again in 1939. McKesson was a
deputy county counsel and later became a judge of the superior court. Several other presidents came from the middle level professional and upper
rank administrative classes in the county service.

When the membership became large and the program extensive in 1933,
the board of directors employed an executive secretary. The position was
elevated to general manager in 1940 and assigned to represent the association before the board of supervisors, to public groups, and to the citizenry.
Wallace W. Braden, the first general manager, had been a supervisor's
field deputy and an assistant superintendent of the charities department.
He was generally thought to be ambitious for public office, and this factor
led ultimately to his removal in 1952.

The Third Period, 1952-1969. The 1953 election of officers, when an in-
surgent group defeated the incumbent leadership, was a critical event in
the history of the LACEA. The challengers based their campaign on the
premise that the board and officers must be responsive to membership
desires, saying:

We promise to restore to the Council its intended function of representing the
membership. Under the present board it is forced to operate as a rubber stamp din-
ner club under an agenda prepared by the Board of Directors and the management. We stand for greater Chapter recognition, and we don't mean occasional
visits by insurance salesmen.[7]

The new controlling group assigned more activities to chapters established where county work locations were concentrated, and it contracted
with the county registrar of voters to conduct association elections. It limited officers to two consecutive terms. An increased percentage of the
board membership was recruited from lower management and supervisory

positions. Elected officers put in considerable time on association affairs, but only the president was granted an expense allowance.

Structuring the institution to achieve the group's major goals is a perpetual problem in an organization that seeks to recruit and represent members working in all occupations and assigned by management to widely scattered locations. County departments were the main representational units in the LACEA structure, and members in each department elected representatives to the council on the basis of one delegate and an alternate for each one hundred members. A department chairman presided over unit caucuses which instructed the representatives who attended council meetings. Approximately sixty percent of association members worked at the county administrative center in downtown Los Angeles, but the remainder were at institutions and field stations scattered throughout the county. Chapters cut across department lines and provided representation on a geographic basis.

The council met quarterly to recommend policy to the board of directors, propose by-law changes, and nominate candidates for association offices. The board of directors, the major policy deciding body composed of four officers elected by the membership and sixteen chosen by the council, met once a month. Both the council and the board made use of standing and special committees to broaden members' participation in association affairs.

When the board sought a new staff director in 1955, it selected Frederick H. Ward, who had long experience in government personnel work and had represented the Architects and Engineers Association. Ward served the association at a time when it began to encounter serious competition from unions and when state legislative proposals on employer-employee relations demanded great expenditure of expertise and time. He became an influential figure state-wide in intergroup negotiations and legislative planning by association representatives. A short time after Ward retired, Victor Hochee, a member of the staff, was promoted to the directorship and guided the LACEA through its transition from an independent association to a union local. He was forced out of office in 1974 during a factional struggle within the union.

The LACEA staff expanded slowly in the early years, then grew as the organization undertook a more active role in employer relations. In 1928, one person performed the duties of secretary, editor of the magazine, and business manager. By 1941 the staff comprised only five positions: a general manager, three full-time secretaries, and a part-time clerk-bookkeeper. It grew to eighteen in 1953, and doubled in the next ten years.

The LACEA demonstrated in 1958 its newly sought independence from management influence when it sued the county board of supervisors following a wage dispute. Section 47 of the county charter required the governing board to pay county employees salaries equal to the rate of wage prevailing in the community for comparable jobs. For several years, the county in company with several other jurisdictions had conducted a wage survey to determine prevailing rates for selected bench mark classes of jobs. The findings of this annual study provided the base on which the board's salary ordinance was constructed. Board members were unable to agree on the findings in 1958, however, and they merely extended the existing salary rates. The association filed a class action suit and won a unanimous decision in the state Supreme Court.[8] The case became a classic ruling for those California jurisdictions whose charters or statutory rules required payment of the rate of wage prevailing in private employment.

Throughout the first four decades of its history the LACEA experienced relatively little competition, but in the 1950's it began to face challenges to its dominant role. From time to time, departmental and occupational groups developed a sense of separate identity and organized their own associations. The employees of the county road and public works departments and the flood control district joined the Architects and Engineers Association. County fire department personnel went through several stages of organizing a departmental unit and ultimately established a local of the International Firefighters Association. The sheriff's deputies also made several efforts to organize a peace officers association. Many persons who joined departmental or occupational groups retained their LACEA membership because of the insurance and benefit programs, and dual membership became a fairly common practice.

When a merger of the LACEA and a union was suggested in the early 1960's, the association's leadership, believing that a majority of its constituency was cool toward union ideology and tactics, rejected the proposal. In 1968, when the county board of supervisors considered an ordinance that would establish bargaining procedures coupled with exclusive unit representation, the LACEA expressed strong opposition. After the board adopted the plan, the association sought to have the courts declare it invalid and incompatible with state legislation.[9] LACEA also argued that dual membership in employee organizations, affording members both countywide and occupational representation, had been the prevailing practice in this county and that exclusive representation would destroy this advantage. It lost its case in the court of appeals.

The association decided then to compete in the unit representation elections held under the new system, but it lost the first two elections.[10] A considerable portion of the countywide work force appeared to favor the association, but majorities in some specific units chose the union style of employer-employee relations when presented a choice of bargaining representatives.

The Fourth Period, 1969-1975. The LACEA received its first union affiliation proposal in 1969 when the AFSCME offered it a charter as a council or cluster of union locals. The existing AFSCME local represented only 2,000 county employees, however, and the association rejected the plan.

Soon thereafter, the LACEA began discussions with the Service Employees Union, whose locals represented 7,000 members and had worked alongside the association for several years. The two organizations signed a memorandum of understanding in June, 1969, covering jurisdictional claims and operations. The LACEA was assured of its status as an organization representing most of its existing members and any others who might choose it in an election. New locals were to have considerable freedom to determine their policies, and LACEA staff personnel were to be assigned to service them. The SEIU agreed it would charter new locals containing LACEA members only when the members specifically elected the choice. LACEA was chartered as LACEA-SEIU Local 660, but was given no jurisdiction over the existing four SEIU locals that represented certain groups of county employees.

The election held in March, 1971, among LACEA members to ratify this agreement demonstrated both apathy and confusion. Only a small portion of the 30,000 members claimed by the association participated. The vote was 5,295 yes and 3,006 no, although the State Conciliation Service, administrator of the plebiscite, reported invalidation of more than 2,500 ballots.[11]

Two months after the agreement was ratified, the general council of the new unit voted almost unanimously to rescind the no-strike provision in its constitution and to add a phrase saying that the organization aimed to advance the political welfare of the public employees.[12] The members approved these changes by a vote ratio of 20-1. The officers said they did not contemplate that the association would take strike action, but that the new policy would permit its twenty-two associated bargaining units to do so if necessary. The move appeared to be mainly a muscle-flexing gesture to build membership and to counter efforts by rival organizations. The organization threatened to strike in 1974, but cancelled its plans when the board of supervisors approved a new wage agreement. During the same period, however, the Local 660 conducted a strike of its members employed by the county sanitation district.

The merger agreement was renewed in January, 1974, and thereby the largest, and one of the oldest, independent local employee associations in the state shifted identity and became a union local. The organization revamped its by-laws in July, 1974, to conform with union structure and procedure. The representative general council was replaced by a general membership meeting which elected a twenty-one member board of directors for three year terms. The board was to elect the president, vice-president, secretary, and treasurer for one year terms. Standing committees provided in the by-laws were the executive, nominating, civil rights, and political education units. A significant change established a city division, which became an umbrella to cover city employee groups recruited by affiliation, merger, or direct solicitation. Two classes of membership and dues were provided, one for those whom the organization represented as the elected bargaining unit spokesman under the county employer-employee relations ordinance, and another for those represented by other procedures. The by-laws also stated the union's goal to obtain legislation authorizing an agency shop policy that would require all employees of a unit represented by a recognized bargaining agent to contribute to the agent's finances.[13]

OTHER COUNTY EMPLOYEE ASSOCIATIONS

When independent local public employee associations were surveyed for the first time in 1963, forty-nine of the fifty-eight counties had a general association similar in organization and operating style to that in Los Angeles County.[14] Most counties reporting no organized unit were rural ones such as Alpine and Del Norte.

The county associations recruited employees from all occupations and from management and professional ranks as well as from clerical and semi-skilled classes. Most had established credit unions, group insurance programs, and discount purchasing arrangements. Many, however, were unable to finance an extensive service program and employed a staff consisting of a paid executive secretary and one or two office employees. The executive officer carried the multiple burdens of recruiter, administrator, consultant, and lobbyist. The responsibility for policy development, grievance negotiation, and presentation of general wage proposals to the board of supervisors fell mainly to elected officers, who were themselves county employees and therefore vulnerable to administrative pressures.

The county associations generally eschewed taking overt action on candidates, although San Luis Obispo County was a major exception to this generalization. It acted openly during the 1960's to sponsor candidates for supervisor, and it waged election campaigns as a means to gain its objective of influencing county employment and salary policies.

The majority of the county employee general associations confined membership to persons on the county payrolls and did not attempt to recruit and represent those employed by cities or other units. In some instances, however, they included employees of special districts. Several proposed representing all public employees in a county in order to achieve some economies of scale, to increase political strength, and to prevent national affiliated unions from getting a foothold. The Public Employees Association of Riverside County was an example where geographic factors tended to favor this plan. The county population was distributed among several partially urban areas which were scattered over a wide county territory. Although a large percentage of county employees held jobs at the county seat, many were assigned to administrative sub-centers located many miles from this headquarters. County employees in the sub-areas often had closer personal and employment relationships with city employees than normally existed between the two groups in other jurisdictions.[15] SCOPE, the Sonoma County Organization of Public Employees, is another example where a group of city employees elected a county association as its bargaining representative to city governments. It established its right to represent city employees under the Meyers-Milias-Brown Act by a suit against the city of Petaluma,[16] and it reached agreement with the Sonoma County authorities regarding county workers.[17]

The Los Angeles County Employees Association was less successful in opposing the spread of unionization of city employees. It offered to supply city associations in the Los Angeles suburban area with staff services in wage and grievance negotiations and the Santa Monica Employees Association contracted with it for a brief time, but the arrangement proved to be unsatisfactory and was not renewed. Shortly thereafter the Santa Monica group affiliated with AFSCME.

Nine associations in San Joaquin County, representing teachers, police, and city and county employees formed a coordinating council to discuss a unified approach to local employer-employee relations.[18] Most such alliances were formed to meet a peculiar situation, and depended mainly on personal relationships between figures active in the participating groups.

The independent general associations in several large counties began in the 1960's to negotiate merger agreements with unions. The first to do this was the Contra Costa Association, which joined the AFSCME. It disaffiliated later, however.[19] The Humboldt County association also turned to the AFSCME in 1966. Each sought to enjoy the negotiating skill, financial backing, and political strength of a national union and the local labor council. The trend toward merger picked up momentum when the Los Angeles County Employees Association joined forces with the SEIU in 1971. This action was soon followed by that of the Civil Service Association of San Francisco and the Santa Clara and Alameda County associations, all large bodies.[20]

THE ALL-CITY EMPLOYEES ASSOCIATION OF LOS ANGELES (ACEA)

ACEA, which became the largest municipal employee organization after it was formed in 1922, has some of the same characteristics of formal organization as the LACEA but has a different operational history. A small group of middle rank administrative personnel at city hall started this organization to counter the entrepreneurial activities of some persons who had formed benevolent associations, which charged relatively high dues and traded on the organizers' purported political influence with city officials.

The ACEA organizers recruited members from all occupations and departments other than water and power, police, and fire. They also established branch units to attract employees at the sub-city halls. The bulk of membership in the early era was provided by such low salaried employees as those in the street maintenance, inspection, and sewer divisions of the public works department.[21] This gave the ACEA a higher percentage of ethnic minorities than most general associations exhibited until well into the decade of the 1960's. Heads of divisions and departments also took part in the organization's activities. Moreover, the persons who formed the ACEA remained in city employment and were active in the association throughout their careers. Several rose to high civil service positions. This factor gave strength and continuity to the development of the organization, but it also led to tension when newer city employees expressed the belief that the leadership was resistant to change and that the organization did not offer sufficient attractions to the newer elements in the work force. To provide greater protection for its funds, the ACEA incorporated in 1932 as a nonprofit corporation.

The association was actively interested in pension legislation from the start, its retirement committee establishing close relations with the appropriate city council committees. It presented its first pension plan in 1936 via a petition signed by 48,500 persons. The council responded favorably, but the mayor vetoed the ordinance. The association next presented a charter amendment backed by a petition containing almost 180,000 names. The council placed this proposition on the ballot, and the ACEA conducted a successful campaign for voter approval. Litigation became necessary, however, to compel the council to appropriate sufficient funds to administer the system. Throughout its later history, the ACEA continued to be the prime mover of charter amendments to govern pension benefits and their funding. It did this uniformly by presenting proposals to council committees and the council and then financing the voter campaign from assessments on its membership.

The association instituted a group, prepaid medical plan in 1932, and followed that with a federal credit union, and with group life, health, and accident insurance plans. It took twenty-five years to establish a city employees' cafeteria, however, because of opposition from a city council member who owned a food vending business near the civic center. The ACEA promoted social activities, discount purchase arrangements, and theater ticket and travel arrangements. A magazine provided a vehicle for communication and advertising. Association meetings were often used to provide incumbent council members with favorable exposure to substantial numbers of city employees.

Throughout most of its history, the association maintained close relationships with council members and committees. It also lobbied with the Civil Service Commission, departmental governing boards, and departmental general managers.[22] It concentrated heavily on salary, seniority, and job protection matters.

Despite the normally close relationship with elected officials, the association chose to sue to compel city action on some occasions. A major instance of this was in 1962, after Mayor Yorty vetoed the annual salary ordinance, alleging that the council had not voted sufficient taxation to finance the expenditures. The state Supreme Court capped a series of actions in the lower courts when it ruled to force the city to pay 2.75 million dollars to make up the salary increments denied 10,000 employees.[23]

The ACEA method of organization placed large responsibilities on a president, elected annually by the membership, who served as executive officer as well as chairman of the policy board. Five elected officers constituted an executive cabinet and a large board of directors served as the policy determining body, reacting to proposals and plans presented by the president. This body, comprising almost two hundred persons, was elected by members in the several departments, bureaus, and divisions of the city work force. The formula used to distribute seats was intended not only to recognize membership numbers but also to prevent domination of the organization's affairs by the very large departments. A series of standing committees provided opportunities for many members to share in the organization's activities. During its history as an independent association, the ACEA never developed and used its full-time staff in a way comparable to its counterpart, the LACEA.

The ACEA teamed with associations from other cities to work on state legislation of interest to all public employees and in 1966 it joined the ACE, a state-wide coalition of associations.[24] In return it requested the other associations to support legislation affecting Los Angeles city pensions.

The AFSCME and the SEIU gained footholds in the Los Angeles city work force in the 1960's and began to challenge the ACEA, whose members divided sharply on the subject of collective bargaining and relations with unions. Some favored the union type of representation; others preferred to continue the long established civil service procedures and the close relations with the city council. The unions began pushing by 1970 for a city employer-employee relations ordinance based on collective negotiations. The mayor and council discussed the proposal for several years but delayed action because of indecision among the employee organizations about the probable impact on their interests.[25]

In June, 1971, the ACEA executive board recommended that the members accept the AFSCME invitation to affiliate and the proposal was approved by a very narrow margin, 4,653 yes to 4,139 no.[26] A dissenting group blocked action temporarily by a suit, whereupon the board decided to drop the affiliation plan and proposed a new arrangement whereby the ACEA would become part of an AFSCME joint council and retain its identity.[27] After further discussion, AFSCME announced the grant of a charter to an ACEA-AFSCME Joint Council 60 in December, 1972. The new unit was to be the exclusive bargaining agent for all AFSCME members employed by the city except those in the water and power department. The ACEA by-laws, constitution, officers, and dues structure became those of Council 60.[28] This alliance experienced a stormy existence, however, and broke up in 1975. The ACEA resumed its independent status.

The Civil Service Association of San Francisco (CSASF)

The Civil Service Association of San Francisco, organized in 1902 shortly after the city-county adopted a civil service program for employees other than police and firemen, grew ultimately to claim approximately eight thousand members.[29] Organized in a city noted for its pro-union attitudes, the CSASF existed for seventy years in an accepted niche. Over half its members were also dues paying members of craft and trade unions, attracted to dual membership by the CSASF benefits. Craft union members relied on their wages being set in accord with a charter section that required the city-county to pay the prevailing rate of wage, and looked to the CSASF to secure other employment benefits for them.[30]

The association conducted its business through semi-monthly membership meetings and a governing board composed largely of persons holding lower supervisory jobs who were elected on an at-large basis. The CSASF program and methods of operation in other respects were quite similar to those employed by other nonaffiliated associations.

When the board of supervisors began to consider an employee relations ordinance, the CSASF officers advised their constituents that the organization's future would be served best by affiliation with a strong labor organization. They negotiated an agreement with the Marine Engineers Benevolent Association, and in February, 1971, the members voted 3,238 to 779 to accept the affiliation. The CSASF retained its dues structure, organization, and autonomy within the union, and received promises of assistance in bargaining and financial support.[31] Unions whose members held dual membership in the association complained, however, that MEBA was raiding their members and thereby violating AFL-CIO regulations. The complaints were soon overshadowed by other events. MEBA and AFSCME undertook to establish a joint council in 1972, allegedly without consulting the CSASF officers. Granville DeMerritt, CSASF executive secretary, urged his organization to disaffiliate from MEBA, and the membership adopted his proposal.[32] A short time later they again followed DeMerritt's advice and voted to merge with SEIU Local 400. Dues of the two organizations were adjusted to a figure midway between that paid previously in both. The newly merged unit became the largest force in the city general civil service, representing approximately ten thousand city-county workers.[33]

INDEPENDENT ASSOCIATIONS IN OTHER CITIES

The general associations in most other large cities employed the ACEA and CSASF organizational pattern and mode of conducting relations with elected city officials and central administrators. One major difference was that the other associations did not have sufficient membership or funds to employ full-time staffs. Hence, most organizational and representational duties were carried by elected officers and appointed committee members. Lack of expertise in personnel matters and inadequacy of information on which to base the proposals they made to the city council and administrators were frequent sources of frustration. The organizations' effectiveness often depended on the talent and dedication of a few individuals who projected themselves into leadership roles.

An organizational issue that continually arose in many cities concerned the relationship between police and fire organizations and the associations representing the so-called miscellaneous employees. The police group in some cities cooperated with the general association and often provided the leadership for both organizations. In some smaller cities, the general association represented the fire, police, and miscellaneous employees alike.

Relationships between most general city associations and the city government depended often on the attitude and administrative style of the city's chief administrator. General associations of miscellaneous workers in most cities concentrated their limited efforts on making annual presentations to the council or on making an occasional drive to modify certain personnel rules and practices. A few examples illustrate some variations in the managements' styles and associations' reactions. A succession of city administrative officers in Inglewood worked diligently for many years to keep employee groups from formulating issues that might lead to confrontation and thereby publicize a role for the organizations. Administrators and employees alike regarded the associations as channels of general comunication, not as negotiators of demands. Administrators who held office later found a more complex situation and were often placed in confrontation with the association. The condition led to adoption of formalized negotiations. Manager-association relations in Santa Monica, where employee organizations had been active for many years, varied from harmonious to threatening. The city manager who held office between 1962 and 1973 employed a management style that often produced heated confrontations with employee groups. The three employee associations became active participants in the political move to oust the manager. The general association affiliated with the AFSCME in 1970.

FEDERATIONS OF INDEPENDENT ASSOCIATIONS

Recognition of a mutual need for a vehicle through which the many, relatively small, independent associations could aggregate their strength and seek legislative action led to the formation of state-wide federations. A second purpose was the development of information about classification practices, salary levels, and related matters of public employment for use by the constituent associations in discussions with local managements. Most of these federations were inherently weak and were able only partially to accomplish their purposes. Although their membership totals were sometimes impressive, their financial resources were small; therefore their guidance and service programs were limited. Moreover, the fact that they were composed of associations that represented diverse memberships and jealously guarded their independence forced them to accept only broad, general programs for common legislative action. A central problem for all the federations involved representation in the policy determining body. Allocation of seats on the basis of number of members in each association gave such units as the Los Angeles County Employees Association, the All-City Association of Los Angeles, or the California State Employees Association overriding control. Any formula that gave the smaller jurisdictions a balanced portion of the seats rested on the good will of the larger associations. The primary factor that kept the associations together in the federations was fear that national unions would take over the dominant role of advocate for the public employees, particularly with respect to state legislation.

The oldest of the general federations is the League of County Employee Associations (LCEA), organized in October, 1939. It reported having forty-one local associations affiliated with it in 1963, representing a total of 65,000 county employees.[34] By 1969 its membership had grown to forty-eight affiliated units with 85,500 total members.[35] A persistent issue throughout its history was the allocation of votes among the large and small associations. The formula used for several years gave the smaller associations more voting power than the larger ones.[36] It was changed in 1970 to conform to the one-man, one-vote principle, except that the huge Los Angeles County Employees Association agreed to cast votes equal to only one-fourth of its 34,000 members. The large associations withdrew, however, when they merged with unions or formed other alliances enabling them to win local representation elections.

The league opened its membership to all public employees in 1970, although it continued to regard itself as primarily a federation of associations.[37] It changed its name to California Public Employees Federation (CALPEF) and augmented its staff to provide more information service to its constituent associations. Membership continued to erode, however, dropping from a one-time high of 150,000 to 35,000 in 1973.[38] Merger proposals from the SEIU and the Marine Engineers Benevolent Association were rejected and the associations remaining in CALPEF expressed their intention to continue as independent bodies making a joint legislative effort.

The city employee general associations followed the example of the county groups and formed a California League of City Employee Associations (CLOCEA) in August, 1947. Its purposes were identical with those of the LCEA, namely, to seek legislative action pertaining to municipal employment policies and benefits, and to provide information about classification and salary practices to its members. The structure was a loose confederation.

Membership in 1963 was 103 associations, representing an estimated total of 18,000 city employees. The figures swelled to 177 associations with

68,800 employees represented in 1968, but thereafter the number of affiliates declined. To forestall further decline, CLOCEA began to assist its members in organizing, negotiating, and conducting employer relations. Six employee groups in Southern California sought these services immediately,[39] and in 1973 ten city employee associations in Los Angeles County employed CLOCEA to negotiate with their employers.[40]

In 1974, however, the CLOCEA affiliated with the Service Employees Union, and became the city division of Local 660 of the Los Angeles County Employees Association.[41] It retained its policy-making board and staff but gained union backing in negotiations. At the time it affiliated, CLOCEA represented fifty-five local associations.

An over-all coordinating association, known as the Associated California Employees (ACE) was instituted in June, 1964, to mobilize strength against the organizing drive started by the national unions affiliated with the AFL-CIO. This body was essentially a protective alliance trying to develop unity of advocacy to the legislature on behalf of the general associations. Affiliated with the ACE were the California State Employees Association, California Teachers Association, the League of City Employees Associations, the California School Employees Association, the California State Firemen's Association, some individual county and city associations, and police and fire groups.[42] It performed a fairly effective role as a coordinator of associations' legislative plans and as a vehicle for exchange of views between the constituent staffs for approximately ten years. Retirement of some of the leading figures and internal changes in many of the organizations caused the ACE to fade out.

When congressional legislation and federal administrative regulations of state and local governmental employment practices began to appear, the independent associations organized the Assembly of Governmental Employees in 1952. This organization's major objectives have been to develop and sponsor legislation which will benefit the independent associations, to protect the merit system of personnel administration, and to provide a vehicle for exchange of information among its member organizations. It claimed 700,000 members in 1973. Among its largest affiliate groups are the California State Employees Association and the California School Employees Association. Others are the Ohio Civil Service Employees Association and the American Association of Classified School Employees.[43]

The assembly conducts a convention annually and maintains a Washington office. It has advocated an extension of the Fair Labor Standards Act to cover state and local employees, has urged removal of Hatch Act restrictions on political activities, and has sponsored a Public Employee

Merit System Act as a counter proposal to the Public Employees Relations bill sponsored by the American Federation of State, County and Municipal Employees and the Public Employee Coalition.

POLICE ASSOCIATIONS

Police associations first began to appear in the larger California cities during the 1920's, notably in Los Angeles, San Francisco, Long Beach, and Oakland. A survey of thirty-two organizations in 1962, however, showed that two-thirds had been organized after 1945.[44] The associations were found most often in the large departments of central-city and suburban municipalities. Cities with less than 12,000 population or fewer than fifty police employees seldom had police organizations.

Only slightly more than a fourth of those existing in 1962 had been formed for the purpose of negotiating with the employer regarding police working conditions. About a third said their main current objective was to improve salaries, hours, and working conditions. Several had been created to raise funds to supplement pensions or to provide aid to widows and orphans of officers injured or killed in the course of their employment. Approximately half were purely social or community service organizations that provided pistol ranges or fostered boys' clubs. Among the services provided association members were arranging for group medical plans (thirty percent), securing group life insurance (forty-six percent), and managing a credit union (five percent).

The relations between city police associations and the municipal administrations appeared to be amicable and departmentally oriented in 1962. Sixty percent enjoyed payroll dues deduction privileges. The officers of half the associations said their most frequent contacts with top-level administrators were with the chief of police, whereas only eight percent said they had most frequent contacts with the city manager. Most reported they approached either the department head or the city council regarding salaries and hours; relatively few said their main contact on these subjects was the city manager. In the context of this behavior pattern, it is interesting to note that most police associations did not seek alliances with other city employee groups regarding wage demands and preferred to plead their case alone.

Although most police associations had high-ranking officials in their membership, group officers were drawn predominantly from the lower departmental ranks. The police units differed from the general associations in that approximately a third assigned the responsibility for selecting a president and other officers to an elected executive committee. Peace officer associations also tended to be more loosely structured than general associations. They were geared to exercise influence within departments that were highly traditional and that possessed a strong sense of group loyalty, but they were poorly prepared to cope with a centralized management composed of professional, analytically thinking persons. They have demonstrated considerable ability and willingness to put up money, however, usually contributed as one-time donations or dues deductions, to pay for professional campaign management in promotion of charter amendments and to pay for attorney fees in litigation against the employing governments.

The California Highway Patrol Association (CHPA)

The CHPA, composed of state employees, began as an affiliate of the California State Employees Association but developed its own structure and programs. It is one of the few police organizations in the state to employ an executive secretary and to maintain a headquarters. The size of its membership and the geographic spread of its roster necessitates a type of organization different from that of a city or county association. One of the main CHPA activities is legislative advocacy. A notable example of its success is the peace officers' retirement legislation adopted in 1968.[45] The plan permits patrol members to retire on half pay at age fifty-five, with twenty or more years of service, and allows special death and disability benefits. The provisions are sufficiently liberal that other state-employed public safety personnel and local law officers have sought comparable benefits. In 1970, the legislature extended the plan's coverage to enable local governments that contracted with the state retirement system to give their public safety employees the benefits previously granted the Highway Patrol.[46]

On one occasion, in 1972, the CHPA sought to get a new pay setting procedure for its constituents by promoting an initiative constitutional amendment, after it had been frustrated by Governor Reagan's refusal to approve salary increases. The plan was defeated at the state general election, however.[47]

The Los Angeles Fire and Police Protective League

The Los Angeles Fire and Police Protective League, though unique because it represented two safety groups, was for fifty-three years probably the most influential police association in California. The league in its original form was a product of reactions between the city's police and firemen and the official leadership when the uniformed personnel attempted to form unions in 1919. Pressured by the central area business community to stop the unionization drive among the city employees, the mayor and a business group sponsored the creation of separate, nonaffiliated fire and police benevolent associations which merged in 1921.

The strength of the organization derived in large part from the enormous size of its membership, recruited from two large occupational groups, each of which had traditions of mutual interest in group protection of members. The league could achieve unity in support of its demands as long as it was committed to programs that equitably benefited both occupations. The cornerstone of its demand structure rested on its insistence that the city maintain reasonable parity between the police and firemen in salaries and retirement benefits, and that it keep the rank structures of the two forces nearly parallel. Deep strains developed within the league's membership, however, when police compensation in other cities began to rise more rapidly than the firemen's pay.[48] The firemen's union, re-established in Los Angeles in 1953, repeatedly charged that the police dominated the league and failed to propose adequate benefits for the firemen.[49] League spokesmen started to demand collective bargaining for police and firemen in the 1950's, but when the city council began to discuss a municipal employer-employee relations ordinance in response to pressure from city union groups, the inability of the police and fire personnel in the league to work together became clear. Two chapters, one for firemen and another for police, were created in an effort to hold the organization together, but after a short time the parent body was renamed the Los Angeles Police Protective League, and the patrolmen and sergeants chose it as their negotiating representative.[50] The firemen selected the fire fighters' union.

Throughout most of its history, the original Fire and Police Protective League chose to work behind the scenes in city hall, lobbying with council members, the mayor, and members of the police and fire commissions on matters pertaining to salaries, hours, benefits, and working conditions in general. It avoided endorsing candidates for office and concentrated primarily on program matters. During most of its history it had the approval of higher-ranking officers in both departments, and it often worked in close conjunction with the command hierarchies to develop and provide the tactical support for proposals that required the approval of the police and fire commissions, the mayor, and council. During several administrations, the league was the chosen instrument of the departmental hierarchy to conduct the skirmishes with groups critical of the police force.

The league's work was performed by men who were active-duty members of the two departments. Leadership posts were customarily alternated and the president was usually either an inspector of police or a fire captain. The incumbent drew partial compensation from the league for time and expenses incurred in the organization's affairs. A committee system helped develop the association's policies. Two police inspectors, William Parker and Edward Davis, became chief of their department, and fire captain Louis Nowell won election to the city council after service as league president.

The league found initiative petitions useful means during the 1920's to place charter amendments relating to salary formulas and work-hour arrangements on the city ballot when the council or mayor were not sympathetic. In later decades, however, the league's relations with the elected officials and influential interest groups at city hall were such that charter amendments relating to police and fire pensions and similar matters were submitted to the electorate by the council at the league's suggestion. The league collected campaign funds and managed the drives to win voter approval (see chapter seven).

In salary matters, the league, like other employee groups representing members in the council-governed departments, sought to maintain good relations with the city council's personnel committee. A comment by a political writer for the *Los Angeles Times* epitomizes the situation that existed for many years:

Today, Councilman [Billy] Mills, head of the Personnel Committee, is considered the employees' best friend on the council. "We're pleased with the Personnel Committee," said Capt. Weber of the Fire and Police Protective League. "We don't win all the time, but something can be worked out."[51]

The three-member personnel committee considers all salary and personnel matters, usually after holding public hearings, and makes its recommendations to the council. Because the committee chairman normally serves as the floor strategist to mobilize councilmanic votes on committee recommendations, his attitudes and political ability are of concern to the city's employee organizations.

As long as the state legislature refrained from pre-empting the field of police and fire personnel policy matters, the league focused its attention on the local political processes. When the policy making action began to shift toward the state legislature in the decade of the 1960's, however, the league, like many other local public employee organizations, began to send advocates to Sacramento. It also became a major influence in the statewide Peace Officers Research Association (PORAC) after that unit was formed

in 1953. Its representatives often appeared with PORAC spokesmen to testify on proposals concerning police salaries, organization rights, hours, and
benefits. It also co-sponsored the Carroll amendment on police organization rights in 1963, and it was deeply involved in the 1969 legislative fight
over SB 1414, which dealt with police compensation and training
standards.

The change in the league's local tactics, from quiet, behind-the-scenes
lobbying to harsh, public declaiming before the city council and in press
conferences, began to appear in 1969. The new public posture was revealed
when the league proposed that uniformed personnel be given cash payments in lieu of unused sick leave.[52] Its spokesmen publicly attacked members of the council finance committee and suggested that work disruptions
might result if the council continued to delay or reject its proposal. The
league president was quoted as saying:

Although the protective league has never engaged in job action to settle labor disputes, there is no doubt that it worked successfully in Vallejo and Oakland. . . . We
will do everything within the law to get the benefits, but we're not going to take one
step beyond the law.

Another spokesman approached the matter somewhat differently, saying:

Fifty percent of the police membership is under five years on the job. They're a militant group. They're a new breed. They're no different from the people walking
around carrying picket signs. Our young membership is talking unions and strikes.[53]

The suit filed by the league in 1969 to compel the city to meet with its
representatives in accordance with the George Brown Act was consistent
with both statements.[54] The league, like other police organizations
throughout the state, began to resort more frequently to litigation. An
example of this tactic is the suit demanding that the city pay for the forty-
five minute per day lunch break allowed by departmental regulations or
recognize that an eight-hour work day included lunch time.[55] The league
won in superior court but was reversed by the court of appeals.[56] In 1971,
the league filed a suit as a bargaining tactic to compel the council to grant
a 7.8 percent raise in police and fire salaries instead of the 5 percent voted
for other classifications. In essence, the court was being asked to act as
arbitrator. The council had sought to set aside the formula it had adopted
in 1955 for determining uniformed personnel salaries. The mayor vetoed
the action, however, and the firemen and police ultimately received a 5.5
percent increase.[57] The league returned to court in 1973 seeking to extract

retroactive pay, computed according to a classification and pay plan recommended by a consultant firm employed by the city, but not adopted by the council until six months after the beginning of the fiscal year.[58] It also sued to block Chief Davis' order withdrawing the use of official cars after duty hours. It alleged the practice had existed so long that it had become an employment benefit and could not be altered without consultation with the police association.

During the period that the league was turning to the courts to arbitrate employment-practice disputes the issue of police unionism arose, as it had twice before. Representatives of police associations in eleven large cities announced adoption of a national union constitution and an application for an AFL-CIO charter.[59] Chief Davis reacted immediately with a request to the mayor and council to adopt an ordinance forbidding members of the police force to form or join a union and engage in strikes.[60] The council declined to adopt the proposed ordinance and the national police union did not materialize, but the events produced tensions within the Fire and Police Protective League.

Adoption of an employer-employee relations ordinance by the city caused the league to restructure, separating its police members from the fire fighters. Although the patrolmen and sergeants chose the Police Protective League as their bargaining representative in a unit election, the league continued to prefer dealing with the city council through the personnel committee rather than to negotiate with the city administration. This tactic was reinforced by the league's support of council candidates who demonstrated a friendly attitude on police employment matters. Money was contributed to campaign funds and volunteers were recruited to assist in precinct work. The league also continued to exhibit an active interest in state legislation pertaining to a very wide range of peace officer concerns.

Peace Officers Research Association of California (PORAC)

PORAC, a statewide association of police, interested initially in welfare and health programs, was formed in 1953 by representatives of police departments in the San Francisco-Oakland area. Its founders proclaimed that their main objectives were to promote the professionalization of the police service and to stimulate mutual cooperation between law enforcement agencies.[61]

During its second developmental stage the association included representatives from local associations in San Diego, Los Angeles, San Bernardino, and Riverside Counties, and the Bay Area.[62] It reported a total of eighty-six affiliated associations comprising 18,000 members.[63] Later it claimed to represent three-fourths of the total of city police and deputy sheriffs.[64]

In most of its activities, PORAC worked in close association with the Peace Officers Association of California, a very large and influential group composed of sheriffs, chiefs of police, district attorneys, and other law enforcement officers, which had been formed in 1921. The two groups developed a code of police ethics, which was given wide circulation, and worked to establish a state Commission on Peace Officers Standards and Training.[65] The statements of both organizations regarding policies and objectives were heavily laden with references to professionalism in police training and operations.

One of PORAC's major objectives in its early years was to act as a gathering agent for information on police salaries and benefits, which it distributed to its affiliates for use in the local jurisdictions. It also sought state legislation to improve police compensation state-wide. Using the standards and training program as its base, PORAC sponsored a bill in the 1969 session (SB 1414) which proposed the most radical change in salary setting and state-local relationships introduced to that date. It proposed to require all cities and counties to compensate law enforcement personnel according to uniform schedules set by the legislature. Pay levels would be gauged according to the amount of training each officer possessed, determined by certificates issued by the Commission of Standards and Training. Although the authors sought to have the legislature declare the state's intention to finance a portion of the cost of this program, the League of California Cities and the County Supervisors Association were able to defeat the bill.[66]

The PORAC board, frustrated in the state legislative process, decided to retaliate against the League of California Cities. It encouraged its affiliate, the San Francisco Police Officers Association, to seek an injunction to prevent the city-county of San Francisco from paying dues to the league.[67] The association alleged the league used tax funds paid by member cities to finance its lobbying against legislation in which the police officers had a financial interest. The trial court denied the injunction, but both parties appealed for a definitive ruling of law. The court of appeals ruled that payment of dues financed by taxes was constitutional and did not involve delegation of the city's authority to the league, because any city council could use public funds to support or oppose whatever legislation it determined to be in the public interest.[68]

Unable to accomplish its objectives through legislatively mandated salary formulas, PORAC began to propose legislation that permitted compulsory arbitration of police employment interest disputes, a subject which was under intensive study throughout the country. It sponsored SB 333 in the 1971 session, by Senator Dills of Los Angeles County, which again brought the league and PORAC into collision. The league's spokesmen contended that compulsory arbitration of interest disputes interfered with the prerogatives of elected officials to make decisions for which they were responsible to the electorate.[69] PORAC was defeated at the state legislative level, but the Vallejo and Oakland police associations were able to secure adoption of the plan in their respective cities by local action. The Sacramento and San Francisco police groups were unsuccessful in their local efforts.

STATE-WIDE GENERAL ASSOCIATIONS

THE CALIFORNIA STATE EMPLOYEES ASSOCIATION (CSEA)

The CSEA, the fourth oldest organization of state employees in the nation, formed in 1931, is outranked in age only by the Civil Service Employees Association of New York (1910), the New Jersey Civil Service Association (1911), and the Colorado State Civil Service Employees Association (1928).[70] Early in its existence it became not only the largest association composed solely of state employees, but one of two that had recruited the largest percentage of the respective state work force.[71] It has claimed as high as eighty percent of the state's employees, although the statistical bases for such calculations were never free from controversy. The core of CSEA membership is made up of those employees whose recruitment, classification, compensation, and disciplinary matters are under the jurisdiction of the State Personnel Board. The association also has recruited members from the University of California faculty and support staff and from comparable groups in the state colleges and university system,[72] competing with faculty associations, the American Association of University Professors, the American Federation of Teachers, and unions that organized support-staff on some campuses. Although each of the two higher education systems draws its principal financial support from state budgeted funds, its academic governing board, not the State Personnel Board, determines the employment policies.

Throughout the main portion of its history, the CSEA did not undertake to recruit city or county employees, as the New Jersey and Hawaii associations did. When many local government employers joined the state retirement system and some also contracted for service from the State Personnel

Board, CSEA leaders considered expanding the scope of recruitment but decided against it.[73] In 1972 it offered city and county employee organizations an opportunity to affiliate. The Sacramento County Employees Association contracted for legislative and technical services but did not seek affiliation.[74] The CSEA also sought in the 1960's to provide the independent associations greater political strength and to provide a counter to union organizing by helping found the ACE,[75] discussed previously.

The association from its beginning built its structure on chapter units because state employees were distributed among numerous administrative centers. field stations, and offices scattered throughout a large state. Although the founders of CSEA were located in Sacramento, they worked with others in Los Angeles and San Francisco in their organization planning. The association by-laws authorize the board of directors to grant any group of twenty-five or more members a charter as a chapter. Each subordinate unit functions under its own rules but these may not conflict with the association's by-laws or the decisions of the general council.

CSEA organizers have also recognized that regions are important to the organizational politics of an employee association. The original by-laws established several posts of regional director. These officers, elected by the members within the respective regions, whose number reached twenty in 1962, have two clusters of responsibilities. They direct recruitment, assist in forming new chapters, and exercise general supervision over the chapters in their regions. They serve on the state-wide board of directors which governs association affairs between annual sessions of the general council.

The board is composed, in addition to the regional directors, of three functional directors of personnel, organizational activities, and general welfare, who are elected at large, and the president, vice-president, junior past president, secretary, and treasurer. In addition to constitutional committees on civil service and personnel, on law and legislation, and on organization, numerous standing and special committees assist the board in developing policies. Members anxious to participate in CSEA work and policy development are drawn into the committee system and the general council. The ultimate ambition for many is to be elected to the board of directors.

The general council, made up of chapter delegates, regional delegates, and association officers, meets annually to elect the major officers and to determine general policies. Consistent with California political traditions and respect for regional interests, this body alternates its meetings between northern and southern sites. Chapters or groups of members submit resolutions for council consideration prior to the meetings. The council may adopt resolutions by majority vote, but the CSEA constitution requires a

two-thirds majority for by-law changes. Adoption of constitutional amendments requires approval by a two-thirds majority of the council and a plain
majority of the chapters.

The size and diversity of the state's work force and its geographic distribution present substantial organizational problems to the CSEA leadership, which desires to maintain the organization as the dominant, if not the
exclusive, voice of the state employees in employment policy matters. It
began a policy in the 1960's of granting formal recognition to occupational
groups and of encouraging them to articulate the peculiar needs of their
members, but it offered the staff services and representational strength of
the parent organization to keep them within the CSEA framework. The
directors and the headquarters staff strove to reflect the interests of the occupational groups as well as the traditional state-wide viewpoint of CSEA
demands to the legislature, the State Personnel Board and Public Employees Retirement Board.

The president, who is elected annually, has extensive appointment
powers and traditionally provides a major leadership role, defining the
directions the association takes and conducting relations with external
groups and institutions. A few presidents have been re-elected for a second
term. Most have been middle level administrators or professionals in state
service. They have risen in the association through the hierarchy of elective
offices, gaining increased recognition and following at each step. The 1972
election was a turning point in the association's history in several respects.
Dr. Leroy Pemberton of the San Diego State University staff was nominated from the floor of the council on a platform that supported collective
bargaining legislation and greater political activism by the CSEA. He defeated two candidates, including the incumbent who was seeking a second
term.

The headquarters staff has been headed for many years by two major
positions, the executive director and the chief counsel. In the early period,
the director served as general spokesman and performed the entire range
of duties: organizational work, development and administration of staff
services, and legislative lobbying. As the organization grew in membership
and service programs, personnel was added and functions became more
specialized. Robert Thomas, who served as executive director during the
1940's, set the pattern for the director's role. He was succeeded by Samuel
G. Hanson, who began an apprenticeship under Thomas and served from
1946 to 1969, the period of greatest association growth and closest relationships with the legislature and governor. The board has selected a series of
incumbent general counsels to become executive director. After Hanson
retired, Thomas Jordan followed Hanson and Loren V. Smith replaced

Jordan. Smith resigned in 1972, when he disagreed with President Pemberton and the board over an initiative constitutional amendment the association sponsored. William W. Taylor replaced Smith but he, too, left after a disagreement with the board in 1975. The general counsel is the chief legal advisor to the association and its officers, but he also usually does much of the legislative and administrative advocacy. The executive director and the general counsel have been about equally visible officers.

CSEA employs a large staff of personnel specialists, as well as attorneys and clerical workers, to handle grievance appeals and to monitor State Personnel Board actions. Many of the employees have been hired from the state civil service. The concentration of staff in Sacramento was challenged when the members in other regions began to demand prompt and continuous service, and this has caused the board to try various arrangements of field assignments.

CSEA service programs have been similar to those developed by the larger associations of local government employees: credit unions, group life, medical, surgical and hospital insurance policies, discount purchasing, and travel arrangements. For many years, CSEA has assisted members making grievance appeals or defending against department disciplinary actions. These services have involved making presentations to department managers, hearing officers, and the State Personnel Board.

The most widely publicized activity of the CSEA has been the legislative advocacy on behalf of the entire state work force on employment security, salaries, fringe benefits, and retirement matters. Work with respect to employment policy, salaries, and benefits begins with the presentations to the State Personnel Board and its staff. Article twenty-four of the state constitution assigns the board extensive responsibility to recommend wage and benefit decisions to the governor. CSEA endeavors to work closely with the governor's representatives, with legislative committees, officers, and members. The association has maintained generally good relations with department heads, department personnel officers, and major executive officers. On the other hand, the university board of regents and the trustees of the state college and university system have resisted recognizing the CSEA as a spokesman for support-staff employees under their jurisdictions.

During the first thirty years, CSEA behavior was typical of a general association. It was prudent in its demands on the state for salaries and benefits; the staff director and officers often advised the general council and members to temper their demands to match current economic conditions. The association also tended to support across-the-board percentage increases in salaries because it represented members employed at all civil service levels and occupations. Eventually it changed both tactics and demanded salary increases commensurate with increases in costs of living and made differential salary recommendations based on comparisons of compensation paid to occupations and job classes in the private sector.

The rebuff by the governing bodies of the two higher education systems, plus the threat of competition by unions for representation of state employees, caused the CSEA to push in 1960 for legislation recognizing the right of state employees to organize and be represented. Its so-called California Plan was based on eight points: (1) recognize the right to organize, (2) recognize representation, (3) establish organization recognition procedures, (4) create councils where interests are not clearly defined, (5) undertake negotiation and arbitration, (6) use governmental rather than industrial procedures, (7) disavow the strike weapon, (8) preserve and extend the merit system of public employment.

The George Brown Act, adopted by the legislature in 1961, embodied the essence of points one, two, and three. Although the legislature approved statutes requiring local governments to meet-and-confer with their employees, it declined to pass regulations governing state employer-employee relations. The CSEA therefore advocated that the state recognize the right of an organization comprising a majority of the employees to negotiate binding agreements with the State Personnel Board, Board of Control, and the State Retirement Board. It also urged that a state employee relations office be created and authorized to negotiate all matters not covered by the other three bodies.[76] Finally, it proposed that the state adopt fact finding and compulsory arbitration.[77]

The State Personnel Board, in response to a request from the legislature, recommended that the state establish meet-and-confer procedures for all matters that involved state-wide policy considerations, but submit subjects that were within the jurisdiction of department management to collective negotiations. It suggested that a state employee relations commission be created to assist in selection of representation units and to decide claims of unfair labor practices.[78] The CSEA countered this proposal with a plan that the governor act as the management representative and negotiate with recognized employee organizations on employment matters.[79] Ultimately Governor Reagan provided by executive order a limited base on which the state government conducted meet-and-confer relations with its employees.[80]

CSEA policy toward work disruptions underwent a change similar to its reversal on collective bargaining during a span of approximately ten years. It amended its constitution to renounce the right to strike when it proposed the California Plan in 1960, apparently hoping to dampen fears concerning its proposals about negotiations.[81] In 1967, however, Sam Hanson, its executive director, recommended repeal of the no-strike article as a means to strengthen the association's tactical position in state bureaucratic politics; but the general council rejected his proposal.[82] Some portions of the membership continued to advocate repeal, citing the California Nurses Association's successful job actions in 1966. The general council again rejected a resolution to repeal the no-strike article in 1968 but substituted an amendment demanding direct participation in the formulation of pay scales and working conditions.[83] The militant mood among state employees, fanned by disputes with the Reagan administration, generated sufficient strength that five resolutions to remove the no-strike provision were introduced at the 1969 council session. After extensive debate, the council approved withdrawal by a vote of 630 to 192 and sent the matter to a plebiscite of the 188 chapters.[84] A majority of the chapters concurred.[85]

When Governor Reagan vetoed the state salary increases in 1971, the 3,300 member chapter in Los Angeles voted to sanction a strike, a slowdown, or a sick-in to demonstrate resentment.[86] The CSEA board unanimously authorized a strike vote, despite admonitions from the executive director that an effort to override the veto would be more consistent with CSEA's proven tactics in the past.[87] The override did not materialize and the association went on to place an initiative constitutional amendment on the 1972 state ballot to change the salary setting procedure. Prior to the election, however, employees of the state water project went out on strike for five days with the support of the CSEA board. Governor Reagan's representative negotiated a settlement. Defeat of the association's constitutional amendment cooled the ardor of its more militant members but renewed the debate within the organization over tactics to regain the comparatively comfortable position the CSEA enjoyed prior to 1960.

THE CALIFORNIA SCHOOL EMPLOYEES ASSOCIATION (CSEA)

The California School Employees Association, a 50,000 member nonaffiliated organization established in 1926, concentrated its attention on organizing and representing classified support employees in school districts and public school offices. Public schools in California employ a wide range of occupations: clerical and stenographic, food service, bus operation, custodial, grounds maintenance, warehouse and stock-clerical, building maintenance, building trades, and electronic and data processing. Therefore a general association, such as CSEA, must attempt to balance the interests of white collar and administrative employees with those of blue collar workers and skilled personnel. Its role, in its special field, is similar to that of the

California State Employees Association and the large, local governmental, general employee associations, except that it deals with numerous district employers throughout the state. Like most associations, it also faces competition from unions. In some jurisdictions, notably in San Francisco, the Service Employees Union edged it out, and in several Southern California districts it operated alongside SEIU Local 99 for several years. In some jurisdictions the AFSCME represented some of the classified personnel whereas the Operating Engineers Union and the building trades unions represented the crafts workers. The CSEA was able to maintain a strong position state-wide and in a number of regions for several years because it cultivated the classified school personnel field and also maintained effective legislative relations in Sacramento. When the Rodda Act brought collective bargaining to the school districts, however, the CSEA suffered erosion of strength in many areas. In some districts it won the right to represent all classified employees, but in several large districts it was able to retain only the clerical workers.

The CSEA also competes with the California Teachers Association affiliates and other teacher organizations at the district level for a share of the salary budget. Since the organizations representing certificated and classified employees compete for shares of the same pool of dollars, each tends to view gains by the other as a potential loss to its members' interest. The relationship between the two at the state-wide level is illustrated by the major pieces of state legislation governing employer-employee relations. The Winton Act, largely sponsored by the CTA, established certificated employee councils through which the organized teachers met-and-conferred with district management. But it was silent with regard to classified employees' negotiations. The Rodda Act of 1975, which established collective bargaining in school districts, was supported by the teachers' organizations but was opposed by the CSEA.

The CSEA has been very effective in its legislative advocacy with respect to the myriad of details in the Education Code of interest to classified school employees. Sections of this code which pertain to employee rights and benefits bear the stamp of its legislative drafting and advocacy. Many of these provisions were written to correct situations that had occurred in single districts, although the code has general application.

Two major thrusts of the CSEA legislative program have been support of the merit principle for school personnel administration and the protection of the career service concept. With those ends in mind, the organization supported legislation that permits districts to establish a formal merit system personnel program by a referendum of school employees. It also demanded that the organized employees share in the administration of the system; therefore most of the approximately one hundred merit system school districts operate with a three-member personnel commission, one member of which is nominated by the organized employees. Attempts to repeal the merit system portions of the Education Code and give the school boards full control of personnel administration were fought vigorously by the CSEA.

The association was one of the last large, independent organizations to push for collective bargaining legislation. The delegates to the association's annual conference, held in San Diego in 1973, approved the executive director's recommendation that they seek collective bargaining legislation. They also adopted a companion resolution that expressed a desire to retain the merit system for classified school employees and instructed their representatives to seek legislation to spell out the respective areas of responsibility, to permit collective bargaining and the merit system to coexist.

The association is similar in structure to the other general public employee associations. Its basic organizational unit is the chapter, composed of members employed by a single jurisdiction. Chapter officers are elected annually and formerly carried the major responsibility for conducting relations with the school board and its administrators. Full-time, paid staff employed by the association now carries this function. The annual convention composed of delegates from the chapters is the major policy determining body and elects the statewide officers. Meeting sites are rotated through the major geographic areas of the state.

A board of directors, made up of four officers elected at large and nine elected from regions, determines policy within the general frame of convention directives. A series of committees serve as channels for proposals to the annual convention. Another echelon of association officials, composed of representatives from sixty-six areas, bridges the gap between the state-wide organization and the chapters.

The executive director, Richard C. Bartlett, has played the primary role in shaping CSEA policies. His planning and persuasion were chiefly responsible for the shift of policy to support collective bargaining legislation despite a lukewarm attitude among the delegates. A point he made repeatedly was that other public employee organizations were supporting collective bargaining and that CSEA could not afford to be isolated in the legislative maneuvers.

The association maintains a headquarters in San Jose, three regional field offices, and a Sacramento governmental relations office from which its chief legislative advocate operates. Field representatives operate from the regional offices, providing assistance and representation to the chapters. Each representative is responsible, through a supervisor, to the executive director, but is also bound by instructions given him by the chapter for whom he acts as spokesman to district boards and administrators. This procedure is intended to provide a blend of systemwide and local policies. The strength of the association at the district level depends heavily on the skill and knowledge of the field representatives.

Like most general employee associations in California, the CSEA offers its members a broad array of services, which includes auto-fire insurance, group life insurance, discount purchase arrangements, and a magazine. Chapter social activities also are used as organization builders.

STATE-WIDE SINGLE-OCCUPATION ASSOCIATIONS

THE CALIFORNIA TEACHERS ASSOCIATION (CTA)

The oldest, and often the most active, public employee association in California is the California Teachers Association. Teachers, even more than employees of the general purpose governments, have created numerous organizations to influence public policy. A continuum of events in which these organizations have been involved includes reorganizations, subdivision of units, and mergers.

Organizational historians consider the California Educational Society, which was formed at the urging of State Superintendent John Swett in May, 1863, to be the parent of the CTA.[88] Its membership at the start was entirely in the San Francisco Bay Area. The name, California Teachers Association, was first used in 1891 when groups from the northern and southern areas of the state met in Riverside to urge reform in educational legislation and practice. Two additional regional organizations formed soon afterward but, in 1907, the four area-based groups agreed to form a federation. Shortly thereafter the association purchased a privately owned educational journal and employed an executive secretary.

The State Council of Education, a state-wide CTA policy-making body, was formed in 1910 and has remained the key element for channeling the members' views into association decisions. Three subjects discussed at the first council session have continued to be major items on the CTA's ongoing agenda: legislation to establish and maintain a statewide teachers' pension plan, a teachers' tenure law, and an adequate plan for apportioning state school funds.[89] The fourth, a system of industrial education, has ceased to be a major interest.

The federation formed in 1910 did not eliminate any teacher organizations but operated, until a major reorganization in 1970, as a multi-level conglomerate of local associations and four (later expanded to six) regional sections. It affiliated nationally with the National Education Association. Each section had a council, a board of directors, and a set of by-laws, and each section incorporated in order to facilitate its purchase and management of headquarters property.

Early in its history, the CTA focused attention on the professional development of teachers and the maintenance of high standards of teacher behavior in the classroom and the community. At the same time, the organization concentrated much effort on defending teachers who were harassed or jeopardized in their employment by school boards, administrators, or community groups. It pushed successfully for legislation governing teacher tenure and its sections provided counseling service and legal defense for members.

Services to members, provided through state-wide and sectional units alike, included most of those undertaken by the other large public employees' associations: group life and medical insurance plans, discount purchasing arrangements, travel bookings, and ticket purchases. Job placement services, for both the beginning and the experienced teacher, received much attention. The extensive membership service programs developed soon required the employment of a considerable staff to administer them, provide support for committees, recruit new members, develop public relations, and carry out legislative advocacy.

The CTA experienced an unusual degree of continuity in its directing staff personnel, a factor that contributed considerably to the strength of the organization. Roy W. Cloud and Arthur E. Corey, each of whom served for twenty years, 1927-1947 and 1947-1967 respectively, were strong personalities who performed leadership roles as a series of elected officers and active member participants arrived and departed. Jack D. Rees, who was selected in 1967 and participated in what was perhaps the most change filled period in the organization's history, was succeeded by Ralph J. Flynn from the National Education Association in 1976.

The six sections that comprised the middle level of CTA organization between 1921 and 1970 varied widely in structure, membership, financial assets, and programs, and each was vigorously protective of its individual status within the framework of the state-wide organization's by-laws. Prior to 1967, CTA made no effort to compel by legal action any section council to comply with the state council's decisions. Persuasion was the standard technique employed to achieve coordination, although it often resulted in frustration for all parties.[90]

A considerable amount of friction arose out of sectional rivalries because the several geographic sections of the state experienced different growth rates. The Southern California area gained population with the greatest rapidity in the years that followed the close of World War II. Other sections grew, but at comparatively modest rates. The allocation of seats in CTA governing bodies was based on proportions of the teacher population. Therefore, when the southern section contained well over half the state membership in 1971 it elected fifty-one percent of the council members, whereas the north coastal section was entitled to only ten seats in the 158 member body. The southern section was also able to maintain a staff and a service program that rivaled those of the state-wide CTA in size and scope.

Conceptual and tactical differences also began to exacerbate the frictions within the CTA. The leadership in the state-wide organization, based in Burlingame, placed great emphasis on the long-productive legislative relations, periodic use of initiative petitions, and appeals to the state's voters by campaigns on educational issues. Highly vocal elements in the southern section began to emphasize confrontation with district school boards and the development of bargaining procedures. This attitude was also supported by the staffs and many members in several of the large, urban district teacher organizations affiliated with CTA.

Another issue that tended to polarize attitudes during the decade of the 1960's concerned the role of school administrators in the CTA. Throughout a major portion of the association's history, administrators as well as classroom teachers held membership and took active part in the state and local programs. This factor probably accounted for some of the conservative tinge displayed in CTA's objectives and tactics, but it also gave strength to many of the organization's political efforts. It certainly influenced the choice of alliances with other groups active in the state's political system. During the 1960's, however, fewer school administrators took membership in CTA local affiliates, and elements in some local teacher units sought to bar administrators from membership.[91] The southern section council, for example, instructed its delegates to the state council to vote for a by-law change to bar administrators, but the state-wide body declined to take this action. Finally, in 1971, seven administrator groups comprising 18,000 members merged to form the Association of California School Administrators.[92] This group pursued its own legislative program in which it sometimes cooperated with the CTA and sometimes with the California School Boards Association.

Early in the 1960's, the CTA shifted from its long-stated opposition to collective bargaining and its reliance on lobbying state policy-making bodies. In 1965 it drafted and sponsored AB 1474, which became the Winton Act. One purpose of this bill was to blunt the demands being made by a militant element which was expressing admiration of the American Federation of Teachers' proposals for collective bargaining with district school boards. CTA supporters defeated two amendments intended to bring AB 1474 into line with AFT desires. One proposed to permit teachers to negotiate collective contracts and strike. The other proposed to establish negotiating councils.[93] The Winton Act in its final form established a nine-member negotiating council in each district to meet-and-confer with the district administration. Seats on a council were apportioned among organizations according to membership, a plan that greatly favored the CTA in most school districts.

The CTA began in 1962 to use public censure of districts engaged in unresolved disputes with its local affiliates. This method was first used against the Little Lake District in Los Angeles County, which was accused of having inadequate salary scales and poor leadership resulting in a substandard educational program.[94] In most instances when a local affiliate alleged that the district administration and board had failed to carry on meaningful negotiations, the CTA appointed a panel composed of administrators and teachers to investigate and attempt to mediate disputes without publicity. After repeated complaints that a board was harassing teachers, the CTA board of directors adopted sanctions.[95] The intent of a vote of censure was to urge all teachers to refuse employment with the censured district. In a few instances, the CTA voted a censure in conjunction with a strike conducted by the affiliate.[96] The initiative to conclude a censure action normally was taken by the local affiliate.[97]

The leadership of the teacher associations recognized in the 1960's that reorganization was overdue. Arthur Corey, the CTA executive director, began a study in 1966 before he retired by which he hoped to channel the changes along directions he and his supporters had favored for many years. A preliminary recommendation proposed to consolidate the existing six sections into two, but discussion soon produced the conclusion that complete unification was most desirable. The state council voted by a substantial majority in November, 1970, to restructure the organization as a unit, to dissolve the six existing corporate structures, and to establish a single dues structure to be administered by the central body. Dues were to be doubled to finance increased programs and services. The staff was to be unified also, although the chapters were to be given a voice in the selection, assignment, and retention of employees.[98]

The strongest resistance to the reorganization plan came from elements in the southern section that were predominantly interested in establishing collective bargaining. They were fearful that the new scheme would permit the faction favoring retention of the traditional legislative advocacy and professional negotiation methods to secure control of the entire organization. The dissident attitude was stimulated by developments taking place in the Los Angeles Unified School District. The AFT Local 1021 had been contesting with the district board, the Los Angeles Teachers Association (LATA), and the Affiliated Teacher Organizations of Los Angeles (ATOLA) over collective bargaining as well as salary policies.[99] The 19,000 member LATA and the 3,000 member AFT staged separate but concurrent strikes in November, 1969, and shortly afterward began negotiating a merger agreement.[100] A new body, known as the United Teachers of Los Angeles (UTLA), was proposed to replace the two and to begin operations February 1, 1971. The proposal immediately drew state-wide and national attention, because of the size of the two merging units and because the action might portend the outcome of merger discussions then taking place between the National Education Association and the American Federation of Teachers. Only one local merger, that in Flint, Michigan, had preceded.

UTLA members were to be required to continue membership in one of the two national organizations as well as to pay dues to the local body. The NEA and AFT agreed to subsidize UTLA for any loss of membership resulting from the merger. Discussion of the plan greatly increased the tension between factions in the state-wide CTA and strained relations between the state and national associations. In light of the total situation, CTA officers could do little more than express support of the principle of local determination. When sixty percent of the Los Angeles teachers who participated in the plebiscite on the UTLA plan approved the merger, UTLA-CTA-NEA relations became chaotic.[101]

The two-year period following the merger was an extremely turbulent one. The CTA sued the UTLA for delinquent dues, and the latter sought to have the National Education Association dismiss the CTA from its fold. A rival state organization, the United Teachers Association of California, was instituted and took away two large CTA affiliates. These national-state-local disputes were over organization, finance, objectives, and philosophy governing the teacher association movement. Nevertheless, negotiations at a meeting in Washington in April, 1972, produced agreement on twenty-five points.[102] The NEA recognized the CTA as its sole affiliate in California and the UTLA as its exclusive representative in Los Angeles. The CTA and UTLA agreed to coordinate their state legislative activities. Any disagreements concerning the terms of the Washington agreement were to be submitted to arbitration.[103] Subsequently the rival, state-wide association was disbanded.

A CTA reorganization plan, placed in operation in 1972, vested decision authority in the state council, whose membership was increased to approximately 475 members. The six semi-autonomous geographical sections were replaced by six regions whose functions were to be mainly delivery of service to members. Regional headquarters, directed by an appointed executive officer, were established in Walnut Creek, Sacramento, San Jose, Fresno, Los Angeles, and San Diego. Fifteen regional resource centers were created and distributed among the six regions on the basis of geographic size and number of members to be served. The centers, supervised by a council composed of chapter presidents and state council members resident in the area, were to facilitate discussions. Field offices, staffed by paid CTA representatives, were also to provide means for communications between members and the organizational units. Chapters could request assistance in local negotiations and obtain research information from regional and state-wide headquarters through the field offices or service centers.[104]

Changes in the national leadership of both the NEA and the AFT and abandonment of negotiations to merge those two national bodies served to strengthen the role of the CTA in California school organization politics. It also cleared the way for adoption of a unified dues structure to finance the local, state, and national units.[105]

Teachers' associations in California have tightened their organizational model with respect to financial support of the state and national organizations, but they have retained many of the basic service programs of the original association model. Legislative advocacy also continues to be an important activity. The CTA has also retained, in modified form, much of its traditional concern for professional standards. On the other hand, it has begun to endorse and contribute financial support to candidates for state elective offices. Its affiliates have endorsed district board candidates for many years. After ten years' experience with the CTA-sponsored Winton Act, the association supported the Rodda Act of 1975, which introduced collective bargaining into school district employment relations in 1976. Development of collective bargaining, even in this limited form, portends a situation in which the more significant elements of employment policy will be made in future by negotiation, district by district, rather than by legislation and amendments to the Education Code as in the past.

The California Nurses Association (CNA)

The CNA, a professional association affiliated with the American Nurses Association (ANA) is an example of an organization of professional persons that has experimented with collective bargaining in both the public and private (but non-profit) areas. It has enrolled the vast majority of registered nurses in the state, whether employed by governments or private hospitals, or engaged in private practice. The preponderant portion of its membership is female.

The national association, together with its state affiliates, followed for many years the classic pattern of professional groups in that it concerned itself with establishing standards of nurses' training and practice. It also developed a consensus about the role of the nurse in the institutional and clinical health service programs. A large percentage of its membership was highly motivated to patient care, was proud to consider its occupation a profession, and was expressive of the ideal that financial rewards were secondary to the satisfaction of giving service.[106] The ANA's interest in collective action by nurses to improve their economic status began in 1948, but it assigned the tasks of organizing units and negotiating agreements to the state associations.[107]

The formal structure through which CNA policy decisions are made resembles in its main outlines that of previously described state-wide associations. The House of Delegates, selected by constituent nurses' associations, meets once a year to elect officers and act on by-law changes and other general policy matters. The president exercises considerable influence on the organization's policies, although a series of committees and task forces develops program proposals or supervises association activities. Significantly, the leadership in CNA has been supplied mainly by those in administrative positions and nursing education, despite the fact that the bulk of the membership comprises general hospital nurses.

An executive director and a headquarters staff in San Francisco implement the association's programs. An important service program offers malpractice liability protection and insurance covering disability resulting from accidents or cancer. Field representatives carry the CNA programs to the members and assist the district associations. In 1973, the association's expenditure budget totaled slightly over a million dollars.[108]

CNA members are organized locally according to geographic areas rather than according to employing organizations. Most districts are served by an executive secretary. A regional organization plan was approved by the House of Delegates in 1971 to accommodate the different needs that result from a variety of hospital administrative practices. The private and non-profit hospitals in some areas formed such associations as the Hospital Council of Southern California to standardize administrative practices. Public hospitals in that area, although not members of the council, tended to conform to the council's standards. Groups of hospitals in the San Francisco Bay Area, on the other hand, employed labor relations consultants to negotiate with their organized employees.

The CNA confined itself originally to recommending salary rates for general hospital nurses, but in 1946 it began to negotiate contracts with private hospitals and associations. By 1956 it had made ten contracts with twenty-seven institutions in the Bay Area.[109] In Southern California it developed with the hospital council a series of statements concerning rates of pay. Its basic policy as a representative of nurses' interests was rooted in advice given by Paul St. Sure, a noted Bay Area attorney and its first legal counsel. He recommended that the association actively represent nurses with employers in all parts of the state. He reasoned that hospital management would rather negotiate with a professional association than with any other type of organization and would bargain in good faith to prevent the CNA from withdrawing and leaving the field open to others possessing a different philosophy. He urged, moreover, that the association assure hospitals that the nurses would not strike.

A series of events in 1966 rapidly pushed the CNA into a departure from the latter part of St. Sure's strategy. First, the association endorsed informational picketing by nurses at some Bay Area hospitals. Next, the nurses at the Eden District hospital in southern Alameda County gave notice of intention to submit mass resignations. After two weeks they walked off the job and did not return until the management agreed to a negotiated settlement.[110] The Eden tactic quickly attracted the attention of nurses in county general hospitals throughout the state, where considerable discontent with salaries and benefits existed. Many believed that submitting mass resignations after giving notice was consistent with the traditional CNA policy and with concepts of professional responsibility toward patients and employers. Hospitals were able to reduce admissions and transfer patients to other facilities; supervisors and a small cadre of nurses usually remained to care for acute and emergency cases.

General hospital and public health nurses employed by Santa Cruz County followed the Eden District precedent, and those in Alameda, San Luis Obispo, and Imperial Counties soon did the same.[111] Nurses employed at the Fresno County Hospital chose to conduct a mass sick call-in rather than to offer resignations as a means of pressuring the board of supervisors to adopt salary schedules comparable to those being negotiated in other areas.[112] General hospital and public health nurses in San Francisco gave notice in August, 1966, that they would absent themselves on sick leave unless the supervisors adopted a salary schedule comparable to that recently negotiated in private hospitals. This action was widely labeled a strike, and the Central Labor Council discussed the possibility of giving its support although the CNA was not affiliated with the labor movement.[113] The CNA board of directors announced that, after consulting the ANA representative and being told the state organization was free to make a decision, it would approve a departure from the associations' no-strike policy that it had observed since 1949.[114] The nurses rejected the county's salary proposal a week later and began taking sick leave. After three days, they accepted a new county proposal and returned to work. The second proposal was the result of negotiations between the mayor and CNA representatives, with the executive secretary of the Central Labor Council participating as a counciliator.

This series of skirmishes produced two notable outcomes. One was the negotiation of agreements that set area-wide patterns for nurses' compensation. Those in the Bay Area were made by negotiations between CNA representatives and individual hospital managements, with the State Conciliation Service acting as mediator. In Southern California, negotiations were between the CNA and the hospital council. In both, the agreements were made with representatives of private hospitals, but county governments tended to take note of them in their internal decisions.

A second outcome was the establishment of the association as the representative of registered nurses in wage negotiations as well as in matters of professional concern. The CNA, possessing a tradition as a professional body, has attempted to maintain its independence of the organized labor movement but has showed a willingness to work informally with unions in support of legislation. It was among the early sponsors of state legislation relative to collective bargaining. Its position, supported by the ANA, has been that nurses, as professional persons, should not be grouped with other occupations in representation units in collective bargaining, unless the professionals specifically elect to be so grouped.

The CNA enjoyed considerable success in winning the right to represent registered nurses in the first county collective bargaining elections conducted under local ordinances. In Marin County in 1968,[115] it won in competition with the county general employees' association, and it did likewise in Los Angeles in 1969.[116] It soon began to encounter competition from the unions as well as the general associations, however. In Los Angeles, the nurses switched from CNA to the SEIU Local 660 in 1974. As a result of this competition, the CNA, like other nonaffiliated associations, began to develop an abrasive rhetorical posture in its relations with employers and to advertise its successes in negotiations as a device to recruit members. Its membership increased markedly after 1967.[117]

It continues active in the legislative field, in which it emphasizes its continuing interest in nursing standards and procedures and in the administration of state licensing of registered nurses. The CNA, more than most professional and employee-interest associations, has evidenced a specific interest in facilitating the entry of minorities into its occupation. It has focused its attention on the education and training of minority persons and on broadening their opportunities for employment as nurses.[118]

CONCLUSIONS

The employee associations, as initially developed in California work forces, met the need for a focus of common interest among persons employed in disparate government programs and created a vehicle by which civil servants could stretch the purchasing power of their wages. Self-help, rather than demand that the employer finance all worker benefits, was the basic element in the original philosophy. Opportunity to enjoy a variety of service programs at relatively low cost became one of the main attractions of this type of organization.

Most associations though, at some stage in their development, exhibited an interest in working conditions and rules governing employment. One common action was to seek creation of a government administered retirement system to which employees as well as employers contributed. Most of the systems created were administered by boards, a portion of whose members were elected by the employees. The associations thus developed a vested interest in the protection and growth of these systems. Interpretation and liberalization of benefits became a part of their on-going concerns. Stabilization of government employment conditions, which the civil service system seemed to offer, next became the associations' major goal. Many organizations worked to persuade the governing boards and the voters to adopt a formal personnel system based on the civil service concept. To establish these systems, the organized public employees engaged in lobbying and mounted campaigns to secure voter approval. The political climate in California at the time caused them to avoid making overtures to the political parties. They used initiative petitions to achieve their goals in many instances.

A continuing issue among the general associations was the selection of a program that would satisfy the numerous occupational groups. Establishment of retirement systems and a personnel administration tended to meet the needs of all, but some occupational groups had strong feelings about their status in the work force and the rewards they should receive for their work. In the larger work forces, single-occupation associations formed. Occasionally they sought alliances with other associations; often they followed an independent path. Those who considered their occupation to be a profession looked primarily to their professional society, which was usually heavily concerned with education, training, and performance standards.

The problem of achieving a balance between constituency interests based on occupation, department, or geographic region caused many associations to create relatively cumbersome structures. All were forced to keep their dues low to retain members, hence much of the organization's work was done by elected officers or volunteers. Persons performing organization responsibilities were often dependent on the good will of their supervisors or of the employing agency's governing body. All associations traded on the desire of persons to be recognized by their peers, and created hierarchies of offices and committees to draw members into organization activities. Those who achieved the top offices often became administrators or senior professionals and drifted toward a management point of view.

As association activities proliferated and membership grew, the larger organizations employed staffs, and the executive directors became highly influential exponents of the associations' interests. In the internal politics of associations, however, the director was often the focus of factional disputes.

When the national unions began a campaign among California public employees in the 1960's, the associations responded with renewed efforts to form and strengthen federations. These loosely structured alliances were intended to unify the associations' approach to the state legislature and to provide information to the constituent members for use in negotiations with employers. The federations were fragile instruments because the small associations feared that the larger associations might dominate or ignore the small groups' special concerns. Their legislative efforts, at most, made state legislators aware of the complexity involved in writing uniform state legislation governing public employer-employee relations.

The large associations were attractive targets for union organizers. Discontented elements within them, spurred by a rising level of expectations regarding compensation for work performed, and irritated by the cautious tactics employed by the association leadership, agitated for more aggressive demands on the employers. Some associations assumed a more aggressive stance. Some concluded agreements with unions to obtain the services of negotiators to enhance their strength vis-à-vis other competing organizations. Others negotiated a merger and became a local unit of a national union. Although many members expressed strong opposition to the mergers, only small percentages of the claimed membership voted on the agreements; the factions favoring merger won.

Those associations that have survived have enlarged their full-time, compensated staffs and have reorganized their structures with the intent of increasing member participation. Most of them now take a very active part in the election of public officers. Where collective bargaining has been established, they compete for election as bargaining unit representatives.

III

PUBLIC EMPLOYEE
ORGANIZATIONS:
THE UNIONS

Concerted effort by organized labor to recruit public employees is a comparatively recent experience. Such pioneer leaders as Samuel Gompers and William Green showed relatively little desire to organize or represent state and local government workers. The national and international unions that dominated the American Federation of Labor in its early history were composed mainly of craftsmen employed in the private sector. Each union had recruited its members and carved a niche for itself in the labor movement. Collective bargaining was their means for dealing with employers, and the strike, boycott, and picket line were their traditional strategies for bringing economic pressures to bear in support of their bargaining demands. They considered civil servants to be in a different sphere, operating under separate conditions and facing other problems. A considerable segment of the labor movement felt that civil servants would prove to be a detriment to the union cause, inasmuch as they would not, or could not, go out on strike or respect other unions' picket lines. Most civil servants were white collar workers who were not attracted to the traditional union methods. Moreover, a considerable percentage of them were women.

Ironically, the first union of local government employees received by the A.F. of L., the American Federation of Teachers which was created in 1902 and affiliated in 1916, had a considerable contingent of female members. The International Association of Fire Fighters, organized and affiliated in 1919, was atypical in another way. Its constitution forbade local unions to strike. Both unions contributed comparatively small numbers to the A.F. of L. and their influence in national and state labor councils was slight, until many years later. The A.F. of L. also chartered a national union of police, but its experience with this organization was so turbulent it reinforced the wariness many in the labor movement felt toward unions composed solely of public employees.[1] Such blue-collar unions as those of carpenters, plumbers, and painters took in workmen who were employed by state or local governments, but they did not charter separate local unions for them.

The American Federation of State, County and Municipal Employees, which affiliated with the A.F. of L. in 1936, encountered stiff resistance from the older craft unions, apprehensive that a general union representing all occupations among state and local employees would encroach on their traditional jurisdictions.[2] It has continued to be embroiled in jurisdictional quarrels.[3] This union sprouted from the Wisconsin state employees' local of the American Federation of Government Employees (AFGE),[4] and its first president, Arnold Zander, came to it from a job as Wisconsin Civil Service Commission examiner. Its stated objectives, namely, to support the merit system in public employment, to promote efficiency in government service, and to advance the social, economic, and general welfare of the public employees, were considerably different from those of the old-line craft unions of the A.F. of L.[5] Early in its history it added a fourth objective, to establish government workers' retirement systems.

The assistance given public employee unions by the California Labor Federation, the A.F. of L. body responsible for coordinating the affiliated unions in the state, was relatively meager during the early attempts to unionize public employees. The following excerpt from the 1944 secretary-treasurer's report is an example:

In response to a request from Brother Arnold Zander . . . your Secretary agreed that Brother Hyans [a CSLF staff member] might work with him during any spare time available from his [other] activities.[6]

During the same year, Secretary Haggerty also worked informally to resolve a dispute between the city council and fire fighters of Fresno over a city charter provision requiring payment of the prevailing rate of wage.[7] In his next annual report he stated:

The Federation has assisted Harry Wolf, General Representative of AFSCME, in this union's campaign to bring state employees into the A.F. of L. No financial help was needed, but full support, advice and publicity was furnished wherever asked.

The state federation's attorney also aided fire fighter locals in Long Beach and San Francisco with claims against their city-employers.[8]

A more active effort to recruit and service state and local workers was made for several years by the Congress of Industrial Organizations, which was organized after its unions split from the A.F. of L. in 1935. Some units of teachers, state employees, and city workers also deserted the California State Labor Federation and affiliated with the new body.[9] The CIO locals demonstrated a more militant approach to the public employers than those affiliated with the A.F. of L.

After twenty years of rivalry, the A.F. of L. and CIO reunited in 1955. Their state counterparts in California required another three years to negotiate a merger. One factor that helped bring about the national reunification was concern over the steady decline in total union membership. Many conditions in the national manpower and labor market situation had changed in the 1940's and numerous analysts concluded that the labor union movement had not kept pace with the changes. Shortly after the mergers were concluded, the AFL-CIO leaders decided that a nationally supported recruiting campaign was essential if either the organization or its historic mission of representing the working person's interests was to survive. This perspective was clearly stated by C. J. Haggerty to the California Federation of Labor convention in 1960:

As a matter of necessity, the labor movement has come to recognize...[that] its survival as a potent force in our economic democracy may well depend upon the successes obtained in organizing the growing army of white collar workers who now actually outnumber the so-called 'blue collar' labor force. Among these white collar workers are the millions of public employees who constitute a significant group whose peculiar problems are as great as their potential for organization. As public employees they lack many of the protections of law, which employees in the private sector of our economy now take for granted. We must recognize that because they are employees of government they are continually plagued with legislative problems. If we in the labor movement on the one hand declare an interest in helping public employees, we must on the other hand, make an effort to assist them in the solution of their problems. By the same token our commitment to assisting them has carried with it an obligation to make a special effort to help their weak and struggling organizations assume their rightful role and place in the trade union movement.[10]

The AFL-CIO leadership selected the white-collar workers as their prime organizing targets and, when they analyzed the national employment statistics, they were impressed by the fact that state and local government work forces were growing at an exceptionally rapid rate.

The 1961 AFL-CIO convention approved a proposal that the national body sponsor a general recruitment drive. Six months later a planning group submitted to the executive committee a plan for a pilot project to organize government employees and other non-union workers in a major area. It recommended that the first site be the Los Angeles-Orange County area of California. After the unions in the target area reached an understanding about jurisdictional claims, the executive committee approved the plan. The AFL-CIO headquarters and regional staffs conducted training sessions for organizers in the unions that were to participate. The campaign that followed, which was financed and supported by more than fifty national and international unions, was reported to have brought in 12,000 new members in a six-month period.[11]

The 1963 convention authorized the AFL-CIO officers to sponsor state legislation which would provide state, county, and municipal employees collective bargaining and arbitration, and would condemn statutes and local ordinances that forbade or discouraged union organizations among these workers.[12] The meeting held two years later went a step further when it approved a resolution presented by Walter Reuther, head of the Auto Workers Union and chairman of the AFL-CIO industrial union department, and pledged to work aggressively for legislation which would grant public employees the right to organize, to select their own representatives, and to mandate the public employers to bargain. It also agreed to sponsor federal legislation that would embody the principles of the Wagner Act and would give teachers the right to bargain collectively. Furthermore, it instructed local labor unions and central labor bodies not to support efforts by non-union firemen to win improved salaries and working conditions.[13]

California union delegations to these conventions took an active part in formulating the AFL-CIO statements. The central labor councils of San Diego, San Joaquin, and Ventura Counties, for example, offered resolutions which were combined with others to form the statement adopted by the 1967 convention.[14]

The national officers moved cautiously to create a headquarters structure to represent and service public employee union interests within the AFL-CIO. They opposed a resolution at the 1965 convention to establish a special department to provide research, legislation, and organizing support for these unions, saying they preferred to wait for the public employee unions to ask for this assistance.[15] Throughout most of the 1960's, the public employee unions were served by the industrial union department headed by Walter Reuther, the former CIO leader.[16] A Government Employees Council, composed of thirty-one unions, served for many years as a planning group to prepare legislative programs.[17] In 1971, the AFSCME became restive and formed an alliance with the National Education Association, the non-union teacher organization, to create the Coalition of American Public Employees, whose purpose was to sponsor federal legislation on behalf of state and local employees. Three other unions joined the coalition a little later. Finally in 1974, the AFL-CIO executive council created a public employees department to which the twelve unions representing public employee members transferred.[18]

The structure, philosophy of operation, and strategic plans for the national bodies of the several unions that have organized and represented state and local employees in California are important elements for understanding the unions' activities in the state political system. The local unions and their state groups work within the frame of their national organizations and often draw upon them for political support.

THE AMERICAN FEDERATION OF STATE, COUNTY AND MUNICIPAL EMPLOYEES (AFSCME)

The AFSCME, the largest union of public employees in the nation, pioneered attempts to recruit and represent all occupations employed by state and local governments. Its history at the national level is divisible into two eras, that of Arnold Zander and that of Jerry Wurf, the two presidents who have headed the union since it was formed in 1936. The Zander period was rooted ideologically in a mixture of trade union concepts associated with the early history of the labor movement in the United States and principles and concepts of the merit system civil service. Zander's strategy bias tended to steer the AFSCME toward an emphasis on state legislative action and organization of local unions, mainly in large work forces. During this era, the union measured its success toward winning its objectives in modest increments.

Zander's personal approach to problems of intra-union relationships was characterized by tolerance for divergent views and by accommodation to the numerous group interests that churned within the national union.[19] At national union conventions, he remained neutral in factional struggles to elect vice-presidential candidates and he put his maximum effort into persuading delegates to support his administration's program proposals.

The nationwide public image of the AFSCME during the Zander era was that of a white-collar, civil service organization which exhibited the attitudes and value judgments associated with professional and clerical employees. The AFSCME was never totally a white-collar union, however. Many of its local unions were entirely blue-collar in membership, and several police locals were chartered at an early date. The AFSCME leadership firmly recognized a need for close association with the trade union movement, but it insisted that public employment involved unique problems that required special approaches. At every convention prior to 1960, the delegates, at Zander's urging, adopted resolutions calling for extension of the civil service system in state and local governments. In 1954, however, the convention advocated for the first time adoption of state legislation to authorize collective bargaining in the public service.[20] Throughout his administration, Zander advised local unions to avoid strikes, although he did not completely rule out their use by workers, except police. The union constitution forbade police members to strike.

A favorite Zander program that did not fit traditional trade union concepts was the moderate-cost housing project for union members. Projects were launched in several areas, including three in Los Angeles. Opponents claimed this program drained financial and manpower resources of the union away from the organizing and negotiating tasks which they believed were basic to union success. The housing program was one of the first to be scrapped when the Wurf regime took office.

The AFSCME membership grew steadily during the Zander administration, although the heaviest concentration of locals and members was in the Midwest and in portions of the Atlantic coastal region. The national union was never able to get sufficient financing to be able to conduct a strong recruitment drive. Convention delegates repeatedly refused to authorize increases in dues and per capita payments to the national organization. Consequently, recruiting was done to a large extent by local officers under the general coordination of regional vice-presidents of the national body. Zander and a few national staff members worked to organize local units where demand arose. Complaints that the national headquarters did not provide sufficient service, particularly to smaller local units located at considerable distance from the AFSCME headquarters in Washington, D. C., caused friction within the organization and produced some erosion of membership from time to time.

When the AFSCME undertook to get a foothold among state employees in California, it faced a formidable competitor in the California State Employees Association. It formed local unions in several state hospitals and in the prison at San Quentin.[21] Much later, it mounted another specific campaign to enlist state employees when it tried to capitalize on a split in CSEA ranks over the integration of social security benefits with the state administered retirement program. The union sponsored legislation to permit a favorable linkage of the two programs and opened recruitment offices in Oakland and Los Angeles to service state workers in those areas. Its membership continued to be concentrated in the health care institutions, however.[22]

It gained more substantial niches in some city and county work forces.

Local 122 in San Bernardino, Local 127 in San Diego, and Local 146 in Sacramento County were among the earliest units organized and each came to be influential in the AFSCME state-level councils in California. Other units were formed in San Jose, Fresno, Los Angeles, and San Francisco.

Interest in unionization, both in the private and public sectors, rose during the years of World War II when plants employing thousands of workers were set up to produce war materials. Inasmuch as many of these new plants were located in California, the unionization trend affected the employment situation in such areas as San Diego, Los Angeles, and San Francisco-East Bay. It was during this period that the AFSCME extended to California its interest in organizing local police unions. The police in the city of Santa Monica formed a local in 1940.[23] Those in Long Beach, Burbank, San Jose, and the deputy sheriffs in Los Angeles County followed a few years later.[24] AFSCME chartered a local in the Los Angeles city police department in 1943 and reportedly recruited approximately eight-hundred members in three years. Police in Oakland tried to form a unit in 1956.[25] Opposition within the communities caused most of the police locals to dissolve after short periods, however. The police commission in Los Angeles, after three years, ordered the uniformed officers to forego membership in any labor organization and, when the courts sustained the commission's action, the local was disestablished.[26] The San Jose union was the only one in California to continue for several years.

The AFSCME was more successful in absorbing independent general associations of public employees. It became the first nationally affiliated union to do this when the Contra Costa County Employee Association, a 1,200 member group, voted in 1960 to affiliate and accept a charter as Local 1675.[27] President Zander made a special trip to California to seal this agreement. Shortly thereafter the local achieved its goal of enrolling a total of 2,000 members by recruiting among employees of several cities, school, and special districts in a three-county area.

The move to dislodge Zander as president and change the thrust of the national union was first mounted at the 1960 convention. The rebellious faction was led mainly by delegates from some metropolitan area councils that employed full-time administrators and provided support activities to their local unions, thereby overlapping the programs of the national union. The two major issues at this convention were an increase in per capita payments made by local unions and councils to the national body, proposed by Zander, and a constitutional amendment to permit election of national vice-presidents by members in the regions rather than by the entire delegate convention. The big-city councils were opposed to the first and favored the second. The convention defeated the dues increase and the leadership sidetracked the amendment by getting it referred for further study.[28]

In the 1962 convention, Jerry Wurf, the director of the New York City council and a former member of the national union staff, ran for president but failed to win a majority. The anti-Zander faction, however, captured the post of secretary-treasurer, the second most important position in the union organization, and won several seats on the executive board. The big-city bloc also defeated a proposal to increase per capita payments.

The Wurf-Zander power struggle ended at the 1964 convention when Wurf won a narrow majority and his supporters took over a majority of the board positions after a tumultuous floor fight. Zander was voted a pension as president-emeritus. Soon afterwards, Wurf projected himself nation-wide as the primary spokesman for militant organized public employees. In a series of attention-catching speeches via the national news media he stated a forceful case for legislation authorizing collective bargaining for public employees. He also boasted that where legislation was not forthcoming, his union forced employers to negotiate through strikes and other pressures, in reference to experiences in New York City and a number of eastern communities.[29] AFSCME-led strikes by black sanitation workers in Memphis and Charleston helped to symbolize Wurf and his union to many workers, discontented with existing employment conditions, as champions of poorly paid minority workers, willing to challenge traditional citadels of power.

Consolidation of the new president's control over the direction of union organization took time. Not until 1966 were the convention delegates persuaded to approve an increase in the national body's annual income and an expansion of the national staff to recruit, organize, and provide service to local unions.[30] The constitutional amendment governing selection of regional vice-presidents was approved and much of the disciplinary functions formerly exercised over local unions by the executive board were shifted to a new judicial panel appointed by the president. Finally, in 1972, the delegates extended the term of office for all elected national officers to four years.[31]

Wurf, impatient with the slow progress made in obtaining state legislation recognizing collective bargaining and arbitration, has organized coalitions of public employee organizations that sponsor congressional legislation intended to establish a national policy which would supersede the states' role. Although he has achieved recognition of the enhanced status of organized public employees in the AFL-CIO by winning a vice-presidency of that body, he has been reported on several occasions to be taking actions not supported by the president and executive board.

Tension can develop between a local union, particularly a medium sized one located at a distance from national headquarters, and the national organization. An example of this occurred in Sacramento in 1967. Local 146, one of the oldest AFSCME units in California, had been accustomed to speak for a wide range of employees of Sacramento County in a manner not unlike that of the nonaffiliated general association. It was then engaged in discussions with the county board over a tentative employer-employee relations ordinance, but was encountering severe competition from the Service Employees Union that had recruited a large percentage of the social workers and was pressing for a different model of ordinance.[32] Furthermore, the SEIU was threatening to call a strike in support of social worker demands. When the national executive board of AFSCME announced a plan to place the local unions in California under a state-wide council to strengthen the union's program and to require locals to pay increased per capita dues, the officers of Local 146 rebelled and alleged that interference by the national organization was causing a loss of members.[33] After they met with President Wurf in Los Angeles, they told the press they thought they had been assured their organization could remain independent of the new council.[34] A month later, however, the national board directed Local 146 to amend its by-laws and come under the jurisdiction of Council 149.[35] At a later meeting in Los Angeles, delegates from eighty-one locals adopted a council constitution, elected officers, and planned a state-wide membership drive.[36]

Local 146 elected new officers and, as counseled by President Wurf, remained neutral during the SEIU social workers' strike against Sacramento County. With the assistance of the national staff and the state-wide council, it soon regained much of its vigor in Sacramento County and prepared to operate under the ordinance adopted by the county board in April, 1970. An arbitrator established eighteen representation units and Local 146 chose to contest in four of the largest ones. It did not compete with the SEIU for the social workers or the hospital and institutional workers, but it was challenged in the four in which it chose to stand by an alliance known as SOURCE, composed of the county employees' association and the Operating Engineers Union Local 3. In the ensuing election, Local 146 won in the office-technical, medical center, and operations-maintenance-inspection units, comprising 3,300 employees, but lost the supervisory unit, comprising 1,100 employees, to SOURCE.[37]

The AFSCME under the Wurf regime continued to affiliate several general associations. The first of these was in Humboldt County, in the far north-coastal part of the state. The county employees' association had persuaded the county board to adopt a civil service ordinance in 1964 but later clashed with the board over a work-week increase.[38] To gain assistance in this dispute, the association turned to the League of County Employee Associations and to the AFSCME. It also hired a full-time staff person. When it was unable to achieve satisfaction from the county board, the association voted a strike and asked Wurf to provide union assistance. He appealed to the Humboldt County labor council and the unions in this highly organized area to support the strike.[39] When the Teamsters refused to deliver supplies to the county general hospital, all county government services, except sheriff and fire department, closed for several days.[40] The dispute was soon negotiated, and the association affiliated with the AFSCME.

The Santa Monica Employees Association was the first to affiliate in Southern California. Previous to the action, the association had gone through a fifteen-day strike with the assistance of the Los Angeles County Employee Association and had not been pleased with the outcome. Although the city association's directors had recommended a renewal of the agreement with the county body, the ultimate decision was to affiliate with AFSCME.[41] The city administration, which had opposed the city-county association relationship, soon negotiated an agreement with the union to cover city library, clerical, and white-collar employees.[42]

The AFSCME managed its biggest coup in 1971, when the huge Los Angeles All-City Employees Association voted to link with it.[43] The union had had two locals representing certain city employees for several years, but the affiliation agreement gave it access to an organization that could become the bargaining representative for most employees except those in the water and power, police, and fire departments. This agreement, however, was dissolved at a later date.

Other alliances with the general employee associations also proved to have limited life. Local 1675, the successor of the Contra Costa County Association, disaffiliated in April, 1969, after a lengthy dispute with the national organization on several matters. The association (CCCEA) was revived but took the name of Public Employees Union Local 1. A faction that desired to retain Local 1675 contested the disaffiliation action in court but was told that the CCCEA was a voluntary organization and could withdraw in the same manner it had entered the national union in 1960.[44] A portion of the Contra Costa County work force returned to the AFSCME in 1973 when the 600 member United Clerical Employees of Contra Costa County voted to affiliate. It was chartered as Local 2700, and was given wide jurisdiction to recruit members.[45]

William Lucy, who had been president of Local 1675 in 1965, moved to the national organization in 1966, becoming the associate director of the legislative and community affairs department and later the executive assistant to President Wurf. He was elected secretary-treasurer in 1972, becoming one of the first blacks to fill an elective national union office in the United States.[46]

In forty years of organizing local and state government employees in California, the AFSCME has experienced lows as well as highs. It has established local unions in almost every geographic section and has represented most occupations. Although it has units in many of the larger cities and counties, as well as in the state employment, it has also gone into the small and medium sized jurisdictions.

THE SERVICE EMPLOYEES INTERNATIONAL UNION (SEIU)

The SEIU represents wage earners in a wide variety of occupations in both the private and public employment sectors. More than one-fourth of its national membership total is employed by governments and all but a handful of those are on state or local payrolls.[47] Organized in 1921 as the Building Service Employees Union, this organization's original clientele comprised workers employed in office buildings, hospitals, and rest homes. They were mainly elevator operators, switchboard personnel, janitors, cleaners, porters, parking garage attendants, and stadium employees. The word "building" was dropped from the union title in 1968 because of inferred limitation to the union's organizing scope. The current constitution sets forth a lengthy list of occupations the union claims as constituents.[48] The organization is best characterized as a general union; it recruits blue-collar and white-collar workers alike.

The career of the current president, George Hardy, illustrates the broadening interests of the SEIU and explains something about the extent of influence this union has in California public employment. He and his father, Charles Hardy, were members of the theatrical janitors Local 9 in the San Francisco Bay area when they helped form BSEIU Local 87 in 1936 to represent office and department store janitors in downtown San Francisco.[49] The younger Hardy formed the state council of the union in 1937 and began soon afterward to organize public employees. He headed local unions in San Francisco and Los Angeles and became a vice-president of the Los Angeles County Labor Council. He served as secretary-treasurer of the state-wide council from 1937 to 1948, leaving to become a representative of the international union. He succeeded his father as a vice-president, and in 1971 was elected general president when David Sullivan of Boston resigned. He has been re-elected at each quadrennial convention of the

SEIU and has become a vice-president of the AFL-CIO. Aggressive organizing and recruiting by SEIU agents under Hardy's direction has made this union the largest affiliated with the AFL-CIO in California as well as the largest union of public employees in the state.[50]

The SEIU constitutional structure is similar to that of the AFSCME and other national or international unions that encompass a variety of occupations. The convention of delegates which meets every four years, or oftener if called by the president, is the general policy determining body. Seats in this assemblage are apportioned to allow each local union at least one delegate and to give the larger ones seats in proportion to their membership. The delegation from each local is authorized to cast a number of votes proportionate to the dues-paying members of the unit. The general president, secretary-treasurer, seven vice-presidents, and five board members are elected for four-year terms. This group constitutes the general board, which is the governing body that functions between conventions. The union constitution empowers the general president to grant and suspend charters of local unions, appoint organizers and representatives, and conduct the affairs of the union in consultation with the general board.

The local unions appear to play a more prominent role in the SEIU than do similar units in other unions representing workers in both the public and private sectors. Possibly one explanation for the SEIU success in recruiting public employees and negotiating affiliation agreements with the independent associations is the amount of autonomy given the local unions. The bulk of the paid staff is employed by and serves the local unions. For example, in 1970 the international headquarters employed twenty-six professionals and the 350 locals had a total of six-hundred.[51]

Local unions in California are grouped into four councils, consisting of a state unit whose headquarters is in San Francisco, a joint council in the East Bay and two in Los Angeles. A function of the state council, on which all locals have one seat, is to determine the union's legislative program.

The locals are structured in a variety of ways. Local 535, for example, represents the social workers employed by several counties.[52] Local 390 is made up of a diverse aggregation of occupations from several cities and districts, and the county governments in Alameda and Contra Costa Counties. Local 99, located in Southern California, represents classified employees working in a variety of occupations for school districts. Local 660 comprises chiefly the Los Angeles County employees, formerly members of the county employees association, who elected the SEIU as their bargaining representative. Other locals represent hospital workers or probation officers. Locals range in size from approximately two hundred members to several thousand. Even prior to establishment of collective bargaining, most

SEIU public employee units represented only non-supervisory workers. Several were composed of persons employed in the lowest-paid classifications.[53]

SEIU local unions in California publicized their position in the local government work forces by a series of strikes in 1966. Local 535 conducted walkouts by social workers in Los Angeles, Santa Barbara, and Sacramento Counties. Local 434 led the Los Angeles County General Hospital support workers and Local 390 conducted a similar operation in Alameda County. Local 347 headed a strike of sanitation workers in the city of Los Angeles. The militancy of this union, calling attention to its entry into the civil service area, is expressed by George Hardy in his vice-presidential report to the national union convention in 1968:

Now the greatest number of strikes are on the West Coast. It hasn't been in private industry. It has been in some of the soft jobs, the Civil Service field. The social workers have been taking it on the chin. The most educated people in the labor movement have joined our union, and they believe in democracy.... This is like the old times—these militant white collar educated people went to jail for their union.... The garbage workers, the sanitation workers who have been kicked around for years, had a one-day walkout about three weeks ago, and boy, after Memphis, Tennessee [strike], they made a settlement quick.[54]

Use of the strike tactic to gain attention was used again in March, 1974, when Local 400 launched an action against the city-county of San Francisco. A major portion of all municipal services, including sewage treatment, were closed for several days with the assistance of other unions that recognized the SEIU picket lines. An employer-employee relations ordinance had been adopted, but no unit representation elections had been held. The dispute ostensibly concerned salaries, but many observers viewed the strike as a move to demonstrate the SEIU ability to win a favorable settlement and thereby impress city employees about to vote in unit elections.[55]

SEIU local unions have also used litigation extensively, often selecting disputes that receive a maximum amount of publicity for the sponsoring agent. In most cases the litigants were either holders of the lowest paid jobs or were large aggregations of workers who labored under very trying circumstances for relatively low pay. This tactic appears to be consistent with George Hardy's statement to the 1968 national convention about union concern for the "thoughts of the poor people, the minorities, the downtrodden, the people who have to survive on the lowest wages paid."[56]

The union's legislative actions stress demands for approval of both collective bargaining and political activity by public employees. When the international union launched its program in 1968 to organize public employees, it proposed a four-point set of objectives: (1) obtain authorization for union shop conditions, (2) prohibit the indiscriminate use of injunctions against peaceful picketing and strikes, (3) modify the federal Hatch Act and adopt state and local legislation that would give public employees full rights of political participation, (4) obtain fringe benefits for public employees equal to those enjoyed by private sector workers.[57] Its legislative advocacy in California has held consistently to these objectives.

The SEIU made its most spectacular membership expansion in this state between 1971 and 1973, when it negotiated affiliation agreements with several large, previously independent associations. The first was with the 30,000 member Los Angeles County Employee Association. This was followed by one with the Santa Clara County Employees Association.[58] In November, 1972, the Civil Service Association of San Francisco, with 14,000 members, also voted to affiliate with the existing SEIU Local 400. Next, the Kern County Employees Association, with 4,100 members, consolidated with Local 700 in March, 1973.[59] At virtually the same time, the Alameda County Employees Association voted to affiliate with a newly chartered Local 616. It had rejected a similar proposal two years previously.[60] Each of these actions brought large numbers of dues paying members onto the SEIU roster, and placed the union in a strategic position to win representation rights in the state's largest local work forces when the jurisdictions adopted employer-employee relations ordinances.

Some smaller associations that have affiliated with SEIU are the Albany Municipal Employees Association, the Alameda County Water District Employees Association,[61] and the Santa Barbara City Employees Association.[62] Local 400 in San Francisco also negotiated a memorandum of understanding with the city school board to represent seventy percent of the classified school staff of that jurisdiction.

The SEIU has extended the geographic scope of its influence beyond the metropolitan central areas of Los Angeles, San Francisco, and the East Bay, where it has been influential for more than twenty years. The Orange County court clerks, for example, selected Local 434 of Los Angeles in 1973 as their representative.[63] County employees in Marin County had previously elected the SEIU. As this union has established its presence and gained power centers in such counties as Kern, Santa Barbara, Orange, and San Mateo Counties, it has built communication links with the suburban and sub-metropolitan areas of the state. It has further diversified its occupational mix, and it has opened a niche in the state government's work force.

THE AMERICAN FEDERATION OF TEACHERS (AFT)

The American Federation of Teachers has had a long career in organizing and representing classroom teachers. It began in 1902 as a local group in Chicago which fought with the school board and city officials, and it became a national union in 1916.[64]

The original objectives of the federation were to raise the standards of the teaching profession and to achieve the democratization of the school administrative system. The leaders and members from the beginning used political action, including candidacy for public office, support of candidates, lobbying, and appeals for voter support. They have been concerned with a wide range of issues, but tenure, salaries, and leave policies have uniformly had high priority on their agendas.[65] The AFT's main operational objective has been to conduct direct negotiation with district school boards. Its philosophy, throughout a considerable portion of its history, is expressed in the following:

One of the most important reasons for the organization of the teacher's union movement was to protect classroom teachers against arbitrary and unjust acts on the part of the lay educational authorities and their administrative officers. But this opposition to autocratic educational administration on the part of the Federation does not imply a lack of appreciation of the necessary and important function of educational administration. Actually the teacher's union movement presupposes the existence of local educational authorities with their executive and administrative officers, for the plain fact is that without them we could not have a public school system. In our complex, industrial-urban society, the function of the administration in education is as essential as the function of teaching. The problem is one of developing proper relations between authentic organizations of teachers and the school boards with their professional staffs. . . . The record clearly shows that in the absence of independent teachers unions, there is a tendency for both school boards and superintendents to think of teachers as employees in much the same way as many think of factory employees, that is, as 'hired hands' who are supposed to do what they are told without questioning.[66]

After the AFL and the CIO merged in 1955, the teacher's union was drawn into the orbit of Walter Reuther and the Industrial Union Department. Reuther was greatly interested in unionizing white-collar workers, especially the teachers. He gave the AFT considerable financial and organizational assistance during his tenure in the AFL-CIO.

During a long period of AFT history, two wings coexisted in the organization. One, situated mainly in big Midwestern cities, responded to a succession of Chicago based leaders who opposed strikes but favored aggressive political action. The other, dominated by Local 5 in New York City, was not only abrasively militant but espoused a more radical political and social philosophy.[67]

The New York group, also known as the United Federation of Teachers, had taken over the teachers' union in that city and had developed it into the largest local labor union in the nation by 1962. Operating from this strong base, and under aggressive strategists, they won control of the AFT at the 1964 national convention and ousted the Chicago leadership set. With the aid of AFL-CIO industrial union department funds, the teachers' union began a nationwide drive which pushed its roster to 425,000 members by 1974. It also chartered a large number of new local unions. Moreover, it dropped the no-strike clause from its national constitution.

The AFT has been led since 1964 by a series of New York City based presidents. Charles Cogen, first elected in 1964, was replaced in 1968 by his mentor, David Selden, whose major presidential strategy was to seek merger with the National Education Association. He also pushed the experimental effort to merge Local 1021 in Los Angeles with its bigger competitor, the NEA-affiliated Classroom Teachers Association. After the national merger negotiations were broken off by the NEA, Selden was defeated for re-election as AFT president by Albert Shanker. Shanker, the charismatic and highly publicized figure among the union teachers, who was simultaneously head of the New York City organization, president of the New York State Teachers Federation, and a vice-president of the AFL-CIO, virtually replaced Selden as the AFT policy spokesman two years prior to the election.

AFT locals were first organized in California in such medium sized and large cities as Sacramento, San Francisco, Los Angeles, Fresno, Oakland, and Long Beach. Moreover, most of the local units formed prior to 1960 were in the northern portion of the state. Their membership rosters continued to be modest, however, seldom exceeding fifty names.

The California State Federation of Teachers, which serves as a state-wide coordinating and legislative action body, was formed in 1941. It has supported such legislation as the Moretti bill in 1973 and 1974 to establish a single, comprehensive, collective bargaining system for all public employees. Like most of the local unions, it has consistently affiliated with and participated in the policy discussions of the general state labor federation.

The AFT national organizing drive, started in 1964, began to show results in this state within four years. Charters were granted to new local unions in all parts of the state. Small cities and districts, as well as large ones, were reached in this thrust. In many instances, however, the new locals comprised a mere handful of persons hopeful of gaining cohorts. The AFT also stepped up its efforts to recruit among college teaching staffs. San Francisco State and San Jose State locals became especially visible during the unrest in those schools during the 1960's. Community colleges, state colleges and universities, and some University of California campuses formed AFT locals by 1970. The college units merged in 1971 and became the United Professors of California, a central agent for unionized collegiate staffs.

The AFT has achieved its major California organizing success in San Francisco, where it represents approximately half of the classroom teachers. This unit conducted a strike in 1974 which closed many of the city's schools for several weeks and ultimately induced the non-union group to join the walkout. In the Los Angeles District, where the United Teachers: Los Angeles, formed by a union-CTA merger in 1968, represents the largest aggregation of teachers, it has been vigorously opposed by several non-union associations. In the majority of districts throughout the state, the AFT has been outvoted by teachers who favor the California Teachers Association.

THE INTERNATIONAL ASSOCIATION OF FIRE FIGHTERS (IAFF)

The fire fighters were the first single-occupation group of city employees to organize nationally. They received a charter from the American Federation of Labor in 1918.[68] From the inception of their national organization, the fire fighters participated actively in local labor councils and state federations. Concurrently, the IAFF was successful in maintaining a unique status in two respects over half a century of association with the labor movement. It stood committed, until 1968, to a policy which forbade its local unions to use the strike weapon in their relations with government employers. It also experienced almost no encroachment by other unions. Both features have changed since 1968. Mounting pressures from some of its members, notably those in New York City, have caused the IAFF national convention to delete the strike restriction from the union constitution. Furthermore, the Teamsters Union, which is not affiliated with the AFL-CIO, has made inroads to the IAFF preserve in the firehouses.

Throughout most of its history, the IAFF has maintained a small international headquarters staff in Washington, D. C. The relatively low per capita tax paid by the local unions to support the international organization did not enable the latter to maintain more than a minimal organizing and promotional staff. The bulk of the duties and responsibilities were allocated to the president. The convention, which met biennially and was composed of delegates from the local unions and state councils, determined the union's general policies and elected the international officers. An executive committee advised the president in the interim between conventions. Several vice-presidents represented the international's presence in their respective regions and were generally responsible for recruiting and organizing. This echelon of officers, however, was composed of men who were active-duty firemen in their local departments and could devote only such time to union work as could be arranged with local employers.

The international's headquarters staff was active chiefly in the preparation and distribution of information about fire fighters' salaries and employment practices for use by the local unions in their presentations to local employers. Some critical observers have referred to the headquarters as a library organization, a somewhat unfair label.[69] The international president put in much effort on state legislation pertaining to safety regulations, firemen's retirement plans, and similar subjects vital to the fire fighters' welfare.

Two strongly held traditions in the fire fighters' organization have contributed to many of the organizational disputes. One has been the high degree of autonomy accorded the local unions; the other has been the heavy reliance at local, state, and regional levels on elected officers who were active-duty firemen, rather than on professional staffs of organizers and negotiators. In the latter characteristic, the fire fighters have been atypical among the unions.

Tensions arising from the strike issue and from relationships between the international headquarters and local units kept the union in turmoil during the early part of the 1960's. The 1966 and 1968 conventions produced major changes in the union's philosophy, tactics, and leadership personnel. The strike issue was debated extensively in the 1966 convention and at the next meeting the membership voted to amend the union constitution, after several locals had defied President Buck and the international board and gone out on strike. Election of a new president, a raise in per capita payments, and an increase in the number of vice-presidents who were given responsibility for directing recruitment in their regions presaged important changes.[70] The headquarters staff was expanded and trained to assist local unions with negotiations.

Organizational matters continued to raise disputes within the IAFF for some time. Episodes that occurred in 1970 and 1972 illustrate some of these. A major struggle at the 1970 convention concerned revision of the voting method employed at the biennial meetings. Local unions in small cities were demanding that the international body provide them more services and grant them a degree of recognition that was disproportionate to their membership numbers. Many small locals were unable to send delegates to the convention where union policies were decided. The locals from the big cities dominated the convention sessions and consequently had a controlling voice in determining programs and policies, but were not as dependent on the headquarters for assistance. The big-city locals continued to have a major influence, however. At the 1972 convention, delegates from West Coast locals sought to obtain a regional office staffed by specialists who could assist with organizing and negotiations. They contended that there were 8,000 unorganized fire fighters in their region, and that such unions as the Teamsters and Operating Engineers were raiding the IAFF's special field because the latter lacked the strength to keep up.[71] They said that an international office located in Washington was too removed from the scene to meet the region's needs. The proposal was defeated.

Despite these disputes, the IAFF organizing campaign, which began in 1967, has produced a marked increase in the number of local fire fighter unions in California as well as in the rest of the nation. Moreover, the rhetoric used by fire union representatives, both in local negotiations and in legislative hearings, has become increasingly strident and even belligerent. The number of concerted sick calls and outright strikes has also increased.

A number of characteristics of the governmentally administered fire fighting program in California are particularly relevant to the development of firemen's organizations, including unions. Full-time, compensated fire departments were established in California cities relatively early in the history of the state. The volunteer fire companies, so prevalent throughout American communities, did not multiply in California as extensively as in other regions. The state fire marshal reported in 1974 that California was one of the few states to have more paid departments (571) than volunteer ones (462). The numbers of persons involved is impressive: 28,750 paid firemen, 5,200 part-time members, and 13,908 volunteers.[72]

Fire fighting in this state is not an exclusively municipal function. Several counties have maintained organized forces for many years to suppress fire in grain fields and mountain watersheds. Since the 1920's, suburban fringe areas have created fire protection districts, often associated with the county fire departments, to cope with structural fires. The State Department of Natural Resources has stationed a considerable fire fighting force in suburban as well as mountainous portions of the state.

California fire fighters in some of the larger cities joined the IAFF relatively early in the life of the organization and also affiliated with the state and local trade union bodies. Oakland Local 55 received its charter in

1918, San Diego Local 148 in 1924, and Richmond Local 188 soon thereafter. Locals formed in San Francisco and Los Angeles were forced by official opposition to turn back their charters and were not re-established until many years later. Unionization of the fire forces progressed slowly at first. Twenty-one years after the first IAFF unit was formed, only six had been added to the three previously named. They were Long Beach, San Jose, Stockton, Santa Ana, Sacramento, and Santa Barbara.[73] As late as 1961, the IAFF had established footholds mainly in the large metropolitan or suburban cities, whereas the independent, nonaffiliated firemen's associations had sprung up in cities having populations of 20,000 to 70,000.[74] In some large-city departments, the union competed with an independent association for members and for opportunity to influence city employment policies.

In 1938, the union firemen established a state-wide coordinating body, the California Federation of Fire Fighters, one of the first state bodies chartered by the IAFF. It meets annually in a convention composed of delegates from the local unions to decide its legislative program and to elect officers, who serve as its legislative advocates and advisors to local unions. A. E. Albertoni, of Oakland Local 55, was the organizing architect of this body. Kenneth Larson, of Los Angeles County Local 1014, who served as executive secretary and legislative advocate from 1958 to 1972, was another major figure in the union's legislative history. The Fire Fighters' Act of 1959, which recognized the right of firemen to organize and join organizations of their choice, was adopted during that era. Larson demonstrated a second role of the state federation in 1970 when he coordinated union support for Sacramento Local 522 in strike action against the city.

The organizing campaign begun in 1967 by the international union produced a marked increase in the number of local unions in California. Locals were formed in many cities smaller than the IAFF had previously been able to enter. In some instances, small-city locals merged to form a countywide body possessing larger resources. By 1972, however, many IAFF locals in California contained fewer than fifty members.[75] Nevertheless, more locals were established in large jurisdictions, with the result that ten large local unions comprised the bulk of the membership in California. San Francisco Local 798 and Los Angeles County Local 1014, with more than 1,500 members each, headed the list. Los Angeles City Local 112, reconstituted as Local 748, expanded its membership enormously when city firemen left the Fire and Police Protective League and selected the union as their bargaining representative.

Local 1014 exemplifies a type of organization used to extend IAFF influence into small-city fire departments, to aggregate membership, and to maximize resources. Its primary membership is composed of employees in the unified county and fire protection district department, which provides structural fire protection in urbanized but unincorporated areas and serves the mountain and desert portions of the county as well. It also gives full protection to numerous incorporated cities that have joined the county fire district. Local 1014 has increased its membership in some instances by absorbing city firemen whose departments have merged with the county district. It has also won the court-recognized right under the 1959 statute to represent firemen employed by a city that is not a part of the county system.[76] A few cities have transferred their fire departments to the county system to avoid dealing directly with the union in city employment policy making. Local 1014 has also assisted firemen in several independent cities where issues of prime interest to union firemen throughout the country were being considered, such as creation of a consolidated public safety department or establishment of police salaries at a level above that of firemen.[77]

IAFF locals in California have employed litigation periodically to challenge local administrations and to enforce provisions of statutes the union has sponsored. Those in Merced County and the cities of Palo Alto and Los Angeles went to court in 1960 to enforce the 1959 statute that established the right of firemen to join organizations of their choice. The Vallejo local pressed its claims for arbitration and interpretation of the city charter, whereas the San Francisco and Los Angeles locals sued their respective cities to enforce charter provisions concerning their wages.[78] The Pasadena unit challenged the legality of the procedure the city used to select the fire chief.[79]

Strikes by IAFF locals have been comparatively infrequent, although their spokesmen have threatened walkouts. The most publicized incidents were the strikes by firemen of Vallejo in 1969, Sacramento in 1970, and San Francisco in 1975.[80]

Four employment policy subjects, police-fire wage parity, consolidation of police and fire departments to form public safety units, a shortened work week, and compulsory arbitration, have been major concerns of the IAFF for several years, both nationally and in California. Parity between firemen and police wages existed for so long that it became a tradition. Management in several cities challenged this tradition in the early 1960's, however, proposing police salaries ahead of those paid fire fighters. The move was based in many instances on the recruitment situation, in which applicants for fire jobs were numerous and those for police work were scarce. It also resulted from job analyses in which budget and personnel specialists found that approximately one-third of the time spent by personnel at fire stations was devoted to recreation, sleeping, and passive duties, whereas police personnel were steadily involved in law enforcement. Many police departments in California had endeavored to raise the formal educational requirements of their officers with the objective of creating a law enforcement profession. Although fire fighters' knowledge requirements increased greatly in sophistication, the tasks performed continued to be regarded as those of skilled workmen rather than of professionals, in the general sense of that term. The IAFF members reacted heatedly to all proposals to depart from the traditional wage standard.

Berkeley, the first city in California to break with the tradition, provides an interesting example of systemic reactions to a key decision. When the city raised police pay above that for the parallel fire classes, the IAFF local promoted a charter amendment by initiative petition to require the city to continue to observe parity. It lost at the ballot boxes. The San Francisco police also were aroused because the new Berkeley pay rates exceeded those paid them, and they pushed through a charter amendment which required the city-county to pay its police rates equal to the best in any major California city. The San Francisco firemen were determined to keep pace, and won an initiative charter amendment that assured them parity with the police. The issue continues to arise periodically in San Francisco and in other cities. It first arose in Los Angeles in 1967, when Mayor Yorty recommended a greater raise for police than firemen and was supported by the Fire and Police Protective League. IAFF Local 748, which at that time had only a fraction of the fire department personnel on its roster, attacked the plan vociferously and charged that the plan had been instigated by a statewide conspiracy among police associations. The outcome of that episode was that the city council gave both departments the same rate of wage increase.[81] The parity issue is not publicly debated in the 1970's, but it remains ever present in negotiations.

The plan to establish public safety departments that would perform fire suppression duties as well as law enforcement is likewise not as prominent in the 1970's as in an earlier period. A few public safety units have continued to operate, but most experiments proposed during the 1960's have been abandoned. The IAFF's unequivocal position throughout has been that only qualified professional, and therefore specialized, fire fighters should be employed to suppress fires.[82] Probably the most publicly fought battle over a consolidation plan occurred in San Diego in 1961-63. The city manager, when pressed to reduce the firemen's work week from sixty-three to fifty-six hours, responded with a plan to create a consolidated public safety unit.[83] The IAFF local solicited assistance from the international union and recruited allies among a number of local political interest groups to win a unanimous vote of the city council to shelve the plan.[84] The defeat of this proposal, combined with setbacks on some other issues, caused the manager to resign.

The firemen's work week has been atypical of public employee work schedules for decades. This has been due partly to the necessity for maintaining fire station crews in readiness around-the-clock to respond to calls. It is also a product of the traditional practice of requiring the on-duty crews to live at the fire station for periods of sixty or more hours and permitting them comparably long duty-free periods after a shift is completed. Most public employees work a fixed number of hours per day, whether during daylight or night hours, and may return home after work hours.

The California Federation of Fire Fighters and the IAFF nationwide tested a number of strategies during the 1950's and 1960's to reduce the work week without challenging the basic plan wherein fire crews live at the stations. During the 1950's, some of the local unions in the larger California cities sought to achieve their goal through initiative petitions to amend city charters. The major interest state-wide, however, was in obtaining passage of state legislation that would set a maximum number of hours a government employer could work its fire crews. An alliance of firemen's organizations, IAFF locals and nonaffiliated associations, made an all-out legislative drive in the 1961 and 1963 sessions. It obtained appointment at the first session of an interim legislative study committee, which held hearings throughout the state and surveyed the existing practices. This committee, headed by Assemblyman John Knox of Contra Costa County, proposed a bill (AB 1194) which became known as the 56-Hour Bill in the 1963 session. Although the proponents were able to get the bill through the Assembly, the opponents, chiefly the League of California Cities, defeated it in the Senate. After that attempt to set a mandated state-wide policy failed, the IAFF turned again to local action and eventually to collective bargaining and compulsory arbitration of interest disputes.

The IAFF announced in 1972 an objective to obtain congressional legislation to authorize compulsory arbitration of interest disputes in which fire fighters were involved. State legislatures in Pennsylvania, Michigan, and Hawaii required local governments in those states to go to arbitration when they reached an impasse in bargaining with fire and police organizations. Bills to achieve a similar objective failed in the California legislature, however. IAFF locals in Vallejo and Oakland succeeded in getting a charter amendment and council ordinance adopted which gave them arbitration rights, but firemen in San Francisco and Sacramento failed in similar efforts.

THE BUILDING AND CONSTRUCTION TRADES UNIONS

Several international unions have recruited and represented public employees but have not, in most instances, formed separate departments, councils, or local unions of public workers. Prominent among these have been the building and construction craft unions of carpenters, painters, plumbers, and electricians. Many public employees were members of their respective craft unions before they entered public employment and have retained the affiliation after appointment to the civil service.

The Building Trades Councils, composed of various unions in the building industry, have been influential elements in salary setting among the larger local government jurisdictions. Working in conjunction with the central labor council of the particular area, the building trades unit has effectively advocated the prevailing rate of wage concept which relates public salaries to wage levels paid in the community for comparable levels of skill and responsibility. These combinations of labor organizations have caused several cities and counties to adopt sections of their charters which require the government-employer to follow this practice. In the Los Angeles metropolitan area, for example, both Los Angeles city and county, which have this type of charter provision, have calculated salaries for their skilled trades employees in accordance with a formula developed during the 1950's by administrative agreement with the building trades unions. The formula is based on wage levels set by regional industry-wide contracts negotiated between the Associated General Contractors and the construction unions, adjusted to reflect differences in fringe benefits paid by the governments and the building industry.[85] In some other areas, notably Alameda County, a similar plan is used to determine public employee salaries.[86]

THE INTERNATIONAL UNION OF
ELECTRICAL WORKERS (IBEW)

The IBEW is a part of the building trades group in local public employment wage setting negotiations in most jurisdictions, but in those cities that operate publicly owned utilities it has demonstrated a special interest for many years. IBEW Local 18 is an outstanding example. It is a pioneer in the California labor movement, having been first chartered in Los Angeles in 1893 as Local 61 and later consolidated and retitled. When public ownership of the electrical system serving customers in the city of Los Angeles was proposed in 1905, the union supported the proposal.[87] The close relationship that has existed between the water and power department and Local 18 for the greater part of the electrical system's existence has been described by George Smith, the unit's business agent at the time of the union's 75th anniversary, in the following terms:

[M]ost of our members are employed by the Department of Water and Power, and we have a system of year-round negotiations with management of the DWP. It isn't formalized, and no written contract comes out of it.

The relationship has been influenced greatly by the fact that the Water and Power Defense League, the chief fund raising and political action unit for support of charter amendments governing the operating policies and powers of the department, has been a muscular arm of the union. The league, particularly during the early history of the DWP, played a very active role in city council and mayoral elections. A Los Angeles political analyst has summed up the situation in this fashion:

Councilmen and city officials say Local 18 is one of the two most influential city employee organizations . . . an AFL affiliate, [it] represents some 5,500 cable splicers, electrical mechanics, pumping plant operators, repairmen and others who work for the Los Angeles Department of Water and Power. . . . At election time, the active members combine with 3,000 retired members for campaign work.[88]

Local 18 strongly supported the concept of departmental independence from mayor and council control. The five-member commission which heads the department was responsible for determining salaries paid its employees. Although most of its employment practices were governed by civil service policies set forth in the city charter, the department personnel office was in reality independent of central control for many years and was able to draw many employees away from the council-controlled departments. Much of this independence has diminished in the 1970's, however, and in 1977 the municipal voters vested all salary setting responsibility in the mayor and council.

Local 18 began a relationship with the Pasadena municipal electric system similar to that which it enjoyed in Los Angeles. The informality of that relationship ultimately produced an interesting, but negative, outcome for the union when the AFSCME recruited members in the Pasadena system in 1970. The IBEW appealed to the AFL-CIO, claiming its jurisdiction was being violated. An arbiter found that the AFSCME had in fact encroached but had not violated the AFL-CIO standards, inasmuch as in the absence of a negotiated contract Local 18 had no formally recognized status in the Pasadena department.[89]

Since that time, Los Angeles and Pasadena have adopted employer-employee relations ordinances that establish formal procedures. Local 18 has become the bargaining representative for most of the classifications it previously represented informally. It also serves as negotiator for city utility employees in Azusa and Burbank.[90]

IBEW Local 1245 in Oakland is another example of a unit representing public employees.[91] It has functioned in that city for more than twenty years and has recently negotiated agency shop arrangements with two irrigation districts in Alameda County on behalf of district employees.[92]

THE INTERNATIONAL UNION OF OPERATING ENGINEERS

The International Union of Operating Engineers, an organization with approximately 400,000 members nationwide, is a mixed union which organizes and represents public as well as private sector employees. In California it represents members employed by counties, cities, and school districts in all types of personnel transactions, although the number of members employed in any one jurisdiction is often not large. It has broadened its membership interest in recent years, and now includes white-collar, professional, and uniformed employees as well as blue-collar workers. The union divides its public employee representation in this state according to geographic regions.[93]

Local 3 has been assigned the northern portion of the state and has been especially aggressive in the Sacramento-San Joaquin Valley areas. It claimed 4,000 public employees in its territory in 1973.[94] Its constituents were uniformed personnel in three counties and eleven cities and nonuniformed personnel in eight counties and eleven cities, five school districts, and two special districts.

Local 501 is responsible for organizing and representing Southern California public employees. It reported a membership in 1973 of approximately seven-hundred nonuniformed personnel employed by two counties, two cities, two school districts, and two university campuses.[95] Like many public organizations, the Operating Engineers union has engaged in litigation on behalf of its members. Local 3 sued Fresno and Madera counties in 1973 and, in the latter case, overturned a county policy that had recognized an independent employees' association as the sole representative of a countywide unit of employees.[96]

THE INTERNATIONAL BROTHERHOOD OF TEAMSTERS, CHAUFFEURS, WAREHOUSEMEN AND HELPERS OF AMERICA (TEAMSTERS)

The Teamsters, an independent, international union, ejected from the AFL-CIO and noted for aggressive action in the private sector, has become active in organizing and representing public employees. It seeks to enlist any number, no matter how small, of members in a work force and seeks to enlarge its foothold by skillful maneuvers. In several instances it has negotiated an agreement to represent an organization of local government employees in bargaining, although it does not gain many members. In 1973, it purported to represent workers in more than thirty public jurisdictions in California.[97]

The Teamsters, like the Operating Engineers, divides the state into two geographic areas for purposes of organizing and representing public employees. Local 960 serves northern California and Local 968 operates in the southern area. Local 960 works through three divisions, one of which represents correctional officers in thirteen state institutions, another serves employees of the city-county of San Francisco, and the third represents administrative officers in the San Francisco school system. At one time it also had an affiliation agreement with the San Francisco deputy sheriffs' association.[98]

Local 986 has been particularly active with police officers and fire fighters. In organizing the latter, it has invaded the traditional stronghold of the IAFF, an affiliate of the AFL-CIO. In 1974, the Vernon Police Association voted to designate the Teamsters as the bargaining agent, and in 1976 the much larger San Diego Police Association entered a similar relationship. In 1973, the Teamsters were reported to be the negotiators for twelve city and one county fire fighters' groups, for miscellaneous employees in seven cities, for a city airport department, and for three school districts.[99]

THE LABORERS INTERNATIONAL UNION OF NORTH AMERICA (LABORERS)

The Laborers union is also a mixed union which has only recently become active in the public sector. Approximately ten percent of its membership nationwide is among public employees in sanitation and street departments.[100] It has competed sharply with the AFSCME in several areas of the eastern United States but has not been widely accepted in California. Local 261, for example, represented approximately half the clerical, professional, and supervisorial employees of the city of Tracy in negotiations and a strike in August, 1969.[101] The union also represented San Francisco municipal gardeners and street sweepers during a strike in April and May, 1976.

THE MARINE ENGINEERS BENEVOLENT ASSOCIATION (MEBA)

The Marine Engineers, a relatively small international union with headquarters in New York City and few affiliates, became prominent in California public employee affairs in 1970, when it began to represent several large, previously independent public employee associations.[102] It offered professional knowledge and experience in collective bargaining and financial support of organizing, and it permitted each organization affiliating with it to retain its identity. These features proved attractive to large associations that were seeking alliances by which to protect themselves from unions that were attempting to take over through consolidation.

The California Association of Professional Employees (CAPE) was the first to affiliate with MEBA in 1970. It comprised approximately 3,700 engineers, architects, surveyors, and inspectors employed in the Los Angeles county and city engineering departments and the county flood control district. It had been one of the prominent associations in those jurisdictions for several years.[103] This association's action was soon followed by that of the 9,000 member San Francisco Civil Service Association.[104] The CSASF leadership soon became dissatisfied with the arrangement and brought about a merger with the SEIU.[105]

MEBA continued its success story throughout 1971, however. The 1,200 member Municipal Employee Association of San Jose signed with it in April; the 1,500 member Fresno city association and the 1,100 member Oakland association did likewise in July.[106] In each instance, the associations' members voted approval overwhelmingly. Each local group appeared to be interested primarily in gaining the service of experienced negotiators and in preparing for negotiations over local employer-employee relations ordinances which contained collective bargaining procedures.

THE CALIFORNIA LABOR FEDERATION, AFL-CIO

The California Labor Federation, organized in 1904 as the California State Federation of Labor, coordinates the local unions of the international bodies that make up the AFL-CIO within the state. It is financed by annual per capita payments from its affiliates, and its biennial conference of delegates elects its officers and determines policy and the agenda for legislative advocacy. In 1972 it represented 1368 local unions and 148 councils, comprising more than a million workers.[107]

The federation's chief executive officer and legislative advocate, John F. Henning, was elected in 1970 to succeed Thomas L. Pitts (1960-1970) and C. J. Haggerty (1943-1960). Henning had served as California's Director of Industrial Relations under Governor E. G. Brown, Sr., and as Under Secretary of Labor in President Kennedy's administration.

In the AFL-CIO plan of organization, county central labor councils are the foundation structures, representing the labor movement at the community level. Their executive secretaries have been referred to as the voice of labor in their geographic areas. They frequently accept appointment also to numerous public committees and boards as a combined community service and public relations responsibility on behalf of organized labor. The Los Angeles central labor council is one of the largest units in the nation, and those in San Francisco and Alameda rank well up on the scale of size. Their executive secretaries are prominent figures in the labor program. A central labor council executive secretary often makes the presentation of wage proposals to major city councils or the county board on behalf of the union members. Increasingly, this officer acts as a conciliator in work disruptions that involve public employees. Unions affiliated with the AFL-CIO, moreover, are required to obtain the approval of the central labor council, as well as of the international officers of their own organization, before going out on strike.

The resolutions pertaining to organized public employee interests adopted by the state federation at its biennial sessions provide a good index of the legislative program. During the decade of the 1950's, the preponderance of resolutions dealt with civil service in general or State Personnel Board matters. The 1960 convention, for example, supported a resolution by the Fire Fighters which sought to establish civil service tenure for employees of fire departments throughout the state. A 1963 proposal demanded a change in the state administered civil service oral examination procedures. The 1966 convention, however, dealt with virtually the last resolutions pertaining to civil service per se. Of forty-five propositions considered on that occasion, three concerned civil service. One called for the repeal of the federal Hatch Act which restricted public employees' political actions, and the remainder related to public employee retirement, sick leave, and other benefits. Eight related to the right to organize or to collective bargaining.

The federation's interest shifted noticeably from civil service to collective bargaining and related procedures, beginning with the 1968 convention. Its spokesmen at the legislative session held that year helped to put into law the Meyers-Milias-Brown Act, which required local governments to meet-and-confer with employee organizations.[108] The convention resolutions adopted thereafter pertained mainly to civil rights, a subject on which the federation first took action in the 1950's, and to collective bargaining. The executive council stated in 1972 that one of the federation's major priorities was to win full collective bargaining rights for public employees.[109] In line with that policy decision, the federation has given preference in its support for a statute that would provide a comprehensive system applicable to all public employees in the state. It supported the bill sponsored by Assembly Speaker Moretti in 1972 and 1973, and that presented by Senator Dills in 1975.

CONCLUSIONS

Although some employees of the California state and local governments were union members prior to 1959 and 1961, when the legislature recognized the right of civil servants to form or join organizations of their choice, the growth of membership has been greatest since those dates. The growth is partly the result of an organizing campaign begun by the AFL-CIO in 1961 to organize white-collar and government wage earners. The first major target for that drive was the Los Angeles-Orange County region of Southern California. Numerous individual unions have continued to make individual efforts in that area and throughout the state. The major recruiting efforts focused first on the work forces of large central cities, districts, and counties in the metropolitan areas. Since 1970, several unions have extended their efforts to non-metropolitan jurisdictions throughout the state.

An unusual part of the union recruitment story is the capture of established, previously independent general associations. The relationship between an association and a union began, in numerous instances, when the association sought the help of the experienced negotiators and the financial support promised by a national or international union to strengthen its position vis-à-vis the public employer. Most associations also hoped to maximize their strength for competition with other organizations that sought to represent employees in the same work force. In most instances, the alliance resulted in a merger and the association became the nucleus of a local union or council of unions. Sometimes the association switched allegiance to a second union. Sometimes the relationship was severed after considerable controversy.

As the larger local government work forces have formalized employer-employee relations under the Meyers-Milias-Brown Act or local ordinances, the unions and associations have undergone a sorting out process. Unit representation elections and other processes which determine representation have tested the ability of each organization to survive.

The public employee union picture changes frequently. Two AFL-CIO affiliated international unions, the AFSCME and the SEIU, which represent public employees engaged in a wide range of occupations, vie for the role of dominant spokesman for unionized civil servants in California. Both have established strength in the major metropolitan areas and have extended their influence into some other parts of the state. Neither has large numerical memberships among state employees. The AFSCME organizes and represents only public employees, whereas the SEIU is a mixed organization of private and public sector workers, although its public sector locals are composed entirely of public employees. Three other international unions from the private sector are challenging these two in California. The Operating Engineers union represents public employees through locals whose members are mainly industrial workers; the MEBA has negotiated agreements with several large associations but has not attempted to set up a local union structure. These competing international unions are affiliated with the AFL-CIO and therefore their jurisdictional strife is subject to some in-house review. Another international union, the Teamsters, is not affiliated and therefore can recruit at will. It has shown periodically its intent to search out and represent public employees in several occupations, including those in police and fire departments.

Such single-occupation unions as the AFT and IAFF have grown considerably in members and local unions since 1968. The IAFF's historic monopoly in the fire fighting field is now being challenged by the Teamsters and the AFT is in constant competition with the nonaffiliated California Teachers Association.

The California Labor Federation provides a major channel through which public employee unions and those representing private sector workers can negotiate a census on demands to be made for state legislation. This body historically has concentrated its attention on matters that interested industrial workers, but since approximately 1960, like its associate, the AFL-CIO, it has reflected a much broader mixture of working-persons' interests. It has pushed hard since 1968 for state legislation to establish a comprehensive state-administered decision system based on collective bargaining for all public employees. Each individual union, however, has its own structure by which it determines its special legislative agenda. On numerous occasions, the interests of one union have been at variance with those of another in the AFL-CIO family.

Clearly public employee unionism in California is a plural force. It is not monolithic and, although it exhibits a degree of unity on some issues, it is subject often to internal strains and to slippage in strength.

IV

THE CALIFORNIA
POLITICAL SYSTEM

The state and its local governments constitute a political system through which decisions on public policy are developed. They are at the same time employers. Conflict is inherent because many of the performers in the decision process on public employment policies are not in a position to act as arbiters between competing political forces, as they do in other matters.

The present purpose of analyzing the state political system is to understand how it works when it determines public employment policy. The formal structure of the fifty states and their local governments are similar, but certain differences in detail significantly influence the operations of each. Custom and political interaction combine to determine the subjects about which each state makes policy and the substance it gives to those subjects selected.

This chapter is concerned with major aspects of the California political system as they pertain to the development of policies relative to conditions of public employment and employer-employee relations. The informal processes combine with the formal structure to make up a functioning system.

The California system offers many gateways through which organized public employees make demands concerning employment policy. These include not only the legislature, governor, local boards, and executives, but also civil service or personnel boards, and the courts. In California, more than in most states, organized groups may appeal to the voters by means of initiative petitions. Following state Supreme Court decisions in 1968, public employee organizations began to participate in the election of legislative and executive officers.

For approximately forty years the political parties, customary catalysts of interests in American politics, were weak participants in the state and local policy-making process. The vacuum created in the state political sys-

87

tem by their weakness was filled by a myriad of interest groups. Organized public employees constituted one set of groups, and those who opposed their demands, either by objections to specific proposals or by longer-range resistance on economic or philosophical grounds, constituted another. Also among this opposition were organizations of public officials who performed the role of employers. Groups such as the League of California Cities, the County Supervisors Association, the School Boards Association, and the Irrigation Districts Association appeared on the scene relatively early and demonstrated skill in presenting their views. Similar sets of employer groups exist in other states, but few match those in California in organizational strength and influence on the policy making process.

The Progressive Movement in California politics in the early part of this century fostered a strong tradition of local home rule, for counties as well as cities, which was translated into formal law as well as custom. When the organized local employees were frustrated in attempts to influence local employment policies, they sought state legislation that would mandate rules or standards for all local governments. The organizations of officials tried either to defeat these proposals or to develop alternatives that would give local administrations more freedom to work out special arrangements.

Political reform ideologies and theories of governmental administration that dwelt on the values of a strong executive and a professional bureaucracy were greatly influential in California state and local governments during the first half of this century. They made an important impact on formal structure and on operations. Most executives and central administrators schooled in these theories strongly resisted the demands for participation in policy decisions by organized public employees. The clash between the two sets of interests has resulted in some adjustments in the formal structures, but greater changes have occurred in relationships and operations. Further modifications of political and administrative structures demanded by the proposals for collective bargaining between public employers and employees would raise substantial problems.

A less important but interesting aspect of the California political system is the development of numerous intergovernmental agreements for purposes of mutual aid or of sharing the costs of public works construction and operation. Some blur the identification of the employer responsible for making employment policy. Some enable a governing body that grows weary of coping with employee problems to shift responsibility, along with the program, to another government. Others enable government-employers to render aid to a jurisdiction whose employees are on strike, thereby strengthening management's position in the dispute.

THE STATE EXECUTIVE

The governor of California is a key figure in making employment policy for the state government, and many of his decisions are also crucial for the determination of those affecting local governments. The office, when judged in terms of formal powers vested in it by the state constitution, is rated one of the most powerful among the fifty states.[1] Moreover, incumbents of this office, beginning with Hiram Johnson (1911-1916), have used political techniques as well as their constitutional powers to exert leadership in policy making. Only a few have specifically sought to take the leadership in public employment problems, however. One was Earl Warren (1943-1953), an outspoken supporter of civil service. Edmund G. Brown Sr. (1959-1967), governor when such issues as whether public employees should have the right to organize and whether the state should adopt formal employer-employee relations procedures first came under extensive debate, was broadly sympathetic to the employees. Ronald W. Reagan (1967-1975), opposed collective bargaining for public employees, assigned state patrolmen and firemen to aid the city of Vallejo during a fire and police strike, and approved a settlement of the first strike of state employees. He also declined to authorize state salary increases one year. Edmund G. Brown Jr. (1975-   ), personally intervened in legislative negotiations to try to get agreement on a comprehensive bargaining bill but did not succeed. He drew employee criticism when he authorized only minimal salary increases.

Formal constitutional powers of the office give the governor the opportunity to determine legislative output on spending and all other state transactions. They also offer him the opportunity to manage a major portion of the state's administrative apparatus. The grant of these powers is not wholly of recent origin. One of the more significant tools, the item veto, was authorized in 1908. It enables a governor to eliminate or reduce appropriations either in the omnibus state budget bill or in any statute that proposes to spend state money. A constitutional amendment adopted in 1922 makes the governor responsible for preparing and introducing the state budget. The combination of item veto and budget preparation authority places the governor in a very strong position to determine the spending level and the allocation of funds among programs and objects of expenditure. Although the legislature frequently increases the total budget above that presented by the governor, the latter participates in the adjustments. Moreover, the record shows that a gubernatorial item veto has been overridden by the legislature only once, as long ago as 1939. Equally significant is the fact the legislature seldom overrides the governor's veto of non-fiscal bills.

The governor, under a plan begun in 1966, is aided in the supervision of the state bureaucracy by four deputies, each of whom presides over a cabinet agency composed of numerous departments whose top administrators are, for the most part, appointed by the governor. He exercises considerable influence over the departmental program operations through these deputies. The number of offices the governor may fill by appointment is limited chiefly to high level, policy-making positions. Some serve at his pleasure; others are subject to confirmation by the state Senate. Governor Reagan chose to delegate responsibility for state employee relations to the secretary of the Agriculture and Services Agency. E. G. Brown Jr. operates in a different manner, taking a direct part in negotiations, assisted by members of his personal staff who are specialists in employee relations.

Patronage opportunities in the overwhelming percentage of state jobs were removed from the governor's grasp in 1938 by a constitutional amendment sponsored by state employees and supported by organized labor, leaders from both political parties, and a wide spectrum of groups. State employment affairs are directed by a five-member State Personnel Board whose members serve by appointment of the governor and by confirmation of the Senate for ten-year terms. Terms are staggered for the purpose of ensuring that only a governor re-elected for a second term can appoint a majority of the board membership. The constitution prescribes the duties of this board and places the vast majority of state employees in the classified system. A statute gives the board responsibility for determining the rates of wage that prevail in the employment market and for recommending to the governor salaries for each job classification in the state bureaucracy. This body is responsible for maintaining equitable salary relationships between the various classes in the state service.

The Board of Regents of the University of California and the Trustees of the State University and Colleges system, the two largest employers of personnel in the state government, exercise authority over employment and salary setting of the academic and support employees in their respective institutions. Members of both boards are appointed for relatively long terms by the governor, subject to Senate confirmation.

The governor identifies himself with a political party and is elected by the state-wide electorate. The direct primary method of nominating party candidates for state offices compels those seeking the gubernatorial office to court the support of major groups and to raise the initial campaign funds without the support of the party organization. Unofficial bodies within each major party have attempted to exercise some influence in this process by giving pre-primary endorsements to favored candidates. Only in the general election do the formal party organizations perform their traditional roles. It is agreed, however, that endorsements and financial contributions from organized groups play a very significant part in the winning of primary and general elections. The support sought or accepted by the candidate tends to indicate his policy intentions when he reaches the office. In the 1974 election, for example, the winning Democratic candidate, E. G. Brown Jr., accepted contributions from the state labor federation and several public employee organizations and stated that he favored the adoption of collective bargaining. Houston Flournoy, the Republican candidate, was supported largely by business contributors and indicated that he favored some changes in the meet-and-confer procedures in government-employee relations but did not support collective bargaining for public workers.

The governor is expected to present a legislative program at each session of the legislature. His ability to achieve favorable action depends on his popularity and ability to negotiate with opposing or uncommitted legislators, as well as on the number of members identified with either party in the two houses. Governor Warren, a moderate Republican, was opposed on several legislative items by the ultra-conservative members of his own party, although he felt that his greatest opposition came from lobbyists.[2] Divided government has been the rule for almost forty years. Most Republican governors since 1935 have faced a Democratic-controlled lower house. Governor Reagan, for example, had only one two-year period during his tenure in which his party enjoyed a numerical majority in both houses. In his final two years, the Democrats led both houses. The senior Brown had greatest difficulty with the lower house where the Democratic Speaker, Jesse Unruh, was anxious to restore legislative power in state politics and hoped to achieve the governorship himself. The younger Brown had the unusual experience of dealing with a legislature in which his party held almost two-thirds of the seats in both houses.

A CHANGING LEGISLATURE

The California legislature, like its counterpart in other states, suffered for several decades a low public esteem and an inability to identify or grapple capably with policies having state-wide significance. Despite constitutional prescriptions of legislative-executive parity, it was overshadowed by the governor. The situation was due to several factors. One was the distrust of legislative bodies that lingered with memories of corruption in the 1890's and early 1900's, despite the Progressive reform accomplished in 1910. Another was a heritage of the Progressives' espousal of non-partisanship.

Although they failed to make election to the legislature a non-partisan process, they weakened the parties so much that all vestiges of party responsibility for organizing the legislature, sorting bill proposals, and identifying issues of state-wide significance were lost for almost fifty years. Party organization returned to the Assembly in 1935 but was not firmly in effect in the Senate until 1968. Party labels were virtually meaningless in the legislature until approximately 1963. Interest groups replaced the parties as the force that made the legislature move through its constitutionally limited biennial sessions. According to many observers, ten or twelve influential lobbyists representing financially powerful interests controlled the main outlines of legislation enacted for several years.[3] The structural revisions in state government which enhanced the powers of the governor also shifted to the executive the challenge to identify state-wide issues and to determine what initiative would be taken with respect to them.

A third aspect was the malapportionment of the legislature caused by the federal plan, adopted by initiative constitutional amendment in 1928, in which seats in the Senate were apportioned among the counties and those in the Assembly were apportioned on the basis of population. The result was that the rural and mountain counties elected the majority of senators and the three major urban areas, Los Angeles, San Francisco, and the East Bay, elected the majority in the Assembly. The Senate was controlled by conservative Republicans and Democrats, whereas the majority of the Assembly were liberal Democrats. Legislation pertaining to public employment matters sponsored by employee organizations usually were approved by large majorities in the Assembly but were buried in Senate committees. For almost twenty years, the Senate Committee on Governmental Operations served as the conservative control mechanism that stopped or drastically amended most pieces of legislation intended to set state-wide standards for local employees' compensation or hours or suggested any type of collective bargaining procedure. Regional rivalry in state politics was so great that several attempts to repeal the federal plan were defeated by coalitions of voters in the San Francisco area and those in northern rural and mountain counties. The malapportionment was finally broken by the decisions of the U.S. Supreme Court, headed by former governor Warren, based on the one-man: one-vote principle. Senate reapportionment in 1968 made possible the election of some labor-supported members from metropolitan areas, although the reapportionment also brought a considerable percentage of new members from suburban communities that did not favor legislation sponsored by labor-affiliated groups.

The leadership of the two houses is another factor that helps determine the fate of bills in the legislature. The Speaker of the Assembly appoints the chairmen and members of the committees in that house and determines the routing of bills to committees. He also exercises a major influence in the preparation of rules that determine the number of committees and the procedures for considering bills. During the era of low party strength, speakers were chosen to all intents by the lobbyists who assisted their favored candidate to line up sufficient votes from members of both parties. Organizations and interests that were parts of this coalition had ample opportunities to influence the make-up of committees to which their bills were to be referred. The party caucus and the practice of selecting the speaker on partisan lines reappeared in the California legislature in the 1958 session with the selection of Ralph Brown. While Speaker Unruh, who became speaker in 1963, appointed some Republicans as committee chairmen, he followed a strong party line. He also achieved a national reputation as a parliamentarian and modernizer of the state institution. He reduced the number of committees, added committee and house staffs, and improved the procedures of the lower house. The revision process which came to a peak under the Unruh leadership helped revive popular respect for the state legislature and led to other changes. Legislative salaries and benefits were increased, the annual session was adopted, and the California legislature became a more effective, coordinate branch of state government that now operates virtually year-round.

Change in the Senate leadership came more slowly than in the Assembly, due in part to the lateness of the reapportionment of that body. During the federal plan era the leadership was held by a group of wealthy rural or small-town senators who operated in a club-like atmosphere. After reapportionment, formal leadership was vested in a five-member rules committee elected by the forty senators to make committee appointments and to direct the institutional work of the house. The chairman of this committee is the president pro-tem of the Senate. This officer has been subjected to challenge from time to time, and on two occasions the incumbent has been toppled before the end of the legislative session.

One conventional procedure remains remarkably constant, despite the series of legislative changes. Each member of either house introduces bills on any subject, whether constituency-serving or state-wide in effect, without deference to the party leadership. Many introduce numerous bills at the request of interested groups and these do not necessarily reflect the legislator's personal convictions. Unlike most highly partisan state legislatures, the California body did not develop until approximately 1970 the practice in which the legislative party leaders draft most of the major legislation. Speaker Unruh, however, drafted some significant pieces of legislation and used the power of his office to push them through. Since that start, every speaker, regardless of party identification, has done somewhat the same. For example, Speaker Robert Moretti in 1971 and 1973 held up all bills pertaining to public employee collective bargaining and gave priority to his own comprehensive bill.

Members of both parties introduce legislation pertaining to civil service and related employment matters. Liberal Democrats have tended to sponsor collective bargaining bills, although some moderate Republicans have also done so. Conservatives in both parties offer bills to outlaw strikes or to do away with teacher tenure. Individual members continue to mobilize votes for their bills with the assistance of lobbyists and fellow legislators and to steer their general-interest proposals through the committees and to the governor's desk. Consequently a considerable number of legislators choose to develop legislative reputations and political careers by specializing in such fields as employment policy or employer-employee relations. Assemblymen George Brown and Charles Meyers, Democrats, did this in the early 1960's. The success of individual members is due in part to the relatively high turnover in legislative membership and the consequent low importance of seniority. Moreover, committee chairmanships are not awarded on seniority in a committee or the legislature. Committee chairmen, however, often use their position to affix their names to legislation that has been modified extensively by their committees. Assemblyman John Knox did this with the Firemen's 56-Hour Bill in 1961, and Gordon Winton with the Winton Act, which established formal employer-employee relations in the schools. More recently, George Milias and James Hayes, both moderate Republicans, did the same with bills defining employer-employee relations in local governments. Senator Ralph Dills has drafted and led the legislative drive for several bills on collective bargaining, and Senator Albert Rodda wrote and negotiated passage of the schools' collective bargaining law that bears his name. Both were Democrats of considerable seniority and chairmen of standing committees.

The legislative committee system deserves two further general comments. One is that the rules of both houses since 1974 have tended to require two or more committees in each house to study and act on major legislation. One reviews mainly the substance, the other examines the financial implications. Both may make amendments or reject the bill. This practice tends to produce more thorough study, but it also complicates the legislative process. The other comment is that legislative committees, over several years, tended to create separate subject matter bailiwicks. Legislation pertaining to schools, whether it pertained to child lunches or to employment, was referred to the education committee in either house. Bills having to do with local government employees might go either to the committee on city and county government, composed mainly of former councilmen, or to industrial relations, composed of legislators from high labor-influence districts. Each set of committees (Assembly and Senate) worked within the framework of a separate legal code. The education committees saw things in terms of the Education Code, municipal affairs saw things as the Government Code, and industrial relations saw things as the Labor Code. Thus the structure of the legislature tended to institutionalize a series of pigeon holes into which state policy was fitted. Recent changes, not only in committee structure but in legislative thinking, have overcome some of this condition.

APPEALS TO THE VOTERS

Politically active groups are also able to intervene in the California legislative process by means of initiative petitions, thereby by-passing both the legislature and governor. The initiative procedure was first adopted for city governments in 1903, and in 1911 it was extended to state matters. To place a statute before the voters by petition, a sponsoring group must secure the signatures of registered voters equal to five percent of the total vote cast for all candidates for governor at the previous general state election.[4] A number equal to eight percent is required to submit a state constitutional amendment.[5] On an average, two initiative propositions qualify for each general election. Organized public employees have sponsored several that pertain to employment policy. Most notable is the constitutional amendment adopted in 1938 which established the state civil service system. The California State Employees Association and the State Highway Patrol Association each presented amendments in 1972 that would have drastically revised the procedure for setting state employees' salaries. Both measures failed of adoption.

The initiative is normally a device used by organized groups unable to obtain legislation they desire because of previous opposition in one legislative house or the governor's veto. It is also used on some occasions when a group believes it can get voter approval without the proposal being subjected to the amendments and compromises normally encountered by a bill in passage through the legislature. An initiative statute or amendment is placed on the ballot as written by its sponsors and may be approved by a majority of the votes cast on it. If adopted, the proposition can be amended or repealed in future only with the consent of the electorate.

Usually candidates for governor and incumbent governors avoid taking a public position on initiative propositions. There are exceptions, however.

In 1961, the "Right to Work" proposition was supported by William Knowland, the Republican, and was opposed by Edmund Brown, the winning Democratic candidate. Governor Reagan proposed an initiative in 1971 to limit taxation by school districts, cities, and counties and was opposed by the teachers' association. He also publicly opposed the 1972 initiatives sponsored by state employee organizations.

The initiative and its companions, the referendum and the recall, are products of the Progressive reform that swept California politics between 1910 and 1916. No state referendum has qualified since 1952, and recall of state officers has seldom been tried, but referendums and recall elections occur with some regularity in local affairs. The initiative petition, on the other hand, seems to be an established part of the state legislative process.

THE JUDGES AND EMPLOYMENT POLICY

The state judiciary is another authoritative institution called upon with some frequency to decide policy matters involving public employment. In most instances it does not initiate action. Aggrieved parties bring a case to court by suing an identified defendant. In accord with judicial procedure, the court decides between the contesting parties in the light of the issues and facts produced and is guided by precedents established in the decisions of similar cases.

The California judiciary, like that in other states, is composed of three levels possessed of jurisdiction to decide matters that relate to public employment matters. The first is the superior or county court, whose jurisdiction is confined to cases arising within a county. It is also the primary trial court to which cases involving the entire gamut of legal problems are brought. In the rural counties, one judge constitutes the court, and all cases are tried by him unless he is disqualified for some reason. The superior court in the metropolitan counties is composed of many judges, a condition that permits specialization. Cases are assigned for trial by a master calendar judge selected for that task by his peers. Most superior court judges achieve their position by gubernatorial appointment to fill a vacancy, although some reach the bench by defeating an incumbent in an election. Judges appointed by the governor must face the county electorate at the next general election held after they take office. Most judges are reelected for several terms. Members of the superior court bring a variety of experiences to the judicial process. Many have been involved in local politics or have held state office. Several have been legislators or local officials. They are required to be attorneys and to devote full time to judicial affairs, but their knowledge of law and judicial procedure varies widely.

One aspect of decisions by the superior courts deserves special analysis because it is peculiarly involved with employer-employee disputes. This involves the issuance of temporary restraining orders and injunctions against strikes and picketing. The procedure used in these matters is different from that previously discussed. For example, a city's employees decide to strike in a dispute over wages or conditions of employment and to establish a picket line around a municipal building. The city government may choose to request a temporary restraining order of a superior court judge, alleging that the strike and picket line is illegal and interferes with the city's performance of a function mandated by state law or jeopardizes the peace and welfare of the community. The judge has considerable discretion, unless limited by statute, to determine the action to be taken. If he is convinced there is immediate danger to public welfare, he may issue the order without first notifying and hearing the striking workers. The hearing may come at a later time or may be postponed until the city government requests issuance of a permanent injunction. In the meantime, if the workers do not do as directed by the judge's order, they may be arrested for contempt of court and jailed until their innocence or guilt can be determined at a preliminary hearing and trial. In several of the public employee strikes in the 1960's, city administrations chose to enforce restraining orders vigorously but learned that this action was counterproductive because it stirred to intervention many outside groups not previously concerned. The resulting controversy caused settlement of the original disputes to be postponed. In later disputes, several administrations have sought court orders, hoping the action would warn and deter strikers while settlements were under negotiation. In some instances, however, the judge who issued the original order took note of violations and brought to trial the officers of the organization that conducted the strike or individuals who committed acts of violence.

Most decisions by superior court judges are appealable, usually to the court of appeals, a body comprising more than fifty justices who work in teams of three (called divisions). The state is divided into five appellate districts and cases arising from a superior court go to one of the appellate divisions in that district. The justices of this court are appointed by the governor for twelve-year terms. At the next general election after appointment, a judge must submit to a district-wide vote of confidence if he wishes to continue to serve. The same requirement applies to subsequent terms. This procedure has resulted in virtual life tenure for justices of the court of appeals. Many of these officers have served previously as superior court judges, but a fairly large percentage have held legislative or executive office before appointment to the court. Justices of the court of appeals consider their freedom to interpret the law in most cases to be limited by precedents established by the state Supreme Court. If no relevant precedent can be discovered, they tend to be cautious and await clarification from the higher court. Consequently public employees who have hoped to broaden public policy by appealing to this level of court on matters arising from disputes with their employers have been disappointed in a high percentage of cases. The decisions are read with considerable interest by a wide audience, because a ruling by a division of the court of appeals becomes the guide for lower courts and administrators throughout the state until the Supreme Court arrives at a different conclusion. Occasionally, however, two divisions of the appeals court reach different decisions concerning the same point of law, creating some confusion and hastening attempts to get the matter to the Supreme Court.

The state Supreme Court has original jurisdiction in a number of matters, including such judicial items as habeus corpus and mandamus, but it is selective in the choice of cases it takes directly or on appeal, partly to keep its workload within manageable proportions. Most appeals from superior court decisions go first to the court of appeals. Appeals from the latter are likely to be accepted if they raise significant points of law requiring settlement — in other words, if they have not been dealt with adequately by previous decisions of either the appeals or Supreme Court. The Supreme Court is composed of seven justices appointed by the governor for twelve-year terms, subject to review by a Board of Judicial Qualifications composed of the attorney general, the senior presiding justice of the court of appeals, and the chief or senior justice of the Supreme Court. On one occasion, this body rejected an appointee. In practice, the justices have a virtual life tenure, but retirement at age seventy is available and supported by custom. A justice may be removed at any time, however, by the court on recommendation of a commission created by statute to consider complaints concerning the competence of a justice. One justice was removed for age-connected health reasons in 1977.

California's highest court has achieved a distinguished collegial record for competence and scholarship, notably during the period that began in the late 1930's and extended into the 1970's. It has also been noted for its liberal or innovative interpretation of the state constitution and legal doctrines, particularly with respect to the rights of individuals. The background of the four chief justices who served during this forty-year period illustrate some of the types of experience contributing to the court's decision process. Phil S. Gibson (1940-1964) served as the governor's finance director and had little previous judicial experience prior to his appointment as chief justice. Roger J. Traynor (1964-1970) was a noted professor specializing in tax and administrative law prior to going on the court. He was elevated to the chief's position when Justice Gibson retired. Donald R.

Wright (1970-1977) served for many years on the superior and appeals courts before being appointed chief justice. He retired on reaching the age of seventy and Governor Brown appointed Rose Bird, the Secretary of Agriculture and Services in his cabinet. Miss Bird was not only the first female member of the high court, but was also the youngest to serve. She had no previous judicial experience. The other justices reflect a mixture of backgrounds in judicial experience, private practice, and state executive offices.

THE LOCAL EMPLOYER-GOVERNMENTS

California adopted a basically simple design of local government in its 1850 constitution and has retained most of that scheme. The constitution established counties and provided for creation of municipal corporations or cities. It avoided the multi-tiered pattern of villages, towns, and townships found in many Atlantic coast and middle western states. The legislature was directed to create a state system of schools and it established a series of districts administered by locally elected boards to employ teachers, levy a school tax, and administer the schools under a detailed statutory law code, supervised by elected county superintendents and an elected state superintendent of instruction.

The original simplicity of the pattern began to blur when the legislature exercised its discretionary authority to create additional forms of local government and established an astonishing array of special districts, the majority of which are authorized to perform only a single function. A few that have been permitted to choose a broad spectrum of functions have developed into quasi cities, but they lack general law-enforcement powers. Some water districts, such as the Metropolitan Water District of Southern California and the East Bay Municipal Utility District, are relatively large-scale employers. Two or three transit districts also employ large forces. The majority of districts, however, are taxing entities that employ few workers. Most water districts, and some others, have their own governing bodies, but a large percentage of districts are closely associated with county government, having been created to finance services in rural or suburban communities. Until approximately 1950, the state legislature prescribed no employment policies for special districts created either by special legislative action or under procedures set up in general statutes. It left the hiring of agents and the enactment of policies to govern their employment to the discretion of district boards. When some of the larger district work forces became embroiled in employer-employee disputes in the 1960's, a few special statutes were enacted. Eventually all districts were subjected to some state employment legislation.

Historically, city governments have been the largest local government employers because the urban population required such services as police and fire protection and waste disposal. To these functions have been added park and recreation programs, street and drainage system maintenance, and public health protection. Several cities operate water distribution, electric power supply, and bus enterprises, and coastal cities maintain harbors for commercial shipping and marinas for pleasure craft. Many have voluntarily transferred such functions as weight and measure inspection, property tax assessment and collection, restaurant inspection, and public health service to the county government, thereby reducing the size of their work forces. Others, notably in Southern California, contract with the county for almost all services, including police and fire. Those municipalities employ a small managerial and clerical staff to supervise contract operations and to provide information service.

The structures of city governments, through which their community interests are channeled and administrative programs are managed, vary considerably because California has permitted its municipalities to exercise considerable leeway in this matter. The majority are governed by general statutes enacted by the state legislature. Their basic structure consists of a five-member council elected by the voters at large, an elected clerk, and other officers and employees appointed by the council. The controlling statutes provide for a number of options, however. The mayor may either be a member of council elected by the other members or may be separately elected, but this officer has little independent executive authority under either option. Most cities have made the clerk appointive. Council members are paid small fees for their services and they transact most official business at weekly, biweekly, or even monthly meetings. The council appoints and removes department heads by majority vote. Many cities during the 1930's began appointing a chief administrative officer to prepare and administer the city budget and to exercise some central control over personnel administration as the council's staff officer. Several now assign extensive central managerial authority to this officer, both by formal ordinance and by informal arrangement, thereby making the C.A.O. in fact a city manager.

Those cities that operate under the general statute are permitted to choose one of several options for the recruitment and supervision of employees. They may delegate considerable responsibility to department heads. In many instances, the city clerk serves as the central personnel clerk. Several chief administrative officers have achieved extensive control of personnel management. Also, since 1936 the cities have been authorized to create a civil service system and to appoint a personnel commission that determines much of the policy and supervises the implementation of personnel rules.

A substantial number of other California cities operate under a municipal charter prepared initially by a specially elected charter commission and approved by the voters. Charter amendments may be offered by the council, by a charter commission, or by initiative petition. The concept of a home rule charter was conceived in the 1878-79 state constitutional convention and was intended to enable the larger cities to escape the legislative interference that had greatly disturbed many urban citizens. San Francisco was the first to adopt a city charter, but several medium sized municipalities followed during the Progressive era in California politics. The law governing charters has been amended since and any city, regardless of size of population, may adopt a charter if its voters choose to do so.

Many cities adopted charters in the early years because they sought authority to organize their governments according to local desires. Most large cities wished to elect a mayor to whom they could delegate executive powers. In some instances, notably in Los Angeles, the prevailing political attitude favored the election of council members by districts rather than at large. Moreover, numerous charter cities created citizen commissions to supervise departments, and they set up elected controllers to serve as the guardians of the city's fiscal probity. When the legislature broadened the general law governing cities and permitted a choice of options, it greatly reduced the attractiveness of charters as means to innovate through structure.

The most significant attraction of a charter has always been the fact that it gives a city comparative freedom to decide which functions it will undertake and how it will perform them. Cities operating under the general law, by contrast, are required to seek amendment of the governing statute if they wish to perform in a manner not authorized or described in the state law. Inasmuch as the state constitution strictly limits the legislature in its use of special legislation, the general-law cities must gain a consensus among themselves before they can persuade the legislature to adopt a major innovation. A prime example of the situation is the history of adoption of local civil service systems. Chartered cities, beginning with San Francisco in 1898 and followed by Los Angeles in 1903 and Berkeley in 1907, created civil service programs tailored to fit the situation prevailing in each community. During the Great Depression of the 1930's, employees of many general-law cities demanded that the city councils establish a civil service procedure to stabilize city employment and to give employees legally recognized rights. Legal advisors pointed out that this could not be done unless the legislation were amended. The legislature was prevailed upon, but only after extensive debate and considerable compromise, to adopt emergency legislation enabling the cities to respond to the demand.

In the early history of municipal home rule in this state, the state Supreme Court followed the practice of strict interpretation and denied cities' efforts to innovate if (a) the charter were not minutely precise in its grant of authority to the city council or municipal officers, or (b) if the city appeared to encroach on policy matters in which the state government had a substantial interest. This judicial attitude caused two broad developments: (1) it caused most cities to write detailed charters and to engage in frequent amendment to specify new procedures or to approve new programs; (2) the state constitution was amended several times in efforts to broaden the range of freedom given the charter cities. The ultimate change declared that a municipal charter provision relating to a municipal affair was to prevail over a conflicting general state law. Introduction of the term "municipal affair" returned the problem of defining state-local relations under municipal home rule to the courts.

The state Supreme Court has declined to spell out a broad definition of home rule and has given interpretations in a series of decisions. Consequently the definition remains flexible and subject to new applications when events produce new sets of facts and issues. The chartered cities contend that decisions concerning the employment, assignment, compensation, and supervision of their work forces are municipal affairs, and in a 1932 case the Supreme Court agreed that the rate of compensation paid city workers was a municipal affair.[6] When employee organizations pressed the legislature to mandate employment procedures for all local governments and to set standards governing fire fighters' hours or training of police officers, the chartered cities contended the legislature could not make the statutes applicable to them. The court of appeals ruled, however, that the statute which recognized the right of fire fighters to organize was a valid exercise of legislative authority and did not interfere with the cities' right to employ and supervise their fire departments.[7] The Supreme Court permitted the ruling to stand, tacitly approving it.

State-local clashes over jurisdiction to set controlling policy have not been confined, of course, to matters relating to employment. They arise often on law enforcement, traffic routing and control, and conservation of water, air, and land resources. Social and economic conditions have changed since 1915, when the final municipal affairs amendment to the constitution was adopted, and human perceptions of needs have apparently changed. Subjects that were considered earlier to be proper ones for exclusive municipal decision are looked at quite differently in the 1970's. For example, the courts ruled in early decisions that the power to set speed limits on streets forming part of a state highway was a municipal affair. Later experience with traffic control caused them to reverse that interpretation. In an attempt to provide a broad set of boundaries for policy determination, the courts and the legislature have developed the concept of state pre-emption of a policy field. Defined simply, this concept permits the state to pre-empt a field of policy-making if the courts are satisfied from the legislative record that the legislature and governor concluded, after study and debate, that the matter was of state-wide significance and took deliberate action. In some instances, the courts have applied a test of exclusive pre-emption, ascertaining whether the legislature had pre-empted an entire field of regulation which it had previously either shared with or left solely to local governments. When the legislature adopted a statute regulating certain political activities of public employees, the attorney general advised that the state had pre-empted certain phases of the subject but had left other points open to local governments' rules.[8]

The cities governed by general law and those operating under charters have worked in concert for many years to articulate a common set of interests in policy relating to local affairs. The vehicle for this purpose is the League of California Cities, which was organized in 1898. Almost every city in the state is on its membership roster. Its legislative advocacy program often favors issues most meaningful to the elected officials of medium sized cities, but the leadership has studiously avoided taking positions that offend the representatives of the very large cities. The large cities send their own legislative advocates to Sacramento to deal with matters of special interest but they seldom work at variance with league positions on matters agreed upon at the annual convention. Los Angeles, San Francisco, and San Diego mayors and council members take prominent parts in the league's offices and committees. The league's membership is composed of city governments but the mayors and council members, meeting as a section of the organization, exercise a dominant role. City managers, attorneys, and department heads also comprise sections that consider problems of special interest to the administrators.

The league's policies are developed through committees which report to the annual convention and regional subgroup conferences. Policies adopted at the convention are refined for action by a large executive committee whose membership is carefully balanced to include voices from most significant elements within the league's constituency. The top officers change annually, but the progression through the hierarchy is governed by rules and traditions which ensure that persons who reach the top will have had extensive experience in municipal and league affairs. The leadership role in policy formulation is jealously retained by the mayors and council members.

In its early years, the league performed such traditional functions of associations of officials as publishing a journal, sponsoring conferences, and providing information to the officers of member cities. Only a portion of the cities in the state were members, consequently the league was successful only in a limited way at Sacramento. It was reorganized in 1935 and new leadership infused a spirit that has continued since. It has continuously exercised an impressive influence on legislation affecting local governments. When collective bargaining and its related concepts were first introduced in the legislature, most elected city officers and appointed administrators were adamantly opposed to any plan that diminished the authority of officials to determine the formal policies governing conditions of employment or compensation. The league convention, committees, and regional subconferences have provided important forums for the airing of views, study of experiences, and determination of strategies in local operations as well as in the state legislative process. The league has been served by a competent staff whose headquarters has long been in Berkeley, with offices in Los Angeles and Sacramento. Richard Graves, Richard "Bud" Carpenter, and Don Benninghoven, the executive directors, and a small staff have provided continuous input to the organizational work and the policy development process. The executive directors have been highly respected legislative advocates in Sacramento. Carpenter and Benninghoven worked during the era in which the league's attitudes toward employment legislation were discussed most extensively. Their advice to league members and their advocacy of league positions in legislative sessions have been consistently powerful influences.

California counties perform dual functions. They are surrogates of the state to enforce its laws and to perform additional tasks assigned them by state legislation, and they also operate as local governments, particularly serving those areas outside the incorporated cities. The prevailing constitutional concept did not conceive of counties as self-governing units. County officers were expected to perform only those activities specifically authorized or assigned by state legislation. Moreover, the statutes usually prescribed in some detail how the tasks were to be performed. It was assumed that county government was performed in a uniform manner in all parts of the state. This assumption was at least partially negated by the fact that most county officers were elected by their neighbors. Hence they were responsive to community standards and values rather than to state-wide norms, except when they were directed by a judicial decision to conform closely with a statutorily prescribed procedure.

The traditional model of county government began to change in 1913, mainly as a result of the Progressives' determination to enhance the place of local government in the California system. This state was the first to extend the home rule idea to counties, when it adopted a constitutional amendment in 1913. County electors were authorized to prepare and adopt county charters, but they were not given the degree of freedom that had been extended to cities. The principal benefit realized from county home rule is a legal freedom to innovate with the structure of county government. Numerous offices have been consolidated and many have been made appointive. Several counties, notably Los Angeles, Alameda, and San Diego, have established county civil service systems to govern employment of county workers. Several have created central administrative offices, both by charter and ordinance, to coordinate sprawling bureaucracies.

A second constitutional amendment, adopted in 1915, provided impetus for a more significant change in county government than home rule accomplished. This action authorized counties to undertake municipal functions and thereby enabled those in which suburban development took place to devise means for providing services. A few counties, notably Los Angeles, decided to create a wide array of municipal programs in the fringe areas outside cities and to finance many of them from the county general tax fund. Many others chose to confine their municipal-type programs to those communities where residents were willing to authorize the creation of special districts. Either decision caused the county work force to expand beyond that necessary to administer the state-mandated programs.

County governments are today the largest local government employers in the state because of the array of functions either mandated to them by state law or undertaken by county decision. Many labor-intensive programs are assigned to the counties, such as general hospital care, public health medical, nursing, and inspection services, and administration of welfare. Many federally aided welfare programs rely on the counties to provide their basic field administrative staff and its first-line management. Law enforcement in areas outside the cities is the mandated responsibility of the county sheriff. Court-related programs staffed by marshals, court clerks, probation officers, and jail attendants add greatly to county work forces. Property assessment for purposes of taxation is assigned to counties, as is property record-keeping and the administration of state elections. When fire fighting, park and recreational services, planning and zoning, and road construction and repair programs are added to this list, a large multi-occupation work force results.

County governments are headed by a five-member board of supervisors elected by districts on a non-partisan ballot, although party affiliation of candidates often figures in the campaigns. There is no executive head of the county; the board as a whole appoints department chiefs, oversees county administration, and adopts the county budget. A member of the board is selected as chairman and performs ministerial and ceremonial duties. The office of supervisor is a part-time office in all except Los Angeles County; consequently, a substantial amount of authority for administration has devolved to the department heads. The sheriff, district attorney, and tax assessor are independently elected and they perform duties prescribed by state law, although the supervisors determine the number of employees, amount of equipment, and size of support funds allocated to each department.

Los Angeles County was the first to develop a chief administrative office to prepare a unified budget and to advise the board of supervisors about management of the county administration. It also created a staff of budget and management analysts as a part of this structure. The C.A.O. remains, however, an aide to the board and possesses little formally delegated authority. In practice, this officer exercises extensive managerial influence so long as he retains the confidence of a majority of board members.

Other counties have followed the Los Angeles example and almost every one now has a chief administrator. Many have employed persons trained by Los Angeles County. Sacramento and San Mateo counties have accorded their central administrator a number of powers and responsibilities by charter prescription.

For many years elected officials of the fifty-eight counties have exercised considerable influence in Sacramento with respect to county affairs. The County Supervisors Association, which dates from 1911, is their principal agent. It is composed entirely of county board members; unlike the League of Cities, the association has not brought administrative officers extensively into its activities. The CSAC policy-making structure is similar to the league's in other respects, but is not as complex. It established a small staff in Sacramento in 1950 to provide research and information services for the counties, to arrange the annual conferences, to serve the numerous committees through which CSAC conducts its affairs, and to conduct legislative advocacy. CSAC officers also perform much of the legislative work. The League of Cities and CSAC often cooperate on matters affecting state-local relations and home rule, and they usually take similar positions on proposals relating to public employment and employer-employee relations.

CSAC has been involved in a number of disputes with the state labor federation. Its executive board distributed to the counties in 1967 a proposed model county personnel ordinance which set forth a policy statement and proposed procedures for conducting employer-employee relations. The head of the state labor federation described the publication as anti-labor in tone because it did not provide for direct two-party negotiations.[9] He urged all county labor councils to express opposition to its use by the county boards in their areas. Nevertheless, most county ordinances adopted at that time reflected general similarity to the CSAC model.

School district government is independent of the cities and counties, although many districts and the city in which they are located serve the same people. Schools, cities and counties tax the same parcels of property to obtain a large percentage of their income. The school districts also compete in the labor market with the cities and counties to employ clerical, custodial, building maintenance workers, and bus drivers. The schools are in their own special sphere in the employment of teaching and administrative personnel. Nevertheless, the combined instructional and support payrolls reveal many districts to be large employers. The fact that they have two sets of employees tends to create some unusual employment problems.

The districts perform under a remarkably uniform formal organization, which is the product partly of nationwide school historical traditions and partly of specific state legislative prescription. Each district is headed by a board, usually composed of five members elected at large on non-partisan ballots. Boards in some large cities have a few more members. There is no elected executive although a board member is selected to serve as chairperson. Board members serve part-time and meet usually for weekly or bi-weekly evening sessions. The real executive of the school district is the superintendent, a professional educator, who is employed by the board under contract for fixed terms, usually for four years. One of the hotly discussed issues in many districts arises from the board's dependence on the superintendent for information, policy proposals, and for implementation of its decisions. Part-time board members, responding to or reflecting group pressures in the community, clash with the superintendent, who has a power base of his own and a set of values and concepts that often are at variance with those of board members.

In the initial employment of teachers and administrators, school boards are limited to choosing candidates who hold state-approved certificates of fitness measured in terms of education and training. With reemployment for a fourth year, a teacher achieves a tenure status which is protected by law against arbitrary attack. Selection, assignment, and compensation of teachers and the determination of class size are all subjects for district board decisions.

At the request of the workers, approximately one hundred school districts have established a merit system civil service type of personnel administration for their support employees. In these districts a personnel commission is responsible for making rules, examining candidates, classifying positions, and hearing appeals on disciplinary actions. It also recommends salary rates to the district board. In most districts the district appoints one commission member, the largest employee organization nominates a second, and these commissioners select a third.

The school boards, like their counterparts the city and county governing bodies, have created an association for the purpose of developing a consensus regarding a legislative agenda. The main subjects for several years have been teacher employment, collective bargaining, and state aid to district schools. The California School Boards Association is similar in many respects to that of CSAC in its structure and mode of operation. It develops its policies through committees which report to the annual conference. An executive committee and officers provide the leadership to focus members' attention on key subjects, formulate proposals, and implement those approved by the convention. A small staff assists.

INFLUENTIAL IDEAS AND CONCEPTS

Ideas and concepts influence the structure of governments and shape the operations that follow. Three sets of ideas, each especially influential in state and local administration in California and in the public employment policy decision process, have been selected for brief discussion. These concepts are administrative management in a separation of powers framework, professionalism, and a civil service merit system of employment.

A basic constitutional theory of American government, rooted in the history of this country, places a high value on the separation of powers to prevent the arbitrary and despotic exercise of official authority. The establishment of administrative programs, therefore, calls into question the respective responsibilities of the executive, legislative, and judicial branches to determine policy and supervise administrative operations. When the concept of collective bargaining was proposed in the 1960's as a procedure for determining government employment policies, the theory of separation of powers presented a substantial challenge. Collective bargaining, as developed in industry, is based on a concept of two-party confrontation and negotiation. Popular terminology gives the parties the titles of management and labor. Each party is considered to be equal in status at the bargaining table and, after agreement has been reached, each is presumed to be able to assure the other that terms of the agreement will be respected.

If the concepts of collective bargaining are to be transferred to the public work forces, who in fact performs the role of management? In governments committed to the theory of separation of powers, is there a management in the sense customarily recognized in corporate-structured industry? As preparation for consideration of that issue, it is well to examine what developments have taken place in state and local governments before collective bargaining was proposed.

When the state and local governments undertook an increased number of social and economic service programs at the beginning of the twentieth century, administration became a significant part of the government process. Observers of this development began to advocate theories and principles of management, and many concerned themselves with reform of the structure of government. Others considered process to be more important than structure, while still others applied methods of scientific analysis in efforts to understand what was taking place. Much of this diverse set of ideas found its way into the organizational environment in which public employees work and in which employment policy is shaped.

The administration of California state and local government programs was influenced for several decades by principles and concepts produced by the "scientific management" and the "governmental efficiency and economy" schools of thought. These overlapping bodies of thought were respected in intellectual and management circles throughout the nation during the first half of the twentieth century. Woodrow Wilson's essay on public administration, published in 1887, is considered to be the progenitor of the efficiency and economy approach to government policy, although Frank Goodnow, Luther Gulick, Lyndall Urwick, Frederick Cleaveland, and Louis Brownlow were noted figures in its further refinement and popularization.[10] Henry Taylor, an industrial analyst, is generally credited with being the founder of the scientific management approach.[11] The Commission on Efficiency and Economy, whose report by Cleaveland was presented to President Taft in 1912, stressed the desirability of making the chief executive the supervising director of all administrative agencies in a government. It recommended that an executive budget be developed to provide the legislative branch with a set of recommendations for government expenditures.

Hiram W. Johnson, the Progressive governor of California in 1912, was stressing a similar plan in state government, although he was limited to the exercise of executive control over state expenditures by means of informal political influence. His personal prestige was sufficient to swing legislative votes on executive-suggested appropriations and he sought to manage expenditures by giving directives to his carefully chosen appointees on the board of control, a statutory fiscal reviewing body. Formal change did not take place until the electorate adopted a constitutional amendment in 1922 that gave the governor responsibility for preparing a budget. This responsibility gave him considerable leverage to determine the number of employees and the level of expenditure for salaries. Each governor since 1922 has chosen a budget director, often with a corporate business experience background, who becomes his closest associate in the day-to-day management of state affairs. This officer heads the Department of Finance, staffed by civil servants experienced in budgetary and organizational analysis, which operates as a central management as well as budget-preparing agency.

The efficiency and economy school also emphasized executive control of the bureaucratic structure. Its central premise was that the chief executive should be authorized to initiate and design plans to group employees within the bureaucracy in ways he deemed best to improve performance or to facilitate executive control of program operations. This concept clashed, however, with two historic and constitutionally protected practices in state government. The state constitution has established four constitutional officers and charges them with certain administrative duties that are to be performed independently of the governor. Moreover, the state legislature has participated in the process of creating other administrative agencies and assigning duties to them. Consequently, the California legislature was slow to respond to proposals that the governor be permitted to reorganize administrative units, despite the fact that the federal commission headed by former President Herbert Hoover, a California resident, had given the concept of reorganization great prestige.[12] A statutory commission, composed mainly of business executives, has operated in California state government for several years, recommending changes in state organization and procedures to achieve efficiency and economy. Not until 1964 did the legislature authorize the governor to initiate reorganizations through submission of an executive plan, which would become operative if the two houses failed to nullify it within ninety days. Each governor since that date has used the procedure on several occasions. The combination of reorganization authority and cabinet supervision, discussed previously, has produced a moderately tight system of executive control over state administration and has enabled the governor to act as chief of management, but within rather severe limits.

The political leadership in a large percentage of California's cities during the first half of this century also favored a set of concepts advanced by advocates of the efficiency and economy school. The Municipal Reform Movement, for example, had the same ideological base that contributed conceptual ammunition to the Taft Commission. Advocates in this movement proposed that a mayor with strong legal powers should head the government of large cities, that municipal finance should be administered according to a budget, and that control of purchasing and contracts should be centralized. The National Municipal League, a New York-based reform organization, was especially interested in city charters and ballot reform to reduce the number of elected officials. Its major mission came to be advocacy of the council-manager form of city government, first employed in Staunton, Virginia. The plan entailed the election of a relatively small number of council members, usually five but seldom more than nine. The council selected a manager to direct or supervise all aspects of municipal administration. The plan's early proponents gave much attention to the business corporation analogy in which a board of directors and an executive officer managed the firm's operations.

Municipal reform advocates in California often used the league's model charter as their reference. These reform advocates were idealists motivated by middle-class values. Many were engaged in business or professions associated with the business community and were not attuned to political activities dependent on organizing precincts, ringing doorbells, and getting out a mass vote to win elections. The corporation analogy suggested by the council-manager plan attracted them because its proponents claimed it would produce more efficient and economical governing than would a mayor and council elected by patronage politics. Moreover, when the council-manager plan was first adopted in California cities, the non-partisanship concept of state and local affairs was compatible with the political philosophy dominant throughout the state, held in high esteem by the politically active and influential elements.

California was among the first states to see the council-manager plan adopted in its cities, and it proliferated rapidly. A tradition of appointing a chief central administrator to exercise a considerable degree of authority in personnel management developed in the 1920's and grew more firm in each decade thereafter. If one makes exceptions of the two largest cities, Los Angeles and San Francisco, it can be said that by 1935 almost all cities in the large and medium population categories employed managers to head their administrative structures. By 1973, *The Municipal Year Book* listed 270 of the 411 California cities with appointed central administrators.[13] Not all managers possess full authority to determine personnel practices, however; many share these responsibilities with a civil service commission appointed by the council. Although managers in many cities continue in office for long periods, the average tenure record is approximately seven years. Those dismissed are more often cut off because of factional power struggles in city hall than for management errors or failure to develop broad and imaginative program plans.

San Francisco created an office of chief administrator responsible to the mayor for supervising the performance of several departments. Los Angeles developed an office responsible to both the mayor and the council as the chief budget officer and management analyst. This office became the center for salary studies and exercised important influence on numerous personnel actions. Nevertheless, the executive and legislative institutions in these two central metropolitan cities retained important political influence over matters pertaining to employment policy.

The much-heralded analogy that equates the council-manager and administrative officer plans with private sector corporate organization is misleading. County and city governments do not seek to make profits, the presumably central motivating force that influences corporation behavior. Their major purpose is to provide services to community residents. Moreover, the citizens of a community do not necessarily have a continuing consensus about the priorities they wish given to the services that a city or county undertakes. Nor does a city or county sell its services in the marketplace where several vendors compete. Government revenues, for the most part, are derived from taxes, and different sets of taxpayers have different preferences for expenditures to return satisfactions in replacement for payments made. Therefore, state, city, and county administrators operate in an environment in which conflicting political demands constantly challenge the goals and values they cherish as civil servants.

In sum, the appointed managers in California local governments are seldom able to exercise the degree of control over planning, production, and operations that the top executives in corporate firms customarily exercise. The relationships between management and the policy-making bodies, and between them and the so-called stockholders of the enterprises are different in the two organization models in practice. Nevertheless, a considerable degree of centralization of authority and decision making did develop informally in local governments, because the corporation analogy was sincerely believed by numerous influential figures in the local government process, and this influenced the manner in which most local governments operated in this state.

A different type of concept, but one compatible with the efficiency and economy school of thought, is embraced in the term "professionalism." The bundle of meanings that adheres to this term extends far beyond government employment and management, but it is possible to limit the discussion to its application in these fields. The term is often used in a variety of ways, and equally often is abused. It is employed here in a limited sense. To be a professional, one is normally required to possess a body of knowledge and skill that is fairly well defined and that is recognized by other members of the profession. Much of it is acquired through formal programs of instruction influenced, if not directly controlled, by the profession. Members of a profession share similar sets of values relating to their occupation and to the methods by which they perform their skills. These values and skills tend to set the professionals apart from the nonprofessionals engaged in the same general occupation. Although many professionals in society are self-employed and are deemed to have considerable control over their own behavior, a professional person who performs his occupation in government service is, by definition, employed by an organization that has its own rules and makes demands on its members. One of the inherent problems of the professional in government is that his peer group sets standards to govern his performance and ethics, and these may conflict in important instances with the demands made on him by his employing organization. Therefore, one of the attributes of professionalism in government employment is often a certain transiency, born of the willingness or necessity to move from one employer to another. The profession-centered city manager, health officer, planner, legal officer, probation officer, or personnel analyst may well perceive that his or her career is less rooted in success in one's work force than it is in one's personal reputation for competence, measured according to the respective profession's standards. To the extent that his occupation is a profession, he finds employment for his particular skill and knowledge in various parts of the nation or, periodically, in the private sector.

The concept of professionalism has been widely employed in state and local government in California for a period of fifty years. City managers were among the first to articulate its premises with regard to local government. They were also among the first to establish an international organization to foster such aspects of professionalism as training, skill development, and professional ethics. A state-wide group of public managers has also been active for years, fostering a group consciousness among its members, influencing the selection of new entrants into the profession, making suggestions to educational institutions for the preparation of young persons for careers, and helping to create public acceptance of the role of professional administrators. Persons employed in occupations closely associated with managers, as budget and personnel analysts, or fiscal and purchasing officers, have shown similar activities. A semantic rather than a substantive question is whether these groups are distinct professions or subdivisions of a large professional category.

Professionalism has not been confined to any one level of government. State officers and employees have embraced the concepts and practices as enthusiastically as city employees. County administrators have been somewhat slower to manifest professionalism, but some, such as those in Los

Angeles County, have been pioneers in organizing professional associations, and most of the initial appointments to top positions in other California counties have come from this Los Angeles group.

School teachers and administrators may well claim to be the first self-designated professionals in state and local governments; certainly their occupational group exhibits more formal characteristics of professionalism than do city managers and others outside the school systems. Criteria for education and methodology in school administration have long been defined both by state government and professional associations. Moreover, California teachers and administrators are licensed by the state and may be punished for nonconformity with the rules, many of which are supported by professional bodies. The National Education Association, for example, has vigorously advocated the professionalism of public school personnel for many years. The California Teachers Association has also been deeply engaged over a long period in debates about teachers' ethics as well as the relationship of teachers with school boards, and teachers with pupils.

As the state and its local governments have expanded and upgraded numerous publicly administered programs, such as hospitals, mental health programs, health care activities, air and water pollution research and prevention enforcement programs, they have recruited highly educated and skilled persons who were involved in their respective professions and who acknowledged the conceptual role of professionals even before they became government employees. Consequently, the percentage of persons in California state and local government employment who identified themselves with professions, and who used the terminology and thought forms associated with those groups, mounted rapidly during the 1960's and 1970's.

Some occupations employed in California state and local governments debated their professional status throughout a fifty year period, but society generally remained skeptical about granting them this status. One cogent example is the law enforcement occupation. The term "professional" was first applied to police and law enforcement personnel in California in the 1920's by a small aggregation who wanted to raise performance standards and to change many parochial attitudes that had prevailed among law enforcement officers. One of the pioneers who enjoyed an international reputation for some time was August Vollmer, chief of police in Berkeley. Another whose influence and status was visible for a longer time was Earl Warren, who began his advocacy from the office of Alameda County district attorney and continued it when he was state attorney general, governor, and Chief Justice of the United States Supreme Court. Vollmer and others like him worked mainly with city police forces. Warren and his associates worked with investigative and prosecutor staffs. Each sought to reach all branches of law enforcement agencies. They shared a common interest in establishing curricula and schools of police science, setting entrance requirements for appointment of law enforcement personnel, fostering continuing education and training programs, and stimulating discussion of the many facets of police ethics and behavior. The state Department of Education began in the 1930's to establish courses of study for police, financed mainly by federal vocational aid. Numerous community and state colleges installed police science curricula at later dates, and both the University of California, Berkeley, and the University of Southern California offered formal programs. The Peace Officers Research Association of California (PORAC), an influential, state-wide organization that numbered Earl Warren among its early sponsors, has maintained a statement of objectives throughout its history describing itself as an association of professionals.[14] Its stated code of ethics compares closely with that of other professional bodies.

Professionalism among salaried occupations may be said in a non-pejorative sense to be largely self-serving. Increases in educational requirements for entrance into public school teaching or law enforcement have been advocated on numerous occasions to the members of these groups as a means to gain better salaries, greater social prestige, and more freedom for the individual employee to exercise his particular craft without close supervision. Licensing, or other means of regulating and controlling entrance into a professionalized occupation, has often been seen as a means to limit the number of persons able to compete in a specialized labor market, thereby influencing salary levels.

If there has been a self-serving aspect to professionalism, there also has been an altruistic feature. Two themes equally emphasized in the literature, teaching, and discussion of professionalism in government occupations are devotion to a high standard of job performance and concern for the social consequences of the work being done.

Some advocacy of professionalism among government employed persons has perhaps been uncritical, naive, even self-serving. Certainly the whole concept with its numerous interpretations has come under intense discussion and criticism in the 1970's. Much of the criticism has focused on the supposed elitist consequences of professionalization, namely, the attitude that only professionals were qualified to express valid views on government and bureaucratic policies. In many public work forces, the higher salaried, professional positions were held by university educated whites, and the lower paid, more routine jobs were filled by ethnic minorities or whites with less impressive educational records. Tensions arising from these conditions raised issues and problems in the 1970's never dreamed of in the 1930's.

The concept of professionalism has had important consequences for employer-employee relations. Professionals have tended to have ambivalent attitudes about the role of their organizations in employer-employee relations. They have placed great value on their individual status in the work organization and their freedom to determine work methods. They have not been attracted to unions and have tended to regard those organizations as potentially encroaching on their interests. When legislation to govern employer-employee relations has been discussed, professional groups have insisted that their constituents be permitted to choose whether they would be grouped with non-professionals in a representation unit or would be represented by a separate agent.

Professional administrators have tended to oppose the establishment of formally recognized procedures for employer-employee relations, particularly those established by state or federal legislation. This view is epitomized in a policy statement issued by the executive board of the International City Management Association:

> Local governments are the most appropriate bodies to set policies on their personnel relations and should do so in an equitable way.
> State government may choose to regulate local personnel relations, but only to the extent of providing legislative uniformity.
> There should be no blanket guarantee that public employees in all states and localities can be organized and bargain collectively. This should be a state-by-state decision, and made in the best democratic tradition.[15]

The third set of influential concepts relates to the civil service and the merit system of employment. The civil service concept was introduced in California by a coalition of the Progressives, the council-manager plan advocates, the short ballot enthusiasts, and several general-interest civic groups. Its installation in many places was spearheaded by organized employees. The first objective of the civil service reform movement was to eliminate the use of public jobs as election victory spoils, and to prohibit the coercion of public employees to contribute money and time to support party candidates for office in exchange for job favors. A second major objective, which developed gradually, was to ensure the selection, promotion, and retention of public employees on the basis of individual, demonstrated personal merit. In its early history, the civil service program did not depend on group action to recommend policy options or to defend the individual employee's interests. When employee organizations began to take part in civil service decision-making, they were accepted as an interested group that could be heard, along with others, prior to the making of official decisions by the personnel commission. They were also accepted as agents representing an individual employee's interests in a disciplinary hearing. The civil service system remains committed, however, to the idea that the demonstrated merit of the individual is the significant element in personnel operations.

Only in job classification does the merit system civil service submerge the role of the individual into that of the group. Classification is a procedure whereby individual jobs are analyzed and grouped with others requiring similar knowledge and skill and bearing a similar level of responsibility. Related classes of jobs are grouped into series and hierarchies of classes, with the end result being a totally classified work force encompassed in a comprehensive plan. A major premise of a classification plan is that all jobs and classes in a specific work force bear a relationship to all others in the same force. In sum, a classification plan seeks to define and recognize job relationships and to balance a network of systemwide relationships. The classification process also provides the underpinning for two significant elements of personnel administration. It establishes the standards that govern the amount and type of experience, education, and levels of skill that applicants for each class of jobs must demonstrate. It also provides the base on which compensation for each class is determined.

Equally basic is the proposition that candidates for classified public jobs should establish their fitness through job related tests conducted under as nearly equal conditions as possible. Public service tests vary in method and complexity according to the level and nature of the duties of the class of job. Some parts of the tests are completely objective, but some have markedly subjective features, although much technical effort is made to confine the subjectivity within defined limits.

Another prime feature of the merit system civil service is the concept of career employment in which an employee is accorded specific employment rights and benefits upon completion of a prescribed probationary period. The probationary period, a practical extension and application of the testing process, is crucial both to the merit and career employment concepts. Among the rights an employee gains at the conclusion of a successful probationary period are procedural protections against arbitrary dismissal or other penalties. Classified employees under the merit system can be dismissed, demoted, suspended, or reprimanded, but only in conformity with procedures that permit a third party to scrutinize the action and referee a test of the validity of management's allegations in an adversary-type hearing to ensure observance of due process rights.

Substantive and procedural features of the merit system and civil service in the state and local governments are set forth in rules promulgated by a personnel commission after public hearings at which all interested parties may testify. Rule changes may occur frequently but must conform to requirements of notice and hearings. Most rules also provide applicants and employees the right to appeal from administrative decisions on many personnel transactions. Although rule making is an open process that provides an opportunity for many interests and philosophies to make an impact on public policy, in fact only three groups normally seek to be heard: personnel technicians, management representatives, and employees. Debate is usually between either the professional staff and management, the personnel specialists and employees affected by the proposed rules, or employee representatives and management spokesmen. Other interests in the community seldom participate, although in a few communities the League of Women Voters sends observers.

Most personnel commissions are composed of three or five members appointed by either the executive or legislative body for fixed terms, the objective being to ensure a high degree of commission independence from the management.[16] Appointments to some commissions are made by officials of another level of government. The principal example is that of public school personnel commissioners, who are appointed by state officers. The structure of the merit system civil service in most California jurisdictions is based squarely on the American constitutional theory of checks and balances. The commission is responsible for ensuring that legislatures as well as executive and administrative officers adhere to the statute or local charter law governing employment practices. Equally basic is the concept that the commission shall conduct its transactions by means of rules which may be adopted or amended only after public hearings. By law, exceptions to rules cannot be made to fit individual convenience. Moreover, the decisions of personnel commissions are appealable to the courts and, although the California courts are disinclined to substitute their judgment for that of a commission, commission decisions are occasionally reversed when an individual employee's rights have been prejudiced or insufficient evidence has been considered.

The merit based civil service was first introduced in California in city and county charters. The state established civil service by statute in 1913, but after several years of misuse, the statute was withdrawn and an article was written into the constitution by initiative petition and popular vote. More than one hundred school districts, including some of the largest employers, apply a merit plan to their support employees under a section of the Education Code. It is generally agreed that the civil service move-

ment found a fertile field in California public work forces. A very high percentage of the public employees are governed by rules and practices consistent with its concepts.

Development of staffs possessing advanced education and training to
administer the technical aspects of examinations and job classification has
added a strong element of professionalism to personnel administration
under the merit system. Consequently, one of the perennial issues debated
is whether professional personnel administrators approach administrative
problems with an excessive emphasis on technique at the expense of a clear
view of public purpose.[17] There is not much doubt, however, that administration of the merit system depends on technical skill. It also depends on a
conception that its public purpose is to achieve a balance between the
interests of employees and those of the public that receives services and
pays for the support of state and local governments.

During the decades of the 1960's and 1970's, merit system civil service
programs have come under tremendous dual pressures, not only in reaction to the educational requirements that were established when public
employment opportunities were limited and the number of school gradu-
ates was large, but also in reaction to the civil service insistence on neutrality with respect to race, sex, and national origin of candidates. Until the
decade of the 1970's, subjective observation showed that state and local
work forces were overwhelmingly composed of whites and that the supervisory, managerial, and professional positions were occupied almost exclusively by males, except in nursing and welfare programs.[18] Non-whites
were employed chiefly in sanitation and custodial jobs; women were mainly
in clerical, nursing, and social work. The neutrality concept, commend-
able in its intent, was unfortunate in one respect. It hid the fact that the
executives and key administrators were responsible for the selection and
assignment of employees from civil service eligible lists. Until the appointing officers, and the legislators or governing boards that exercised supervision over them, changed their attitudes and behavior, the commissions
and personnel staffs had limited power to make changes. The affirmative
action programs, created to get larger percentages of non-white minority
members and women into public employment and higher paying positions,
have been achieved where the management and the personnel administrators have worked cooperatively. Personnel administrators have also re-
examined the education and experience qualifications in class specifica-
tions and have rewritten examinations to make tests more nearly job-
related.

The merit system is also involved in a three dimensional tugging match
that results from the interface between the personnel commissions and

their staffs, the executive and administrative officers responsible for appointing and supervising employees, and employee organizations. Administrative officers, individually and in associations, urge that they be given greater authority to select, promote, and discipline employees. Many who have established their credentials as professional administrators possessing considerable integrity argue that they can protect the public interest in employment matters and that they abjure the type of abuses the civil service was established historically to uproot. They claim that the civil service insistence on competitive examinations slows the filling of positions and does not permit flexibility in advancement and promotion of workers trained by management to fill jobs requiring judgment and responsibility. If personnel administrators allocate resources to schedule routine examinations to have eligibility lists always available, they face the probability that lists for many job classes may be used not at all or only after considerable delay. Turnover in some classes is erratic, and management frequently chooses to reorganize rather than fill some vacancies. Job candidates complain that they must wait a long time after examination before being called for appointment. Smooth performance and selection depends on continuous cooperation between management officers and the personnel department.

Friction arises between management, the merit system personnel agency, and employees over classification of specific positions. The personnel agency analyzes a position in terms of duties, responsibilities, and level of skill required regardless of which employee occupies the job. Management focuses on individuals. It uses classification to build up a job held by an employee it deems capable of performing more complex tasks and, through this accretion, to justify awarding higher compensation. This action clashes with the merit system concept that all employees who have the requisite experience and training should have an opportunity to compete for advancement to more complex, responsible, and better paying jobs. Organized employees generally support the merit system principle in this matter, and they watch suspiciously any delegation to public management of authority over classification, alleging that management uses classification selectively to reward favored employees and to thwart those not favored. For example, in small work forces with job classes comprising one or two positions, management sometimes reorganizes the unit and revises the requirements as a means of ousting employees who have displeased top administrators or elected officials. Middle management and specialist jobs are particularly vulnerable to this tactic. Reorganization of work units and reallocation of duties are management prerogatives that the merit system administrators are usually not legally authorized to challenge.

Employee organizations do not dispute examinations for entry level positions, but they register strong opposition to examination policies that bring recruits from outside the service into higher level jobs. Furthermore, they vigorously advocate the right of those in public employment to advance to higher levels and to retain their employment until they reach retirement eligibility.

In criticizing the merit system, employees have long censured the rule-of-three, which permits an employing management officer to select any of the top three names on a list of eligibles established by competitive examination. Merit system policies give management this flexibility, recognizing that testing procedures are not sufficiently precise to guarantee that the top candidate will always be the best qualified to perform a specific job. Employee organizations frequently charge that management manipulates the lists to obtain candidates it likes, passing over qualified individuals it does not like. Employees have aimed their most heated criticism, however, at the use of supervisors' appraisals of employee competence for promotion. Many merit system agencies request these appraisals and assign them some degree of weight as a part of the promotion examinations. Employee organizations generally oppose this use, alleging that supervisors are able through this device to manipulate promotions. It is a subject often clouded by rumor, half-truth, and hyperbole, but it is a prime example of a three way conflict that exists under the merit system. Managers and supervisors usually contend that the authority to determine promotions within the work force under their supervision is a necessary part of management responsibility. Employee organizations tend to insist that managers and supervisors should have no voice in the promotion procedure other than to make appointments from an eligible list.

Organized public employees have pushed for collective bargaining legislation not from discontent with the merit system or civil service as administered by quasi-independent boards and staffs, but from frustration over compensation, benefits, and hours. These particular issues are determined by elected legislative bodies and executives rather than by merit system personnel agencies. Grievances arising from many other supervisor-employee relationships have been appealable to quasi-independent boards under the merit system civil service, and employee organizations have made abundant use of these procedures.

V

THE POLITICAL RIGHTS OF
GOVERNMENT EMPLOYEES

George Washington Plunkitt, the erstwhile Tammany Hall commentator, said when asked to explain his success in politics:

I stick to my friends high and low, do them a good turn whenever I get a chance, and hunt up all the jobs going for my constituents. There ain't a man in New York who's got such a scent for political jobs as I have.[1]

That conception of politics lingers on today, causing confusion about what political rights public employees should be permitted to exercise. Much of the confusion is due to carry-over from the reform movements of the late nineteenth century that, in trying to root out the influence of Plunkitt and his associates, characterized political activity almost solely in terms of partisan election tactics and patronage.[2] Political activity is also a part of the process of making policy. The policy process involves sorting and adjusting the competing demands on an appropriate institution such as a legislature, a city council, or a commission which ultimately produces a decision. Policy outcomes affect citizens in a variety of ways. Some gain satisfactions, others lose in some measure. Some others may scarcely be aware that a decision has been made, because the impact of it on their perceived interests is either slight or the effect is delayed. Political action can be expected from those who anticipate either satisfaction or adverse results from a proposed policy decision. Political action takes numerous forms in which the individual citizen or the group seeks to influence either directly or through surrogates the outcome of the decision process.

Making public policy to control land use in an urban environment, or to regulate the practice of medicine or law involves political action. So does policy-making that governs the conditions of employment or fixes the compensation of government employees. Land developers, apartment property owners, architects, and builders frequently are members of local planning commissions that make decisions affecting their livelihood. Professional associations of medical and legal practitioners take a specific and direct interest in the making of statutes and rules governing admission to their professions and the standards governing their practice. Moreover, the members of the regulated professions usually compose the state boards that license practitioners and enforce professional standards. Nonetheless, the question of permitting government employees to participate directly in the decision-making process when their occupational welfare is affected continues to be vigorously debated in California as well as throughout the nation.

Virtually no one contends that public employees should exercise no political activity. The controversy is over how much activity and which political actions should be permissible. Some persons argue that government is a unique type of employer, and that those employed by it must recognize that they cannot participate in making the rules governing their own employment.[3] A second, more pragmatic attitude views government employees as comprising politically motivated interest groups that seek to influence statute-making by lobbying legislators and legislative committees. Those holding this view advocate limiting employees, both as individuals and as groups, to the exercise of minimal political action, such as writing letters to their legislators or city council members and employing spokesmen to address legislative hearings on their behalf.[4]

A third analysis bypasses the issue of participation in the traditional forms of political action, suggesting that if two-party bargaining were used to determine policies about compensation, hours, and working conditions, public employees would no longer be interested in lobbying, campaigning for candidates for elective office, or contributing to campaign funds.[5] They appear to ignore the fact that this bargaining process is another form of political action, and that two-party bargaining in government cannot be taken out of a political context. The organized public employees' strength in the bargaining process is gauged in terms of their ability to influence the officials who ultimately vote government budgets and taxes. Moreover, in a state political system the traditional political actions are sometimes used as counters to bargaining. For example, in New York state in 1973 business and finance groups, reacting to the unusual success of New York City employee unions in gaining greatly increased retirement benefits through locally negotiated contracts, proposed that the state legislature roll back and limit these gains. A coalition of city unions then appeared in force at Albany to protect its gains by legislative lobbying. Collective bargaining in the public sector cannot be realistically examined without reference to its political setting.

Another view concerning political activity by public employees maintains that political action is an inherent right of citizenship in a democratic polity, and that it may not be denied or seriously limited merely because a person has accepted employment in the government bureaucracy. They see no justification for enacting statutes or administrative rules that treat public employees significantly differently from other citizens.[6] Some contend that educated, socially concerned, and sensitive persons will not be attracted to public administrative service if the political rights of civil servants are seriously curtailed or, if such persons are attracted for other reasons, they will become dissatisfied and disruptive.

California state and local government employees have demonstrated extensive interest in various forms of political action, but their perception of what constitutes legitimate, effective action changes periodically. Likewise, public policy determining what is legitimate political action by public employees changes periodically. Over a space of approximately eighty years, each of the views previously described have been examined and implemented to some degree.

Most of the range of issues that relate to public employees' political rights have been debated. Some of these issues are:

1. Should public employees be restricted explicitly concerning political activities?

2. Should more severe limitations be placed on some employees than others because of the nature of their work, their status in the work force, or some other reason?

3. Should some types of political activity be forbidden, but some others be permitted, and still others be encouraged?

4. Should the responsibility to define and enforce restrictions be left solely to supervisory administrators? If so, what type of review should be exercised over these administrators' decisions?

5. Should the policy be decided by politically responsible policy making bodies or officers, such as a mayor, governor, city council, or legislature? Should the policy decisions on this subject be ratified by the voters and be expressed in local charters or the state constitutions?

6. Should local preferences in community relationships be permitted to produce diverse policies and procedures with respect to this subject, or is the subject one that requires uniformity of treatment throughout the state, and therefore should it be defined by state legislation? If the state legislates, should it confine itself to a mandate of basic policy guidelines with the details left to be developed by individual agencies, or should it set forth policy and procedure in detail?

7. Are public employee political rights protected by the state and federal constitutions in essentially the same manner as those of citizens not employed by government? If so, what are the limits on the authority of an agency that seeks to regulate employee conduct for the purpose of ensuring effective performance of public services?

The process by which these questions have been debated and public policy decisions reached supports the generalization expressed by Robert A. Dahl in *A Preface to Democratic Theory:*

A central guiding thread of American constitutional development has been the evolution of a political system in which all the active and legitimate groups in the population can make themselves heard at some crucial stage in the process of decision. . . . It is clear that the politically inactive members of a polyarchal organization cannot directly influence the outcomes of decisions. Hence if a group is inactive, whether by choice, violence, intimidation, or law, the normal American system does not necessarily provide it with a checkpoint anywhere in the process. By 'legitimate', I mean those whose activity is accepted as right and proper by a preponderant portion of the active.[7]

Many California public employees have long remained inactive by choice. But when they were few in number and unorganized some were made inactive by law. As some organized and sought to be active they were restricted by law and were offered what other persons deemed to be an adequate checkpoint in the employment decision process, the procedural protection of the civil service system. When that took place, it was reasoned that civil servants did not need to take political action in their own behalf.[8] The fact that civil service did not extend to all state and local employees did not lessen the ardor of those who advocated this view. For those who wished to be more active, yet remain civil servants, the problem continued to be how to persuade "the preponderant portion of the active" that their claim to participate was a legitimate one.

The discussion of the right of state and local employees to engage in political action began shortly after the Congress adopted the Pendleton Act in 1883, which forbade federal employees to support actively partisan candidates for national office or to contribute funds or effort to candidates or parties. An opinion written by Chief Judge Oliver Wendell Holmes of the Massachusetts high court in 1892 expressed the dominant attitude of the time:

The petitioner (a city policeman) may have a constitutional right to talk politics, but he has no constitutional right to be a policeman. There are few employments for hire in which the servant does not agree to suspend his constitutional right of free speech, as well as of idleness, by the implied terms of his contract.[9]

If, as Holmes implied, the restrictions of the employment regulations clashed unbearably with the employee's desire to enjoy all the rights of a citizen, the worker could turn to another occupation, including self-employment. Few persons saw reason to think that public employees suffered discrimination at the time, because private employers in the 1890's did not tolerate employees talking politics while on the job, unless it were part of a program the employer described to foster his own views.

The first explicit expressions of public policy in California restricting the political activities of persons on city payrolls were written into a few city charters, beginning with San Francisco in 1898. They paralleled the Holmes decision but did not cite it as a guiding precedent. Each statement, whether developed by a city council or a specially elected charter commission, was ratified by municipal voters. It was "the voice of the people," not a hidden bureaucratic decision.

The San Francisco city-county charter adopted in 1898 was explicit as well as selective. Although it placed all city-county employees under civil service, it forbade policemen, firemen, and the commissioners who headed the police and fire departments to accept membership in partisan nominating conventions, to belong to political clubs, or to seek votes for or manage a campaign on behalf of candidates for partisan office. Soliciting assessments for political purposes was also proscribed. The mayor was directed to dismiss any member of either department who violated these rules.[10]

Charters in a few communities extended the San Francisco prohibitions to all appointed city officers and employees,[11] while others restricted only the police.[12] None of the others granted civil service job protection, however.

The introduction of civil service reform, nevertheless, did not uniformly produce restrictions on local civil servants' political activities. When the municipal voters in Los Angeles, Long Beach, and Berkeley approved civil service amendments to their city charters, no limitations on political action were included.[13]

A major example of the opposite practice was the Los Angeles County charter, the first county charter in the United States. It placed almost all county positions under civil service procedures with respect to appointment and job tenure, leaving the elective officials very slim patronage, and it forbade any employee in the classified service to participate in any political activity other than voting or expressing opinions privately.[14] The charter language left no doubt that the prohibition applied to all elections, not solely to those involving county offices. Clearly the board of freeholders intended to create a completely neutral (and neutralized) civil service whose members were to relinquish other political rights as citizens in exchange for protected tenure in their employment.

Enforcement of this plan proved to be a problem. The charter originally made the civil service commission responsible for investigating complaints and dismissing employees who violated the charter. This placed the commission in the position of being investigator, prosecutor, and judge! The procedure was changed, by charter amendment and commission action, to shift responsibility for bringing charges against employees to the department heads. This produced a situation in which only those employees were liable to be charged who engaged in political acts disapproved by the department head. Deputy sheriffs who worked for the re-election of the incumbent sheriff were not accused of violating the charter. Uniformed firemen who went house-to-house in an unincorporated area to persuade voters to oppose incorporation of a city were not criticized by the fire chief, despite written advice from the county counsel that the actions violated the charter. Only when the marshal authorized deputies to campaign during duty hours for a candidate for county supervisor, falsifying time records to cover up the violation, was a criminal prosecution begun and the marshal convicted and removed from office.

Two changes made in the political system of California between 1903 and 1916 had a more significant impact on the political activity of local public employees than did civil service reform. They offset most of the previous restrictions. One was the removal of state and national political party designations from the city, county, and district ballots. The other was the adoption of the initiative and referendum, and the recall of public officers.[15]

The demolition of city political parties closed a well worn path previously trod by employees seeking the center of community political power to obtain job preferment. But even in those localities where civil service made the municipal worker's job relatively secure, elected officials continued to determine his salary and other benefits. Therefore, the employee remained interested in who won elections. The nonpartisan primary offered a new opportunity for groups of city employees to help preferred candidates without belonging to political clubs. Moreover, employees of several cities took action, either by putting pressure on the council or by circulating initiative petitions, to secure civil service laws in their communities.

The initiative and referendum offered an even more significant means for public employees to take political action without violating most existing prohibitions. Political party organizations in California seldom have involved themselves directly in the initiative and referendum processes. Circulating petitions and campaigning on behalf of a policy proposition did not involve work with a political party or candidate. Moreover, organized public employees usually could promote or defeat legislation that affected their interests without overtly threatening an officeholder's status. For example, they could file a completed petition with the city council or board of supervisors and, if the governing body accepted the proposal, no further action would be necessary. If the governing body declined to act, however, the law required the proposal to be submitted to local voters at the next regular election, or to a special election if the petition were signed by a specified percentage of registered voters. An initiative proposition adopted by a majority vote of the electorate would become law without further action. Therefore, the council members could not be considered responsible if the results were later to prove controversial.

Municipal police and firemen saw the advantages of using initiative petitions. Between 1907, when those in San Francisco established formulas for determining their salaries, and 1922, when the Los Angeles Fire and Police Protective League won adoption of an initiative charter amendment to establish one of the most liberal municipally administered pension systems in the nation, the two large-city groups demonstrated a new model of political action.[16] Pasadena police and firemen[17] and Sacramento police followed this example. San Diego police and firemen were able to persuade their city council to place on the city ballot a pension plan which the municipal electorate approved.[18]

Organized policemen and firemen found that the initiative law also gave them a vehicle to protect their gains from attack by opposing officials. The law required any amendment or repeal of initiated ordinances or charters to be approved by the voters. The Los Angeles firemen were able to defeat the city council's attempt in 1916 to repeal the initiative two platoon ordinance, and the Pasadena police and firemen were able to persuade the voters to reject the council's plan to repeal their initiative salary ordinance. Nevertheless, Los Angeles employees discovered that the initiative process had shortcomings which management was able to exploit when the pinch of the economic depression was felt in 1933. When the Los Angeles tax returns declined, the mayor and council presented police and fire employees with the option of accepting a ten percent cut from the ordinance-set salary scale or suffering a reduction-in-force. Members of both departments accepted the salary reduction for a five-year period to avoid layoff of newer employees. They discovered later that the city's fiscal administration ultimately had collected most of the taxes delinquent during the salary reduction period, and they sued to regain the money they had lost. The courts rejected their claims, however, ruling that the salary reduction agreements had been made voluntarily.[19]

A type of formula used by organized police and fire fighters in initiative charter petitions directed the city to set pay rates comparable to those paid by specified cities or the county government. In a number of instances, those in suburban cities linked the salaries with those of the central metropolitan city. The city councils and groups opposing the formula concept raised two issues which were ultimately presented to the courts. Is the determination of municipal pay rates the exclusive prerogative of the council and such officers as the city manager, or must it be shared with the city's voters? Does the adoption of a formula requiring the city to pay salaries comparable to those paid by specified other governments delegate city policy making to the officials of the other jurisdictions, or does it set a policy standard, i.e., comparability with other employers? Two panels of the court of appeals approved formulas proposed by police and firemen in chartered cities, saying that salary setting was a policy decision the voters could legitimately exercise. Moreover, one panel said that a formula which required salaries equal to those paid in another jurisdiction established a policy standard and did not improperly delegate the decision making authority.[20]

Municipal ownership of utilities also produced some situations that caused employees to be active in local politics with the approval of their immediate supervisors. The Progressive Movement in California did not explicitly advocate public ownership, but such prominent reform leaders as Dr. John R. Haynes in Los Angeles and James D. Phelan in San Francisco worked hard to inaugurate it in their respective communities.[21] Numerous cities organized water departments, several began electric power systems, and a small number acquired transit systems. Public ownership of water distribution systems was not a controversial subject in most cities' politics, but electric power and transit systems often underwent lengthy struggles before they achieved an assured place in city administration. The San Francisco street railway and the Los Angeles city electric systems both encountered particularly vigorous and determined opposition for many years. The municipal utility employees were drawn into city politics to defend their employing organization and to support its expansion.[22] The management and the employees had a greater incentive to join forces against common opponents than did similar elements in the more traditional government programs. Management encouraged the employees to take the field in councilmanic and mayoral election contests and to perform active roles in getting initiative and referendum petitions signed.

Both elements regularly negotiated alliances with other local political action groups, often with organized labor, to lobby council members and city executives on matters pertaining to the utility.

The Great Depression of the 1930's produced a series of laws that restricted the political activities of state and local public employees more than most previous rules had done. High rates of unemployment caused large numbers of persons to turn to their local governments, the state, and soon to the federal government for jobs. Political preferment took on a significance it had not had in California since the 1890's. Moreover, partisanship was suddenly restored. The resurgence of the Democratic party under the national leadership of Franklin D. Roosevelt had immediate repercussions in California state politics. The conservative wing of the Republican party, accustomed to dominating state politics after Hiram Johnson left the governorship in 1916, was threatened by new challenges. The gubernatorial contest in 1934 between Upton Sinclair, Democrat, and Frank Meriam, Republican, was one of the bitterest in California history.

In this politically charged climate, employees of a number of general law cities urged their city councils to establish a civil service system, fearing that without some procedural protection they might summarily lose their jobs. They were informed that the cities lacked authority to do so, whereupon representation was made to the legislature for a grant of appropriate authority. Republican legislators, in control in both houses of the legislature, were willing to authorize civil service status but were afraid that city employees might support legislative candidates identified with the Democratic party. The bill that was ultimately adopted, introduced by James Utt of Orange County, Republican, was permissive in one respect.[23] It authorized, but did not mandate, general law cities to adopt a civil service system by ordinance, but it also required a city that chose to do this to limit its employees' political activities. The author evidently considered employee political rights to be trade offs for a grant of some degree of job security. A city was to prevent its employees from participating in county as well as municipal campaigns, accepting office in a political club or organization, serving as poll watchers, or distributing pamphlets or handbills for city or county candidates. No civil servant could solicit signatures to petitions of any type, nominating, initiative, or recall. Dismissal was declared to be the appropriate punishment for anyone engaging in these prohibited activities. The statute balanced these restrictions with an affirmative statement approving membership in and attendance at political club meetings, candidacy for elective office, and voting.

City employees did not react to the issues presented by the Utt bill because almost no employee organizations existed in general-law cities at that time. After eight years' experience with the statute, however, enough pressure was built up that the legislature restored to city employees the right to use direct legislation with respect to rates of pay, hours of work, retirement, civil service, and other subjects pertaining to working conditions. The amendment added two new restrictions, namely, that political activity must be conducted after hours, and that no employee could engage in that action while dressed in the uniform required for work in his or her department.[24]

The circulation of initiative petitions governing compensation soon produced so much controversy that the League of California Cities urged the legislature to reamend the law and withdraw recognition of the right.[25] Several city councils aggressively attacked fire and police ordinance proposals. At least one declined to place a salary-setting initiative on the ballot, causing the organized firemen to sue. The court of appeals upheld the cities' contention. It ruled that because the state had pre-empted the subject in a later statute governing general-law cities and had assigned responsibility to decide compensation policy solely to the city councils, initiative petitions could not deal validly with the subject.[26]

Legislative policy concerning political activity of state employees was also affected by Depression-era politics. The subject surfaced in a legislative committee study that accused the executive branch of subverting state employees.[27] A state civil service statute had been enacted in 1913 as a part of the Progressive reform legislation.[28] It had set some limitations on state employee political activity modeled on the federal Pendleton Act. It had also forbidden other persons to solicit contributions from state employees for political purposes, or to promise promotions or salary increases in exchange for votes. The controller was directed to withhold salary warrants from any state office-holder found in violation of this law by the civil service commission. There is no record, however, that any enforcement action was taken. The statute proved to be innocuous for several reasons. Civil service applied only to a small portion of the state work force. Moreover, the state's bureaucracy had expanded after 1913 and the law did not apply automatically to new agencies. The weak party organization and lack of cohesiveness which resulted from the Progressive reforms made the governor turn more and more to patronage for leverage to mobilize votes in the legislature in support of his programs. The Civil Service Commission report for 1933 showed that of 23,223 state employees, only 9,827 had civil service status. Nearly half the total were in exempt positions and another one-tenth were listed as temporary employees.[29] The legislature had made an ineffectual move in 1929 to tighten control over state employees by prohibiting those in the classified service from engaging in "improper political activity," a phrase whose definition was left wholly to the civil service commission. Any employee violating this vague rule was to be disciplined.

Between 1930 and 1941, a bipartisan coalition of conservative state senators was in almost perpetual conflict with the governor. When the national laws prohibiting the manufacture, sale, and consumption of liquor were repealed, this coalition was so suspicious of Governor James Rolph's desire for patronage that it forced placement of the new state liquor control agency under the supervision of the Board of Equalization, a tax agency headed by five independently elected officers. The tension mounted when the national government provided funds to be administered by a State Relief Administration to assist the unemployed. An intense and prolonged struggle between the legislature and governor over control of this new agency continued during the Rolph, Republican, Meriam, Republican, and Olson, Democrat, administrations. When the 1938 election put a Democrat, Culbert Olson, into the chief executive's office for the first time in more than fifty years, the clash intensified. Olson's opponents claimed that his regime was using the State Relief Administration for patronage purposes, and, in a charge unprecedented in California, that the governor favored collective bargaining for the SRA staff.[30] Demands on the new governor were tremendous and his handling of them proved to be less than skillful. The conflict came to a peak in 1940 when the Senate's so-called economy bloc forced adoption of a "Little Hatch Act" prohibiting political action by the agency's employees as the price for its approval of appropriations enabling the SRA to continue.[31] This statute was short-lived, however, because the SRA was liquidated in 1941.

The dispute in California over appointments to newly created state agencies providing work relief, employment placement, aid to the aged, children, and handicapped, was but a segment of the larger, nationwide controversy. The national controversy produced consequences for state and local government employees. The U.S. Senate was disturbed over President Roosevelt's use of executive power to appoint persons to serve in the numerous new administrative agencies created as part of the New Deal program. Led by Senator Carl Hatch of New Mexico, Congress adopted the Hatch Act in 1938, placing extensive restrictions on federal employees' political activities. In 1939 it extended similar restrictions to state and local employees engaged in programs financed wholly or partially by federal loans or grants.[32] Workers were forbidden to take an active part in managing either state or national partisan campaigns or to coerce other employees to contribute to a party organization or candidate. They were assured, however, that they continued to have "the right to vote (as they choose) and to express opinions on political subjects and candidates."[33] The Hatch restrictions did not apply, so far as state and local employees were concerned, to nonpartisan elections or to campaigns relating to policy restrictions.

The U.S. Civil Service Commission was assigned responsibility to determine the appropriate disciplinary action, and a disciplined employee could appeal the commission's decision to the federal courts. The state and local supervising officers were placed in an awkward position inasmuch as they were made responsible for filing charges against an employee who violated the restrictions. The employing jurisdiction could be penalized by loss of federal grants equivalent to the salary of the offending employee if the supervisor did not take action and if the commission, as the result of a federal investigation, found an employee guilty. Both the states and the employees complained often about the lack of clearly stated guidelines and definitions of improper activity. The guidelines or definitions existed only in an uncodified collection of commission statements and decisions.[34]

California's acceptance of federally funded programs in social welfare, education, employment, health, and highway construction brought a large number of state and local employees under the jurisdiction of the Hatch Act and the U.S. Civil Service Commission with respect to regulation of political activity. Equally importantly, the Social Security Act, which governed federal-state relationships in the broad area of welfare administration, required state and local agencies administering funds under its terms to conform with merit system rules relative to employment, promotion, training, and compensation established by the Social Security Administration. The California state government was in the process of setting up a new state-wide personnel agency, but most counties, which were to become the field administrative agencies of the social welfare programs, had no personnel systems at that time. Existing statutes did not authorize general-law counties to establish civil service or merit system procedures. More significantly, county officials had not indicated any interest in the subject. Nevertheless, if California were to qualify for federal funds, legislation acceptable to the Social Security Administration had to be enacted. The statute adopted in 1939 covered a minimal scope, as a subhead indicated, "authorizing adoption of a limited civil service system."[35] It also gave county boards of supervisors optional authority to write restrictions on political activities by employees not subject to the Hatch Act provisions or the Social Security Administration standards.

Reorganization of the state civil service system, begun in 1934, reached a climax of formal action in 1937 supported by an unusual coalition of groups that had been disturbed by the impact of the turbulent political and economic conditions on the state work force. The first to act was the newly formed California State Employees Association, which was desirous of finding a means to stabilize state employment on behalf of its members.[36] Another was the California Federation of Labor. In another quarter of the political spectrum, the Commonwealth Club, a San Francisco non-partisan civic club with state-wide membership that included many influential professional and business persons, renewed its previously expressed interest in the state government. After considerable discussion between these and other groups, a conclusion was reached that an initiative constitutional amendment establishing a greatly strengthened civil service system was the preferred approach.

The state employees' association provided most of the manpower to obtain signatures to the petition, although in counties where no CSEA chapter existed, the captains of the Highway Patrol directed petition circulating.[37] The joint effort rounded up signatures in every county. When the petition qualified for a place on the ballot, Governor Rolph was persuaded to appoint three prominent persons to write arguments for publication in the official ballot-explanation pamphlet. He chose Earl Warren, district attorney of Alameda County and an influential figure among law enforcement officers, Will C. Wood, a former Superintendent of Public Instruction who had masterminded a 1920 initiative on school support, and Manchester Boddy, publisher of the *Los Angeles Daily News* and a notable in the Democratic party. Ralph W. Taylor, executive secretary of the Agricultural Council of California, a powerful and conservative farm lobby group, gave the amendment a further boost by publishing a strong supporting statement in more than two hundred rural newspapers.[38] No organized opposition presented itself and the electorate approved the amendment overwhelmingly at the same 1934 general election in which the rough Sinclair-Meriam gubernatorial contest was decided.

The amendment placed a large portion of the state work force in the classified service whose personnel transactions were to be administered by a five-member personnel board appointed by the governor and confirmed by the state Senate for ten-year terms. The board, which was expected to be relatively immune from direct pressure from either the governor or the legislature, was given extensive rule-making and administrative authority. The amendment was not completely self-executing, however, and a considerable amount of implementation depended on legislation. Despite assiduous lobbying by the State Employees Association and other supporters, the task of writing an implementing statute proved too complex for the 1935 legislative session. Amendments adopted late in the session gave Governor Meriam a reason to veto the bill. At the 1937 session, his supporters were able to assure him that his appointees would be blanketed into the classified service and a statute was approved.[39]

The new civil service statute prohibited assessment of civil servants for support of candidates or parties and forbade anyone to coerce state employees for political purposes — policies remarkably similar to those expressed by the 1913 statute! The officers of the CSEA were disappointed with this and urged the new State Personnel Board to adopt rules that would further restrict political activities. They sought specifically to forbid state employees to participate in any political organization involved with nomination and election of candidates to state office, to use public facilities for support of a candidate, to support a candidate in return for favors, or to edit or publish any political paper committed to support of a candidate for state office. The personnel board declined to adopt the proposal. By implication the board deferred to Attorney General U.S. Webb, who, by reason of long service, was unusually detached in viewpoint. He had given a written opinion in 1935 in which he said:

The propriety of political activity must in large degree depend upon the circumstances of the particular instances. It is generally admitted to be not only the privilege but the duty of an American citizen to be politically active, and it has not been supported that employment in state or municipal service, whether civil service or otherwise, would prevent or prohibit an employee from the exercise of the political right, including a reasonable and well ordered activity in behalf of those political principles which he favored, or in the support of those candidates whose success he believed would contribute to the general welfare. Whether an employee in a particular instance exceeds the limits indicated must be determined . . . by a consideration of the facts and circumstances bearing upon the particular activity.[40]

Interestingly enough, the CSEA took a certain type of political action which, when challenged by its critics, gave the attorney general an opportunity to enlarge his advice concerning public employee actions. The CSEA avoided taking sides in the campaigns for elective offices in 1938, but engaged heavily in opposition to two state-wide initiative proposals its officers believed threatened state employee interests. Proposition 20 proposed the Henry George Single-tax Plan and Proposition 25 was the Townsend Old Age Pension Plan. CSEA opposed both on the ground that they jeopardized the state's fiscal stability. Its journal editorials advocated defeat of the propositions and its executive director toured the state to address state employees on the subject. When opponents challenged these actions, Attorney General Webb issued a statement saying the activities were consistent with state policy. He said, in part:

It would not be consonant with our form of government to deny to those citizens and electors of the State who may be holding office or employment in the State Service the right to give expression of their views on proposed constitutional amendments or propositions submitted to the voters at a state election. The right is reserved to the people of the State to amend the constitution and to enact or reject proposed laws regularly submitted to them. Freedom of action in this regard should not be denied any class of voters in the absence of definite laws clearly limiting such right and privilege. There is nothing in the language of the State Civil Service Act referred to which should be construed as denying to persons holding civil service positions the right to support or oppose proposed legislation or constitutional amendments submitted to the electors of the state.[41]

Earl Warren, who became governor in 1942, had previously established a record of support for the civil service concept and of respect for equitable protection of individual rights under due process procedures. He gained control of the State Personnel Board early in his first term when two members resigned and a third vacancy occurred in normal course, and he soon made the legislature and the bureaucracy aware of his views. The governor's strong interest was significant both for civil service administration and for state employees' political rights. The 1937 civil service act expressed the policy that each state officer and employee must devote full time and attention during working hours to his state office or employment.[42] It is reasonable to conclude that state employees were not expected to engage in political activity on state-paid time.[43] Another section of the statute, however, said that a state officer or employee shall not engage in any other activity or enterprise inconsistent, incompatible, or in conflict with his duties as a state officer or employee.[44] This statement was intended evidently to warn against actions that produced conflict of interest; nevertheless, it was possible that supervising administrators would interpret it unevenly and arbitrarily limit employees' political actions after hours. It did not give employees any clear notice concerning what actions might be construed to be improper.

Legislation enacted later required each agency head to publish a tentative draft of rules and to conduct a public hearing prior to their submission to the State Personnel Board for approval. Approved rules are published in the state Administrative Code. The procedure not only has enabled administrators to shape rules to fit the agency's program needs but it has allowed employees and supervisors to contribute to the rule-making process. A few examples show how the procedure has been applied. A member of the Highway Patrol has been authorized to hold an elective office as a school board member. Likewise, a deputy real estate commissioner has been given permission to serve on a city council, as long as the hours of service do not overlap with those required by his state employment and he does not participate in decisions that involve matters he deals with as a state employee.[45]

Participation by an employee of the State Motor Vehicle Department as a member of his party's county central committee has been cleared as legitimate.[46] The attorney general has summarized the rule applied to state employees: The right to engage in political activity after the hours of employment is deemed to be a privilege of citizenship which should not be denied, in the absence of express or necessarily implied statutory limitations, or unless the particular activity is harmful to the state government.[47] This rule has applied, however, only to state employees whose compensation was financed by state funds. Those paid from federal funds were subject until 1975 to the Hatch Act's more restrictive requirements.

School district employees, like those in cities, counties, and the state, came in for legislative attention during the Depression era. Prior to that time, the state had expressed no policy concerning their political activities, despite the fact that the combined instructional and support staffs of the school districts made up the largest segment of the public work force in California. The first break in this silence came in response to a local demand from Los Angeles for a mechanism to stop the patronage activities of the school board faction known as "The Four Horsemen." The legislature adopted a statute which applied to the one district, the largest in the state. It created a civil service type program for the support employees and prohibited the governing board from soliciting contributions or political service from any classified employee or candidate on an eligible list, directed district officers and employees not to coerce any employee to support or oppose any political group, and forbade the classified employees to engage in any political activities during their hours of employment.[48] Subsequent additions to the Education Code authorized other districts to adopt similar merit system procedures with the attendant restrictions on political action.

The teachers and school administrators, on the other hand, did not experience any legislative restraint on their political activity until almost twenty years later. Teachers have been active politically, supporting school board candidates in many districts, for several years. State-wide aggregations of teachers have been active since 1920, when Superintendent Will C. Wood managed a coalition of teachers, administrators, parents, and others to amend the state constitution by initiative and to establish formulas for distribution of state school aid. Moreover, the California Teachers Association advocates have been recognized for several decades as some of the most effective lobbyists in the capitol. Although groups that advocate economy in school district expenditures have often complained of teacher political activity, few local boards have attempted to establish explicit rules comparable to those enacted by city councils, county boards, or the legislature.

The CTA staunchly defended the right of school personnel to participate in the electoral process as citizens, although it recognized that certain limitations were legitimate. Moreover, it appears to have been the one public employee organization that sought to develop a set of guidelines for its members concerning political action. Its ethics committee in 1954 answered its own rhetorical question, "what are the ethical responsibilities of teachers in relationship to the public in participating as adult citizens in political decisions involving the welfare of the youth in their charge?" in this manner:[49]

To meet the responsibility to the pupils, the teacher does not use his classroom privileges and prestige to promote partisan politics.... To meet the responsibility to the profession, the teacher maintains active membership in professional organizations and works through them to attain objectives which will advance the status of the profession; exercises his right to participate in the democratic processes which determine school policy.... Once policy is determined, he supports it.

The statement declared that teachers possess full citizenship rights and responsibilities, and urged members to work for the election of qualified candidates for school board seats, although it cautioned that moderate action was wise. It declared that the professional teacher had an obligation to present facts about educational issues and to avoid personalities in school elections.

The state legislation, adopted in 1954, was unusual in that it forbade district school boards to enact or enforce any rule to limit off-duty political activity by school employees.[50] Moreover, the bill was adopted by unanimous action in both houses. The action grew out of a dispute in San Francisco over a school board order prohibiting its employees from engaging in politics relative to the election or appointment of district officials.[51] The American Federation of Teachers had proposed to challenge the order in court, but the CTA went to the legislature with the bill which was adopted. The statute confirmed the district boards' authority over teacher conduct during duty hours, but made it clear that teachers were free to act on their own time. This policy remained in effect until a 1977 revision of the Education Code removed all statements regarding political activities and left the subject open for district board ruling.

NEW POLICY CONCERNS, 1950-1965

An overriding concern of many persons during the decade of the 1950's was the prevention of subversion among government employees. Following an example set by the national Congress, legislative and administrative bodies in many parts of the nation prescribed loyalty oaths for public employees. In California, this action began at the city and county level. When questioned about the propriety and legality of the local rules, proponents of the oath sought a state mandate to require all public employees to take the oath as a condition of employment. The state's voters at the November, 1952, general election approved a constitutional amendment prescribing the oath.[52] An applicant or employee was required to declare that he had not been a member within the previous five years of any organization that advocated the overthrow of government by force or violence. An implementing statute adopted in 1953 prohibited any public agency in the state from employing anyone who declined to sign the prescribed oath.[53] An employee who refused to sign was subject to dismissal, and one who signed falsely was liable to prosecution on a felony charge.

The amendment and implementing statute set precedents in two respects. This was the first official action in this state to deal exclusively with the political beliefs and affiliations of public employees and to mandate a common policy for the state and all local governments.[54]

At the close of the 1950 decade, union labor began to press for removal of restrictions on public employees' political activities after working hours.[55] After the A.F. of L. and the CIO merged in 1955, the organization launched a new political action drive. It created a new political arm, COPE, to endorse candidates, collect and distribute campaign contributions, and coordinate action. In California, the state labor federation and its associates defeated a right-to-work initiative statute in the 1958 general election.

Beginning in 1959 and culminating in 1965, it sponsored a series of bills, most of which sought to establish a comprehensive state-wide policy applicable to chartered cities and counties as well as local units operating under general laws and the state government. Independent associations, particularly in Los Angeles and Alameda Counties where the county charters severely limited employees, also joined in support of some of these bills.[56]

Several factors produced the pressure for this type of legislation. Most of the local governments employing large work forces had established explicit formal restrictions on employee political action. Most were chartered counties or cities.[57] Disputes had arisen in several counties over the right of employees to become candidates for office.[58] In most instances, boards of supervisors were determined to prevent employees from becoming candidates for the office of supervisor or sheriff. In Los Angeles County, the employee association and several unions had joined forces in 1956 and 1962 in a losing effort to amend the county charter.

Another factor was organized labor's growing interest in employment conditions in special districts. None of the statutes that governed special districts expressed any policy concerning conditions of employment or employee conduct. District governing bodies were free to establish policies formally and informally without reference to state-imposed standards. Most of the statutes, though appearing to be general in application, were actually special acts adopted in response to demands from community based groups preoccupied with legitimatizing their authority to perform certain functions and to levy taxes. Some employed few persons but several became relatively large employers. The Metropolitan Water District of Southern California, the Imperial Irrigation District, and the East Bay Municipal Utility District, for example, had not only become sizable employers but had experienced management-employee disputes. As more special districts were proposed for urban communities, unionized trades, such as electricians and operating engineers, began to find employment in this type of agency.

The attempt to promote comprehensive legislation that would override existing policies of chartered cities and counties faced opposition from the League of California Cities and the County Supervisors Association as well as from groups that objected for ideological reasons. Chambers of Commerce in the metropolitan areas, representing business employers, also opposed. Most of the legislation was introduced in the Assembly and given passage there but was blocked or heavily amended in the Senate. Those bills introduced by Nicholas Petris, Democrat, of Alameda County in the 1961 and 1963 sessions were closest to the model preferred by the unions, but they were stopped in the Senate.

The bill introduced by George Danielson, Democrat, of Los Angeles in the 1963 session was changed greatly before it became a statute. Its history illustrates how the legislative process produced a disjointed policy statement that left all parties unsatisfied. AB 2947 began with the amended wording of the Petris bill from the previous Senate session. A long preamble expressed the belief that democracy would be enhanced if public employees had full opportunity to participate in the political process, particularly in state-wide and national elections. It declared participation by state and local employees to be a matter of state concern, therefore it intended pre-empting the regulation of public employee conduct by expressing a state policy. Local ordinances and charter provisions inconsistent with its provisions would be void. The statute exempted school employees, however, leaving them subject to the Education Code exclusively.

The Assembly approved the Danielson bill by the substantial margin of 43-11. Three Republicans joined the Democratic majority, but the negative vote was entirely Republican.[59] The bill ran into trouble in the Senate, where its declaration of intent to pre-empt the field was removed, thus turning the purpose completely around. The local government officials' spokesmen demanded this if they were to modify their objections to the bill. A subsection which prohibited employees from participating in political activities while in uniform, based on an existing section of the law applicable only to general-law cities, was also added. In its final form the bill dealt with four topics. It forbade any public officer or employee to solicit or receive political contributions from fellow employees and proscribed entry to or use of public facilities for the purpose of seeking political contributions. It forbade the use of public office or authority to influence another person politically, and it forbade any officer or employee subject to civil service or the merit system to take an active part in campaigns for offices in his employing government. Officers and employees were authorized to be candidates, however. A fourth prohibition concerned participation in recall elections. [60]

An opinion given by the attorney general soon clarified the impact of the new statute. [61] It applied to chartered cities and counties as well as to those operating under general law and superseded any local policies that conflicted with it. But removal of the clause stating the intent of the legislature to pre-empt the subject field left local governing bodies free to enact regulations on other aspects of political activity not covered by the statute. Moreover, the statute applied only to cities, counties, and special districts. It did not apply to the school districts or the state government.

The results were not viewed by all public employees with equal satisfaction. The Electrical Workers Union in Los Angeles complained that the statute took away from employees in that city privileges previously enjoyed under city policy. The Los Angeles County labor federation urged the state body to attempt again to secure legislation that would limit regulation of employee political activity solely to working hours. [62] The nonaffiliated Los Angeles city employees' association also was anxious to have the statute modified to enable it to collect money for a campaign to change the pension section of the city charter. [63] Two Los Angeles assemblymen competed to offer legislation at the 1965 session to accomplish the association's purpose. George Danielson succeeded in amending his 1963 statute to add a new section pertaining to solicitation of funds.

Parliamentary rules and procedures help to explain the outcome of the policy debate. The Los Angeles city employee association, the party mainly interested in the Danielson bill, wished to get its pension plan on the 1965 city ballot, but under ordinary procedure a statute adopted at this session would not become effective until January 1, 1966. Therefore, it was necessary to attach an emergency clause to the bill, enabling it to be effective as soon as passed by the legislature and signed by the governor. But an emergency bill requires approval by two-thirds of the membership of both houses, rather than by a simple majority. To attract this number of votes, the author was forced to accept two amendments of some significance. One permitted local governing bodies to prohibit solicitation of funds during working hours, the other authorized them to prevent persons from entering work premises to seek contributions. After these changes were made, the bill moved through the Assembly by a vote of 67-1 and, after an attempt to alter it failed, the Senate waved it on with a 32-3 tally.[64]

Passage of the 1965 amendments ended the legislative drive to secure a uniform and liberalized policy statement concerning public employee political activities. Proponents of revision were convinced they could accomplish little more on this subject through the legislative process. Not only had the legislative process ignored broad principles in its pursuit of policy, but the judiciary had taken the responsibility to determine the basic elements of this policy subject.

Speaking for a unanimous state Supreme Court, Chief Justice Phil Gibson wrote in an opinion given in 1963:

> ...the United States Supreme Court has on several occasions applied the principle that where the curtailment of First Amendment rights is concerned the state may prevail only if it can show that it has a 'compelling' interest in limiting those rights.[65]

He went on to say that even if a compelling state purpose is present, the restriction must be drawn with narrow specificity in matters involving constitutional freedoms. The restrictions imposed by a governmental entity must not be broader than required to preserve the efficiency and integrity of the public service.

Applying the criterion it had specified, the court found the entire section of the Alameda County charter pertaining to political activity and a section of the San Francisco city-county charter to be in violation of both the state and national constitutions.[66]

Two cases had reached the court during the same session and were argued at virtually the same time the legislature had passed the original Danielson bill. The one from Alameda County had been brought by a doctor who headed the county alcoholism control program, contesting his dismissal by the board of supervisors for violation of the charter section which prohibited classified employees from participating in political management. Though employed by Alameda County, he had acted as chairman in an adjacent county of the speakers' bureau for re-election of the incumbent governor. The county civil service commission had upheld the board's action but the superior court had ruled the charter section to be unconstitutional and the county appealed to the Supreme Court. The other case, from San Francisco, involved a section of the charter which specified that any classified civil servant forfeited his employment if he became a candidate for public office. A deputy sheriff had chosen to be a candidate for sheriff and, after he failed to gain his objective, he sued to regain his former job. The Supreme Court decided the two cases together, and found that in neither case had the government made a convincing showing that there was a compelling need to restrict the employee's First Amendment rights. Ironically, it was the San Francisco charter, which had been the first to set specific limits on city employees' political activities, that provided one of the bases for the court to enunciate sixty-five years later a constitutional principle governing those restrictions.

The immediate effect of the two decisions was to render inoperative those sections of the county charters in San Francisco, Alameda, and Los Angeles which were sweeping statements of restrictions on political activities. It also caused employees and administrators in many other counties and cities to re-examine local charters and ordinances to determine if those rules might be deemed also to be overly broad. Inasmuch as the new legislative enactment applied to both charter and general-law cities and counties, the state policy was to prevail on the subject of political activity, except on those matters not covered by the statute. A period of readjustment followed the announcement of the Supreme Court decision and the passage of the statute.

Three additional decisions by the state's high court in a space of four years further delineated the constitutional guidelines. Two cases arose from disciplinary actions by administrative officers and one from a union's efforts to prevent enforcement of a governing board's explicitly written policy directive. In two instances, the governing body's authority stemmed from general state legislation rather than from a locally approved charter. In the third, it rested on a charter. In both disciplinary actions, the employee in question possessed no statutory or charter-granted protection to job tenure.

The most significant of the three was *Bagley* v. *Washington Township*.[67] The Washington Township Hospital District, the employer in this case, had been organized under a public hospital district statute which permitted a local governing board to negotiate the terms of employment policy with its employees, but did not authorize any type of civil service procedures. Political conditions in this southern Alameda County district had been tumultuous from the time the unit was formed, and unionized work-

ers frequently disputed the board's view that employees served at its pleasure. Frustrated in attempts to negotiate with the elected board, several
employees joined in a move to recall three board members. The trustees
countered by announcing that:

Participation by district employees in any political activity for or against any candidate or ballot measure pertaining to the district is unlawful . . . and may constitute
grounds for disciplinary action and/or dismissal.

An administrator sought to implement this order by attempting to persuade the plaintiff in this case, a nurses' aide, to discontinue seeking signatures to the recall petition in her off-duty time. When she refused to stop,
he dismissed her from service. Thereupon the hospital workers' union assisted Nellie Bagley to sue.

Unlike the Holmes court seventy-four years previously, the California tri-
bunal regarded the central issue of the case to be determination of the employee's constitutional rights. Said Justice Tobriner, writing for the majority, "The public employee surely enjoys the status of a person protected by
a constitutional right." The court said that although Bagley possessed no
statutorily granted tenure rights, and although there is no constitutional
right to public employment, admission to that employment may not be
made conditional solely on any terms that the employer chooses to impose.
The latter may impose restrictions, but it has a heavy burden to defend
them and to meet the tests prescribed by this court in the 1963 cases. The
court elaborated on the tests to be applied. First, the political restraints
involved must relate rationally to the enhancement of public service. Second, the benefits which the public gains by the restraints must outweigh
the impairment of the constitutional rights, and finally, the employer must
show that no alternatives less subversive of constitutional rights are available. It found the district had not met these tests. It considered the action
of the district board and its administrator to be a totally impermissible demand that the employee waive her constitutional rights as a condition to
continuing in public employment. Furthermore, it found the section of the
Danielson Act which prohibited employees from engaging in recall campaigns, on which the board rule was based in part, to be an improper restraint on the employee's constitutional rights.

In yet another case from Alameda County, the court declared that the
political rights of public employees rest on the constitution rather than on
civil service laws or a local charter. The county board had dismissed an
assistant county health officer while he was still a probationary civil servant
on the ground that his membership in the "Ad Hoc Committee to End Dis-

crimination" was incompatible with his employment. The county charter granted civil service tenure only to employees who had completed their probationary service, and the county administrators therefore had taken the position that management could dismiss a probationary employee for any reason that appeared suitable to them and the civil service commission accepted this concept. The state Supreme Court's response was that "the ultimate boundaries of plaintiff's rights are set not by the Alameda County Civil Service Commission but by the Constitution of the United States." The county had made no effort to carry the burden of proof demanded by the rule spelled out in the Bagley case, therefore the court sustained the employee.[68]

Recognition of a public employee's right to sign or circulate recall petitions to force members of the governing board into special election, as the Bagley case did, opens up a considerable area for political action. If an employee may circulate recall petitions, surely he may do the same for initiative, referendum, and nominating petitions. If any employee may advocate the defeat of an incumbent, elected supervisory officer, he may also seek to elect a preferred candidate at a primary, general, or recall election. Legislation that goes beyond prohibiting political activity during work hours, on the work premises, in uniform after hours, or that prohibits coercion in the raising of campaign fund contributions, appears not to meet the burden of proof demanded of the public employer by the court in the Bagley decision.

A Los Angeles school case is an example, however, of a problem arising during work hours that may not be ruled out. The local board had adopted the following policy:

No political activities shall be engaged in on school premises or on property owned by or in the possession or control of the Los Angeles City School Districts, except as provided under the Civic Center Act. Employees shall not engage in such activities.

The teachers' union had sought to obtain signatures during duty-free lunch periods to a petition pertaining to school finance addressed to the governor, superintendent of public instruction, and the local board of education. When administrators refused to permit the activity, the union sought an injunction. The district introduced testimony to show that the circulation of petitions in school lunch rooms would cause controversy between teachers and would produce disruptive results. The Supreme Court was particularly impressed in this case by the fact that the petition was a plea for the redress of grievances, an historic citizens' right. It was not convinced that the predicted disturbances would be any more disruptive than those generated by differences of opinion on other major subjects. It said, "The danger justifying restriction or prohibition must be one which 'rises far above public inconvenience, annoyance or unrest'." It ruled that in the absence of a showing of clear and substantial threat to order and efficiency of the schools, teachers should not be prohibited from circulating a petition concerning public school finance during duty-free lunch periods on school premises.[69]

Political action and the exercise of First Amendment rights are not always encompassed in petitions, election campaigns, or lobbying. Protests and criticisms of officials' decisions are other forms of expression or action, although they are less frequently identified with public employees' behavior. Most theories about administrative organizations deal with such problems as the reduction of interpersonal friction within an organization. The classical concept of a bureaucratic hierarchy tends to deny that a subordinate may criticize an administrative superior to persons outside the agency. Much contemporary theory, however, supports a more open system and regards most dissent as healthy organization behavior. A case which originated in the city of Berkeley illustrates a clash between the customary application of the bureaucratic principle and the state courts' growing concern with sweeping prohibitions on public employees' exercise of their citizens' prerogatives. The Berkeley city administration had been attempting to disengage itself from the traditional practice of linking police and fire salary schedules. Management desired to increase police salaries more rapidly than those paid firemen. In the midst of the controversy, a veteran fireman wrote a letter to the editor of the *Berkeley Gazette* in which he criticized the city administration's actions, claiming the police department had "fooled" the city manager, personnel officer, and council into thinking there was a serious recruitment problem when the situation was caused by the department's own short-sighted policies. Following publication of the letter, the city manager suspended the fireman for violating the departmental rules which directed employees to refrain from criticizing adversely the actions of any superior and from expressing disapproval of the policies and practices of the department. The fire fighters' union challenged the administrative action in the courts and the court of appeal found the personnel rules to be overly broad. Inasmuch as the trial court had determined previously that the letter did not contain offensive, defamatory, or obscene statements or incite violence, the court ordered the city to reinstate the man, clear his record, and compensate him for the salary lost through the suspension.[70] The court carefully distinguished the situation here from one met in an earlier case where the dismissal of an employee who was also editor of an employee organization paper had been upheld. In that case the

man had allegedly exhorted member-readers to strike if the board of supervisors did not meet their demands.[71]

The changes in policy regarding political activities that have come about
through the judicial process have been the products of organized action by
public employees. Although the cases arose out of threats to specific public
employees, and the decisions interpreted the constitutional rights of individuals, employee organizations supported the litigants financially and
supplied them with champions in the courts. The jurists' philosophy and
reasoning produced the written opinions, but judicial attitudes towards the
subject reflected, at least in part, the scholarship and reasoning the attorneys presented in their briefs and arguments before the higher courts.
Equally importantly, the California Supreme Court worked with precedents provided by the federal courts.

CONCLUSIONS

The assumption that public employees should be limited in their political
activities because of the nature of their employer, the government, has
been widely held. There has not been agreement, however, regarding the
extent of the limitations, so policy development has been disjointed. Initially, individual employees were forbidden to participate actively in partisan elections or to contribute money or effort to support candidates. The
stated purposes of these restrictions were to prevent employees from trad-
ing political support for job preferment and to protect employees from
coercion. Both purposes gained wide popular support, which remains firm
today, although the strategy for achieving them has changed. These prohibitions were revived and amplified in local charters and ordinances and
by state and federal legislative action during the Depression era of the
1930's.

Introduction of nonpartisan local elections and creation of the initiative
petition procedure by the Progressives in 1910-13 enabled employee organizations to participate extensively in employment policy making, through
support of nonpartisan candidates and through initiative petitions, without violating the rules prohibiting partisan activity. The official policies
were very uneven, however. Employees of the state, the school districts,
and the chartered cities were less restricted by state law than were those of
the general-law cities. The cities and counties with the largest work forces
tended, however, to create the greatest restrictions by local board and
administrative rules. Key administrative officers often exerted influence
informally on employees under their direction.

During the 1950's, the so-called Cold War Era when McCarthyism was rampant in American politics, public employees were subjected to special requirements which compelled them to sign loyalty oaths and affirm that they did not belong to subversive organizations. This action produced an unanticipated side effect. It focused attention on the application of standards uniformly to all public employees in the state. When organized labor and some independent associations sought uniform legislation to limit the public employers' regulation of political activities to the hours of work, an opposing coalition brought about a compromise that produced a complex and disjointed policy statement.

Litigation pursued by employee organizations elicited from the state Supreme Court statements of judicial standards based on the First Amendment to the federal constitution which ruled out sweeping restrictions on employee political activities. Each employer-government that seeks to enact rules restricting these activities must carry the burden of proof to show that the restriction is necessary to preserve the efficiency of the public service and that no less restrictive policy will accomplish the purpose.

An employing government may forbid political activity by employees or others during official working hours and on government premises. It may forbid the wearing of their official uniforms by employees when they engage in political activity. Some activities, such as performance of a public office during the employee's free time, may be restricted if it results in conflict of interest or interferes with job performance. The distinction between a person's rights as a citizen and as a public employee has been narrowed markedly.

Public policy, which began with a concern to limit the individual employee's actions in search of preferment, must now emphasize regulation of group action through employee organizations. Employee organizations have become significant factors in state and local decision-making on several subjects, including compensation and conditions of employment.[72]

VI
THE RIGHT TO ORGANIZE

The right of public employees in California to form and join organizations of their choice and to be represented by them for the purpose of influencing employment policy is now broadly assured, but it was accomplished only after long, occasionally bitter controversy. Subsumed in this generalized guarantee is protection from interference by the employing authority with the employees' selection of an organization. The right is acknowledged by a series of state statutes which collectively covers all categories of public employees. The Fire Fighters Act in 1959 was applicable only to one occupational group. The George Brown Act of 1961 stated a general policy for all state and local employees. Several other statutes, including the Winton, Meyers-Milias-Brown, State Employee Organization, and Rodda Acts, reiterated the basic provisions of the George Brown Act and elaborated on provisions governing representation and communications between management and organized employees.[1]

The right of public employees to organize was debated in California for approximately fifty years before it was given legislative approval, despite the fact that employees of several jurisdictions had formed organizations. The issues perceived, and the attempts made in the past to formulate public policy with respect to them, have left residual attitudes that continue to color discussions about the entire range of public employer-employee relations in the 1970's. The issues debated at various times during the fifty-year period are summarized in the following questions:

1. Should any state or local employees be permitted to organize or join an organization that seeks to influence public employment policy?
2. Should each employer-government be permitted to establish its own policy and prescribe its special form of organizational behavior, or is the relationship between public employers and employees a subject that requires the state to formulate a policy applicable uniformly throughout the state? If the state makes the decision, should it confine itself to expressing basic principles and leave the definition of details and procedures to the employing governments, or should it inject its influence and decision making machinery fully into the subject?

3. Should there be one comprehensive policy or should there be separate policies for different types of employee organizations, the distinctions to be based on the occupation of the members, on programs, or on tactics used to achieve the organization's objectives?
4. If there is to be more than one policy, what criteria should be applied to each?
5. If each employer is allowed to make a policy, at what decision making level should the choice of policy or action be made? Should it be made by the department heads, an administrative board or commission, an elected executive, or some combination of executive and legislative offices? Should the policy be decided within the bureaucracy, or should it be determined through the full scope of the political process? That is to say, should the policy be expressed through disciplinary actions taken by administrative officers against subordinates or by an explicit statement of policy and procedure applicable to all employees and developed through open, public discussion?
6. Are alternatives to be examined calmly and policies to be stated before an incident occurs, or is the decision to be made in a series of ad hoc crisis actions that reflect the relationships and attitudes developed during a confrontation between aggravated parties?

Most of the attempts to establish a policy on this subject in California were made after public officers had clashed with groups of employees in disputes heard well beyond the corridors of city halls or county court houses. The decision-making tended to be episodic, although with the repetition of incidents the elected officials, key administrators, and employee organizations began to make their respective attitudes and preferences known. Specific policy statements emerged gradually and opinions crystalized slowly on a choice between administrative officers, elected officials, the judiciary, and the state legislature as the vehicle to resolve the issues.

Local governing bodies, as well as the state government, for many years chose to make no formal statements regarding employee organizations or the right of employees to join them. In most instances, the decision was left to the department heads, mainly police and fire chiefs, or the chief executive, such as the mayor or city manager. The reason for this legislative non-action appears to have been that the governing boards were fearful they would be drawn into a commitment to negotiate if they made a formal policy statement recognizing the right of employees to organize. They hoped to keep their options for action open by remaining mute.

The reluctance to make positive policy statements is illustrated by the discussions that took place in Santa Monica in 1946 when a new city charter was prepared. The city government had been involved in a stream of controversies about employer-employee relations. The municipal bus drivers had struck in 1942 and had sought a court directive to compel the city commissioners to recognize the Brotherhood of Railway Trainmen as their bargaining representative. The court of appeals had ruled that the city lacked authority to engage in collective bargaining.[2] A CIO union had gained a foothold in three departments in 1945, and was threatening a strike over salary matters. The city commission declined to meet with the union representatives, but employed a consulting firm to prepare a new salary plan. In this environment, a freeholder charter commission began to prepare a new city charter, and one of its committees submitted a draft of a proposed city labor policy which would assure municipal employees the right to organize without interference or coercion by local officials. It also proposed to authorize civil servants to designate representatives, who need not be city employees, to present petitions to the city council on their behalf relating to wages, hours, and working conditions. A clause in the statement specified, however, that the city council could not divest itself of its decision powers. In sum, the city was asked to recognize explicitly the employees' right to organize and present demands, but the council's authority to decide policies was not to be diminished. The local press opposed this plan, alleging that it would encourage unionization of the city work force. Other opponents contended that no statement of labor policy was needed, because the employees were protected by civil service and a liberal pension system. Despite the opposition, the charter commission approved a modified draft by a majority vote and the electorate approved the charter.[3] Santa Monica thereby became one of the very few cities in California to have an explicitly worded, publicly stated policy on the subject of the employees' right to join organizations of their choice.

Sixteen years later, only 16 of 271 cities, or less than six percent, had adopted any policy statement with respect to employee organizations.[4] The statements can be classified in three types. In one, the city's employment policy booklet said the city manager followed an open door procedure whereby any employee or employee representative could discuss any grievances or matters of interest with him. A paragraph from another administrative manual is typical of the second:

Inasmuch as the City employees are joined together in an organization known as the Municipal Employees Association to promulgate their welfare and interests, and since it is the desire of the City Council to set salaries and wages fairly, in the best interest of the employees and the community, the council therefore adopts a policy that in all matters affecting the discussion and negotiation of wages and salaries, it recognizes the Municipal Employees Association as the only organized group who can speak in behalf of the interest of the greatest number of City employees.

A third approach, taken by three cities with relatively large work forces, is illustrated by the following excerpt from an administrative employee handbook:

> All city employees have a free choice as to whether to join or not to join any employee organization. The City's policy is not to advise or interfere with any employee in that choice. Some City employees belong to the Municipal Employees' Association. Some belong to a union. Some belong to various professional societies, associations and other organizations. Some do not belong to any employee organizations. The choice is yours to make on your own. The only condition laid down by the City is that no employee may join or belong to any organization which advocates the overthrow of constituted authority by force, violence or other unlawful means. You have taken an oath to this effect as required by law.
>
> It is against the City's policy for any City employee to coerce or intimidate any other employee into joining or refraining from joining any employee organization. Any employee guilty of attempting to coerce or intimidate any other employee concerning these matters will be subject to disciplinary action.

Several cities and counties gave employee organizations a form of de facto recognition by permitting the payroll officers to grant employees' requests to deduct dues from their paychecks. The dues check-off privilege often was used discriminatively, however, to give preference to a particular local association and to oppose unions.[5] Few local employing jurisdictions adopted policy statements that established criteria to govern recognition of organizations and the granting or withdrawal of check-off privileges. Virtually all decisions were made on an ad hoc basis.

Recognition of the right of firemen and police to form or join unions touched off the most heated controversies of all. Even in these instances, the general governing bodies tended to refrain from adopting explicit, formal policy statements and left the responsibility to the mayor, a department head, or an administrative commission. In a sense, the matter was kept within the bureaucracy and was dealt with as an administrative, disciplinary matter rather than as a subject for policy discussion and community decision.

Attitudes concerning unionization of firemen differ somewhat from those relating to police personnel, therefore analysis of the steps that led to adoption of a policy governing those two occupations, as well as others, must be discussed separately. Moreover, the fire fighters were the first group to demand and get formal statutory recognition of their right to join organizations of their choice.

THE FIRE FIGHTERS

Many fire fighter organizations in California began as benevolent societies or initiative petition circulation groups. The Los Angeles Firemen's Benevolent Association, incorporated in 1906, was one of the first and it received tacit approval of city officials.

Official attitudes toward fire fighter unions tended to be quite different, however, from those expressed about associations. San Francisco provides a notable example. The San Francisco fire fighters first organized as the David Scannel Club in 1913, but when they formed an IAFF local in 1919, the Fire Commission ordered them to refrain. The commission's acting president issued a statement in which he said:

The union of uniformed members of the Fire Department is, in my opinion, opposed to the public interest, and for that reason should not be sanctioned by the Board. The strike is the means by which labor unions enforce their demands and without the power to strike organized labor would never have accomplished the great advance which it has achieved for the working man. A union which would not strike would be a union only in name. But a strike of the firemen which might be called at the beginning of a big fire would expose the city to destruction.

The commission by a 2-1 vote forbade the firemen to join a labor union or to affiliate with one that had the power to strike. Despite the fact that the IAFF constitution forbade strikes by its locals, the firemen assessed the political situation in the city, which was rebuilding after the historic 1906 fire, and decided to dissolve their union.[6] They promptly turned to political action and secured an initiative charter amendment which increased their salaries.[7]

The Los Angeles IAFF local, chartered in 1918, came under intense opposition from city officials and the business community. Fire Commissioner A. C. Denman, who was president of the Southern California Iron and Steel Company, led the campaign to persuade the firemen to drop their union.[8] He and Chief Ralph Scott met with the union officers and expressed the fear that the firemen might strike in support of other unions involved in industrial disputes, leaving the city without fire protection. The two officials told the firemen they were confident that salary increases would be given if they gave up the union. Coincident with this discussion, the chamber of commerce adopted a resolution, published in the *Los Angeles Times,* which expressed the same fear of unionism in the fire department. The Merchants' and Manufacturers' Association joined the discussion and said:

The Association is strongly backing efforts to increase firemen's salaries and settle all just grievances. We supported the movement for the two-platoon system and we have already expressed to the City Council our belief that the firemen's salaries are inadequate and should be raised—and they will be raised.[9]

The Central Labor Council sought to stiffen the firemen's resistance to the pressure for dissolution of the union. It purchased advertising space in the afternoon newspapers to proclaim that forty-thousand laboring men in the city supported the firemen's union.

Mayor Snyder was in a difficult position inasmuch as the charter designated him the chairman of the fire commission. He had been elected a short while before with labor support and had appointed the editor of the labor paper to the fire commission. Nevertheless, he joined Commissioner Denman to vote a ban on union membership.

The official preference for an association was soon made known when Chief Scott announced the dissolution of the union. He stated that the city administration would offer no opposition to the creation of a mutual benefit and protection association. Shortly thereafter the city council approved increased salaries for all firemen, the additional funds to be provided by a newly levied business license tax. This action was followed by the merger of the police and fire benevolence associations to form the Los Angeles Fire and Police Protective League, which exercised great influence in the uniformed services' employment matters for many years. For more than twenty years, the league received the support of the downtown business community.[10]

Unionization of fire departments in other large California cities did not stir the degree of community opposition shown in San Francisco and Los Angeles. Unions were formed in only nine cities in twenty-one years, however. These appear to have been tolerated rather than explicitly accepted and recognized. On the other hand, a majority of large and medium sized cities had a nonaffiliated firemen's association.

The unionization issue was reopened in 1952 in the residential suburb of South Pasadena, a medium sized bedroom community populated largely by professional and business persons who commute to Los Angeles or neighboring suburbs. It had been one of the first cities in the state to adopt a council-manager form of government and in 1952 enjoyed the image of a firmly managed municipal corporation. Trade unionism was scarcely compatible with the way of life embraced by most persons actively involved in its civic affairs. A prediction that a large majority of citizens would approve the city council's explicit prohibition of membership in a union affiliate seemed very safe. Ordinance no. 1107 forbade any city employee from becoming a member of an organization identified with an association of workers or a labor union "which admits to membership persons who are not employees of the city or whose membership is not exclusively made up of employees of the city." Nevertheless, passage of the ordinance in December, 1951, touched off a controversy that soon spread beyond the city and into state-wide political debate.

The South Pasadena situation clearly involved a rivalry between two employee groups that represented diametrically opposite concepts of organization and that possessed divergent organizational goals. The South Pasadena City Employees' Association, formed in 1947, considered itself the spokesman for all the city's employees. It claimed 115 members, a large portion of the work force, and included department heads and city council members as well as rank-and-file workers. The accomplishments its 1951 officers boasted about indicate the limited scope of its program. These were completion of a classification and salary survey that supplied the data to support a general salary increase, sponsorship of a blood bank drive, promotion of a first aid course for the civil defense program, and establishment of a coffee booth in the city hall.[11] On the other end of the spectrum stood the firemen, many of whom were recent war veterans. These men were restive because the city's personnel practices were slow to produce employee benefits. The rising cost-of-living generated by the Korean War made city wage scales inadequate. Moreover, coffee booths and first aid courses were not new benefits to firemen.[12]

The situation also grew out of a clash of views concerning the status of public employees and their relationship with the government-employer. At public hearings on the ordinance, city council members declared that a union was not necessary to protect the interests of the firemen because it could do nothing for the men that the city's management could not do. A statement released to the press by the city manager expressed the official position:

The city council has no quarrel with the unions generally. They have a valuable place in private enterprise but have no place whatever in public employment. Fair treatment of public employees does not require the intervention of labor unions, as in the case of private employment, for such treatment is, in the public field, compelled to a considerable extent by law.

The employees overlook the fact that by voluntarily accepting employment with the city of South Pasadena, they assumed the obligations incident to such employment and impliedly agreed to accept same under the conditions as they existed.

Police and fire departments are in a class apart. Both are at times charged with the preservation of law and order; they owe the public their undivided allegiance.

The firemen replied with a manifesto of their own:

We as returning war veternas feel we have a moral right to belong to an organization which does not advocate the overthrow of the government or does not divide the loyalty of the citizens of South Pasadena.[13]

They threatened to test the legal validity of the ordinance but did not carry through.

The council and city manager began to negotiate informally with the firemen through an assistant city manager, who was assigned special responsibility to supervise the police and fire departments and to discuss fringe benefits with rank-and-file members. After a month of discussion, the management agreed to give both the firemen and police a ten percent salary increase, to award the firemen additional paid holidays and days off, and to reduce the firemen's work week from seventy-two to sixty-six hours. These adjustments were to be contingent on the men's withdrawal from the union. The men promptly accepted the terms.[14]

Firemen in many other California cities immediately interpreted the results of the South Pasadena action to be a threat to all public employee unions, and more especially to fire fighters' organizations that moved aggressively with respect to employment conditions. Oakland IAFF Local 55 and Los Angeles Local 748 easily won adoption of resolutions at the California State Federation of Labor convention in August, 1952, instructing the CFL legislative advocates to push for statutes that would guarantee public employees the right to organize. The Oakland resolution urged that the legislation apply to charter as well as to general-law cities. South Pasadena was under general municipal law, but Oakland and Los Angeles were governed by charter. Similar resolutions were adopted at each of the next six conventions. The Federated Fire Fighters of California also began an extensive organizing drive in 1956 under the leadership of president A. E. Albertoni, who was also IAFF 10th District vice-president, and increased the number of local unions to thirty.

The IAFF and the AFL-CIO found the political conditions in the 1959 legislative session sufficiently favorable that they could anticipate some success for their legislative program. The Democratic party had won both the governorship and a majority of seats in each house of the legislature with the assistance of organized labor. The AFL and CIO had merged and were in an improved position to push a legislative program. The fire fighters' bill, AB 618, was introduced by Assemblyman Lester McMillan, a Democrat from Culver City, a Los Angeles suburb with a considerable union population. Moreover, the bill was referred to the Assembly Committee on Industrial Relations, a unit whose majority was made up of big-city legislators with voting records favorable to labor legislation. Reference to this committee, rather than to the Municipal and County Government Committee, guaranteed that trade union procedures and concepts would be written into the bill while it was in committee.

The original version of AB 618 merely declared that neither the state nor any local subdivision could deny or limit the right of fire fighters to join any bona fide labor organization of their choosing. The committee expanded this wording and added guarantees that firemen had the right to organize, to bargain collectively, to enter into written contracts, and to engage in arbitration. When it appeared that the additions would block all further consideration, they were dropped. When the bill emerged on the floor of the Assembly it contained only the right-to-organize provisions. It was approved by a vote of 62 to 7, several Republican members voting with the Democratic majority.

When the bill reached the Senate, the Committee on Local Government added a no-strike clause. The vote for final passage proved to be difficult for the proponents, however. When Senator Richard Richards of Los Angeles, the bill's floor manager, first requested a roll call, he could muster only eighteen affirmative votes, three short of the required majority of the membership. When he requested reconsideration two days later, five additional aye votes had been rounded up and the bill passed by a count of 23-11. The party affiliations of participants in this roll call are difficult to identify, because the custom of cross-filing was still in effect in 1952 and many senators had won nomination by both parties. Nevertheless, nineteen of the twenty-three members voting aye listed their primary affiliation as Democrat, whereas seven of the eleven voting no listed themselves as Republican. Governor Brown signed AB 618 and it became operative in September, 1959, as part of the state Labor Code.[15]

This was the first statute in California to recognize explicitly the right of any group of public employees to organize. It was also the first to forbid any group of public employees to strike.

The task of implementing the new policy proved to be a difficult one. The statute neither created enforcement machinery nor assigned specific responsibility for enforcement to any existing state administrative agency. It declared a policy but left the interested parties to seek whatever enforcement authority they could find. Under the circumstances, the courts appeared to be the main instruments through which to test the policy.

The first tests came when management in one locality ignored the statute and another claimed exemption because it operated under a home rule charter. The situation in the Merced County fire department illustrates a reaction that prevailed in several communities. The county fire chief reportedly had said that he would not tolerate unions in his department. He had made numerous speeches to the men of his department advocating that they join the County Employees' Association in which he held membership. Furthermore, he permitted the association's representatives to solicit memberships during working hours. Despite the fact that the Merced Board of Supervisors had adopted an ordinance which conformed with the new Labor Code provisions, the chief professed not to be aware of the board's action. He dismissed a captain who was an officer of the IAFF local for soliciting members. The officer had neither job security nor an administrative forum to which he could appeal the chief's action, because the county had no civil service law. The IAFF therefore chose Merced County as a target and filed suit to enforce the new statute. The results proved to be highly satisfactory to the union, because the court of appeals ruled that the legislature had granted fire fighters a right which "cannot be whittled down by unfair practices, threats or discrimination on the part of those in command." It went on to say that the employer could place no restriction on the employee's right to discuss self-organization, unless it could show evidence that the action was necessary to maintain production or discipline. Moreover, it stated that an employer who vigorously attempts to influence employees either to refrain from joining a union or to abandon membership in one already joined abrogates their rights. The court declared it would not tolerate discrimination against employees who exercised the right to organize.[16] This was indeed strong judicial language.

A second major challenge came from the chartered cities. Several maintained that the statute could not apply to them because employment was a municipal affair; others argued that the statutory language did not specifically mention charter cities or counties. Some refused to recognize the fire fighters' organization and declined to discuss employment policies with them, but others took more aggressive stances.

In Palo Alto, departmental administrators and the council opposed the union. Departmental rules, enacted fifteen years previously, denied firemen the right to join organizations. The fire chief maintained that supervisory personnel should not be members of organizations that represented lower ranks, and he directed a captain to resign from the union. The city council declined to discuss employment matters with the union. When the unincorporated IAFF local filed suit, the city challenged the legal status of the union to sue as an agent for its members. It also claimed exemption from the statute.

A dispute in Los Angeles, which parallels in time the one in Palo Alto, was primarily between the union and the department's senior officers. The fire commission's rules provided procedures governing recognition of employee organizations and handling of grievances. Moreover, the commission had recognized the union and six other organizations and had discoursed with their representatives. Contention was rooted in the long-standing rivalry between the large, officially favored, nonaffiliated association and the smaller, more belligerent union. The union submitted evidence of instances in which high ranking department officers had threatened to transfer firemen to less desirable assignments unless they joined and continued membership in the nonaffiliated organization. The officers had stated publicly that union members could not expect to achieve promotion in the department.

Both Palo Alto and Los Angeles governments insisted that the statute did not apply to them because it violated the constitutional grant of authority to chartered cities to decide matters of municipal affairs. Moreover, they contended that control of employment in the fire department was a municipal affair.

The state Supreme Court demolished both cities' contentions in a unanimous decision.[17] The court perceived the statute to be a legislative effort to create a uniform state-wide labor relations policy and assure uniform fair labor practices. It concluded that the state did not deprive the cities of authority to manage and control fire departments' operations, which was a municipal affair. It reasoned also that because the statute authorized fire fighters to form organizations for the purpose of representing their members, "an action of law on behalf of such members is one form of such representation." Moreover, in its judgment, an unincorporated union local had as much right to sue on behalf of its members as did an incorporated one.

The two decisions firmly established the right of firemen to organize without interference from local management. The firemen gained nothing, however, with respect to procedures for negotiating with employing authorities concerning wages, employment conditions, or grievances. Initiative petitions, lobbying, and presentation of demands to department heads and city councils remained the vehicles available to them to influence local employment policy making.

THE POLICE

The discussion of police unions has been just as lengthy and diverse as that pertaining to fire unions. American municipal police began to unionize in 1919, during the period of labor-management turbulence that followed the close of World War I. Costs of living had soared and wage adjustment was tardy. Manpower was plentiful as large numbers of returned war veterans anxiously sought employment. Organized labor, released from the restrictions of wartime governmental control over wage negotiations, aggressively sought to extend its constituency and to establish collective bargaining as the accepted procedure for conduct of labor-management dialogues. Many commercial and industrial firms in the large cities experienced strikes. While these disturbing events took place, the police of thirty-five cities organized groups and applied to the American Federation of Labor for charters.[18]

The reactions of public officials to the police unionization effort varied widely, as official action in four cities illustrates. In Portland, Oregon, where one of the first attempts was made, Mayor Baker adamantly refused to recognize the right of police to organize either in a local association or a union. He expressed a belief, soon repeated by many others, that any extramural organization would divide a policeman's loyalty and render him incapable of performing neutrally in industrial labor-management disputes. The police union members replied that union membership would not interfere with their law enforcement, but would enable them to understand the laboring man's viewpoint.[19] The dialogue did not lead to disruption of municipal services.

A tragically different result occurred in Boston, Massachusetts. The state-appointed police commissioner in that city refused to recognize the police union as the representative of those asking for wage increases. He suspended nineteen officers who had been active in organizing the union. A large portion of the force struck in protest against this action. Vandalism and criminal activity mounted during the first three days of the strike, and the governor called in state guard units. Four civilians were killed in skirmishes with the guardsmen. AFL President Gompers offered to act as negotiator and requested President Wilson to call a national conference on labor problems. Commissioner Curtis refused to receive the striking policemen's offer to return to duty and declared that they had abandoned their positions. Governor Coolidge asserted that the dispute was for the commissioner to settle unilaterally and that the proposed Presidential conference would be irrelevant.[20] The commissioner ultimately recruited a new force by offering increased salaries and an allowance for the purchase of uniforms.[21]

In Washington, D.C., the three-member presidential commission that administered the federal city refused to permit the local police to form or join a nationally affiliated union, but Chairman Louis Brownlow, a former news reporter and confidante of three presidents, stated that the commission:

... approve[s] heartily of the principle of collective bargaining, and they [the commissioners] welcome the organization of members of the police force for purposes of collective negotiation, mutual support and organized effort to increase their salaries or improve their working conditions.[22]

The Washington commission forestalled the threatened police strike and avoided the bloodshed and turmoil experienced in Boston.

Mayor Snyder of Los Angeles chose a course of action that differed from both the Coolidge-Curtis and the Brownlow tactics. The situation he faced was one in which police salaries were much lower than those offered by private employers. Department leadership was poor and department morale was low. The rate of turnover in the office of chief was almost as high as in the lower ranks. Members of the department, many of whom had been railway union members prior to becoming policemen, formed an organization and applied for an AFL charter.[23] The *Los Angeles Times* expressed an editorial opinion the day the Boston police strike began that Los Angeles would be better off with no police department than with a unionized one. It reminded the city officials that the paper was on record in favor of increases in police pay.[24] The chamber of commerce reacted to the Boston strike by drawing up a detailed resolution in which it stated its opposition to unions in the police and fire departments. It urged the police commission to bar unions and to dismiss any police who might have joined one.[25] Fifty business leaders met with the city council for lunch at the chamber of commerce and agreed to a sharp raise in business license fees to pay increased police and fire salaries.

The mayor directed Police Chief Home to assemble the 450 police at a downtown hall to discuss ways to organize a Police Relief Association. Accompanied by three members of an informal advisory committee selected by the downtown business community, Mayor Snyder addressed the group, saying he would spare no efforts to aid members of the department through the proposed organization.[26] The business representatives reiterated the pledges their associates had made to the city council. Chief Home said that funds raised by the sale of advertising in a semi-official publication could be used to finance the proposed organization. The meeting concluded with the selection of the captain who commanded the central police station to serve as temporary chairman of the Police Relief Association. Shortly thereafter the police and fire associations combined to form the Fire and Police Protective League. This organization, by maintaining close relationships with elected officials and leaders of the central business area, was able to promote charter amendments that established a police and fire pension system and set the formula for determining salaries for approximately twenty years.

The police in Long Beach created a Police Relief Association in 1922 patterned on the Los Angeles model. Commercial advertising in the association's brochure paid the organization's expenses.[27] Police in several other cities soon developed associations comparable in structure and goals to those of the Los Angeles and Long Beach bodies. The police union issue appeared to be settled.

In 1937, however, the controversy was renewed when the American Federation of State, County, and Municipal Employees began to unionize California police departments. Members of the Santa Monica department formed a local in 1940 and the Long Beach force organized one in 1945, but both units disbanded after a few months.[28] Burbank city officers and the Los Angeles County deputy sheriffs maintained locals a bit longer.[29] Each organization met opposition from department heads, supervising officers, and the nonaffiliated organizations.

The AFSCME in 1943 chartered Local 665 in the Los Angeles police department, composed of officers holding temporary wartime appointments as well as some permanent civil service personnel. The local membership after three years was reported to be approximately eight-hundred. Relations between the union and Chief C. B. Horral were never peaceful and often erupted into bitter exchanges of polemics. Concern over police unions heightened during a strike in the motion picture industry in 1946. The incident began with a jurisdictional dispute between unions. Police from Burbank and Los Angeles as well as the county sheriff's forces were called to restore order at studios in Burbank. Some public officials speculated aloud in the press whether police union members could be disinterested law enforcement officers when members of industrial unions were involved in disputes. A legislative subcommittee assigned to investigate the motion picture strike held a hearing in downtown Los Angeles at which a member of the county legal staff, who had advised police commanders at the strike scene, charged that strategies planned at the police command post had been leaked to the strike leaders. Although the committee received no detailed information about police misbehavior, it recommended that legislation be enacted to prohibit any police officer from becoming a member of any labor union. The legislature did not act on the recommendation, however.[30]

While the legislative inquiry was going on, the city council adopted an ordinance authorizing the payroll office to deduct dues for several employee organizations, including police Local 665.[31] Mayor Bowron vetoed the ordinance, saying "a labor union of police officers is repugnant to the very principles of democracy." He indicated, however, that he would sign a new ordinance if it excluded the police union from dues check-off. The council attempted to override his veto but fell short of the required three-fifths majority. In his weekly radio broadcast the mayor stated that he intended to ask the police commission to ban unions. Five days later the commission, by unanimous action, adopted a resolution prohibiting department peace officers from holding membership in any organization that identified itself with any trade association, federation, or labor union and admitted members who were employed by any other employer than the Los Angeles Police Department.[32] Members of any such organization were given thirty days in which to divest themselves of membership.

The union promptly filed suit for an injunction, alleging that the board lacked legal authority to issue such an order. The union lost in superior court and appealed, but the decision by the court of appeals demolished the police union in Los Angeles. The court also made comments that appeared to approve actions by any appointing officer to prohibit public employees from organizing. The court's majority opinion said categorically that police unions were, by definition, destructive of the constitutional principles of government, and held that the police commission could deny its employees the opportunity to join an organization by declaring the action to be contrary to the public interest.[33]

City Attorney Chesebro immediately issued a memorandum to Los Angeles administrators advising that any local board or department head could break up any union of city employees by promulgating a declaration that membership in the union was contrary to public interest and directing the employees to divest themselves of membership.[34] Chesebro failed to note, however, that the court had been cognizant of the fact that the Los Angeles city charter gave the police commission unusually extensive supervisory responsibility of police employees.

The court of appeals opinion and the Chesebro memorandum greatly influenced the decision in Oakland and the manner in which it was made when controversy erupted there in 1956 over a police union. When Chief Vernon learned of the plan to organize, he issued a departmental order prohibiting officers from joining any labor organization and gave those who had joined fifteen days in which to dissociate themselves. He was especially sensitive because ten years earlier the city had experienced a general strike of private sector unions. The city's use of police to escort strike breakers at a downtown store had left bitter memories in the labor ranks. The business community was equally disturbed about the growth of unionism.

In response to a proposal from the Central Labor Council that the city management permit a six-month experiment with police unionization,

Chief Vernon stated his position in three points that summarized the views of those who opposed police unions: (1) police must be impartial in labor matters, (2) a police department is a semi-military structure in which there can be no sharing of loyalties, (3) police unions are illegal, according to judicial opinion. The chief said he would resign before he would permit a union to be formed in the department.[35] The city manager made clear his support for the police chief. The Central Labor Council sought to get the city council to review the chief's directive at a public session, and the Building Trades Council announced that any council member who wished to be considered a friend of labor should vote permission for the police to join a union. The Teamsters' Local also supported this pressure on the council, although it expressed the view that police should not strike.[36] Inasmuch as three council members and the mayor had been elected with considerable labor support, speculation mounted whether the council would direct the police chief to alter his stand. The city attorney, however, provided the council members a basis for avoiding a public decision. He advised them that the Los Angeles case placed full responsibility for the decision on the department head. The council members, thus assured, voted unanimously not to review the chief's decision. The immediate thrust of the city attorney's advice was to decentralize decision making concerning the freedom of public employees to organize or join organizations. It placed the issue under bureaucratic control. The policy was not to be decided by elected officials after they had examined the various demands made within the political system.

City councils in three medium sized cities adopted ordinances that prohibited police from holding membership in unions. In San Jose and Santa Clara, however, police locals were accepted without controversy. The San Jose chief was quoted as saying that members of the police force had performed their duties during labor disputes without criticism from either labor or the business community.[37]

The police reaction to the Los Angeles and Oakland episodes was substantially different from that of the firemen in the South Pasadena incident. One reason was that members of police departments and sheriff's forces were organized in local benevolent and protective associations sanctioned by department heads. These groups made no overt move to secure state legislation to offset the judicial and administrative decision. Moreover, no national police organization comparable to the firemens' IAFF existed in the 1950's. The American Federation of State, County, and Municipal Employees represented numerous occupations, and the police constituted a minority of its membership in the state and national organization. Furthermore, the AFSCME did not have a strong political base with backing from the state labor federation. Equally important was the fact that a substantial body of opinion was strongly opposed to the concept of police unionism. No efforts were made to legitimatize the right of police to organize until the George Brown Act was proposed and adopted in 1961, applicable to all state and local public employees. This statute treated police as differing from other employee categories. More will be said about police organizations following discussion of the George Brown Act, which recognized the right of all public employees to form and join organizations.

ALL PUBLIC EMPLOYEES

The George Brown Act had a history different from the fire fighters' statute. It was not enacted as the result of any particular event or controversy. It was sponsored by the unions to override the opposition by many local administrators and elected officials to the attempts to unionize public employees, but it presented a concept that the nonaffiliated associations could accept.

One factor that produced the demand for formal recognition of the right to organize was the reaction by nonaffiliated associations as well as unions to the ideology prevailing among elected officials and professional administrators that elected governing bodies had an unlimited right to determine all employment policies without consultation with the employees. A parallel official attitude was that the establishment of any procedure which recognized the status of an organized group as a participant in the decision making process diminished the authority of the elected officials. The unevenness of the relationships that existed between government-employers and their employees, moreover, added impetus to the demand for uniform state legislation. A few governments recognized the right to organize, some forbade all organizations, and some favored certain types of organizations but not others. The officials, in the aggregate, preferred to have no state legislation relating to public employment.

The public employee organizations were divided into rival camps. The California Federation of Labor coordinated the union forces' legislative efforts, although constituent unions also maintained their own legislative staffs and made their own contacts. This group preferred to obtain legislation similar to the National Labor Relations Act and its counterpart state statutes that governed the industrial sector of the economy. Their goal was to get statutory approval of collective bargaining, arbitration, and negotiated contracts. The officers, managers, and members of most associations looked on the unions as threats to their organizations and the modes of procedure they valued. Small associations and single-occupation groups also feared that the large and wealthy associations were planning to absorb them in the struggle to keep unions out of the public work forces. All factions among the employee organizations could accept the idea, however, that a statute which recognized the right of public employees to join an organization of their choice would benefit them.

Assembly Bill 2375 by George Brown, an Assembly member from Los Angeles who had been active in union politics in the department of water and power prior to his election to the legislature, moved through the legislative mill without unusual difficulty, mainly because it proposed a very modest objective.

The speaker of the Assembly referred it to the Industrial Relations Committee, a relatively friendly unit, for the first step. After the bill remained on the committee file for several weeks, the author proposed three substantial amendments calculated to gain support of moderates and to reduce the likelihood of conservative opposition. One specified that any public employee had a right to decline as well as to join or participate in any employee organization. A second declared that the act was not to be construed to apply to public employment the sections of the Labor Code that governed labor relations in the private sector. A third authorized any public agency to prohibit its law enforcement employees from joining an organization not composed exclusively of its employees.[38] The committee adopted these amendments and moved the bill to the floor, where a substantial majority gave approval. The House did not divide strictly on a partisan line; the fifty-two aye votes came from both parties, although all eleven no votes were cast by Republicans.[39]

The Senate Committee on Governmental Efficiency made one further amendment, which pertained solely to state employees, and moved it to the floor where the bill passed, 23 to 4.[40] Governor Brown signed the bill promptly.

The George Brown Act neither challenged nor modified the doctrine that elected officials possessed the authority to determine salary rates and conditions of employment. It simply affirmed the right of public employees to organize and to be represented when employment policy was considered. Any number of persons, no matter how few, and any grouping or mixture of occupations could form an employee organization. Two or more organizations could attempt to represent the same aggregation of persons, and duplicate or overlapping memberships were common in several work forces. The result was that administrators in most large work forces were faced by a large number of employee organizations entitled to recognition under the Brown Act.

The statute directed each governing body to meet-and-confer with the representatives of employee organizations "as fully as it deems reasonable" on almost any subject pertaining to employment. It authorized, but did not require, governing bodies to adopt reasonable rules to regulate the conduct of employer-employee relations, so it established no monitoring machinery. This so-called grant of authority to adopt rules was in reality little more than a gentle nudge to take action. At most, it removed any legal doubt that general law cities and counties could make such rules. It left open the matter of how employers and organized employees were to communicate with each other, although it proclaimed its intent to "strengthen merit, civil service and other methods of administering employer-employee relations *through the establishment of uniform and orderly methods of communication* between employees and the public agencies by which they are employed [emphasis added]."

Professional administrators' perceptions of the value of communications in administrative organizations were illustrated in a survey conducted in 1966. Eighty-six percent of the city managers said they thought public employee organizations could contribute positively to the achievement of a city government's administrative goals, and fifty percent said employee organizations contributed mainly when they served as communication agents.[41]

Jurisdictions in which no organization had been formed, or in which a general association was accepted as the representative of all employees, tended to delay adoption of rules governing recognition of employee organizations. Action most frequently took place on demand of an organized group. The larger work forces, in which several groups had organized, found it necessary to develop some rules. Some adopted a simple plan that required all organizations seeking recognition to file a list of its officers, an address for receipt of communications, and a copy of its by-laws. Those confronted by a number of organizations seeking to communicate regarding employment policies soon began to follow the model adopted by the federal government under the Kennedy Executive Order of 1961, which came to be known popularly as the three-tier plan. An organization that could claim less than thirty percent of employees in a work unit or occupation was given only the right to communicate concerning policies of general application. Those that could establish claim to between thirty and fifty percent of the employees in a common interest group were given limited representation privileges. Organizations in this category often had to share management's attention with another group when discussing matters of interest to the occupation or administrative unit. Organizations that could show they represented more than fifty percent of the employees in a unit were accepted as the sole voice of that group. The George Brown Act, however, contained a provision that tended to undercut all such efforts to sort out the claims of organizations to communicate employee wishes to the employer. It specifically recognized the right of individual employees to decline to join an organization and to speak as an individual.

One of the first questions asked after the George Brown Act became law was whether it applied to the University of California, inasmuch as the state constitution exempts the university from legislative directives regarding its educational programs. Assemblyman Brown sought an authoritative interpretation from the attorney general and was assured the university must comply with this statute.[42] Attorney General Mosk noted that the state Supreme Court had previously ruled that the state's exercise of its police power took precedent over university regulations in matters not exclusively educational.[43] The legislature had declared in the Brown Act that representation of public employees was no longer the exclusive concern of any single public agency, but was a matter of general public concern, hence all agencies created by the state were subject to the statute.

The act authorized employee organizations to represent their members only. Some governing bodies interpreted this wording to mean they could refuse to recognize an organization whose by-laws did not declare that its purpose was to represent employees in their relations with the public employer. The Willits Unified School Board, for example, challenged the status of the California School Employees Association because the CSEA by-laws did not declare representation of its members in employer-employee matters to be one of its purposes. The court of appeals accepted a showing of custom and practice as evidence that the CSEA was a legitimate representative of its members in such matters.[44]

The court also established in the Willits case that an employee organization could sue on behalf of its members as an act of representation, instead of filing litigation in the name of specifically named members as they had been forced to do in previous years. This panel of the court of appeals interpreted the Brown Act regarding the right to organize and represent members in the same manner another panel had interpreted the fire fighters' act.

Other issues raised soon after passage of the Brown Act involved identification of the privileges gained by employee organizations when they were recognized by an employer. A question asking for an interpretation of the State Personnel Board rules is an example. The attorney general was queried if a representative of a recognized organization could enter official work areas during normal working hours and question state employees about work conditions, or if the inquiries must be made only after working hours. He responded that visits could be made with permission of the management if they were reasonably necessary to ascertain the nature of working conditions. Such visits were appropriate to the representation of members.[45]

Another question probed whether an official agency was limited to communicating with employees through a recognized organization when it sought opinions about a proposed policy. The California State Employees Association objected to the representatives of the Public Employees Retirement System meeting with individuals to discuss retirement policies on which the CSEA had taken a specific position. The attorney general ruled that the PERS had acted properly, saying:

the Legislature [did not intend] that only one side of a position should be presented or that members of an organization should somehow be placed in isolation where they could be addressed only by their employee organization and would not be allowed to hear the public employer's side of any given position.[46]

Another ramification of the Brown Act is shown in an opinion of the attorney general concerning use of an employer's internal mail distribution system. A school district had restricted an organization's use of the mail system to communications addressed to its members. The attorney general advised that the restriction violated the George Brown Act because it prevented employees who were not members from receiving information that might enable them to make a decision about joining the organization or choosing between competing organizations.[47]

POLICE ORGANIZATION RIGHTS

The George Brown Act recognized that certain occupations possessed characteristics that might necessitate treatment different from the general group of public employees. Therefore it established a procedure by which separate action could be taken regarding police officers. It authorized the governing body of any public agency to:

adopt reasonable standards, designate positions or classes which have duties consisting primarily of the enforcement of state laws or local ordinances, and may, after public hearing, adopt a resolution or ordinance prohibiting employees in such positions to form or join employee organizations where it is in the public interest to do so.

The key provision was the one which established a procedural requirement that a public hearing be held before the governing body could adopt the prohibition. Police and fire chiefs, or other department heads and administrative commissions, had seldom concerned themselves about such procedural niceties as giving notice to interested parties and holding public hearings prior to promulgating rules governing internal affairs of administrative agencies. The California Administrative Procedure Act of 1949, which directs state administrative rulemakers to employ formal and open procedures, mainly serves as a protection to persons outside the bureaucracy. Moreover, it does not apply to local government rule making.

The closest precedent for this provision in the George Brown Act is the so-called sunshine law, the Ralph Brown Act of 1955, which requires all city, county, and school district bodies to transact business and to reach decisions in open public sessions. It makes an exception of such transactions as those dealing with employment or dismissal of personnel. The news media have strongly advocated this open-session statute.

The George Brown Act observed the home rule principle inasmuch as it permitted local governing bodies the option of approving or limiting the police right to organize. In this respect, it was responsive to the League of California Cities and the County Supervisors Association. It was also responsive to the numerous other groups and individuals that had contended police should be treated differently from other employees. The nonaffiliated local police association concluded, however, that the wording of the section posed a threat to them and soon moved to modify it. Two bills serving this purpose failed in the 1963 session,[48] but the Peace Officers Research Association and the Los Angeles Fire and Police Protective League joined forces in 1965 to push AB 1067.[49] This bill, introduced by Thomas Carroll, a prominent, moderate Democrat representing a San Fernando Valley constituency in Los Angeles County, read as follows:

A governing board may not prohibit the right of its employees who are full-time peace officers (as defined in the Penal Code, sect. 817) to join or participate in employee organizations which are composed solely of peace officers, and which are not subordinate to any other organization.

It sailed through committee and was approved by the Assembly by a vote of 43 to 17; but Assemblyman Waldie, a liberal Democrat from Contra Costa County, obtained reconsideration and proposed an amendment which limited the bill to police organizations "which concern themselves solely and exclusively with the wages, hours, working conditions, welfare programs, and advancement of the academic and vocational training in furtherance of the police profession." The amended bill was adopted by a vote of 43 to 14 and the Senate concurred, 30-0.[50]

The legislative intent of the phrase, "and which are not subordinate to any other organization," is not readily apparent. Presumably it refers to union-type organizations in which the local units receive charters from a national body, subscribe to the national union constitution and by-laws, and pay annual per capita membership fees. Does the term apply, however, to an organization such as the Fraternal Order of Police, which is not affiliated with the labor movement although it charters local lodges, has national policies, and receives some financial support from local bodies? Does it apply to police associations affiliated with the Peace Officers' Research Association (PORAC)? PORAC proponents insist that the state organization does not control local associations in any manner, that it merely implements state-wide the objectives of the police profession.

No effort has been made to probe publicly for an authoritative interpretation of the phrase added by the Carroll amendment. A discussion in the Los Angeles city council in 1970 illustrates the effect the phrase has on local decisions. When announcement of a renewed effort to form a nationwide police union was made through the news media, Police Chief Edward Davis reacted by requesting, with Mayor Yorty's approval, an ordinance to forbid members of the police department to join a union or to strike. The council's personnel committee recommended against adoption by a 2-1 vote. The council gave the matter a public hearing, as required by the Brown Act, at which the Fire and Police Protective League and the Central Labor Council opposed the chief's recommendation. The spokesman for the former said:

We are nonunion, but we are a labor organization and as a matter of principle we must oppose a law which prohibits a person from joining the labor organization of his choice.[51]

Other groups, including the *Los Angeles Times,* counseled that the proposed ordinance would be unwise and counterproductive because it would stir conflict within the department. Only one organization witness spoke in favor of restoring the 1946 police commission order that forbade unions in the police department. The city attorney's advice to the council may have been influential on the outcome. His deputy said the proposal was too broad and he doubted it could meet the test established by the statute. Affiliation with a union did not necessarily cause an organization to become subordinate to the other body.[52] The council rejected the proposed ordinance, seven yes to eight no.

The outcome of a dispute in the city of Coachella in 1967 illustrates some of the consequences when a city council ignores the amended George Brown Act. The police chief of this city had attempted to get the council to improve police working conditions and to settle grievances that members of the department had presented repeatedly. When these efforts failed, he had supported officers who joined AFSCME Local 1239 and he had also joined later. The council did not take the public action prescribed by the statute, but individual council members chose instead to try to force by various forms of political pressure the chief and other officers to drop their union membership. The council also requested the county sheriff to submit an estimate of the cost of a contract whereby his department would take over the city's police work. Before it reached a decision on this plan, however, it acted in executive session to dismiss the chief and issued a statement that continuance of the incumbent "was not within the public interest." The mayor explained, when questioned in the resulting suit, that the council believed it faced an intolerable situation when the police formed a union and threatened to circulate recall petitions against the council members. The city contended that a chief of police in a general law city serves at the pleasure of the council and can be dismissed without cause and without notice or hearing. The police chief in turn alleged that the council had proceeded to intimidate and discriminate against the members of the department after receiving a letter requesting recognition of the union.[53]

Testimony and other evidence convinced the trial court that the council had dismissed the chief because of his membership and activity in the union, and it ordered him reinstated. The court of appeals sustained the lower court, basing its reasoning on the lower court's finding that the chief's right to participate in an employee organization of his own choosing had been violated.[54] Both courts also were influenced strongly by two previous state Supreme Court decisions that had ruled against dismissal of public employees for political activities under orders regarded as being too broad in scope.[55]

Neither court in the Coachella case spoke to the question of whether the council could have dismissed the chief for insubordination if it had followed the procedure prescribed by the George Brown Act and had adopted a resolution prohibiting police officers from joining a union. Nor did they address the point specifically, but they seemed to imply an affirmative answer to the question of whether the section of the Brown Act pertaining to police organizations was overly broad. At base was the fact that the council chose to accomplish its purpose through covert pressure, threats, and disciplinary action without fully exploring other less repugnant alternatives.

The attorney general probably best explained the purpose of the George Brown Act, with respect to general employees as well as police, in his response to three questions put by Assemblyman Carley V. Porter. The questions were as follows: What authority does a local governing board have to limit police officers' time off duty to attend employee organization meetings? What limits are there on its authority to grant permission for officers to conduct organization affairs during official working hours? Is it permissible to change work schedules in such a manner that officers are unable to attend meetings of employee organizations which the departmental management disapproves? Attorney General Lynch explained that the statute authorized a local body to make reasonable rules covering representation of organized workers in discussions with the employer, but the rules could not prevent the officers of an organization from carrying out their representation functions. The employer was not required to permit employees to attend meetings or engage in organization activities during working hours, but any practice that constituted an unreasonable interference with the right to join and participate in organizations or with the right of organizations to represent their members, would receive judicial disapproval.[56]

CONCLUSIONS

Many employee groups had organized prior to the passage of the Fire Fighters' Act in 1959 or the George Brown Act in 1961, but the continuance of most organizations had depended on the good will of department heads, coteries of senior bureaucrats, or the elected officials of each employer-government. The overwhelming majority of local governing bodies had refrained from expressing any explicit formal policy, thereby leaving the decision to key persons in the bureaucratic structure. Employee organizations were often captive bodies in their local political environments.

The two statutes expressed a state-wide, uniform policy that recognized the right of public employees to organize or join organizations of their own choice. The Brown Act also recognized the right of individuals to decline to join an organization and to present an individual claim to the employer concerning employment matters. The two statutes opened the organization process and also gave legitimacy to the nationally-affiliated unions. The Brown Act in particular fostered the multiplication of employee organizations. Any organization that met reasonable standards set by the employer could represent any number of employees. Employee organizations, therefore, competed with inducements to attract and retain members. Employees often took out plural memberships to gain benefits from more than one organization.

The Brown Act left to the individual employer-government the responsibility for establishing reasonable standards to govern recognition of employee organizations and for instituting procedures by which it would communicate with them. The courts recognized that an organization could represent its members by filing suit as well as by discussing employment policy with the employer. Inasmuch as the governing bodies enacted a variety of standards and tried to establish several patterns of representation, the courts were asked often to determine whether a particular standard was reasonable and under what conditions competing organizations could represent their members in discussions over employment policy.

The number of organizations developed in the larger work forces complicated the public management's task of discussing wages, hours, and working conditions with employee representatives. Numerous lawsuits arose out of these situations, so efforts were begun to develop a consensus for new state legislation to set guidelines governing employer-employee relations.

The Brown Act also established a procedure by which employers of law enforcement officers could restrict the choice of organizations made by that class of employees. However, this aspect of the state's policy remains unclear and undeveloped.

VII

POLITICAL ACTION BY
ORGANIZED PUBLIC EMPLOYEES

Organized political action by public employees to influence public employment policy is not a new phenomenon in California. Local employees have participated in this action for seventy years and state employees for forty years. The tactics used have reflected the contemporary civic culture of the state and, as the culture has been modified, civil servants have moved with the changes.[1] When partisanship and machine politics were the dominant characteristics of the political system in the early years of the century, many individual employees played the traditional spoils game. When the direct primary replaced conventions and interest groups began to play significant parts in the electoral and legislative processes, the public employees formed organizations and learned to take part in the newer activities. Although these organizations performed at relatively low intensity levels, most were effective over time in causing legislators and administrators to think specifically of the employees' interest and to institutionalize the administration of hiring, compensation, and retirement benefits. Introduction of the initiative and referendum processes offered the organized groups a legitimate vehicle to seek access to the policy making system by a new route, an appeal directly to the voters via petition.

In the decade of the 1970's, when interest in campaign funds and broadened participatory politics was resurgent, public employee organizations stepped up their lobbying activities. After deliberative discussions, several revised their by-laws to enable them to endorse, contribute to, and support candidates for public office. Individual volunteer citizen-civil-servants, who had previously acted politically quite apart from their employment, were replaced or augmented by paid organizational staffs and volunteers coordinated to produce a managed effort openly identified with an employee association. This was also the era in which confrontation tactics became common modes of political action. Organized employees turned to informational picketing, protest marches, threats of strikes, and actual walkouts in their efforts to influence employment decisions.

175

The leaders who have shaped public employee organization policies and tactics in this state have been pragmatic in their approaches. They have not allied themselves exclusively with any one political party, although they have worked most often with members of the Democratic party. Nor have they tended to follow the example of European public employees who affiliate with a national labor party. They have adopted the tactics of the interest group in political action. They began this type of action during an era in which governing boards and legislatures exercised exclusive authority to determine public employment policies, and they have continued it undiminished since meet-and-confer and collective negotiation procedures were installed in employer-employee relations.

This chapter examines lobbying, appeals to the electorate, and candidate endorsement, three of the traditional forms of political action practiced by organized public employees between 1905-1975. It also analyzes the implications for public policy that result when organized public employees take these political actions in conjunction with collective bargaining.

LOBBYING

The term lobbying, when applied in the American political scene, covers a multitude of activities by groups of persons that seek to influence government policy-making. Its most common usage refers to those activities which relate to a legislative body, but it applies also to efforts to persuade elected or appointed chief executives, or quasi-legislative, rule-making personnel boards to take preferred action. It also applies to negotiations with administrative officers such as department heads. Lobbying with a legislative body includes the preparation, introduction, and sponsorship of bills by one or more members of the legislature, and the provision of information about subjects in which the organization has an interest. It also includes building alliances with other groups through trades of support, keeping informed about the movement of bills, and expressing opposition to proposals detrimental to the organization's program. A considerable part of lobbying consists in making oral presentations at committee or board sessions, arranging for attendance of supporters at hearings, and dispatching letters, telegrams, and calls to committee members expressing support or opposition for a particular bill or rule. A significant portion involves negotiating amendments to bills and to proposed administrative rulings for the purpose of securing as much of the organization's goal as possible.

Public employee organizations in California have sent legislative advocates to Sacramento for a very long time, and no special efforts have been made to restrict those actions. Their advocates are subject to the same regulations that apply to all paid lobbyists. The number of employee organization advocates grows steadily and the cost of maintaining them has reached a substantial figure. The thirty-one advocates registered in 1961 represented two associations of state employees, ten state-wide organizations of local employees, eight state-wide school groups, two local school district associations, and nine organizations of persons employed by single local governments. Forty public employee organizations registered their representatives in Sacramento in 1973-74. Six spent more than $50,000 each in 1976 to influence legislation.[2] The California State Employees Association led this list, and ranked sixth among all major organizations, with an expenditure of $333,895. The others were: California Teachers Association, $210,410; California State Firemen's Association, $193,538; California State School Employees Association, $114,633; Federated Fire Fighters, $75,484; SEIU, $64,128; California Nurses Association, $55,883. The California Federation of Teachers stopped just short of the $50,000 mark, having spent $49,416.

The status of the legislative advocates in the organization they represent also has changed. Most of the large associations were represented in the early years by their full-time, chief staff officer who combined this activity with direction of the permanent headquarters organization. Roy W. Cloud, executive secretary of the California Teachers Association from 1927 to 1947, Robert Thomas, executive director of the California State Employees Association in the 1930's, and Samuel G. Hanson, who followed him from 1946 to 1968, were models of the all-purpose officer.

As organization staffs grew and legislative sessions became more frequent and extended over longer periods, most directors were forced to delegate more of the day to day advocacy at the capitol to associates who functioned from permanent offices in Sacramento. The state employees' association (CSEA), whose headquarters is situated a few blocks from the legislative chambers, is in a particularly convenient position to utilize its staff to the maximum in legislative relations. Most state-wide organizations of local employees have their headquarters in cities other than Sacramento, however. For example, the California Teachers Association (CTA) and the School Employees Association (CSEA) operate from Burlingame and San Jose respectively, but each maintains an advocates' branch in Sacramento.

Several public employee organizations retain advocates who represent several clients in the capitol and accept no responsibility for organizational matters. The Highway Patrol Officers Association, for example, is represented by former State Senator and Judge James D. Garibaldi, who also represents liquor and horse racing interests.

Employee associations and unions alike are accustomed to retaining legal firms to represent them at legislative hearings as well as in litigation. Firms of attorneys specializing in labor relations matters are increasingly employed for a range of services such as legislative advocacy, court representation, and negotiations with employing governments.

Many employee organizations interested in state legislation do not maintain advocates in Sacramento but send their principal officers, legislative committee members, or paid staff members to Sacramento when matters of major interest are scheduled to be discussed at committee hearings or informal conferences.

The Legislative Reform Act, an initiative statute adopted in 1974, and the Fair Political Practices Commission created by it have made some important impacts on state legislative advocates, including those representing public employees. Notably, limitations placed on the amount of expenditures for entertaining legislators have put employee organization lobbyists nearer parity with those representing heavily financed groups. Reports filed prior to 1974 indicated that representatives of public employee organizations spent relatively little on entertainment, compared to that paid by representatives of commercial clients. Notable also was the FPCC effort to reduce the great influence some lobbyists have exercised by their distribution of election campaign funds in addition to their more traditional use of entertainment, persuasion, information, and pressure on incumbent legislators. Lobbyists able to allocate large sums as campaign contributions have exercised enormous leverage over legislators desirous of continuing in office or remaining active in politics. The commission proposed to prohibit legislative advocates from distributing campaign funds. Many advocates representing commercial clients fought this ruling inconspicuously, but John Henning, the secretary-treasurer of the California Labor Federation, was outspoken in his public statements. He contended that the rule would affect most unfairly organizations structured in a manner similar to his. The union executive officer was the person responsible for directing the organization's programs, allocating its expenditures, and representing its legislative interests. He argued that it was impossible for him to comply with the rule and that it was intended to harass and embarrass organized labor. Eventually the rule was interpreted to mean that the legislative advocate could recommend distribution of campaign funds among candidates but could not decide unilaterally or surreptitiously how the funds would be distributed. Inasmuch as the statute and the commission rule became effective at a time when public employee associations and unions alike were launching into legislative election campaign activities on a large scale, they made an impact on the lobbyists' role.

Judgments concerning the effectiveness of legislative advocates are highly subjective. A survey of opinion conducted by the *California Journal* among an equal number of Democratic and Republican legislators in the 1974 session is of some interest.[3] No individual representing a public employee organization exclusively was listed among the twenty most influential advocates, although John Henning of the California Labor Federation was placed in sixth rank. The group rated the California Teachers Association in twelfth place among organizations. Interestingly, Richard "Bud" Carpenter, the veteran former representative of the League of California Cities, was rated second to James Garibaldi as the most influential advocate.

Lobbying by groups possessing large membership is not confined to the work of a legislative advocate or a team of spokesmen. Some public employee groups engage occasionally in the tactic of packing the gallery. This consists in mobilizing numerous supporters from several parts of the state to attend legislative committee hearings in an effort to impress legislators with the intensity of feeling toward a particular piece of proposed legislation. The public school teachers' lobby provides examples of mass committee attendance when school finance measures are discussed. The fire fighters' lobby does the same thing when bills to mandate a reduced work week in city, county, and state fire departments are under consideration.[4] Some of this activity has been replaced by the staging of mass assemblages on the capitol steps, where the demonstrators are addressed by elected officials and photographed by television.

Most state-wide groups of public employees bring local chapter officers and members into their legislative advocacy programs by urging them to maintain continuing relationships with legislators representing their districts. Chapter and local personnel are also called on to assist in getting communications to these same legislators when major items are about to be voted in committee or a legislative house.

Local employees are cognizant that the work of the state legislature is of constant interest to them. They are equally aware that it is advantageous to approach the legislature about subjects that have universal applicability. They can attain their goals more simply by persuading a majority of the members in two houses of the state legislature than by trying to convince majorities in 350 city councils or on fifty-eight county boards. Legislatively mandated police and fire annual leave benefits, for example, were adopted in this state as early as 1891.[5]

Local public employees have often turned to the state legislature to counteract decisions on employment policies made by local governing bodies. Examples of successful efforts are the Danielson bill, governing political activity, and the George Brown and Winton Acts, which recognize the right to organize. Exemplifying a major unsuccessful effort is the 1963 fire fighters' Fifty-Six Hour bill, which sought a reduced work week.

Employees of a single government are often anxious to influence legislation that will affect employment policy in one jurisdiction, despite the fact that the state constitution discourages special legislation for cities and counties. Most often the demand comes from special districts or school districts. Large school districts, like the Los Angeles Unified, frequently offer an amendment to the general Education Code that will apply only to one jurisdiction.

Lobbying in local government differs in several ways from that in the state legislature. Because it is subjected to less regulation, less is known about it. The city of Los Angeles adopted the first lobbyist registration ordinance in California in 1967. Orange County followed in 1972, and the city of San Diego passed a different type of law in 1973. The objective of these laws is to require all paid representatives to register and to disclose their receipts and expenditures. Twenty-five persons who represented city employees before the Los Angeles city council or its committees filed the required quarterly statements in 1972.[6] Only two public employee unions registered with Orange County in 1974.[7]

City councils, boards of supervisors, and school boards operate quite differently from the state legislature. Only a few, such as the Los Angeles city council and the San Francisco board of supervisors, have a sufficiently large membership to warrant the appointment of committees to develop or screen legislation. School boards in a few large urban districts also make limited use of committees, but the entire membership of all local bodies votes in all legislative or rule making actions. Moreover, the Ralph Brown Act, which requires local governing bodies to discuss all but a few specified subjects in public and take action only in open sessions, has done much to give legislative advocates, the press, and the public access to these sessions.

Local councils and boards also meet routinely throughout the year and do not crowd their entire action into a single, continuous session. The Los Angeles city council is one of the few required to meet daily; most local bodies meet either weekly or bi-weekly for sessions ranging from one to six hours. A considerable percentage meet in the evenings, thereby enabling public employees and other citizens to attend without taking time from their employment.

Local council and board members, except those serving the county and city of Los Angeles, are part-time officials, and most are engaged in businesses, occupations, or professions during their term in office. Most do not have individual, government-provided offices or personal staffs to assist them in preparing their legislative activities. Moreover, most local legislative or policy agendas are prepared by a central administrative staff for council or board consideration, although individual members frequently introduce proposals either formally or informally. Public employees as well as other citizens who seek to persuade board members, usually encounter the elected officials in the community and at the city hall, county seat, or school administrative headquarters. Lobbying at this level of government, except in the most populous local units, is not as specialized an activity as it is at the state level.

Local governing bodies that meet during the daytime often debate whether they should require employees who wish to address them regarding employment policy matters to charge the time against their accrued vacation leave, or whether they should grant a few representatives special leave. A lenient policy may draw too much of the work force away from normal duties, whereas an overly strict one may induce the employee organizations to send only paid advocates. Large masses of employees usually attend council or board sessions only when a major issue such as annual salary adjustments is under consideration. Large employee organizations have tended since 1961 to hire representatives to attend the public sessions of the local policy bodies and to maintain continuing contacts with numerous administrators. Organizations composed of employees in small work forces, on the other hand, have tended to send their president or chairman of the legislative committee. Many unions, and such state-wide associations as the California School Employees' Association, send field representatives to maintain continuing relationships with elected officers and administrators of several governments in the same geographic area.

The process through which public employee organizations develop legislative programs that their advocates endeavor to implement has seldom been analyzed in detail. These organizations proclaim that their goal is to assist workers to participate in public policy-making. If they are to be consistent with this goal, the membership must be able to participate effectively in the process by which the organization decides the demands to be made on the political system. An oligarchic organization, whose input to the state legislature or a local governing body is shaped by an executive director and a small coterie of influential officers, may make an impact on public policy, but it will not exemplify the concept of participatory democracy espoused by the public employee organization movement.

Most public employee organizations hold annual meetings, either of the entire membership or of delegates elected to represent groups of members, at which resolutions relative to proposed legislative action are presented, debated, and voted.[8] The resolutions adopted at the annual convention constitute a general statement of interests, purposes, and demands to be refined and implemented by an executive committee or board of directors whose function is to direct the officers and legislative advocates on specific matters. Most public employee organizations, therefore, employ a representative model of participatory democracy rather than a town hall model.

APPEALS TO THE ELECTORATE

When lobbying does not produce the desired results, California public employee organizations have resorted periodically to alternative procedures provided by the state political system. State employees have thrice resorted to initiative petitions when they have been unable to obtain their goals through the legislature and governor. When city councils, county supervisors, or school boards have ignored local employees' requests, the organized civil servants have appealed either to the local voters or to the state legislature for directives to prescribe a preferred course of action. The objective has been to obtain a mandate to curb or channel the authority of the elected legislative bodies. This objective is consistent with the political practices made possible by the referendum and initiative processes and is one pursued by many groups.

The California Teachers Association (CTA) has the most extensive record among public employee organizations for use of direct legislation methods. It has conducted nine state-wide campaigns in fifty-two years in support of its proposals and also has opposed several propositions initiated by other groups. It first launched into direct legislation in 1918, when it defeated by referendum petition a statute that limited increases in local taxes. In 1920, the state superintendent of instruction, the CTA, and a large aggregation of interest groups initiated a constitutional amendment that fixed the formula governing state aid to the school districts. The amendment also directed the school districts to allocate not less than sixty percent of local tax money to teachers' salaries. The percentage of total school support contributed previously by legislative appropriations had declined steadily over a period of years.

When state and local finances were disturbed by the economic depression, the CTA sponsored an initiative constitutional amendment to transfer responsibility for school finance from the districts to the state, and to levy an income tax and selective sales tax to finance the load. Despite endorsements by such prestigious groups as the California Supervisors Association, the Farm Bureau Federation, the State Grange, the State Real Estate

Association, and the State Department of Education, the proposal was defeated at the polls. A scheme limited to fiscal restructuring, proposed by the state controller later that year, was adopted by the voters and remains the basic formula for the state's fiscal structure. The CTA twice proposed initiative constitutional amendments to secure aid for the schools when the school population began to increase rapidly after the second world war. Its officials wrote the provisions in consultation with the state Department of Education, and organized the petition signature-gathering drives to place the measures on the ballot. Its leadership discovered three successful techniques in the 1946 campaign. It obtained endorsements from numerous groups representing many shades of political opinion; it collected far more signatures than required to secure a place on the ballot, which impressed the voters with the popularity of the proposition; and it employed Clem Whitaker of San Francisco, one of the most successful direct legislation campaign managers of the era, to direct the campaign.

The CTA returned to the direct legislation hustings in 1952 to overcome the counterpressures exerted by groups that paid substantial portions of the state taxes or favored other spending programs. Legislative appropriations in support of schools had again lagged. The CTA strategy once more proved to be successful when it gathered a whopping 883,000 signatures to the petition and persuaded a long list of groups to endorse its proposal. Moreover, a large array of metropolitan and small-town newspapers gave their editorial support.

A different method was used in 1964 when the CTA gathered 1.5 million signatures on an initiative petition and persuaded the legislature to increase state aid substantially. The CTA was thereby spared the expense and toil of an election campaign.

The CTA also opposed several initiatives presented by groups that sought to limit all taxation. Taxpayers' groups led by the Los Angeles County tax assessor, Philip Watson, in 1968 and 1972 placed constitutional amendments on the ballot to establish a rigid limit on tax rates. School groups generally opposed these proposals and constituted the major coalition against Proposition 14, the Watson plan, in 1972. The CTA conducted its own campaign against both plans and also contributed $17,000 to the coalition's 1972 campaign organization.[9] It returned to the field again in 1973 to help organize and finance the California Education Congress, representing a new coalition of fifteen groups that mobilized to defeat the tax-limitation initiative proposed by Governor Reagan and associates.[10]

The CTA's biggest direct legislation battle was fought unsuccessfully in the June, 1970, primary. The CTA strategists had reasoned that a school measure would receive much better attention if it were submitted at the primary election in June rather than at the November general election, when the governor and legislature were to be elected. The proposal, initiated by the director, Jack D. Rees, was approved by the salary committee and was sent to a referendum of the CTA chapters. One-hundred-seventeen chapters representing 27,000 members had responded favorably by the time the CTA policy board, the State School Council, met in November and gave its approval. Strategy discussions with the County Supervisors Association soon led to an agreement to present a two-part general tax revision plan that would transfer all social welfare costs from the counties to the state and would increase state aid to schools. The teachers hoped thereby to restore the traditional fifty-fifty ratio between state and district support of the schools.[11]

The CTA Council approved an assessment of $15 per member to fund the campaign, and teacher committees were organized to gather signatures. It soon became necessary, however, to employ a professional signature-gathering firm to complete the work in time to file the petition.

The heavy cost of conducting direct legislation campaigns, even by organizations possessing a membership numbering 138,000 persons, is revealed by the statement filed by the Whitaker and Baxter agency that conducted the campaign. The CTA spent a total of $836,000, of which the petition circulation firm received $44,000. Other expenditures were for such mass campaign activities as outdoor billboard advertising, radio and television spot commercials, newspaper advertising, brochure printing and mailing, bumper stickers, campaign offices, and fees for campaign management services. Moreover, the expenditures listed were in addition to the vast amount of volunteer work by teachers' committees and clubs, and the work performed by the CTA headquarters staff.

The opponents to the CTA-CSAC proposition, "Californians Against A Tax Hoax," spent $150,000, most of which came from $1,000 to $10,000 contributions made by major oil companies, public utilities, and the California Real Estate Association.[12]

The CTA and CSAC, by attempting to revise the state and local government fiscal arrangements, had intervened in the most complicated and disturbed state political problem. The governor and the legislature had struggled with tax revision at two legislative sessions, and every tax-conscious group in the state was alert to protect its presumed interest. Voter attitudes possibly were affected adversely by Governor Reagan's early declaration of opposition to the CTA-CSAC proposal, and by a strike in the Los Angeles Unified School District just prior to the election. Supporters of the proposition could take some solace, however, in two events that followed shortly after the defeat at the polls. The legislature provided more than $100 million in additional money for schools and attempted to revise the formula for fund allocation. The state Supreme Court declared, when reviewing a case, that such a great disparity in ability to support the schools existed among districts as a result of the state school support laws, it was compelled to serve notice on the legislature and governor that a more equitable plan must be devised. [13]

The objective of the CTA's direct legislation campaigns has been to increase tax funds to support a high level of service, an approach that has appealed to a broad segment of the electorate for many years. Moreover, most proposals have sought to assist property taxpayers by transferring a greater portion of the school cost to groups paying state taxes. Although several amendments have raised state-wide minimum salary standards, and all have aimed to increase the district's funds from which salaries are paid, the teachers' self-interest was muted. The combination of strategies produced a high percentage of successes between 1920 and 1968.

The California State Employees Association (CSEA) is, in a sense, the creature of ballot action in the 1930's when state employees urged the state to create a retirement system. Governor C. C. Young had been reluctant to act without explicit voter authorization. The legislature, at his recommendation, placed an enabling constitutional amendment on the ballot in November, 1930, and state employees in Sacramento, San Francisco, and Los Angeles formed a committee, raised $40,000, and employed Clem Whitaker, the San Francisco advertising and campaign manager, to conduct the campaign. After the election, the retirement campaign committee convened an organizing session at Sacramento on February 21, 1931, and launched the CSEA. [14]

The CSEA leadership in the beginning felt that the organization should not favor or oppose particular officers, candidates, or parties. They sought to work with any legislator or executive official who was favorable to the state employee interests, regardless of the stand the officer might take on other matters. At the time CSEA was formed, a new governor, James Rolph, Jr., was engaged in a power struggle with a strong bi-partisan bloc in the state Senate. One of the first acts performed by the founding CSEA president was to call on the governor and assure him that the fledgling organization did not intend to make problems for his administration, and that its objective was to ensure the establishment of a state employee retirement system. The Senate and Assembly soon adopted by overwhelming majorities the legislation to accomplish this goal and, when the governor signed the bill, the CSEA president convened a meeting of chapter presidents to prepare a panel of nominees for the three positions on the governing board required by the law to be filled by retirement plan participants. The governor appointed those whose names appeared at the top of the association's list.[15]

The CSEA leadership, having achieved its first goal, began to prepare for a second basic task, namely, to bring greater stability to state employment by removing the patronage practice from the civil service. The executive board in 1934 authorized the president to appoint a panel to formulate an initiative amendment proposal that would embrace the principles of the merit system and would provide a strong administrative structure to administer the civil service law. A tentative draft was sent to state employees, state officials, legislators, and numerous citizens. The Commonwealth Club of San Francisco, the California Federation of Labor, and several legislators responded. Two features of the first CSEA draft plan most heavily criticized were the provision to reserve one of five positions on the proposed personnel board for a state employee, and a plan to give the board financial independence of the legislature. Neither item was included in the final draft, which was approved and submitted to the attorney general in time to be given a ballot title.

The CSEA chapters conducted the task of circulating petitions. In areas where there were no chapters, members of the State Highway Patrol carried on the work. These volunteer forces secured 167,043 signatures, approximately fifty percent more than required. The association again employed Clem Whitaker to conduct the ballot campaign, but the sponsoring groups had obtained so many endorsements from influential groups that no organized opposition appeared. Seventy-six percent of the voters who cast ballots approved the plan.

Unlike the California Teachers Association, the CSEA did not find continued use of the initiative or referendum procedures attractive or necessary. It concentrated its efforts during the next forty years on maintaining good relations with each governor, the department heads, the State Personnel Board, and the legislature and its committees. Therefore, it did not perceive a need to appeal to the electorate.

One of the few occasions when the CSEA made an active campaign to influence the voters was at the 1938 general election in opposition to two initiatives, Proposition 20, the Single Tax Plan, and Proposition 25, the Townsend Old Age Pension Plan. The CSEA argued that both proposals jeopardized the state's financial stability and, therefore, threatened civil servants' salary interests. The executive director made speaking tours throughout the state to oppose the two measures, and the organization's journal exhorted members to arouse their friends to vote against these ballot items. Most legislators and state officials apparently shared the association's views in this instance, so the CSEA did not run much risk of incurring criticism that might embarrass its future lobbying efforts.

Retirement and salary matters have consistently headed the CSEA list of legislative concerns. The organization was successful from the first stage in building up a membership which comprised a high percentage of the state's work force. It counted on the sheer size of its membership to impress elected officers. Although CSEA officers made no public claim to be able to swing a large bloc of votes to candidates who supported the association's preferences, they implied that the organization was a force to be reckoned with at election time. The CSEA also built up a qualified staff to present technically competent documentation in support of the positions it presented to the legislative committees and the State Personnel Board.

After forty-one years of lobbying, however, the CSEA again turned directly to the electorate in 1972 in an effort to amend the state constitution. This proposal was to change the state's budget process. The State Highway Patrolmen's Association placed a similar measure on the same ballot. This event illustrates a situation that causes employee organizations to turn to the initiative, and also the process by which a strategy is often selected from among several proposed. State employees had experienced a series of disappointments in salary matters and had clashed with Governor Reagan and his chief administrators on several occasions. Several state hospital staffs had been reduced and one institution had been phased out entirely. The legislature had deleted salary increases for academic members of the two state university systems in 1970, and in 1971 the governor had vetoed salary increases approved by the legislature for all state employees.

CSEA membership was divided on the issue of collective bargaining. Many wished to push for a bargaining law; others wished to retain the procedure that had produced satisfaction for so many years, namely, presentations to the State Personnel Board, the governor, and legislative committees. The governor's veto of salary increase in 1971, the first in the state's budget history, caused an unprecedented stir in CSEA ranks. The CSEA president and board prepared to place a collective bargaining law on the 1972 ballot by initiative petition.[16]

CSEA strategists were somewhat encouraged to choose this option for action when the California Poll was published, an opinion survey of state residents taken in August, 1971, by the independent Field Research Corporation. It showed that 58.6 percent of the sample agreed that state employees should get a cost-of-living pay increase, whereas 25.7 percent supported the governor's veto. Those polled divided, however, over how the increase should be achieved. Approximately 40 percent thought the legislature should override the governor's veto, 17 percent believed a tax reform bill that included salary raises should be passed, 20.8 percent wanted to sustain the governor, 21.8 percent did not know how to accomplish the purpose, and 6.9 percent had no opinion. Those polled were similarly divided over the question of whether the state employees should strike to accomplish their objective. The large group, 26.3 percent, opposed a strike under any circumstance, whereas 21.7 percent said state employees had as much right to strike as private employees, and others had various attitudes. Those members of the CSEA who favored bargaining were moderately heartened to find that 51.7 percent of the population polled favored their view, whereas 23.2 opposed it and 17.6 percent were undecided.[17]

The increased militancy in the membership was indicated by the long list of resolutions, constitutional amendments, and by-law changes presented to the 898 delegates who met in Fresno for the annual convention. Prominent on this list was a proposal to permit agreements that established relationships with any organization or union that represented public employees, and one to delete the section of the CSEA constitution that prohibited endorsement of political candidates. Another called for a $4 million organization budget and included support for collective bargaining. Two proposed to establish a strike fund.

The longest and most earnest debate was on the proposed increase in dues and their use. A proposal to double the annual fees failed to receive the required two-thirds majority vote, but a compromise seventy-five cent increase for current activities and a one-year special assessment of $1.75 per month to finance an initiative campaign was adopted on the second day.[18] The aggressive political program gained momentum when Dr. Leroy Pemberton, a San Diego State University staff member who advocated direct political action, was elected president. He was nominated from the convention floor and defeated three other candidates, including the incumbent who was seeking a second term.

A committee submitted a draft of the proposed initiative to the board of directors in November which combined three major propositions: (1) write into the state constitution the policy mandate that the state pay its workers salaries comparable to those paid by other public and private employers; (2) revise the state budget process to limit the discretion of the governor and legislature in determining salaries and (3) establish collective bargaining between state appointing authorities and the organized employees on matters not regulated by the existing civil service section of the state constitution. It proposed to include all employees of the two university systems as well as persons working in state administrative agencies. It directed the governing boards of the higher educational systems and the State Personnel Board to conduct salary surveys pertaining to their respective sets of employees and to report their findings and recommendations to the governor, who was to place the figures in the budget without change. The legislature was to be limited to making changes only by a two-thirds vote of the membership of the two houses, and the governor's veto authority over salary items was to be eliminated.

The CSEA board made some changes in the draft proposal; the chief one removed the language that created a state employee relations board. It left implementation of collective bargaining to be worked out in legislation. Copies were distributed to newspapers, labor organizations, and CSEA members. The board met again in December to hear comments from association members, make some further changes in the wording, choose a Los Angeles advertising firm specializing in ballot measure electoral work to manage the campaign, and launch an appeal for volunteers to circulate petitions and do telephone work.[19]

Strains were beginning to show within the CSEA, however. Loren V. Smith, the general manager, expressed dissatisfaction with the proposed initiative because it would severely limit the authority of the legislature and would jeopardize the relationship the CSEA had long enjoyed. Unable to prevail in the debate, he resigned, and the board of directors named the general counsel, Walter W. Taylor, to succeed him. President Pemberton expressed the prevailing view when he said that the proposed specification of a two-thirds vote of the legislature to change State Personnel Board findings was necessary to ensure that state employees would receive salaries comparable to those performing similar tasks in private employment because governors controlled a majority of legislative votes on money matters. He added, "This would force a governor to pull votes from both sides of the aisle to remove the salary recommendations."[20]

The association's strategists had hoped volunteer teams of CSEA members could pick up the necessary 550,000 valid signatures on the petition, but by April they decided that the work was progressing too slowly and employed professional circulators to complete the task.[21] The petition qualified and was assigned line fifteen on the November, 1972, ballot.

A two-day strike by employees of the State Water Project in May, resolved by negotiations between the governor's representative and CSEA spokesmen, highlighted the employees' discontent but also hardened some opposition. In the initiative campaign, the CSEA argued that the initiative would eliminate the likelihood of strikes in the future. Public employee organizations split on the initiative. Twenty, including the California Teachers Association, Los Angeles County Employees' Association-SEIU Local 660, All-City Employees Association of Los Angeles, San Diego County Employees Association, and the Alameda County Employees Association, endorsed the proposal.[22] The Union of State Employees (SEIU Local 411) and the California Conference of the American Federation of State, County, and Municipal Employees voiced opposition. John Henning, the executive officer of the State Labor Federation, urged all AFL-CIO councils in California to recommend that their members vote no. He expressed the belief that "it could snuff out any real hope of state employees in California ever gaining full free collective bargaining rights."[23] Labor was particularly fearful that the measure would continue the non-affiliated CSEA's dominance as a representative of state employees. SEIU Local 411 had failed to secure sufficient signatures to put its own salary proposal on the ballot.[24]

Another opposing group, the Committee to Stop the Blank Check Initiative, managed by the John Greenagle Associates of San Francisco, conducted the advertising campaign against the CSEA initiative. Its efforts were financed by a few large contributions from banks, made through the clearing house associations in Los Angeles and San Francisco, an oil company, and a small number of industrial and development companies.[25]

The advertising campaign mounted on behalf of Proposition 15 compared favorably in quantity, type, and sophistication with that employed in other ballot measure campaigns. Television spot presentations, billboards, stickers and placards, and direct mailing were used almost to the point of saturation. Several television briefs, however, had double meanings and seemed to express threats that the public peace and welfare would be jeopardized if the measure failed. In any event, the voters rejected both initiatives by a 2 to 1 majority.

The campaign was expensive for the CSEA in several ways. The association spent more than $1.7 million.[26] It also lost 10,318 members, an eleven percent attrition, during the year. For some dropouts the motive for withdrawal may have been the increased cost of membership; for others it may have been disagreement with the strategy and tactics employed by the new regime.

The next general council session, however, approved a plan to endorse candidates for state offices and contribute to campaign funds. After a lengthy debate, it adopted by a two-thirds majority vote a $3.3 million budget that included a political action fund.[27]

Relations between the CSEA, the legislature, and the governor were not adversely affected by the initiative campaign. The governor recommended salary increases for the next fiscal year, saying that employees had been deprived previously by state financial difficulties; the legislature voted slight additions, and the governor accepted the higher amounts without using the item veto.

The enormous expense of conducting a state-wide initiative campaign in the 1970's, when the electorate has become larger and the cost of all communication media has risen spectacularly, may tend to dampen the future interest of public employees in this method. Moreover, the CSEA was not successful in coupling employee interests with a more generalized public interest, as the CTA had done so successfully for many years. Both 1972 initiatives stood isolated as special interest legislation and, moreover, they proposed to restructure the state budget process to favor that interest, a proposal likely to attract opposition from fiscal conservatives of every degree.

APPEALS TO THE ELECTORATE BY LOCAL EMPLOYEES

Organized firemen and police in chartered cities used direct legislation for many years to establish retirement systems, fix wage formulas, and establish rules concerning working conditions and hours. Some have used it in the 1970's to establish compulsory arbitration of employment disputes.

The earliest application of the petition method by public employees was the San Francisco police and firemen's presentation in 1907 of charter amendments that set formulas for determining their salaries. The Los Angeles firemen used the same procedure in 1915 to prescribe a two platoon system of organization in the department and to limit the duty hours. The San Francisco firemen copied their example the next year. The Los Angeles police and firemen turned next to retirement plans, and in 1922 won a liberal municipally administered pension plan with the approval of the business community. Four years later the same groups returned to the voters and obtained an increase in their minimum wage formula.

In the neighboring city of Pasadena, the firemen and police separately circulated petitions to set minimum salaries. They accomplished their purpose through low-key political activity completely congruent with contemporary traditions of nonpartisan, antiseptic local politics. They purchased advertising space in the principal local newspapers to explain their objectives, and, when the American Legion organized a civic parade to drum up interest in the municipal election, both promptly entered contingents carrying banners exhorting voters to approve their proposals.

The Santa Monica police and firemen were unsuccessful in their attempt to force establishment of a municipally administered pension plan, but they got their point across and hastened the decision to open the state employees retirement system to local governmental employees. When they first approached the city commission about a pension plan, they were told that a city having only a hundred police and fire employees was too small to support a successful program. Undaunted, they drafted a proposal and went door to door in uniform to obtain signatures to a petition that placed a charter amendment on the consolidated municipal-state election ballot on November 7, 1938. They set up campaign headquarters in the most heavily populated portions of the city and conducted a vigorous drive for votes. They sent speakers to the service clubs and purchased newspaper advertising space. Some of their tactics were heavy handed. For example, their campaign chairman, a police captain, told a service club audience that if the pension plan were not adopted, the firemen and police would seek to have the city annexed to Los Angeles. In view of the fact that annexation had been the issue in two previous, bruising referendum battles, the statement was of questionable tactical value. Allegations were made that the police stopped automobile drivers in the business district and asked them to accept windshield stickers advocating adoption of the pension plan. The city finance commissioner made his opposition known by speaking frequently to service clubs and civic committees.[28] Faced with strong antagonism by the local newspaper and the business community, the employees' proposal was defeated, but when the state retirement system accepted local employees a short time later, Santa Monica contracted with the SERS to cover its workers.

Many local public employee groups began in the late 1930's to seek formulas by which to determine salary adjustments. They sought a formula that would constrain the governing body to adopt a prescribed rate of wage, because they concluded that the opposing political groups were usually strong enough at annual budget sessions to cause the public sector wage rates to lag behind those in private employment. Union labor had been particularly interested in establishing legal formulas to govern both public salaries and wages paid by private contractors doing work for public agencies. It had been successful in writing a requirement into the Los Angeles city charter adopted in 1928, for example, requiring the city to pay at least the prevailing rate paid in the community for comparable duties. In the early 1950's, several governments in the Los Angeles area agreed on wage rates for those engaged in the building trade occupations. They would pay the wage rates determined by union contracts negotiated between an aggregation of major construction firms and the unions associated with the AFL-CIO Building Trades Council.

Police and fire fighters had few, if any, exact counterparts in non-governmental employment, so they sought other means of comparison. In the city of Los Angeles they demanded a rate of increase equal to the average of increases awarded all other classes in city service. Police and firemen in the central metropolitan cities also tended to compare their salaries and benefits, as well as the rates of increase, with those enjoyed by their counterparts in other central cities. Suburban government employees looked at the salaries and benefits paid by the adjacent central city and by other cities having a comparable population to their own community.

An incident involving the city of Alhambra, a suburb of Los Angeles, and its fire fighters' union illustrates some of the political and administrative problems involved in establishing comparison formulas, although the state Supreme Court approved the procedure employed. IAFF Local 1587 filed an initiative that proposed to set the firemen's salaries at figures equal to an average of those paid the same ranks by the county and city of Los Angeles. The Alhambra council refused to adopt the proposal or submit it to the voters, declaring the plan was illegal because it would delegate the city's salary-setting authority to other governmental jurisdictions. When the firemen sued to force the city clerk to put the initiative on the ballot, the court of appeals upheld the city's interpretation. The state Supreme Court saw the matter differently, however, saying that the proposal declared a policy that the city should pay salaries comparable to those paid by the principal governmental employers in the area.[29] Ironically, the litigation had consumed four years and when the city called a special election, as directed by the court, the voters defeated the firemen's proposal.[30] The conditions prevailing at a special election contributed heavily to the defeat, inasmuch as the firemen's initiative was the only measure on the ballot. The decision was made by a very low percentage of the registered voters, so the combined opposition of the local newspaper and the elected city officials evidently overcame any momentum the firemen had built up by their original petition circulation campaign.

The police and firemen in Culver City, another Los Angeles suburb, accomplished an objective similar to that of the Alhambra firemen, but they were not challenged by a city administration determined to fight in the courts as well as at the ballot box. The voters adopted in 1954 an initiative ordinance that tied police and fire salaries to those paid by the city of Los Angeles.

Berkeley firemen were defeated, mainly by opposition from the city manager and fire chief, when they placed on the 1958 general election ballot an initiative charter amendment to require the city to pay them salaries equal to the average paid by five specified Bay Area cities. The city council took no public stand, but the manager and chief actively opposed it and distributed a brochure setting forth their estimate that the proposal would cost the city taxpayers at least a million dollars per year.

The San Francisco police and firemen were more successful. The police obtained a charter amendment in 1963 that authorized the city-county to pay salary rates equal to the best paid by any city in the state having a population in excess of 100,000. The firemen, determined to maintain their traditional parity with the police, pushed an amendment that required the board of supervisors to pay them rates equal to those given the police.[31] The police amendment was permissive rather than mandatory, but the board approved compensation rates during the next eleven years that conformed with the formula. When they attempted to change this pattern, the action provoked a strike among the police in 1976.

Employees of cities outside the San Francisco-Oakland, Los Angeles-Long Beach, and San Diego metropolitan areas also have shown a desire to find a formula that will link their salary structures with those of other jurisdictions. Most looked beyond their regional labor market because there were no cities of comparable size in the region. Santa Barbara police and firemen, for example, promoted an initiative charter amendment in 1963 that tied their salaries to the average of those in twenty California cities whose populations equaled Santa Barbara's, although the cities did not compete for recruits.[32]

Organized firemen in several cities tried to reduce their work week requirements by means of initiative petitions but were less successful with this issue. Those in San Diego, Alameda, and Oakland tried charter amendments and the Eureka firemen proposed an ordinance, but none was successful.[33] Each group complained about a low voter turn-out, despite a lack of organized opposition. The Burbank Firemen's Association had quite a different experience but was no more successful when it attempted to reduce the work week from sixty-seven hours to fifty-six by initiative petition. The council called a special election and consolidated it with the state general election which also carried a presidential ballot, thereby guaranteeing a large voter participation. It also organized a speakers' committee that canvassed service clubs and voters' meetings to stress the argument that the proposal would cost property taxpayers eight to ten cents per $100 of assessed valuation annually. The argument was very persuasive among the city's large residence-owning population.[34]

Employee organizations in charter cities have combined voter campaigns with persuasion of the city council or charter commission to achieve their objectives regarding pensions, salary setting, and some other matters. This is illustrated by a series of election skirmishes in Los Angeles. In 1970, the city council revised a charter amendment recommended by a citizens' charter commission it had previously appointed. It placed on a special election ballot a proposal that threatened to destroy the Water and Power Commission's historic independent control of the city-owned utility. The council's draft offered benefits to some city employee groups and pleased a number of community groups, but greatly disturbed the water and power employees. The split of interests is shown by a résumé of contributors who gave $500 or more to the campaign organizations. Major supporters of the proposal included the Pacific Lighting Service Company, an executive of the Pacific Telephone and Telegraph Company, a tire company executive, a motion picture executive, the secretary of the Central Labor Council, and the L.A. Retired Fire and Police Pension Improvement Committee.[35] A Citizens Committee Against the Charter Hoax, composed of the water and power commissioners and two city council members, employed a campaign firm that raised more than $86,000, including $15,000 contributed by IBEW Local 18 through its political action arm, the Water and Power Defense League.[36] The proposal was defeated, but the momentum for charter revision was sufficiently strong that the warring groups returned to city hall and hammered out a series of compromises in time to submit them to the general city election in May, 1971. The Citizens Committee for Proposition 1, the new charter revision plan, had the same treasurer as the sponsors of the previously defeated proposal, but the groups from which he collected money this time were clearly different. The list of major contributors shows something about the nature of the compromise reached: the Clearing House Association (banks), Southern California Edison Company (electricity supplier to the suburbs but not to the central city), the gas company, the Water and Power Defense League, the Water and Power Employees Association, the Fire Fighters Local, and an SEIU local.[37] The All-City Employees Association gave the largest single sum, $16,500.[38]

The council submitted two other charter amendments of great interest to segments of the city work force at this same election. One liberalized the pension benefits for employees other than police and firemen. The All-City Employees Association provided the fund raising organization for this proposal and contributed $181,000 toward the successful campaign.[39]

The Fire and Police Protective League served as the chief fund raiser for the amendment that altered rules and benefits in the uniformed forces' retirement system. It employed a political campaign firm experienced in gubernatorial and legislative elections and raised $194,000 in dues deductions from its members. A committee of sponsors composed of state legislators, Congress members, labor executives, and clergymen was organized. A new element in this campaign was the effort to win support in the minority communities through two city council members who represented black constituents. At the conclusion of the successful campaign, IAFF Local 112 publicly thanked the two councilmen and presented them with checks to be given to the Boy Scouts and to a handicapped children's program.[40]

Drives for compulsory arbitration of police and fire employment disputes in Vallejo, Sacramento, and Oakland in 1970-1973 polarized the voters in those communities. Arbitration came to public attention as a result of the police and fire strike in Vallejo in 1969.[41] When the council sought to reward nonstriking members of the departments, the two organizations demanded arbitration and obtained an arbitrator's ruling that countered the council's decision.[42] A charter commission, a member of which was the president of the fire fighters' local, was under instructions to make recommendations about employer-employee relations. It submitted a new charter that contained an extensive policy statement governing personnel administration and that offered an option of establishing compulsory arbitration of disputes between the city and its police and fire employees, and a prohibition of city employee strikes. The voters approved the charter and the option, thereby making Vallejo the first jurisdiction in California to adopt compulsory arbitration of public sector interest disputes.[43]

The Sacramento police and firemen sought compulsory arbitration by circulating an initiative petition for a charter amendment. They collected 15,000 more signatures than required and raised $20,000 from their members, but were defeated in a hotly contested campaign. The organized opposition, comprising builders, savings and loan associations, and investment companies, spent less money than the employee organizations but capitalized on the support of city officials and several newspapers,[44] including one paper influential in the black community, which were critical of the police and fire plan.[45]

The Oakland police and firemen persuaded the city council to place on the primary election ballot a charter amendment to establish binding arbitration. They raised $52,000 to finance the ensuing publicity campaign.[46] They were successful, winning by a substantial margin.[47]

CANDIDATE ENDORSEMENT AND
CAMPAIGN CONTRIBUTIONS

Candidates for office in a weak-party state strive to gain the endorsement of politically active organizations, hoping to impress the independent and uncommitted voters. Organizations give their institutional endorsement after some show of bargaining based on the candidate's past performance, personal reputation, and promises concerning relevant issues. Endorsement is not always a prelude to the contribution of funds, but an endorsement not accompanied by gifts of money, supplies, or volunteer work is insufficient. Nevertheless, candidates as well as observers frequently debate whether an endorsing organization can influence its members to vote in a bloc to support the approved candidate.

Public employee organizations in California until the mid-1970's were diffident about endorsing either nonpartisan or partisan candidates. Endorsement was considered inconsistent with the organizations' strategy of maintaining a nonpartisan image. Several organizations modeled their by-laws and constitutions after those of the California State Employees Association, which prohibited the officers from endorsing candidates for public office. The main objective was to keep in check officers who might be tempted to commit the association without formal approval of a large segment of the membership. The main concern was that if an endorsed candidate were not elected, the winner might retaliate against the group. In several jurisdictions, employees were forbidden by explicit rule to engage in political action. Charters, such as those in Los Angeles and Alameda Counties, frowned on all expressions of political action.

On the other hand, many associations, including the CSEA, gave incumbent officers who had aided their interests what amounted to de facto endorsement. Incumbents who had carried the association's bills or who had participated in particularly important decisions were invited to speak at the annual meeting or delegates convention and were given publicity in the employee newspaper or magazine. No formal endorsement was given at election time, but the prior publicity was a thinly disguised substitute. Non-incumbent challengers, or candidates running in open contests that involved no incumbent, were rarely given this kind of access to the membership.

State Supreme Court decisions broadening the political rights of public employees, and growing militancy among members of several organizations produced a marked change during the decade of the 1970's. The activities of the state wide CTA and the CSEA illuminate the steps in this shift of attitude and tactics. In 1970, a group of politically active members of the CTA organized the Association for Better Citizenship (ABC) to endorse and finance legislative candidates. All agreed that the CTA should neither endorse candidates nor take direct part in electoral politics. The ABC was financed initially by direct contributions. It endorsed seventy-three state legislative candidates in 1970, thirty-seven Democrats and thirty-six Republicans. Choices were made on the basis of the candidate's stand with respect to school support. When the CTA organization was revamped in 1971, the ABC emerged as the formally recognized electioneering arm of the CTA.[48] Three years later, the strategy was changed again. The CTA council took responsibility for endorsing candidates and assigned to the ABC the task of raising campaign funds. Authority to endorse legislative district candidates was delegated to the chapters.[49] The council broke the CTA long-standing nonendorsement tradition by approving the candidacy of the Democratic candidates for the offices of governor, lieutenant governor, state secretary, state treasurer, and U.S. Senator. Fourteen candidates from several parties had sought the CTA endorsement. District endorsement committee delegates approved sixty-eight candidates for the Assembly, fifteen for the Senate, and thirty-four for Congress. The composite slate of endorsements enjoyed a remarkable success. All approved candidates for state-wide and Senate offices, and eighty-five percent of the Assembly and Congressional aspirants won election.[50]

The California State Employees Association general council and chapters changed their by-laws in 1973 to authorize the board of directors to endorse candidates for state offices. Endorsement was defined as giving full organization support to the person approved, requesting members' votes, and authorizing the use of the CSEA name in publicity. Financial contributions normally were to follow endorsements, but support could also be given candidates not endorsed. The CSEA board voted in September, 1974, to endorse the Democratic candidate for governor and lieutenant governor, four Senate candidates, and nine Assembly aspirants, partially overruling its legislative committee recommendation that only the candidate for governor be given financial assistance. A move to give the Republican nominee a minimal financial grant was defeated. At the close of the meeting, the president issued a statement in which he explained that the board had supported the candidate who favored collective bargaining for public employees.[51] It also authorized the legislative committee to give only financial assistance to seventy-six legislative candidates.

Some state-wide organizations of local public employees also began to endorse partisan candidates in the 1974 state election. The Peace Officers Research Association (PORAC) and the California Organization of Police and Sheriffs (COPS), a political action group purporting to represent large-city police officers, endorsed the Democratic nominee for governor.[52] Reactions within these two groups to the endorsement illustrate some of the organizational problems involved when making partisan choices. Dissenters within the Los Angeles Police Protective League sought to recall the unit's representative to COPS, saying that the local group had endorsed only Evelle Younger, the Republican incumbent attorney general who was seeking re-election, and did not choose to comment on candidates for other offices.[53]

Endorsements are made in a variety of ways. The CTA endorses state-wide office seekers with sixty percent approval of the state council, its large delegate assembly. Committees of delegates from chapters in each legislative district interview and endorse legislative candidates. The Committee on Political Education (COPE), the political action arm of the state labor federation and the central labor councils, usually endorses state and local candidates after large multi-union committees interview them or their representatives. Local unions use various strategies. The Los Angeles County IAFF Local 1014 provides one example. It sends its executive board members to participate in COPE interviews[54] and then supplies manpower to get out the vote for COPE-endorsed candidates. Its leaders believe that support of candidates at state, city, and county levels improves the union's strength at the bargaining table, stating that threats to go to the legislature influence county supervisors' reactions to their bargaining proposals.[55]

The Los Angeles County Employees Association-SEIU Local 660 also endorses candidates for offices at several levels of government. Its political action committee endorsed candidates in 1973 for mayor and for city attorney of Los Angeles, for three seats on the Los Angeles Unified School Board, for single posts in three other school districts, and for two legislative seats filled at a special election.[56] Its board of directors endorsed one candidate in 1974 for supervisor in the Third District, two in the First District and forty others seeking various local, state, and national offices in the primary election. It endorsed the Democratic candidates for governor, lieutenant governor, secretary of state, treasurer, and U.S. Senator, the Republican nominees for attorney general and controller, and thirty-five legislative and congressional office seekers in the general election.[57]

Endorsement by membership convention is illustrated by the action of Los Angeles Fire Fighters Local 112 in the 1973 municipal election, although the occasion raises some questions whether this method reflects the members' choice any more accurately than endorsements by committees. Approximately two hundred of the 2,700 members attended, and a plurality of those present pledged support for Councilman Tom Bradley, a black, retired police lieutenant who was making his second bid for the mayor's office, for Burt Pines, a challenger for city attorney, for six incumbent city council members, and for one contender for a seventh seat. This union's endorsement of Bradley signaled some change in fire fighters' politics. Four years before, the president of the local had personally supported Bradley, but his subsequent resignation as head of the union was reported to have been due in part to adverse reaction among the members.[58] Racial integration of the fire department had been an issue for more than fifteen years since former Mayor Poulson, at the urging of the Central Labor Council and other groups, had directed the fire chief to integrate the force and appoint more blacks.[59] When the firemen resisted, the state labor federation supported the mayor after a heated convention debate, including a vigorous argument from Local 112. Attitudes in the department and community remained rigid for several years. Minority applications for firemen's jobs dropped to zero. The department was partially integrated in the 1950's, but the number of minority members declined. By 1973, political bargaining between the firemen and community representatives was beginning to show some results. Bradley was elected mayor and was re-elected easily in 1977. His relations with the fire fighters' union remained fairly even, though the local criticized him considerably in 1977.

Political activity by organized public employees in the suburban and medium sized cities is described very aptly in the following analysis of Los Angeles' suburban cities:

The friendly neighborhood policeman who gave you a traffic ticket on Tuesday may come knocking on your door on Thursday asking you to vote for his favorite candidate for City Council. And the same is true of the fireman, building inspector, bus driver, even the corps of secretaries in various city offices. It is part of a now-familiar phenomenon in many American cities . . . the emergence of municipal employees as political forces in the cities where they work. Both as individuals and through their employee organizations, municipal workers endorse and work for candidates for local political office. They do precinct work, telephoning, pass out campaign literature, and pay for newspaper advertising and billboards on behalf of the people they are supporting. When they have a stake in an issue before a city council, the employees may go directly to the community seeking support for their point of view. . . . While no one, including employee leaders, believes that local workers have enough political muscle to elect councilmen on their own, their significance in the total political structure of most West Side communities is recognized by all.[60]

In jurisdictions of 25,000-100,000 population, groups of politically attuned volunteers working on behalf of selected candidates have an important impact on the outcome of local elections. The expenses involved in a city council election under these circumstances is relatively modest. A campaign fund of $10,000 for a slate of candidates will supply a great deal of newspaper advertising, signs, bumper stickers, and a few, small billboard spaces at strategic locations. Therefore, a total contribution of $1,000 from two or three employee organizations will provide a considerable share of the funds required.

Mayoral and council elections in the metropolitan central cities and supervisorial elections in the large metropolitan counties have become very expensive undertakings. The cost of legislative district and gubernatorial campaigns has also escalated in recent years. Television advertising is commonplace and expensive. Newspaper advertising is essential, and use of commercial billboards to establish name identification of a candidate or slate of candidates is considered to be basic campaign work. Direct mailing of printed literature to large lists of registered voters is used with increasing success by professional campaign management firms employed by major candidates. The list of devices and their costs goes on and on. Consequently, the subject of campaign funds and contributions assumes central importance in state and local elections.

Figures of funds raised by leading candidates in major cities and counties merely show the dimension of the subject. In the 1971 San Francisco mayoral election, incumbent Joseph Alioto raised $525,000 and his general election opponent, Supervisor Dianne Feinstein, raised $222,000.[61] In the 1973 Los Angeles mayoral primary, the incumbent Samuel Yorty collected $190,000 and his principal challenger, Councilman Tom Bradley, received $263,000.[62] In San Diego, Assemblyman Pete Wilson raised slightly more than $97,000 for the mayoral contest and his opponent in the general election, Edward T. Butler, reported receipts of $47,547.[63] Candidates in the city of Sacramento found the expense somewhat lower in 1971. Mayoral candidates raised between $10,000 and $16,000 for the primary, and $22,000 and $25,000 respectively for the general election. Council candidates' receipts ranged from a low of a few hundred dollars to a high of $8,000. The statistical mode of the receipts was between $3,000 and $4,000.[64]

Election campaigns by supervisorial candidates in Los Angeles County, where each district comprises more than a million constituents, are comparable in expense to the mayoral contests in the major cities. In the 1972 election, two candidates, Assemblyman James A. Hayes and City Councilman Marvin Braude, competed in the Fourth District where the incumbent had recently died. Hayes, who won, raised $76,000 for the primary and $237,000 for the general election, whereas Braude collected $88,000 and $175,000.[65] In the Second District, incumbent Dorn raised $181,000 for the primary but was defeated in the final contest. In the 1974 election, when two Los Angeles city council members competed to succeed a retiring incumbent in the Third District, the winning candidate, Edmund Edelman, raised a total of $205,000.[66]

Analysts and reporters of election expenditures have long been accustomed to pointing out that commercial and industrial firms and business related associations have contributed large sums to candidates. A central question often raised is whether the imbalance in ability of other groups to match the financial capacity of business creates an imbalance of influences on political decision makers. A significant response is that the ability of a candidate to raise money usually determines the chance of success and therefore influences the decision to be an active candidate. Major contributions tend to determine who will be serious candidates. Some candidates choose to operate with a large cadre of volunteer workers and eschew accepting large contributions. They have been the exceptions. The conventional wisdom among campaign observers is that the nonincumbent and the less well known candidate needs advertising to establish name identification, hence there is need for money to support a campaign. An equally important question, less often asked, is what influence do campaign contributors exert over officeholders they support? A significant answer is that contributors of large sums can expect to have access to the officeholder they support. The council or board member, legislator, mayor, or governor may not always decide matters the way substantial contributors desire, but the presumption is strong that they are prepared to spend more time listening to a major contributor than to a casual constituent or advocate. In other words, endorsements, campaign contributions, and lobbying are inevitably intertwined.

In this context, the limited data available about organized local public employees' contributions to candidates should be examined.[67] In the 1973 Los Angeles mayoral election, Mayor Yorty received public employee contributions mainly from the police association and from the Water and Power Defense League. Councilman Bradley, who won, reported receiving $2,000 from the AFSCME headquarters, $1,000 from each of two electrical unions, and smaller sums from the fire fighters, operating engineers, and the building trades council. Most of the city employee organizations endorsed Bradley at the general election, although not all reported making contributions. The organizations have been selective in their contributions to council members. In 1971, the All-City Employees Association gave $1,000 and the electrical workers local gave $200 to Councilman Mills, chairman of the personnel committee, despite the fact that he had no opposition. In 1973, Robert Stevenson, who succeeded Mills as personnel committee chairman, was the principal recipient of employee organization contributions. Stevenson's supporters raised $43,052 for the primary and $18,750 for the general election, of which $3,900 came from ten city employee organizations. The largest single contribution was $1,000 from the Police Protective League, but the league also gave $1,500 to Stevenson's opponent, a former policeman.

In two of the three 1972 district contests for board of supervisors in Los Angeles County, county employee organizations contributed comparatively small amounts. In the First District, the County Peace Officers and several local police groups contributed less than $500 each to Assemblyman William Campbell, and the County Employees Association gave Assemblyman Peter Schabarum, the winner, $500. In the Fourth District, two city employee associations gave Los Angeles Councilman Marvin Braude a total of $400. County employee groups contributed much more to Assemblyman James Hayes, who had chaired the Assembly committee that handled local employment legislation in the previous legislative session. The fire fighters' local gave $3,500, the County Peace Officers gave approximately $3,000, the County Employees Association gave $1,000, and associations of lifeguards, probation officers, and county physicians each gave less than $500. In the Fifth District, incumbent Supervisor Warren Dorn received $2,500 from the County Peace Officers, $2,000 from the Physicians Committee, $1,000 from the County Employees Association, and lesser sums from four other employee groups. More substantial sums were contributed in 1974, when the only contest was in the Third District. Retiring Supervisor Ernest Debs endorsed Councilman John Ferraro, but the county employees favored Councilman Edmund Edelman, to whom the County Employees Association contributed $16,000, the fire fighters gave $5,000, and the Probation Officers Union provided $1,500. The aggregate of employee contributions amounted to approximately ten percent of the winning candidate's funds.

Examination of official records of election expenditures in a sample comprising six populous counties, three central metropolitan cities, and four large, suburban cities showed nothing approaching the figures for Los Angeles city and county. In the 1971 San Francisco mayoral race, the only clearly identifiable city employee group contribution was $11,000 given Mayor Alioto's committee by the Transport Workers' Union. In the San Diego mayoral contest, the losing candidate reported receipts of less than $500 each from three employee groups. In the city of Sacramento, the Police Association was a moderately heavy contributor, having given $900 to the runner-up for mayor and having distributed a like amount among three district candidates for council. The AFSCME gave the incumbent mayor's campaign $500. In Santa Monica, the Police Officers Association gave $1,000 to the 1971 winning campaign of a former police sergeant; the fire fighters' local gave $100. At the 1973 election, the police gave $800 to support a slate of three council candidates and the fire fighters gave $600. Other cities showed no reported contributions by employee organizations. County records showed little more activity. In Contra Costa, the fire fighters' local and the county employees' association each gave approximately $500 to candidates in two supervisorial district elections. In Sacramento County, the SEIU and AFSCME contributed less than $500 each to a candidate in one district. In San Diego County, one candidate reported contributions of less than $500 from a deputy sheriffs' association. No employee organization contributions were reported in Orange County.[68]

Information from interviews indicate that most local public employee organizations support candidates by supplying volunteers for precinct work, mailing brochures, and telephoning voters. The organizations in many instances contribute office facilities and staff time for mailing and telephone calling. Campaign contributions of money are therefore comparatively limited.

Campaign contributions made by public employee organizations to state executive and legislative candidates in 1974 and to legislative candidates in 1976 are even more thought provoking. Most contributing organizations have advertised their desire to obtain legislation to establish collective bargaining. The State Employees Association stands consistently at the top of the list of public employee contributors. In the 1974 election, it allocated $39,150 to the state-wide executive offices and $168,380 to legislative contestants, for a total of $207,530. It contributed $14,000 to the Democratic candidate for governor and $7,500 each to that party's candidate for lieutenant governor and secretary of state. Its allocations to legislative candidates ranged from $500 to $7,500. Most recipients were incumbents, although substantial contributions were made to a few preferred candidates in open contests. In one instance, the CSEA supported a challenger who defeated an incumbent senator, a persistent opponent of legislation favored by the organization. In 1976, when all members of the Assembly and half those of the Senate were to be elected, the CSEA distributed more than $260,000 among 104 candidates.[69]

The Association for Better Citizenship, the electioneering arm of the California Teachers Association, contributed more than a half-million dollars to executive and legislative candidates in 1974. The largest sum, $25,000, went to the Democratic candidate for governor, with lesser sums to his associates, the lieutenant governor, secretary of state, and state treasurer. It allocated $10,000 to the Democratic Speaker of the Assembly and gave several other legislative candidates $5,000 each. The sum given most legislators was $500. ABC distributed $198,000 in 1976 among sixty-five legislative and seven district school board candidates.

Unions, largely comprising local government employees, contributed substantially in 1974 to the winning Democratic gubernatorial candidate, who had expressed support of collective bargaining. The Federated Fire Fighters contributed $10,000 and AFSCME gave $17,400, with an additional $3,500 to the candidate for lieutenant governor. Los Angeles County SEIU Local 660 reported making donations totalling approximately $36,000 to state executive and legislative candidates.

Thirty-eight public employee organizations in 1976 distrubuted a total of $865,883 for campaign purposes, a figure estimated by the Fair Political Practices Commission to approximate ten percent of the total campaign funds contributed that year. Four were among the twenty largest contributors. They were CSEA (state employees), second with $260,000; ABC (teachers), fifth with $198,000; IAFF Local 1014 (fire fighters), fourteenth with $95,000; and CSEA (school employees), seventeenth with $80,000.

CONCLUSIONS

Some organized public employees have engaged in political activity to influence employment policy over many years. State employees, state-wide teacher organizations, and employees of several chartered cities have made effective use of initiative petitions and campaign advertising to achieve their purposes. Teachers and other employees of several jurisdictions have participated actively in nonpartisan elections of governing board members. Virtually all organizations have lobbied the employing governments, and groups of local employee organizations have lobbied the state legislature on matters pertaining to a range of local employment conditions. They have fully established their status as interest groups and have shown a behavior consistent with that of other interest groups.

Many employee associations attempted for years to do their lobbying through elected officers, but they shifted to employing full-time advocates who were employees of the organization rather than of the government. The change resulted partly from a recognized need for specialization and continuity, but also from acknowledgment of the fact that the officers were limited by their status as employees of the government they sought to lobby. The change was but one of several that placed organized employees in an adversary relationship with elected executives, legislators, local governing boards, and key administrators.

Entry of public employee organizations into the candidate election process, and their use of endorsements, campaign contributions, and direct participation in elections, is a culmination of their drive to persuade other active political groups of the legitimacy of their claim to participate. It follows closely upon the decisions of the state Supreme Court acknowledging the right of public employees to engage in political action, subject to a showing in specific instances that the challenged action is detrimental to the efficient conduct of public service. The process of granting endorsements to candidates for public office and allocating funds to support selected candidates is not unlike that practiced by other interest groups. Some argue that heavy political activity in the 1970's was temporarily stimulated by employee desire to achieve one stated purpose, the approval of collective bargaining. They speculate that this activity will diminish. A

considerable percentage of the membership of several organizations indicated, when political action was initiated, that they disagreed both with
the goal and the means chosen, but sufficient numbers within the organizations desired the objectives to win plebiscites on the decisions.

The public policy problems arising from the linkage of campaign contributions with lobbying are not peculiar to organized public employees. A
new feature of the problem is that public employee organizations have
joined the ranks of business corporations and individuals doing business
with state and local government agencies. Concern with this central problem has produced financial disclosure laws and statutes defining and limiting campaign contributions made by organizations and individuals alike.
Some analysts and advocates urge adoption of public funding of elections.
Others argue that corporations and labor organizations alike should be forbidden to contribute campaign funds. The latter proposal has at least two
unfortunate features. It tends to favor incumbents over challengers, and
many real estate developers who contribute heavily to local elections do so
as individuals rather than as corporations.

In any event, the public policy debate over campaign funding is separa-
ble, in one sense, from that concerning public employer-employee relations and employment. It concerns all groups active in the political system.

There are features arising from the intensified political activity of organized public employees which, when considered in conjunction with collective bargaining and matters ancillary to it, are unique to public employees.
One is the matter of use, for political action purposes, of funds collected
from employees under agency shop provisions. Another is the combination
of organized political activity with the negotiation of binding, bilateral
contracts resulting from collective bargaining, a privilege that state and
local governments grant no other interest groups. Also unique to public
employees is the grant of binding arbitration to organized police and fire
fighters for settlement of interest disputes with public employers, in the
election of whose officers these organizations have actively participated.

A union shop policy or agreement, uniformly advocated by unions, requires all employees in a unit represented by a recognized, exclusive bargaining agent either to join the organization or to pay an amount equivalent to the dues. Unions argue in support of this policy that all who benefit
from representation by the bargaining agent should share in the expense.
Many students of industrial relations also contend that agency shop is
needed to ensure sufficient regular income to employee organizations that
they can concentrate on being responsible representatives. They assert that
unions made insecure by fluctuating income often act irresponsibly in disputes to attract new members or to hold restless groups within their ranks.

It is logical, however, to make a distinction between those funds used for representation of employee interests in grievance disputes, collective bargaining over wages and employment conditions, and for litigation on these matters, and those funds used for political campaign purposes. Moreover, an elective officer, whether legislative or executive, the recipient of campaign contributions, helps make decisions on many matters in addition to those in which the employee organization has a representational interest. Many persons forced to contribute funds to this purpose by reason of their employment find some of their money devoted to electing candidates they do not favor because of party affiliation or other reasons.

The U.S. Supreme Court, in the case of *Abood* v. *Detroit Board of Education* in 1977, unanimously approved an agency shop arrangement, but also agreed that the funds thus collected could not be used for political purposes if the contributor objected.[70] In the public sector, where employee organizations operate in a political environment, the most feasible method to resolve the dilemma is to require the employee organization to separate those funds used for direct representation with the employer-government from those used for campaign purposes. The latter funds should be financed by dues or contributions from those persons who indicate their willingness to have their money used for that purpose.

Compulsory arbitration of police and fire interest disputes with government-employers takes on new dimensions when it is realized that organized police and fire fighters participate actively in the election of the government officers representing the employer interests. Proponents of compulsory bargaining contend that it is a quid pro quo grant in exchange for the employees' promise not to strike in enforcement of their demands, and that this method removes decision-making from politics. Elected officials and professional administrators argue in rebuttal that compulsory arbitration delegates the responsibility to decide public expenditures to an arbitrator not responsible to the voters, thus depriving elected officials of their legitimate responsibility. The organized employees are engaged in politics in the election of the public officers. Moreover, the strategies used by government officers and organized employees alike, to throw blame for an impasse on the other party and to invoke arbitration, are political acts to gain public support. Therefore, some form of fact finding conducted by a specially appointed commission that reports its findings publicly is a more logical form of dispute resolution, commensurate with the political nature of government operations and decision-making. A publicly reported fact-finders' statement provides a foundation from which public opinion generates pressure on both sides in the dispute. To give an interest group, the organized police or fire fighters, a special procedure for deciding employment policies is to award it a privilege given no other interest group in the state and local political system.

A prime irony in the history of public employer-employee relations is that public employees, after struggling for decades to overcome attitudes and policies that they perceived to be making them second class citizens in the employment policy-making process, use their newly found strength in group political action to seek a special status that goes beyond that accorded other groups in the political system. The use of lobbying, appeals to the voters on policy matters, and campaigning for candidates, when coupled with the exclusive representation of public employees in negotiation of bilateral employment contracts with the employer-government, gives employee organizations a double entry to the public policy-making process not accorded other interest groups. Analysis of the situation is summarized thus:

The cumulative effect of exclusive recognition, union security devices and large bargaining units...will be to produce employee organizations which possess great potential political power.... It is to be noted that the extent to which elected officials are dependent upon union political support is in part a function of the relative indifference of the majority of the electorate. Thus it is difficult to determine at what point the public employer may have 'too readily acceded to' union demands.[71]

The element of special privilege becomes even more pertinent when it is recalled that the collective bargaining process, developed in the private sector, rests upon a concept that bargaining is to be conducted in secret.[72] Secrecy in government decision making is the basic problem to which the demand for the so-called sunshine laws is addressed. The state fair political practices act is concerned with the same problem, although in a less direct manner. The Ralph M. Brown Act, which requires local government bodies to reach their decisions in public, except in personnel transactions relating to individuals, is a well established California policy aimed at limiting secrecy in public decision-making and preventing special access by interest groups to the decision process.[73]

The demand to establish, by explicit legislative authorization, collective bargaining with its associated procedures developed in the industrial sector, runs counter to previously established policies. It is an escalation of interest group demands which extends far beyond those constitutional rights of individuals recognized by the First Amendment.

VIII
POLICY CONCERNING
PUBLIC EMPLOYEE STRIKES

Organized public employees, as well as other groups concerned about public policy, have confronted state and local decision makers abrasively during the 1960's and 1970's in unprecedented tests of political strength. Despite repeated judicial rulings that public employees have no legal right to strike, work disruptions continue to take place in California. The rule has evidently deterred some employee groups, but it has not eliminated work disruptions. Nevertheless, to conclude that strikes have become a way of life in the California public services is to exaggerate greatly.[1] A large number of employing jurisdictions and many employee groups have not thus far been involved in any stoppage.

Discussion is on a surer footing if one confines the subject to strikes as traditionally defined. Official reporting agencies, accustomed to recording industrial strikes over a period of years, find it more feasible to count work disruptions wherein an organized group of workers leaves its work and takes concerted action in an attempt to force the employer to agree to contract terms. Other forms of organized protest, such as mass sick-leave-taking and work-to-the-rulebook, are more difficult to define for statistical purposes and therefore are not usually recorded in official statistics. The mass presentation of resignations and one-day walkouts that do not result in agreements are still more difficult to determine, although they often have an impact on public employment decisions. These four types of action are akin to the protest movements used by innumerable groups that became politicized in the 1960's and 1970's to work out their frustrations with the policy-making system. Some advocates of collective bargaining and negotiated grievance procedures say that these forms of protest will disappear when the proposed procedures are put into operation, although the record of experience in New York and Michigan does not support the contention.

Having expressed a caveat concerning the statistical record, let us examine the situation in this state. Strikes occurring in the first thirty years, 1933-1963, were solely in the publicly owned utilities and transit systems. Metropolitan Water District employees walked off a tunneling job in the San Jacinto Mountains in 1933. The Santa Monica municipal bus drivers went out in 1942 and 1961. Electricians struck the Los Angeles water and power department in 1944, and in 1946 a larger group of trade workers went out. Mechanics of the Los Angeles Metropolitan Transit District struck in 1960 and the bus operators respected their picket lines. The Stockton school bus operators staged a walkout the following year.

General local government services began to be affected from 1963 onward. Maintenance workers of the city of Concord, and operating engineers of the Washington Township Hospital District in southern Alameda County struck that year. Two years later Pittsburg, a small industrial city in Contra Costa County, experienced the first general municipal strike in this state when all except fire and police employees went out.

Governmental work disruptions seemed to reach nearly epidemic proportions in 1966 when employees in fourteen jurisdictions stayed away from their jobs or submitted resignations en masse. Not only was the number of employees and jurisdictions affected noteworthy, but the actions involved professional and white collar workers for the first time in this state. Social workers, registered nurses, and classroom teachers took collective action in a manner previously demonstrated only by blue collar workers, bus drivers, electricians, maintenance workers, and hospital kitchen helpers.

In the five year period of 1970 through 1974, 115 strikes took place within the state and in no one year were there less than fifteen[2] (see table 2). Although the average duration of these stoppages, 9.5 days, was relatively short, an estimated total of 74,573 employees were involved. Forty-eight of the actions lasted only one day, but twenty-four continued for two weeks or longer. Segments of all portions of the state's government had some experience. The state was the target of one strike, which involved a few workers in the water system. The school districts had thirty-eight strikes in the five year period, and the state university was involved in four walkouts of some support workers on two of its eight campuses. Public transportation authorities had to deal with twelve work stoppages whose average duration, 20.8 days, exceeded that experienced in any other segment of public employment. Other local governments experienced forty-nine strikes which averaged 8.4 days in duration. Perhaps most serious is the fact that the safety services began to strike, registering eleven walkouts in this five-year period in addition to taking numerous, less specific job actions, such as traffic-ticket-writing boycotts and mass sick calls.

Table 2

Strikes by California Public Employees, 1970-1974

	Year					5-Year Period
	1970	1971	1972	1973	1974	
Total No. of Strikes:	21	15	19	17	43	115
Average Duration in Days	9.1	9.4	13.9	8.6	8.1	9.5
No. of One-Day Stoppages	4	4	6	8	26	48
No. of Two or More Weeks' Duration	5	4	4	4	7	24
Type of Employer Involved:						
Safety Services						
No. of Strikes	6	2	1	0	2	11
Average Duration in Days	5.5	2.0	1.0	0	10.0	5.2
Public Schools						
No. of Strikes	4	3	1	8	22	38
Average Duration in Days	10.7	21.6	5.0	4.7	2.5	5.4
Transportation Services						
No. of Strikes	5	0	2	2	3	12
Average Duration in Days	16.0	0	4.0	16.0	43.3	20.8
Other Local Governments						
No. of Strikes	6	8	12	7	16	49
Average Duration in Days	6.1	8.0	8.3	10.8	9.0	8.4
State Government						
No. of Strikes	0	0	1	0	0	1
Average Duration in Days	0	0	4.0	0	0	4.0
State University						
No. of Strikes	0	2	2	0	0	4
Average Duration in Days	0	4.5	75.0	0	0	39.7

Based on: Bonnie G. Cebulski, Clara Stern, "A Five-Year Study of California Public Employee Strikes," *CPER*, No. 25 (August 1975), p. 4.

As might be anticipated, the big-employer jurisdictions in metropolitan areas have experienced the greatest number of disruptions, but the smaller suburban governments and non-metropolitan entities alike have had tastes of these incidents. Moreover, the initiative from the organized employees has not originated in a single quarter. A considerable percentage of the strikes in California have been led by such unions as AFSCME, SEIU, IAFF, and IBEW, but a significant portion have also been directed by associations not affiliated with the traditional labor movement. Chief among the latter are the teacher groups associated with the National Education Association. The California Nurses Association and police associations have also contributed to the list of work stoppages. Nevertheless, it should be re-emphasized that many public employing jurisdictions have not suffered work stoppages, and many units of organized employees have not joined in strike actions.

DEVELOPMENT OF A STATE POLICY

State policy during the period covered by this study evidently has been based on the assumption that public employment decisions are shaped by input from many competing interests. Organized employees, possessors of one set of interests, should accept disappointing decisions without resorting to extralegal actions. State law, legislative and judge-made alike, says public employees do not have a right to strike, but it does not specify penalties to be levied against violators.

Exceptions to this general policy have arisen. The state Supreme Court ruled that one group of workers were granted the right to strike when the transit system employing them was acquired by a public agency. In another instance, the federal courts held that certain state employed rail workers came under the jurisdiction of the national rail labor law rather than state law. Should the state specify a uniform policy to guide or restrict official reactions toward state and local employees on strike? Also, how much discretion should local officers be permitted to exercise when they deal with a work stoppage in a city, county, or district work force?

The statutory labor relations policy in California, adopted in 1934 as a parallel to federal law, recognizes the legitimacy of the strike as a tactic of organized industrial workers. Restrictions on its use have been added from time to time, but the policy remains essentially the same. The policy toward public employees is specific, though it is stated indirectly. Section 923 of the Labor Code specifies that none of the rights and procedures outlined in the previous sections for private sector workers are to be construed to apply to public employees.

The initial judicial statement regarding the right of public employees to withhold labor as a tactic in negotiating wages and working conditions was made by the court of appeals in 1938. It concerned a case brought by the Santa Monica city bus drivers, who had asked the court to require the city commissioners to negotiate their wage demands. The court said that public employees had no common law right either to negotiate collectively with their employer or to strike. They could acquire the desired rights only through legislation. In the absence of such action, the workers had no basis to ask the judiciary to intervene in their disputes with public employers.[3] This ruling set the tone of the policy outcomes from the state's political system on the subject for the next several decades.

A complicated scenario of events illustrates the strategies employed by the various parties attempting to influence a definitive state policy. Public employee unions sought repeatedly to persuade the legislature to rescind Section 923 of the Labor Code and apply to public employment the rules governing industrial employer-employee relations. Most such proposals foundered in legislative committee files. Bills proposing collective bargaining for public employees, without reference to the Labor Code but carrying provisions to recognize the right to strike, suffered a similar fate.

Some unionized occupational groups sought to persuade the policy makers that, because their occupations differed from those of other public employees, they should be permitted to strike as a part of bargaining with their employers. One such group was composed of workers employed by publicly owned utility systems financed by rates from service rather than from taxes. They based their contention on a prior distinction made by the courts of this state between the governmental and proprietary functions of chartered cities. Unions representing employees of municipal utilities contended that since their constituents were involved in a proprietary function, their employer-employee relations should be governed by the state labor code. This theory was advanced by the Building and Construction Trades Council of Los Angeles in 1948 when it sought to vacate an injunction against striking employees of the city water and power department. The case was argued on appeal before the same panel of judges that had decided the Santa Monica bus drivers' case, and who said in this decision that the recognition of the proprietary concept for certain purposes did not make the department an analog of an industrial firm in matters of employee relations. The department was a government agency and the employees were government workers whose terms of employment were governed by the city charter provisions pertaining to civil service.[4]

The proprietary function theory was advanced once more in a case involving employees of the state-owned belt line railroad on the San Francisco waterfront, but it was rejected by the state Supreme Court.[5] The court recognized no distinction between categories of government workers in the matter of employer-employee relations. The rail line workers had been treated as civil servants for more than twenty-five years, their salaries having been computed by the State Personnel Board. The union contended that the federal Railway Labor Act superseded this procedure and that a contract negotiated between the union and the harbor board controlled the wage determinations. The state court disagreed. Ultimately the matter was decided in the federal courts on the issue of the applicability of the federal act to a specific set of state employees, and not on the state issue of employment in a proprietary state function. The U.S. Supreme Court held that the state-owned railway was engaged in interstate commerce and therefore Congress had the jurisdiction to regulate its labor practices. Congress had concluded that a regulated system of employer-employee negotiations was essential to maintain stability in the railway industry and had created in the Railway Labor Act a procedure to accomplish this purpose. As a consequence of this decision, a small category of California state employees became exempt from the state rule governing public employer-employee relations.

A second group of publicly employed transit workers was identified by the state Supreme Court as an exception, when it interpreted a state statute governing the acquisition of a metropolitan transit system from a group of private firms. The legislative history that led to this situation is instructive.

Groups in the city of Los Angeles had persuaded the state in 1951 to create a special transit authority to acquire the local rail and bus systems from several firms whose operating personnel and mechanics were unionized and covered by negotiated contracts. New legislation was required when the authority expanded its jurisdiction in 1957 and became a regional transit system. The attitude of most legislators who represented constituencies outside Los Angeles County was that AB 1104, sponsored by Assemblyman Charles Wilson, Democrat, and other Los Angeles members, was politically a local bill. The San Diego delegation, for example, explained in the *Assembly Journal* that they voted aye at the third reading only as a courtesy to the Los Angeles delegation, and they expressed opposition to any similar plan if it were to apply to their metropolitan area. The transit unions threatened to scuttle the bill unless it recognized the relationships and rights they had achieved through negotiations with the corporate employers. Although the bill was amended several times in the Assembly, its employer-employee relations provisions remained unchanged in substance, and that house approved it relatively early in the session by a vote of 68-4.

The portions of the bill on which the state Supreme Court focused when it recognized the right of this set of transit employees to strike had been inserted during the Senate committee stage. A total of thirty-six amendments, twelve of which pertained to labor matters, were proposed in the upper house. Most significant of these changes was Amendment number 11 which rewrote Subsection (c) of Section 3.6 to guarantee employees of the authority the right to organize, bargain collectively, and engage in concerted activities. Subsections (d) and (e) pertained to labor contracts. The Senate approved the much amended bill and returned it to the Assembly, where several amendments other than number 11 were rejected. A conference committee composed of three members from each house met to settle the differences. Three of the six, Senator Richards, Democrat, and Assemblyman Shell, Republican, and Wilson (senior author), were from Los Angeles. Richards and Wilson were generally regarded as sympathetic to labor, whereas Shell was a leading conservative who usually voted against labor sponsored bills. When AB 1104 returned from conference committee late in the session, Subsection (c) was untouched, and the Assembly approved it by a tally of 68-2. The Senate concurred, and the governor signed.

The authority possessed no taxing power; its income was drawn solely from fares. Moreover, the governing board was appointed by the governor and was not elected by any constituency.

Within two years after the adoption of the Los Angeles Metropolitan Transit Authority Act of 1957, the governing board and the unions reached an impasse over contract renewal terms and, when the workers went out on strike, litigation soon followed. The case, decided in 1960, was the first to involve the specific issue of public employee strikes accepted by the state Supreme Court.[6] The court concluded the legislature had adopted language identical to that used in the Norris-La Guardia, Wagner, and Taft-Hartley Acts and the state Labor Code, all of which had been construed by federal and state courts in numerous decisions. It reasoned that when the legislature uses language which has been construed judicially, it must be presumed that the members intend to give the phrases their established meaning. The expression, "to take concerted action," for example, when read in conjunction with other phrases that recognized a right to bargain collectively, must be understood to mean recognition of a right to strike in support of a bargaining position. The court was also impressed by the fact that the union employees had previously enjoyed the right to strike in accordance with the state Labor Code. It speculated that the legislature might have concluded that a grant of the right was necessary to obtain a capable work force in the particular labor market at the time the transfer of ownership took place—an indirect reference to the political context of the transfer. Moreover, it saw no unconstitutional discrimination against other public employees in the legislature's grant of rights to a single category of workers.

This piece of legislation has produced considerable confusion in the debate about public policy toward public employee strikes. Nevertheless, attempts to repeal or modify its terms have been unsuccessful, even during a strike. In the summer of 1974, RTD union negotiations stalled and a strike stretched over several weeks. Governor Reagan convened a special legislative session to consider ways to resolve the dispute, but neither legislative chamber took action, thereby tossing the matter back to the parties at the bargaining table where a contract ultimately was concluded.

On several occasions in the late 1960's and 1970's, employee organizations sought to change the judicial reasoning expressed by the court of appeals in the Santa Monica bus drivers' case in 1938. They contended that the right to strike had not been raised by the litigants in that case, and that the court had expressed dicta which were not germane. They sought an occasion on which to argue the matter as the central issue. The first instance occurred in San Diego in 1969, when AFSCME Local 127 conducted a strike of miscellaneous city workers. The city asked for a temporary restraining order, basing its request on the point that under California law the employees had no right to strike. The trial court judge, Hugo M. Fisher, who had been a member of the state Senate prior to his appointment to the bench, ruled that the previous appellate court rulings were not binding precedents and rejected the city's request, saying:

The Legislature has expressly permitted the organization of public employees for the purpose of pursuing objectives relating to wages and terms and conditions of employment. It has not withdrawn any of the traditional weapons of labor other than the right to strike as to two classes of employees [Fire fighters and police].[7]

The city appealed and pressed for a ruling on the issue of the right to strike, whereupon the appellate court dealt roughly with the trial judge's memorandum statement, bluntly saying it was based on an erroneous interpretation of the law. The panel reiterated the conclusion expressed in the Nutter (Santa Monica bus drivers) case that, in the absence of legislation authorizing collective negotiations, the terms and conditions of public employment are fixed by the governing body through the processes of law rather than by contract. Acceptance of this employment requires acceptance of the processes by which the terms and conditions of employment are fixed.

The union had contended that the judge's denial of the temporary order should be sustained because the city had not shown that irreparable damage would result from the strike. The court disposed of this by saying that the judge had not exercised the discretion permitted him on this issue and had based his conclusion instead on an erroneous concept of the law.[8]

The Supreme Court declined to accept an appeal from this decision, although three justices thought it should have been heard. The court of appeal's ruling stood.

In a second case, arising from the Sacramento County social workers' strike in 1967, another division of the court of appeals also ruled that in the absence of specific legislative authorization, public employees had no legal right to strike. This panel examined the statutes and found no authorization had been granted.[9] Again the Supreme Court declined to accept an appeal.

In a third case, a different panel went further than the others and said that an agreement reached between a school board and a union under the pressure of an illegal strike was invalid. This case began when the Los Angeles school board obtained an order restraining the United Teachers of Los Angeles from leading a strike against the city's unified school district. When the union appealed this order, the court of appeals affirmed the action and reiterated the common law rule.[10] But the teachers persisted with their strike and returned only after both parties agreed to accept a mediator who helped negotiate a memorandum agreement. Before the board took action to implement the agreement, the court granted a petition from outside parties to prohibit execution of the pact. After hearing arguments, the court concluded that the strike had induced the board to make the agreement and that, inasmuch as the strike previously had been found to be illegal, the agreement was tainted. The court of appeals affirmed the lower court's reasoning.[11]

By 1974, when a large number of the employees of the city-county and school district of San Francisco went on strike over a wage dispute, three of the five districts of the court of appeals had ruled that public employees possessed no common law right to strike, and the state Supreme Court had declined to hear appeals from these decisions. The Supreme Court received an appeal directly from a trial court action in this dispute, however. The issue before it was whether the agreements reached by the board of supervisors and school board to conclude the strike and get their employees back on the job were valid. The court agreed unanimously that the two local boards had exercised their respective legislative powers when they adopted the wage adjustments and, in the absence of proof of corruption or personal gain by the officials, the courts had no basis to intervene. The local governing bodies had discretionary authority to settle a strike unless state or local law prescribed specific sanctions which must be exercised. The court reasoned that it had no authority to deny a legislative body's decision because of allegations that the action had been influenced by improper actions of others. The final approval of the action lay with the voters, not the courts.[12] It noted also that California, unlike some other states, did not have a policy specifying sanctions that must be exercised in the event of public employee strikes. It did not comment directly on the legality of the strike.

The effect of the decision was to leave the responsibility to negotiate settlement of a strike to the executive and legislative authorities of the agency involved. It thereby overruled the contrary decision of the court of appeals in the Los Angeles school case. This is consistent with the California home rule tradition. An interesting sequel to the decision is that shortly after its announcement in 1975, the voters of San Francisco adopted charter amendments requiring the dismissal of police or fire employees who strike, specifying sanctions against other classes of workers who participate in a work stoppage. The voters supported the hard line stance adopted by the board of supervisors in the police strike of 1975 rather than the more conciliatory approach taken by the mayor.

Those desiring a strict state legislative rule respecting strikes have been no more successful with the legislature than have employee organizations desiring to rescind Section 923 of the Labor Code. The first bill proposing sanctions against public employees was introduced in the 1941 session by Senator Biggar, who represented the rural counties of Mendocino and Lake. It proposed that any state or local officer or employee who instituted or aided a strike against the employing agency should forfeit his position and all civil service rights. It died in the Senate Committee on Governmental Efficiency. A second bill, presented in 1947 by Senator J. H. Williams of Tulare County, came closer to producing comprehensive legislation on the subject than any introduced prior to 1974. It declared that "a public servant has no right or privilege to strike against the sovereign body" and declared strikes by public employees to be illegal. Amendments developed in committee permitted re-employment of a civil servant after a strike but denied any salary increase for three years and required a probationary status for five years. The Senate approved the bill by a vote of 28 to 7. Six of the negative votes were cast by moderate senators from rural constituencies; the seventh was that of the senator from San Francisco.[13] The bill died, however, in the industrial relations committee of the Assembly.

The only legislation specifically prohibiting strikes by public employees was that adopted in 1959 as part of the statute recognizing the right of fire fighters to organize—a quid pro quo compromise. Moreover, the IAFF, which sponsored the bill, had a no-strike policy in its international union constitution, and no California fire fighter group had engaged in a strike at that date. The statute did not specify penalties to be levied against organizations or individuals who violated the stated policy.

The legislature received a handful of bills relating to public employee strikes at each session subsequent to a series of strikes by social workers, nurses, teachers, and several mixed groups in 1966. Five were submitted in 1967, although only one reached the floor of either house. Democratic sponsored bills fared no better than those from Republicans. A group of Assembly members, led by George Milias, Republican, chairman of the committee handling public employment matters in the 1968 session, proposed a comprehensive treatment of employer-employee relations, but another bill was used to work out the Meyers-Milias-Brown Act that was adopted. The new legislation denied the right to strike by referring to Labor Code section 923.[14]

Several bills prohibiting the right to strike by one or more classes of public employees were introduced by Republican legislators, three in 1969, five in 1970, and one in 1971. Each failed in committee. Early in the 1976 session, Senator Carpenter, Republican, of Orange County offered another bill which proposed to forbid any public employee to go out on strike. He anticipated that public opinion was running strongly against the strike tactic by public employees because of reaction to the San Francisco police and fire walkout the previous summer. The bill failed to clear the Senate committee, however, on a roll call vote.

A new concept was introduced by Speaker Robert Moretti, Democrat, in the 1974 session. It incorporated a plan suggested by a committee of labor relations specialists he had appointed which proposed that the state recognize a limited right of public employees to strike.[15] The public employer and employees would be required first to engage in good faith bargaining and to submit any impasse reached to a fact finding procedure. The plan proposed to amend court procedures relative to restraining orders and injunctions, authorizing the trial courts to hold a public hearing to determine whether a specific strike seriously jeopardized the public safety and welfare. If the court found the proposed action did not jeopardize the public interest, no restraining order would be issued. The commission considered that this plan offered a balance of interests. The employer would be forced to bargain because of the possibility of a strike. Sanctions could be levied against those employees who violated the court's order to desist from a strike that jeopardized public safety and welfare. The Speaker was able to push his bill, AB 1243, through the Assembly but it was never reported out of the Senate committee.

The essence of the Moretti bill was incorporated by Senator Ralph Dills,

Democrat, of Los Angeles County in his bill, SB 275, for the 1975 session. This became the major collective bargaining bill favored by organized labor and its public employee unions in that session. Midway through the session, however, Dills dropped the strike provision in an attempt to get the bargaining portions approved. The effort collapsed in the latter part of the session, whereupon Senator Albert Rodda, Democrat, of Sacramento County and chairman of the education committee, successfully pushed to passage his bill for collective negotiations in the public schools. This bill, known widely as SB 160, dealt with the strike issue by invoking Section 923 of the Labor Code, which in effect denied school employees the right to strike in support of their negotiation demands.

Several factors have undoubtedly influenced the legislators' reluctance to move beyond the simple statement that public employees do not have the right to strike. The judicial ruling made in 1938 and reiterated on later occasions removed much of the sense of urgency for legislative action. It challenged the employee organizations to seek legislative authorization. This was a test of political strength that civil servants were ill prepared to face until 1974. Moreover, many employees and several associations were either not interested or were more committed to other means of presenting their claims.

The legislators addressed the subject of public employee strikes only at intervals, after some particularly controversial work stoppage. The attitude of the voters toward public work disruptions was unclear. Only a small portion of the public had direct experience with a strike of public workers, so there was no solid consensus concerning methods of coping. In communities where the labor movement had been established for several years, sizable portions of the electorate often had indicated tolerance or sympathy for the employees engaged in particular disputes. In those communities where strikes had occurred, citizens had been inconvenienced and exasperated at the time but, until the San Francisco strike of police and firemen in 1975, there had been no concerted or continuous expression of concern and no call for sanctions to be used. Some segments of the political community, mainly newspaper editors and central-area business groups in the metropolitan central cities, had expressed antagonism toward government workers' strikes and urged that sanctions be exercised. National opinion surveys indicated a division in public attitudes, however. For example, a survey made by the Louis Harris polling organization in 1967 showed considerable opposition to strikes by teachers, fire fighters, and police, but another poll, conducted by the same firm a year later and limited to teacher strikes, showed a substantially different attitude (see table 3). A survey by the George Gallup firm in 1975 found that the majority of persons interviewed believed police and fire fighters should not be permitted to strike,

Table 3

Harris Opinion Surveys on Public Employee Strikes

A. 1967 Poll: Strikes by Teachers, Police, Firemen

Opinion	Percentage of Response		
Right to Strike by:	Total National	Union Members	Non-Union Respondents
Teachers			
Favor	41	48	38
Opposed	52	44	55
Not sure	7	8	7
	100	100	100
Firemen			
Favor	35	39	33
Opposed	57	55	57
Not sure	8	6	10
	100	100	100
Police			
Favor	36	42	34
Opposed	56	52	58
Not sure	8	6	8
	100	100	100

B. 1968 Poll: Teachers' Right to Strike

Percentage of Response

Opinion	Region				Association		National Total
	East	Midwest	South	West	Union	Non-Union	
Favor	43	49	53	54	58	45	49
Opposed	47	42	35	38	34	44	41
Not sure	10	9	12	8	8	11	10
	100	100	100	100	100	100	100

but opinion was about equally divided on the right to strike of sanitation workers.[16]

A substantial factor in the legislature's reluctance to spell out sanctions in state law is that professional administrative officers state that such mandates would deprive them of discretion to deal with the employees under their supervision. When confronted with a threatened work disruption, these officers prefer to negotiate informally with the responsible representatives of the employees to prevent the dispute from escalating and stopping the delivery of services to the public. They seek to get the work force back on the job in as short a time as possible, even if no formal penalties are assessed against those who have gone out on strike. They feel it is impractical to attempt to replace a substantial portion of the work force, which would be necessary if the type of sanctions proposed in 1947 were mandated by state law.[17] They are equally opposed to recognizing the right of organized employees to strike. However, many say that if the choice were between taking a strike and being required to accept compulsory arbitration of an interest dispute—a procedure frequently advocated as recompense to workers denied the right to strike—the strike would be more acceptable, because they believe they could get public backing for their position. They believe that compulsory arbitration takes authority away from the legally responsible, decision-making officials.[18]

Most government agencies in this state found it desirable during the 1950's to enact administrative codes covering the procedure and substance of policy relative to the conditions of employment. A common provision of these regulations specifies that an employee's unexcused absence from work for five consecutive working days constitutes grounds for dismissal. Such rules provide a basis for the exercise of administrative sanctions against individual employees involved in strikes as well as in the more routine employment situations. Moreover, it permits flexibility of decision in individual cases.

Employing jurisdictions are subject to some restrictions if they attempt to dismiss employees solely for striking, so long as property is not damaged or the peace disturbed. Federal constitutional guarantees of freedom of speech and assembly broadly protect peaceful picketing by disgruntled workers who wish to advertise their grievances. The courts have upheld a county's decision to dismiss striking social workers when it observed its charter-prescribed procedures,[19] but they have overruled dismissals when the government disregarded the established civil service procedures.[20] They have also sustained a county's ordinance awarding a one-time bonus to employees who stayed on the job during a strike.[21]

Analysis of the events in two strike situations in California local governments, the Sacramento County social workers' strike in 1967 and the San Francisco police walkout in 1975, affirms the wisdom of the legislative policy of avoiding prescriptions of fixed penalties against public employees who leave their jobs in a dispute. Both involved workers performing functions uniquely governmental in nature. Welfare relief administration is mandated to counties by state decision, whereas police protection is recognized as one of the fundamental functions of city government. A strike in a public entity tends to be a highly complex political situation. Many individuals and groups maneuver for influence or advantage. There is tension and conflict of roles between key officials in the employing bureaucracy as well as between the government management and the employee organizations primarily involved. Rivalry between employee organizations for influence on employment policy and recruitment of members is often an important element contributing to the tensions. Actions by persons on both sides of the dispute contribute still further. Groups in the community not originally concerned become aroused to intervene in support of some of the antagonists. The outcomes tend to differ from the initial goals of either management or the employee organization leaders.

The county officers and the union primarily involved in the Sacramento strike were equally inexperienced and were groping in an uncharted situation. Sacramento County has a home rule charter which established a five-member board of supervisors elected by districts. A chief administrative officer served at the pleasure of the board in 1967 and had limited authority to direct department heads who supervised administrative operations. The charter gave the director of social welfare, for example, the responsibility to appoint and remove department employees subject to civil service regulations. A five-member civil service commission possessed charter-granted authority to enact rules and supervise recruitment, examination, classification, and promotion of county employees and to conduct hearings on appeals from disciplinary actions. The county counsel, the chief legal advisor, was appointed by the board and enjoyed civil service status. The district attorney, the county's prosecuting officer, was elected. The Service Employees Union Local 535, which conducted the strike, had signed approximately three-hundred workers in the Welfare Department, proselyting some from the AFSCME Local 146, which had represented many Sacramento County employees for thirty years.[22] Local 146 had appealed to the AFL-CIO, claiming encroachment by the other union. Another SEIU local in the Sacramento area was also involved in another interunion dispute, consequently when Local 535 requested the Sacramento Labor Council to support its proposed strike against the county, the latter refused and attempted to mediate the county controversy.

The dispute with the county began in December, 1966, ostensibly over salaries,[23] but it soon became evident that the union's primary intention was to force the county to engage in collective bargaining and to recognize it as the exclusive representative of employees in the Welfare Department. It was also eager to publicize its advent into the county work force. The county and the AFSCME local had been discussing a draft employer-employee relations policy, to which the SEIU objected. Union rivalry was evident. The SEIU demanded that the wage matter be negotiated and that the State Conciliation Service be brought in as mediator. The county board rejected both demands, taking the position that it had sole authority to determine wages and working conditions by ordinance and regulations. It modified its stance slightly, however, when it recessed its meeting on January 25 for a proposed informal conference with the employees. The union's officers called a membership meeting to consider a strike to begin on February 7.[24] The county counsel advised the board that a strike was illegal,[25] and the welfare director stated that if employees were absent for five days without departmental approval, he would order their dismissal.[26] The supervisors adopted a resolution, prepared by the county counsel, that supported the director's statement. They also authorized the counsel to seek an injunction if a strike occurred and approved one-hundred temporary positions to be used for hiring replacements of any workers who went on strike. Shortly after these actions, the union announced that seventy-five percent of its membership had voted to walk out on February 7.[27]

Both parties sparred and waited during the next few days. The union president offered to postpone the strike if the county would negotiate, and the board chairman countered by saying that the union had submitted no proposals in writing, although several meetings had been held. Union officers predicted that their members would walk off the job despite the restraining order and asked the county to give assurance that workers who went out would suffer no loss of pay or other reprisal.[28]

The county counsel appeared before Superior Court Judge E. F. Sheehy early in the morning of February 2, and obtained a temporary restraining order on grounds that the strike would interfere with county performance of a state mandated function. Counsel announced later in the day that union members who disobeyed the order would be subject to civil and criminal contempt-of-court charges.[29]

During the days before the strike commenced, a union committee met with County Administrator Tarshes on several occasions, although the latter pointed out that the board had given him no authority to negotiate on wages or working conditions.[30] The Central Labor Council attempted to mediate, and the National Association of Social Workers and three other groups asked the county and the unions to discuss the issues, but all failed to gain their points.

On the morning of February 7, members of Local 535 went on strike without the sanction of the Labor Council, a prerequisite according to union rules. Picket lines were set up around county offices, starting at six A.M., and these were soon met by detachments of city police which the county had requested to enforce the court order. Forty-one pickets, including the union local's president and the international's field representative, were arrested after police had orally warned them to disperse. Bail was set at a relatively low figure, but twenty-nine, including some of the leaders, chose to remain in jail for several days to give further publicity to the dispute. Other pickets took up the vigil but adopted a tactic of disappearing when the police arrived and reappearing when the latter relaxed.

During the next few days more than two-hundred persons, including some who were not county employees, appeared on the picket lines and were arrested. At one point, a municipal court judge offered to release several persons without bail if they promised not to picket, but they refused to so promise. County officials stepped up the pace of discussions with representatives of several employee organizations about an employer employee relations ordinance and changes in the county personnel program.

Tension escalated when the district attorney announced that criminal contempt charges were to be filed against the arrested pickets. Private sector unions influential in the Central Labor Council, disturbed at the district attorney's action, now voted to support the strike. Local 535 dropped its demand for mediation, but reiterated its claim to be recognized as the bargaining agent, and also filed appeals challenging the restraining order and the arrests.

Because numerous meet-and-confer sessions had produced no settlements, the welfare department head ordered all striking workers to return to their jobs the following Monday morning or face dismissal charges.[31] When 183 employees failed to return by the deadline date, he dismissed them and was supported in this by an advisory council. The county offered to rehire many of the dismissed workers, but without their previously earned seniority credits. Some went back to work. Those who refused appealed to the county civil service commission but their dismissals were upheld after hearings.

Several social workers' associations not formally affiliated with the union opposed the department's efforts to recruit new workers. When Sacramento recruiters went to other counties for hiring interviews, the union and its sympathizers pressured the host county administrators to deny the use of public facilities and assistance. The county was able, however, to fill its positions and carry out its function.

In retrospect, the county had been caught in a cross fire of rivalry between two unions. Local 535 gained state-wide publicity as a small, aggressive union representing militant social workers. County management responsibilities were widely dispersed to deal with what was essentially a new problem. The chief administrative officer was restricted by the board and had no leeway to make adjustments. The department head had the major responsibility for hiring, supervising, and disciplining employees, subject to civil service rules and procedures which were supported by the charter. The civil service commission and personnel director had independent powers in many personnel policy areas. The county counsel, the board's legal advisor, was able to influence board decisions on major personnel policy matters throughout this episode. He showed no interest in negotiations and recommended a rigid, legalistic stance toward the organizations, the use of court orders, quick deployment of police against pickets, and the filing of criminal contempt charges against those arrested for picketing. The district attorney, responsible for prosecuting the charges, was independent of the board and not directly involved in the other management decisions. The board of supervisors, though a part-time body, tended to play a direct part in strategic and tactical discussions instead of defining the parameters of policy and delegating responsibility to key administrators to negotiate details. After the strike was concluded, the board adopted an employer-employee relations ordinance which provided for exclusive representation of employees in units possessing common interests, and negotiation on wages and certain defined aspects of employment conditions. In the first unit representation election, Local 535 won the right to represent the social workers and AFSCME Local 146 was selected by two of the large representation units (see chapter 3, pp. 63, 66). To a considerable degree, both unions attained their initial goals. The county civil service commission also delegated some of its functions to the personnel officer, who was responsible thereafter to the board of supervisors. The commission retained appellate functions and some rule making authority. Operational activities were largely shifted to management control, although such functions as classification were subject to commission review.

The outcome of the litigation arising from the strike set some important benchmarks, not only for this jurisdiction but for the rest of the state. The court of appeals sustained the county's right to dismiss the striking workers.[32] The county's use of criminal contempt sanctions against the picket line was ruled improper, however, by the state Supreme Court, which concluded that the pickets were acting within their First Amendment rights to express their views and were not preventing the conduct of county business.[33] This decision tended to warn governing boards, administrative officers, and the trial courts alike that restraining orders and injunctions were to be used with considerable care in public employer-employee disputes.

The San Francisco police and fire strike of 1975 illustrates a different set of factors peculiar to government employment. San Francisco, a consolidated city-county functioning under a home rule charter, is governed by an independently elected mayor and an eleven-member board of supervisors. Although elections are nonpartisan, the party affiliations of major candidates are usually well known. Organized labor has been considered for many years to be strong politically in the city. The downtown business community exercises decisive influence in many issues, due in considerable part to the method of electing the board of supervisors from the city at large rather than by districts, where ethnic groups are strongest. Ethnic minority groups were beginning to be actively interested in city employment issues. Mayor Joseph Alioto, re-elected four years earlier with extensive union financial and vote support, was nearing the end of his second term and was barred by the charter from seeking re-election. A city administrator supervised much of the routine administration but the mayor, who had extensive executive powers, overshadowed him. The city's legal officer was elected independently. Negotiations with employee organizations, other than police and fire, were governed by an ordinance recently adopted after more than three years of conferences. The police and fire organizations had insisted they be exempt from this ordinance because they wanted compulsory arbitration of interest disputes, a feature not acceptable to the board of supervisors and regarded by the city attorney as contrary to the charter.[34]

The charter required the civil service commission to recommend salaries annually to the board of supervisors based on a survey of wages paid by private employers for similar duties. Special instructions controlled the commission's findings in the matter of police and fire salaries, however. The police association had persuaded the voters in 1963 to adopt a charter amendment authorizing the board to pay police salaries and benefits equal to the best paid by any city in the state having 100,000 or more population. The fire fighters had also obtained an amendment that directed the board to pay them compensation equivalent to that of the police. For more than twenty years, the board had approved annual salary rates that followed the police formula. The break from this pattern came in 1975, when the city of Los Angeles raised its police salaries to a level that would have caused San Francisco to grant a thirteen percent increase if it proposed to follow its precedents. The board authorized pay increases averaging 6.42 percent for several classes, but announced that it planned to give police, fire fighters, and municipal railway employees no more than 6.5 percent because of an anticipated budget deficit. It delayed final approval of the salary ordinance pending receipt of the civil service department's survey. In the meantime, it created a management negotiation team to meet with police and fire representatives. The team exchanged a few inquiries with the two organizations, but the latter refused to go further and asked for an executive session with the board as a whole. The board declined the request and adopted the 6.5 percent salary rate. All parties had apparently locked themselves into rigid positions.

On August 18, an estimated eighty-five percent of the police force left its posts and the fire fighters followed a day later, despite a court order directing them to refrain from striking. Pickets began to appear around station houses and the city hall. Most of the detective force and the black police officers remained on their jobs, however. The division within the police soon exacerbated relationships and some violent incidents occurred. The news media began to publicize allegations of damage to city vehicles and property, and it printed pictures of armed policemen walking the picket lines. Tension mounted still further when a bomb blast near the mayor's home caused some damage, although responsibility for the act was never determined. A strong reaction against the strikers began to stir. The board of supervisors urged the mayor to request the governor to send state patrol officers and guardsmen, but he declined. The mayor's public statements also varied in tone. Early in the strike he said all strikers would be dismissed if they did not return to work immediately, but later he contended no effort should be made to get them to turn in their weapons. The issues soon became those of the mayoral election. Supervisors Dianne Feinstein and John Barbagelata, candidates for mayor, were especially vocal in opposing the strikers' demands and tactics. State Senators Moscone, Democrat, and Marks, Republican, also candidates, were quick to announce introduction of bills relevant to the situation.

The mayor and board members met with employee representatives in a closed session at a hotel, but the board members walked out after the employees turned down an offer. The mayor left but returned after a few hours and agreed to give the employees the increase they demanded, basing his decision on a section of the charter which authorized him to exercise extraordinary powers in an emergency. He set the effective date at October 1, however, instead of July 1, the date originally demanded. The employees promptly accepted the agreement and returned to work.

Taxpayer suits promptly challenged the mayor's authority to bind the city to terms not agreed to by the supervisors. The board prepared four charter amendments for the city election ballot. One proposed to revoke the emergency powers invoked by Alioto. Another mandated the dismissal of police and firemen who strike and picket. A third directed the city to compute police salaries from an average of rates paid by the five largest cities in the state. The fourth changed fire department work schedules from a twenty-four-hour shift to a plan combining ten-hour day and fourteen-hour night shifts. Its purpose was to reduce the possibility that firemen could hold second jobs. As the election day approached, firemen's "moonlighting" and police and firemen's residence outside the city became highly emotional issues. The mayor submitted two counter propositions patterned on demands by the uniformed forces. One was a policy statement that public safety personnel should be paid at a rate equal to the highest given in the state; the second was an ordinance establishing compulsory arbitration of police and fire wage matters. Both the POA and IAFF locals raised campaign funds to promote these proposals. The Committee for City Pay Reform, financed by the business community, supported the supervisors' amendments. Two major newspapers, the *San Francisco Chronicle* and the *San Francisco Examiner,* also endorsed the latter.

The voters approved the supervisors' charter amendments by approximately 3-1 majorities and turned down those submitted by the mayor. This was a clear reversal of the voting pattern that had prevailed for so many years and that had enabled the organized employees to enjoy a special status.

The mayoral election returns showed a different picture. Senator Moscone, a former supervisor who received organized labor's endorsement, led the field of eleven candidates by a comfortable margin, although he did not receive a majority and was forced to compete in the general election with Supervisor Barbagelata, who had rigidly opposed the police and fire organizations. Moscone won the general election after a bitterly fought contest. One of his first moves after taking office was to appoint a new chief of police, a former head of the Oakland department who had established a reputation as a firm department manager with experience in dealing with police organizations. The new chief was also a moderate in racial and social policies, but many officers who had participated in the strike were hostile to his appointment.

In the aftermath of the strike, Judge Robert J. Drews, who had issued the order restraining the strike, directed the city attorney to file contempt citations against four officers of the Police Officers Association. After a trial, he fined the president and the association for their leadership of the strike. Moreover, critics of the POA within the department claimed that 250 officers had resigned from the association in protest against the conduct of the strike. The president admitted the loss of 150 members.

Several observations summarize the situation. First, the diffused structure of authority in the city-county government prevented management from operating effectively to temper or forestall the dispute. Inasmuch as the board was determined to reverse a long-existing pattern of decisions, preparation and discussions were highly important, but procedures to accomplish this were not established until after the parties had taken rigid positions on the issues. The mayor, an aggressive, articulate, and ambitious politician and a successful attorney, was inclined to respond favorably to all employee demands as the way to resolve the conflict. Moreover, he did not have to face the city electorate at the forthcoming election. On the other hand, two members of the board were basing their candidacy for mayor on their actions on current matters, chief of which was the strike. Both opposed the employees' demands as being unrealistic, although Barbagelata was most vehement on this point. The leadership of the two employee organizations, long accustomed to favorable responses to their demands, miscalculated public attitudes. Moreover, relationships between the two departments and the city's growing minority ethnic groups were very poor. The fact that many police and fire fighters had moved out of the city exacerbated these relationships and made them vulnerable to other voter groups' resentment as well. The situation was ripe for a political struggle in which many contestants sought advantage.

The combination of factors caused the city's voters to pay close attention to the dispute and to react strongly to the alternative choices presented by the two sets of charter amendments. This police and fire strike was not the first in California, nor did the incidence of crimes and fires rise above normal during the strike period, but the event shocked a large percentage of the voters. The election outcome caused some very specific provisions to become parts of city employment policy. Dismissal of any police or fire employee who might strike in future was made mandatory. Formulas to cut back wage and hour levels were established, and the concept of compulsory arbitration as a recompense for loss of the right to strike was firmly rejected.

One organization and its top officer were punished for improper actions, and persons convicted of destruction of public property were dealt with under the penal laws. The new mayor made management changes to strengthen supervision.

The trial courts' image as arbiters of public employee-employer disputes was weakened in such first encounters as the Sacramento strike, because the procedure practiced gave the appearance of being a game strategy.

The employing jurisdiction's key officers were responsible for taking the initiative to seek a temporary restraining order. The order was usually obtained promptly because the court required only a prima facie showing that the threatened disruption would jeopardize the public health or safety or interrupt functions mandated by law. The law allows the judge a relatively broad degree of discretion, consequently officers responsible for initiating a request are tempted to ponder the choice of a jurist to address. In some large counties, however, the judicial organization and the rules governing allocation of duties among the large corps of judges limits the range of choice. The statutory procedure does not require an evidentiary hearing, with all concerned parties present and presenting views and precedents, to advice the judge before the temporary restraining order is issued. The decision rests mainly on the judge's conclusion that the petitioner's presentation is persuasive.

The decision to pursue the matter to the permanent injunction stage rests chiefly with the employer-government's officials. Often they request the court to drop the matter because the strike has ended, some negotiations are being carried on, or the government has agreed to take no further action as part of a settlement.

In many instances, the employer-government has made little use of the restraining order other than to serve notice on the officers of the employee group. When public property has been damaged or a disturbance has occurred, persons have been arrested, thereby setting in motion the process of trial and appeal in which the validity of the actions is tested in the judicial system. The San Francisco police strike in 1975 is one of the few instances in which those who have actively induced employees to strike have been tried for contempt of court and fined after an evidentiary hearing. The courts have seldom taken active steps to obtain information about the outcome of the order issued. In other words, the key elected and appointed officers of the employer-government have controlled the choice of action.

The process by which the government's management decides to involve the courts in a strike situation frequently produces internal tensions. The initial responsibility rests, to a considerable degree, on the city manager, county chief administrative officer, or district school superintendent, although this depends on the allocation of duties in the specific government. The head of the department whose employees are involved may make considerable input to the decision. Each officer is guided by his estimate of the elected board members' attitudes based on their explicit statements and past voting records. The board membership is often not unanimous in expressing a preference for a particular course of action. Moreover, the emotional and political ramifications of a public employee strike are often sufficiently acute that the board members are tempted to assume individual roles in the decision-making. Where there is an independently elected executive, the two branches of government frequently become rivals, seeking credit with varied constituencies for stances taken in the dispute with the employees. A significant factor is the individual official's ambition to use his action or rhetoric as a base to gain voter support in a later election to an office deemed more prestigious than the one currently occupied. This condition was illustrated most clearly in the San Francisco police strike.

An equally intriguing complication in the government decision process is the bureaucratic conflict which arises from several disparate perceptions of what is optimum management strategy. This is based on the legal and informal status, role perception, and intellectual background of such key officers as the legal adviser, the prosecutor, the chief administrative officer, and the department head.

Central administrative officers and department heads, as previously hypothesized, often favor informal negotiations with the workers or their spokesmen in order to minimize the impact of a threatened stoppage and to insure the continuance of as much public service as possible while retaining workable human relations. These administrators are usually loath to take actions that will result ultimately in the loss of experienced workers. The legal counsel tends to approach the situation from a different viewpoint. This officer is appointed by the governing board in most city governments, but in most counties and in the state he is independently elected. The county legal officer also advises most school boards. In each instance, his status is independent of the administrative hierarchy. Furthermore, his training, experience, and customary procedures relate to litigation rather than to administration, and his expertise is in estimating what the courts will decide, in the light of existing precedents, and what is possible to accomplish through litigation. It is reasonable to hypothesize that the legal counsel has less incentive to recommend negotiation and compromise in employer-employee relations than has an administrative officer. The formal opinions given governing bodies by the state and local legal advisers indicate that these officers tend to view employer-employee relations largely in terms of the doctrine of sovereignty of the employer. The legal and administrative officers become bureaucratic rivals who frequently present sharply divergent recommendations to the governing board or take divergent action. Sacramento County illustrates the situation described. Moreover, in that instance, the controversy was widened considerably when the district attorney, an independently elected officer, decided to charge the strikers with criminal rather than civil contempt of court. Although the county board originally said this action would be taken, the choice rested ultimately with the prosecutor. Responsibility was again diffused in that action, as it was in most other phases of the controversy.

INTERGOVERNMENTAL COOPERATION IN POLICE AND FIRE STRIKES

Throughout the history of strikes in the private sector in the United States, organized labor has sought to prevent employers from hiring substitute workers to break a strike. A governmental unit unable to protect the peace and safety of its citizens, however, faces a condition bordering on anarchy. Moreover, the traditional concept of state and local government envisions a system of governments in which mutual responsibilities are accepted. Although elected and appointed government officers are not devoid of a spirit of competitiveness in their relations with other government units, the motive is different from that prevailing in commercial competition in the market.

Intergovernmental cooperation to protect the peace and ensure the safety of citizens in California rests on a long history of policy and negotiated intergovernmental agreements. Governors of most states have summoned the state militia, now comprising units of the National Guard, to assist local authorities in emergency situations. Units of the California militia were called to assist in the San Francisco earthquake and fire in 1906 and in the Long Beach quake in 1933. They were called again to the Watts riots in 1965 and to the disturbances in the San Francisco-East Bay in 1968. Opposition to the use of combat-trained troops in civil disturbances caused the commander of the California National Guard to announce in December, 1975, with the governor's approval, a plan to train military police units in civilian law enforcement.

When the California Highway Patrol was created, groups fearful that it might be used as a strike breaking force, particularly in farm labor incidents, insisted that its authority be limited to policing state highways. Within that policy framework, the CHP and the local law enforcement departments developed considerable experience with cooperative, as well as competitive, traffic law enforcement. In 1970, Governor Reagan went beyond this traditional policy when he sent detachments of patrol officers to assist sheriffs' deputies in Alameda and Santa Barbara counties in quelling mob disturbances.

The state fire protection service was developed primarily to suppress grass, grain, and timber fires, although several units are stationed on the fringes of suburban areas. It works also in conjunction with county departments in several sections of the state.

Interest in planned cooperation between local governments in fighting major blazes stemmed originally from a holocaust in the Berkeley hills in the late 1920's. Los Angeles County and several cities also developed an extensive network of agreements in which they pledged fire and police back-up support in the event of major disasters. The concept of intergovernmental cooperation in rendering emergency services was well established in this state when the California Emergency Services Act was legislated in the war year of 1943, intended to provide a basis for coping with conditions occurring during enemy attacks, earthquakes, floods, and major fires. Organized labor, sensitive to the possibilities that planned procedures for intergovernmental cooperation might be used in strike situations, insisted that a governmental entity be prohibited from supplying emergency services when the emergency involved a labor dispute. Local government officials were primarily concerned about protection from liability for injuries to fire fighters and police who responded to emergency calls and for damage done to private property when giving aid to other jurisdictions.

Intergovernmental cooperation in a public employee strike was first questioned in 1971 when the Vallejo police and firemen went out during a dispute with the city on wages and working conditions. The city council appealed to Governor Reagan for assistance and also requested the Solano County sheriff to provide police protection. The governor ordered the state fire service to send crews and equipment and directed the highway patrol to back up the city's skeleton force and the sheriff. Several legislators immediately requested Attorney General Lynch, a Democrat, to advise regarding the legal basis for these actions, presumably to determine if new legislation were needed. Lynch replied that the 1943 act amply supported the state and county action. The strike was not a labor controversy as defined in the Emergency Service Act. Moreover, he reasoned that a local government could provide the same assistance under mutual aid agreements made in accordance with the Joint Exercise of Powers Act. He said, with respect to the strike:

Since public employees do not have a legal right to strike, we would conclude that any such illegal activity was not a labor controversy within the intent of the Act[s]. We believe that in using the phrase 'other than conditions resulting from a labor controversy' the Legislature was only concerned with the direct and proximate effects of labor disputes between private employers and employees. Hence the state may render whatever aid and assistance is necessary to preserve and protect the public health, safety and welfare in the event that firemen of a city refuse to perform their duty.[35]

No further requests have been made to the state. Mayor Alioto declined to request assistance during the 1975 police and fire strike in San Francisco despite urging by the board of supervisors. No request was made during the Berkeley fire fighters' strike the same year. Governor Brown directed the state fire service to be prepared to protect state property on the University of California campus but specified that no other action be taken.

The fact that the International Association of Fire Fighters has organized a preponderant number of city and county departments raises the question of whether local fire personnel would respond willingly to calls for cooperative work, except in disaster situations. Most cities confronted with fire fighters' strikes have relied on supervisory personnel, volunteers, and other municipal employees to respond to routine fire calls. Police organizations are primarily local in nature and do not present comparable jurisdictional issues, although individual officers may question assignments outside the employing city.

Governor Reagan's action in sending state firemen to assist the city of Vallejo brought out another issue not contemplated in intergovernmental cooperation plans. The state paid its fire fighters a lower wage than did many cities, primarily because state crews dealt mainly with grass and timber fires rather than with those in structures and industrial installations. The State Employees Association advanced the argument that state crews sent into cities to supply emergency service should be compensated equally with those they temporarily replaced. Four Democratic Assembly members introduced legislation responding to the CSEA demand and the bill passed both houses without a dissenting vote but was vetoed by the governor, who expressed the following view:

The powers enabling me to act in emergency situations are necessary to assure the continued functioning of vital and necessary services when the public welfare is threatened for any reason. This authority should not be encumbered by consideration of the compensation to be paid state employees or by the possible stigma of state interference in a local public agency labor dispute.[36]

No move was made to override the veto.

CONCLUSIONS

Discussion in this chapter has focused on the debates about development of a state policy toward strikes in state and local government work forces. The policy currently rests on the oft-repeated ruling of the court of appeals that public employees have no common law right to strike, and on the legislative statement in the state Labor Code that the right to strike granted industrial employees does not apply to public workers. Some employee organizations have sought a specific legislative grant of the right, but only the employees of a transit district, who had it prior to coming into public employment, have succeeded.

The state authorized certificated and classified school employees to negotiate collectively with school districts, but it denied the right of these employees to strike. Several chartered counties and cities have established negotiation procedures as part of their employer-employee relations program, but none has recognized the right of employees to strike. Moreover, San Francisco, Vallejo, San Anselmo, and San Diego voters have adopted charter amendments that forbid police and fire fighters in those cities to strike. San Francisco and San Diego specify that violators shall be dismissed.

Proposals to mandate the imposition by state law of such penalties as dismissal, denial of salary increases for a specified period, or reduction of striking employees to a probationary status, have not been adopted. Government administrators generally have opposed mandated penalties because these directives unduly restrict their discretion when attempting to end a strike and to maintain an adequate, experienced work force to perform the programs for which they are responsible.

The elected and appointed officials who constitute the management of public agencies use a great variety of tactics and strategies to cope with strikes.[37] Governor Reagan's representative moved quickly in 1972 to negotiate a settlement in the one instance of a strike in the state work force. Most strikes in local work forces have been of less than two weeks' duration and many of them, regardless of length, have been ended by some type of negotiation between the parties involved.[38]

The administrative sanction most commonly employed by public management is dismissal for unauthorized absence from duty. Where this sanction has been invokved in accordance with local civil service regulations and sustained after a due process hearing by a personnel commission, the courts have upheld its use. Employee organizations, however, commonly make management's agreement to forego dismissal of striking workers a prime condition for the return to work. The state courts have insisted that management respect these conditions when they are contained in a memorandum of agreement.

Local governing boards occasionally undertake to pay a bonus to workers who remain on the job during a strike as a means of encouraging and rewarding loyalty to the employer. The courts have upheld this procedure, although arbitrators have ruled in some instances that the payment violated terms of negotiated agreements. County superior courts are frequently requested to issue a temporary restraining order against a threatened public employee strike, and one is usually granted because the judge has wide discretion and the procedure does not require a complete two-party hearing before a writ is issued. In many instances, there is little serious follow-up after the writ is granted. Some observers believe the temporary restraining order induces employee organizations to negotiate with management more quickly; others contend that it has little constructive effect and more often hardens the resolve of employee leaders to demand as a condition for return to work that no penalties be levied.

Donald Wollett, member of the commission appointed by Speaker Moretti in 1974, advocated that the statutory instructions to the judiciary be revised to narrow the range of discretion permitted judges when issuing an injunction.[19] The instructions urged that the judges be required to hold a hearing to determine the extent of the impact of an impending work disruption on public peace and safety. If the impact were found to be slight, an injunction could not be issued, whereas if the conclusion were that public peace and safety would be jeopardized, an injunction would be appropriate. The commission stated its intent was to create sufficient pressures on both the public employers and employee organizations to force them to negotiate until they reached a settlement. The legislature did not accept the proposal.

Pressure of public opinion and of adversely affected interest groups provides the ultimate deterrent to disruption of public services. The strategies used by all parties in a public employment dispute are essentially political, aimed to attract public support of their views or actions. Management hopes to secure approval of its actions as being just, legitimate, and in the public interest. Occasionally, a segment of management resorts to the use of a direct voter plebiscite, as did the San Francisco board of supervisors in 1975. Employee organizations strive to convince a portion of the public that they have a just grievance against the official decision makers. Only infrequently does either public management or an employee organization wish to draw others into active participation in the resolution of the controversy, as was done by the union in the 1967 Sacramento strike.

Two propositions underlie the discussion in this chapter. One is that government in the California political system exists mainly to provide services and satisfactions to its citizens. The other is that the decisions and actions that lead to a disruption of work in a government work force are not invariably or exclusively those of one party; hence the explorations of penalties to be assessed against those who strike is only part of the necessary inquiry.

Local governments, and to a lesser extent the state, operate as service supply monopolies within defined territorial jurisdictions. Most of their services are financed by taxes paid by a wide range of participants in the political system. The governments compete with each other or with other suppliers of public services only in a general sense, and they are expected to supply their services without interruption, barring such natural calamities as earthquake or floods. Specific programs are reduced or terminated by budgetary decisions made through the normal, constitutional channels and influenced by the lobbying of interested parties, the use of the petition initiative, or by the pressures normally associated with election politics.

The argument that employees engaged in nonessential services should be allowed to strike in support of bargaining demands, and that those in the so-called essential service functions should be granted compulsory arbitration of their interest disputes as a recompense for the denial of the right to strike, clashes with the theory of the service nature of the state and local governments. There is substantial agreement that police protection, fire suppression, and sewage disposal are crucial to the maintenance of an orderly and healthful society in modern urban communities. The corollary, however, that all other functions are nonessential and that interruptions in their performance can be tolerated is inconsistent with the view that service is the basic function of government. Are the latter services nonessential merely because some classes of persons, but not all, are benefited directly by them? A calculus that measures essentiality of a government function in terms of numbers of persons affected by its interruption cannot be accepted safely. Some persons may consider several functions to be less than essential to their personal needs, but others may find the same functions to be quite important to their welfare or gratification. Who can say with assurance that an interruption of an educational or a clinical health program has no adverse effect on the children in classes or the patients awaiting clinical care, or that it affects only those persons? Disruption in either program makes an impact on many others than those immediately involved. It also has a future effect as well as an immediate impingement. If we attempt to assess the impact of a strike in the public service, whether it is measured in terms of damage to property, loss of earnings, or injury to human well-being, we must consider many intangibles that are impossible to calculate.

If the harm to individuals that results from interruptions of government services could be calculated more precisely, there would doubtless be a strong basis to expand the theory of tort liability and to seek damages from those responsible for the injury. The student whose learning program is delayed or set back by the closing of schools might sue for damages or some alternative compensation. The person who suffers a deterioration of health, or whose earning capacity is diminished because timely health care was not available when public health care services were closed or were critically understaffed because of a labor dispute, might litigate. A workable definition of adequate proof of injury and appropriate compensation in such matters provides a significant challenge to public interest law. Some publicly owned utilities, as a public relations gesture, have compensated housewives whose refrigerated food spoiled when a strike delayed the repair of a damaged power line, but there is no known instance of a public transit system having reimbursed ticket holders for jobs missed or for added expense incurred in travel to a job when a strike stopped public transportation.

Who is at fault and, therefore, liable to bear responsibility for the interruption? Is it the employer-government or the organization of striking employees? A few scholarly attempts have been made to determine the cause of some public employee strikes, but they have focused mainly on the actions of the employee organizations involved.[40] Some strikes appear to be the result of a truculent employee organization's relentless pursuit of demands which the employer representatives believe are unreasonable. Some others, however, appear to be triggered by the stubbornness and the arbitrary attitudes and actions of public management officers. Close observation of public employee disputes has, on some occasions, produced the conclusion that public management risked a strike, hoping public reaction would focus against the employee organizations involved and tip the balance of political influence toward the incumbent managers, a political strategy in the most appropriate sense of the term. Regardless of which party is at fault or bears a share of the blame, the impact of most public employee strikes has far-reaching social and economic consequences. It is therefore important to the public interest to prevent strikes or to terminate them quickly.

Fines have been imposed on the officers as well as on the organizations for contempt of court and violation of a restraining order. The court of appeals approved a further step in 1977 when it ruled that the Pasadena school district could sue a teachers' organization for damages caused by a strike.[41] A school district may be considered the corporate representative of the citizens of the district. In California, a school district loses state aid measured by average daily pupil attendance when schools are closed by a strike. But these precedents do not cover the losses to individual students or families which result from disruption to the educational program caused by the failure of management or of organized employees to provide the service for which they are responsible. This is a subject that deserves exploration through public interest legislation as well as through legislative hearings.

Most legislation concerning employer-employee relations, and particularly that which establishes collective bargaining procedures, seeks to define both fair and unfair employment practices applicable to the employing agency as well as to the employee organizations. The central theme emphasizes bargaining in good faith by both parties to reach a settlement. A major element missing in the California government employer-employee scene is an agency or procedure that will reveal to the public accurate information as to whether all parties have negotiated in good faith and have sought fairly to resolve differences over employment policy.

There are at least two alternative methods by which to fill this gap. One is to create a state public employer-employee relations commission to judge the actions of employer-governments and employee organizations. The record of such bodies in other states and of the EERB created by the Rodda Act in California indicates, however, that the volume of transactions handled results in considerable delay in decisions. Furthermore, the conclusions are not translated into information enabling public opinion in the appropriate jurisdiction to develop and bring pressure on the contending parties. The alternative is to create bodies in the various jurisdictions composed of a balanced selection of persons that will have authority to conduct fact-finding inquiries into impasses between the employer-government and employees and report their conclusions publicly. The city of Lakewood, Colorado, has used a similar procedure for several years. Whatever method is employed, the public is affected by a work disruption. Therefore it needs accurate information about the circumstances.

IX

AN EMERGING POLICY

California has moved slowly toward a policy expressed in a series of statutes that supports a limited form of negotiation between employing governments and their employees with respect to compensation and employment conditions. Furthermore, teachers in the public schools have been authorized to negotiate concerning matters of educational policy. A philosophy of participative decision-making, distinguished from one based on the historic doctrine of exclusive governmental sovereignty, has evolved after extensive debate at each step. The process by which this policy has been produced is virtually a textbook example of the disjointed, incremental theory of decision-making propounded by Charles A. Lindblom and David Braybrooke.[1] The lack of agreement among influential groups concerning the goals to be achieved and the means to be employed supplies one explanation of this incrementalism. The state's political system provides another.

Most public employee associations were reluctant to support a concept of collective bargaining developed in the private sector, whereas the unions clamored for it. When such associations as the state employees (CSEA) and the school employees (CSEA) shifted position and called for a form of collective bargaining, they tended to visualize sets of procedures that grouped employees in types of representation units different from those the unions desired. They preferred, for example, more general units that included lower level supervisors as well as supervised employees. Unions wished to separate supervisors from other workers. The California Teachers Association was interested in creating a single, comprehensive representation unit in each teaching work force, but other groups usually sought more narrowly defined units because they were interested in multi-occupation work forces. The major associations were interested in continuing to work through state legislation to get some items of employment policy decided, but unions wished to have policies determined mainly by contract negotiations. These differences were not primarily technical or procedural; they were based on each group's calculus of its self-interest and chances for survival in the complex competition of employee relations politics. Moreover,

241

many members of associations were opposed to the philosophy and traditional practices of trade unionism.

The drive to achieve collective bargaining legislation undoubtedly was blunted for a considerable time by the existence of several procedures that gave many employees satisfactory access to employment policy-making. The civil service systems are major examples. Most were established years earlier by employee demand and were generally defended by organized employees against efforts to weaken them. High percentages of employees of state, county, and big-city forces worked under employment conditions determined in large part through civil service procedures to which they had regular access.

A more specialized example is the University of California faculty consultative system, which has been in effect since 1920. Through the academic senate and its committee systems, the faculty has participated in personnel and educational policy-making. A system of peer review has permitted faculty members a significant voice in decisions about hiring, retention, and promotion. Faculty committees have contributed influential input to tenure decisions.

The California political system also has provided the initiative petition method, discussed in previous chapters, to appeal directly to the voters. Numerous groups of organized employees have made use of this procedure. One product of the initiative, and of lobbying as well, is the requirement expressed in several county and city charters that employees be paid a rate of wage comparable to that paid for similar duties in private employment. The state and several local jurisdictions have adopted the concept by legislative action at the urging of organized workers. When it was first developed, this policy was regarded as a substitute for collective bargaining in public employment. Public salary rates were to be correlated with those negotiated in private employment through collective bargaining.

Lobbying of the legislature, governing boards, executive and key administrative officers, and various commissions has been practiced extensively and with considerable success. Most employee organizations have built up considerable staffs to perform this function.

Litigation has provided another means of access to policy decisions, and several employee organizations have used it with satisfaction to their members. Many decisions, particularly during the 1960's, have resulted in salary adjustments and legitimatization of salary setting formulas.

Collective bargaining appealed to some as a new means by which they hoped to move away from some irksome features they had encountered in existing procedures. The consequences of securing it were not clearly perceived, however. Would its adoption cause most other means of access to policy-making with which they had experience to be swept away, or would it provide an additional means? For example, would such rules as the requirement to pay prevailing rates of wage, which had been interpreted by litigation and procedures developed for its administration, be dropped or retained when collective bargaining came in? The answers to these questions were not clearly perceived by the parties involved with the issue. Reluctance to give up policies and procedures that had been utilized for several years contributed to the controversy over support of the new proposals.

In the political system, the two major parties have assisted the electoral process of choosing legislators and governors, but they have not been really significant conduits and circuit breakers for input from individuals and groups to the state policy decision process. Democratic legislators most often have sponsored bills favored by organized employees, whereas Republicans have presented those designed to prohibit strikes or to dilute some features of the Democratic-sponsored ones. But members of both parties have frequently followed other patterns, and the party organizations have seldom been in a position to punish the aberrant members.

Malapportionment of seats in the state Senate, however, long overshadowed whatever partisanship was displayed toward public employment policy matters. The apportionment formula used between 1928 and 1968 gave the representatives of rural constituencies a vehicle to block legislation urged by such urban-based groups as public employee organizations. Neither reapportionment nor resurgent party cohesiveness in the legislature completely changed the legislative situation. The two houses remained jealous of their institutional prerogatives. More significantly, they were divided on partisan lines in several sessions. The 1974 election produced the first legislature in many years in which a substantial majority of both houses were of the same party as the governor. Moreover, the active participation of employee organizations in this and the 1976 election produced the first semblance of a Democratic-employee organization coalition in state politics.

Public employer-employee relations have figured prominently in gubernatorial politics only since 1968. Governor Edmund G. Brown Sr., a Democrat, approved the George Brown Act of 1961, which recognized the right of public employees to organize, the Winton Act of 1965, which gave school employees the right to meet-and-confer with their employers, and the Meyers-Milias-Brown Act of 1968, which granted similar rights to city, county, and special district employees. He was also favorable toward state employees. A rash of local employee strikes in 1968, as well as defections within the Democratic party, contributed to his defeat for a third term and brought Ronald Reagan, a conservative Republican, to the governor's office. Reagan discouraged passage of legislation pertaining to state employment relations and established by executive order a procedure to keep control in the hands of the governor and his cabinet, a newly created institution. He clashed with employee organizations on several occasions, negotiated a settlement of the first strike in the state service, vetoed the Moscone bill that would have given the public school teachers collective bargaining, and expressed his intent to veto comparable bills if they reached his desk. His treatment of state salary matters caused the California State Employees Association to sponsor an initiative constitutional amendment to change the salary-setting procedure.

Public employer-employee relations did not become a front-rank issue for state-wide voter attention until the 1974 gubernatorial election. Senator Moscone of San Francisco and Assembly Speaker Moretti of Los Angeles sought to win support of the public employee and general labor votes for their candidacy in the Democratic primary election by their leadership of legislative drives to obtain collective bargaining legislation. Both were disappointed when Secretary of State Brown won the nomination. Brown expressed himself repeatedly in favor of comprehensive collective bargaining legislation for public employees and won financial support and endorsements from the largest public employee organizations. He next defeated in the general election Controller Flournoy, who had taken a more cautious approach to the public employment relations issue.

Brown soon took a personal role in legislative negotiations on a comprehensive statute, but backed away when senatorial opposition developed. His interest in the subject appeared to wane for a time, thereby bringing strong criticism of his administration from employee organizations who had supported his election. He approved the Rodda Act in 1975, however, which extended limited collective bargaining to school employees, and the state employees' representation bill in 1977, which gave legislative recognition of a meet-and-confer procedure for employment relations in the state government.

The relatively weak position of the major political parties over a long period of time in the state policy-making process has permitted interest groups to achieve an unusually significant status. The groups concerned with public employment issues have been remarkably evenly balanced in political influence. Significant differences concerning the preferred model of employer-employee relations have divided the employee groups, and no single coalition has been able to dominate the articulation of demands on the policy-making institutions. In sum, there has not been consensus about the tactics to be used in achieving the broadly described goal of increased participation in employment policy-making, nor has there been agreement regarding the specific objective of collective bargaining.

The local government associations, on the other hand, composed chiefly of elected officials but assisted by groups of career professional administrators, have been effective advocates of the government-employer's point of view. Their strategies have not been based on joint lobbying action, however. These organizations initially took the position that the government-employer could not share decision-making with any interest group, that employees accepted the unique conditions under which government personnel policies were made when they accepted employment. This concept was modified to a degree when state policy requiring employers to meet-and-confer with employee organizations was adopted. They continued their contention, however, that the basic features of collective bargaining developed in industrial relations were incompatible with the theory governing relationships in a governmental system. They objected to the concept of exclusive representation by organizations and argued, moreover, that individual employees should have the right to negotiate individual employment conditions if they desired. They believed that numerous areas of employment policy should be decided by elected officials, subject to ultimate voter approval. They insisted that the legislative body's authority to determine basic policy matters must be continued. Agreements reached through negotiation were to be binding upon management and employees only when adopted by the legislative body. The concept of management rights, or subjects reserved from negotiation, was expressed frequently. The local government associations also determinedly resisted the creation of a state agency having strong powers to decide representational units and to force decisions upon local elected officers.

This determination was evident when the Winton Act, presented by Assemblyman Gordon H. Winton, Jr. of Merced County at the request of the California Teachers Association, was adopted in 1965. This act also illustrates the pressures that caused groups interested in one category of public employment to push their legislation when more comprehensive bills foundered. It applied to public school employment only and wrote into the state Education Code directives that school boards meet-and-confer with employee organizations on employment matters and with certificated employees on education subjects as well. The statute was to be implemented solely by conferences between the employers and employee representatives.

The statute primarily reflected the interests of the CTA, which counted in its membership the majority of teachers in most districts throughout the state, although one feature recognized the existence of other teacher orga-

nizations, notably the American Federation of Teachers. It did not, however, make specific provision for organizations representing the support
workers, although it enabled them to meet-and-confer with the district
administration. Two considerations influenced the choice of procedure
prescribed for employer-employee negotiations. The largest district, Los
Angeles Unified, had twenty-two organizations vying to represent teachers.
The preponderance of CTA members in most districts also assured that
organization of primacy in representation if an employee council model of
negotiation were adopted. Consequently, the act required districts containing two or more teacher organizations to establish a negotiating council.
The council seats were to be allocated by the district board in proportion to
the organizations' membership. The concept was not particularly new in
public employer-employee relations. The Tennessee Valley Authority has
employed a similar plan for negotiations with skilled trades employees.
The British national government and local authorities have conducted relations through Whitley Councils for many years. The author of the California statute says that he favored the council plan as a means to delay consideration of collective bargaining, which the Federation of Teachers was
advocating.[2]

The concept and the terminology of meet-and-confer came out of the
Senate Committee on Governmental Efficiency to which the Winton Bill
was referred after passage through the Assembly. The intent evidently was
to employ unique wording and thereby to avoid the introduction of private-
sector collective bargaining by interpretation of legislative language. After
the committee substituted the phrase "meet-and-confer" for "negotiation,"
it reported the bill out with a recommendation for passage. The revision
was accepted by both houses and the bill was signed by the governor.

The Winton Act was implemented slowly, with each of the interested
parties seeking interpretations favorable to its preconceived position.
School boards believed initially that they should meet with teacher representatives or the negotiating council, but were disturbed by the Ralph
Brown Act requirement to transact their business only in public sessions.
Gradually many assigned the responsibility to the superintendent or his
representative. There was great uncertainty about the size of the councils.
Controversy over assignment of seats developed because in some districts
teachers belonged to more than one organization. The CFT was quite un-
happy with the council plan. It sought by litigation to force district boards
to conduct representation elections and to require teachers to choose their
representative. The courts ruled that the statute did not authorize this procedure.[3] The CFT also tried to persuade several district boards to receive
its demands and to by-pass the CTA-dominated council. The courts said
that the statute required employee organizations to communicate with the

board through the negotiating council, although individual teachers who were not members of an organization could negotiate with the employer directly.[4]

Revisions adopted by the legislature in its 1970 session sought to clarify the meet-and-confer concept and to make a few adjustments in procedure. It said both parties were expected to make a conscientious effort to exchange information and reach agreement. An agreement could be put in writing, but the ultimate decision was to be made by the governing board. In case a persistent disagreement arose, both parties were to meet-and-confer about a procedure to resolve the matter. If agreement were not reached, each party was to appoint a fact-finder and the two would choose a third to chair a panel which would investigate and report its conclusions. Any formal decision reached would be the responsibility of the governing board, however. The size of the negotiating councils was limited to a minimum of five and a maximum of nine members.

Both the CTA and the CFT were demanding repeal of the Winton Act by 1972 and were pushing their separate versions of collective bargaining. The nonaffiliated support employees' organization (CSEA) continued to look to the Education Code provisions governing non-certificated employees' employment conditions. The principle defender of the Winton Act was the California School Boards Association. When its president testified before the panel of specialists preparing a comprehensive employer-employee relations bill, he said:

We believe the Winton Act has served the teaching profession well. For we believe the Winton Act has enabled our schools to function with a minimum of confrontations, shutdowns, and slowdowns, which is a unique situation in a state of geographical, social, and political complexity such as California. . . . The public and school boards will not and cannot support a private-sector collective bargaining bill for public school employees because schools are essentially different in nature from private corporations.[5]

He went on to say that if a collective bargaining statute were developed, it must include:

Abolition of single-step guaranteed increment salary schedules, tenure, merit system and maximum instructional day limitations, etc. The abolition of such protections is necessary because if the ultimate power of the teacher union under the collective bargaining act is to be coercive against a board of education, it is imperative that the board of education be granted the right to hire and fire and to determine hours, conditions of work, and merit pay within the framework of the contract negotiations. School management would need this authority to be effective in the negotiations.[6]

The CSBA delegate assembly at its convention in 1973 adopted a modified position and advocated revision of the Winton Act but stopped short of supporting collective bargaining. It advocated exclusive representation, in place of the negotiating council, and called for an election procedure to determine the representative organization. The scope of meeting-and-conferring was to be limited to wages, hours, and conditions of employment, with other subjects reserved for management decision. Persistent disagreements were to be resolved by mandatory mediation or fact-finding, with recommendations to be made at a public meeting of the board. Grievances, but not interest disputes, were to be resolved by binding arbitration. Agreements were to be expressed in memorandums of understanding that were to be binding on both parties when approved by the board of education. The CSBA plan for the first time called for creation of a state agency to implement the law. It also proposed prohibition of employee strikes.[7]

In the 1973 session, the principal bills on employer-employee relations were SB 400 by Senator Moscone, applicable to the public schools, community colleges, and the two university systems, and AB 1243 by Speaker Moretti, a comprehensive plan. The Moscone bill was introduced at the request of a coalition of teacher groups, a remarkable development in itself. It was a straight collective bargaining bill. When the Moretti plan became mired in the Senate, Senator Moscone was able to muster a 21 to 17 vote approval of his bill, the minimum affirmative vote possible for passage at that stage of the session.[8] This feat is open to skeptical interpretation because the legislators anticipated that the governor would veto the bill, hence political capital could be established with employee voters by an aye vote, but without risk that the bill would actually reach the statute book. On September 28, Governor Reagan returned the bill with his statement of objections:

1. The bill ignored the differences in governance, funding, and traditions of the various types of educational institutions involved,
2. It did not outlaw strikes in the schools,
3. No management rights were specified,
4. The record of California school districts under the Winton Act was, in his judgment, superior to that of comparable institutions in states operating under collective bargaining plans.

In view of the relatively close vote in the Senate, no effort was made to override the governor's veto.

Two major and several minor bills on school employment relations appeared at the 1974 legislative session. Senator Albert Rodda, Democrat, of Sacramento introduced SB 1857, which was later supported by the school board and administrators' associations. It proposed to repeal the Winton

Act, to provide for exclusive representation but prohibit agency shop, and to recognize specified subjects for meeting-and-conferring. It also proposed to establish a five-member state commission to implement the plan. At the request of a coalition of teacher organizations, Assemblymen Alatorre, Keysor, and Berman, all Democrats of Los Angeles, introduced AB 3254, substantially the previous Moscone bill. State Superintendent Riles and Controller Flournoy, the Republican candidate for governor, announced their support of the Rodda bill in August when the Senate approved it. The teacher groups split. The San Francisco Teachers Union, the Fresno Teachers Association and the United Teachers of Los Angeles supported it, but the state-wide CTA and CFT, the School Employees Association, and the Professional Educators Group of Los Angeles opposed it.[9] Both bills failed passage.

One amendment to the Winton Act adopted at the 1974 session introduced an interesting sunshine provision. Sponsored by the California League of Women Voters and introduced by Assemblyman John Vasconcellos, Democrat of San Jose, it required the employee organizations and district governing boards to submit their initial demands and offers at a public session of the board, and it required hearings prior to the commencement of negotiations.[10]

A sheaf of employer-employee relations bills was again introduced in 1975. Senator Rodda, chairman of the Senate Education Committee, presented his SB 160, patterned on his previous SB 1857. Senator Moscone's SB 4 was amended in the Senate Education Committee to carry the provisions of his 1973 school bill. Senator Dills of Los Angeles County, chairman of the Committee on Government Organization, drafted SB 275, which was supported by advocates of the comprehensive approach to public employee bargaining. Assemblyman Berg of Sacramento introduced AB 1781 to grant collective bargaining to state and university employees.

The legislative leadership initially favored the Dills comprehensive bill and Governor Brown pushed for its passage. Agreement was not reached, however, and by the latter part of June the governor withdrew his support. From that point forward, the legislative battle became complex. The supporters of the comprehensive approach re-amended SB 4 to carry the contents of the Dills bill, but that effort proved abortive. They next took over AB 1781, but this bill was defeated in the Senate Finance Committee. Meanwhile, the Senate had approved the Rodda bill prior to the legislative recess, thereby keeping it alive. Senator Rodda sought to get the major school employer and employee groups to consent to his legislation as a start toward improved negotiating procedures. He proposed to put the plan into operation in stages, and he promised to offer amendments in 1976 to clear up any troublesome details discovered during the first implementation steps. The CSBA, ASCA, UTLA, and Superintendent Riles favored the bill from the beginning of the session. The CTA opposed it early in the session but agreed to support when the Dills bill failed. The classified employees (CSEA) supported it during part of the session but opposed it after reaching the conclusion that it was inadequate for their needs. The Professional Educators Group opposed it throughout. By the time SB 160 reached the Assembly floor, the majority caucus and leadership decided to support it. Julian Dixon of Los Angeles and John Miller of Alameda County agreed to assume leadership for its floor management. The bill passed by a 63 to 13 count and four days later the Senate gave it final passage by a vote of 25 to 7. Governor Brown signed it, although he reiterated his preference for a comprehensive statute.

The statute was scheduled to become effective on the following April 1, when the governor was expected to appoint the three members of the Educational Employee Relations Board created by it. The remainder of the act was to take effect July 1, by which time it was assumed the board would be sufficiently organized to begin hearings. The July 1 date caused some confusion because school districts were normally well advanced in considering salary and budget matters by that time. When the governor was tardy in making appointments to the EERB, implementation of the act was postponed in reality until the next fiscal year.

Two features of the legislative strategy are particularly significant. One was the use of broad language relative to features on which the contesting interest groups had been unable to reach accord. Senator Rodda stated repeatedly that the statute delegated to the EERB the responsibility to clarify numerous points by administrative rules and orders.[11] This was a clear statement that the legislature did not attempt to resolve the varying points of view, but instead passed the task to the new administrative board. The author promised, however, to sponsor amendments in the following legislative session, a pledge he was able to keep despite efforts by CSEA and others to change the original scope of the plan by their own amendments. The second strategy feature was Senator Rodda's effort to draft the bill in a manner that would make it usable later as a base from which to extend coverage to other employees. Consistent with that objective, the act was made part of the Government Code rather than the Education Code. The first strategy in particular produced ambiguities in the language; both left gaps unfilled.

One ambiguity arises from the fact that the legislation is written primarily with the problems and interests of the teaching, or certificated, employees of public schools in mind. It provides for exclusive representation of employees under circumstances that encourage creation of district-wide units of representation, an arrangement more suitable to instructional employees than to multi-occupational support workers. It uses the word "supervisors" in a context meaningful to certificated employment but ambiguous to classified worker situations. The scope of representation is limited to wages, hours, health and welfare benefits, leave and transfer policies, safety, class size, employee evaluation procedures, and grievance procedures. Support employees find the list of subjects slanted toward the certificated side.

The Rodda Act also continues an experiment in public employment relations. It carries over from the Winton Act the Vasconcellos sunshine provision, which requires initial proposals to be presented at a public meeting of the governing board and to be given a public hearing before negotiations commence.

Implementation of the Rodda Act depends basically on the ability of the district governing boards to reach agreement with the employee organizations. A district board determines the units of representation in consultation with the organizations. It recognizes the exclusive representative of each unit on request by an applicant organization, although it or a contesting organization may call for an election to determine the representative. The board and an organization may negotiate establishment of an agency shop for organization security purposes. They may also agree to final, binding arbitration of grievances arising from interpretation of a negotiated agreement.

The EERB holds hearings on complaints of unfair labor practices brought by either party and may issue cease and desist orders, but it must seek a court order to enforce its directives if they are contested. The board is not authorized to enforce agreements between two parties. It may appoint a mediator if a board and an organization reach an impasse in interest negotiations. If mediation fails to produce agreement, either party may petition for appointment of a fact-finding panel. The panel's recommendations to the parties in dispute must be made public.

The Rodda Act moves the school administrations and employee organizations a step along the path toward consultative local decision-making, but the legislature has not resolved the differences between the contending parties. Support workers' interests, for example, continue to be sufficiently different from those of the certificated employees that one of the organizations representing the former seeks vigorously to change the scope of the statute.

The Meyers-Milias-Brown Act, adopted in 1968, is another example of a statute worded vaguely because the legislature preferred to approve a partially resolved plan rather than to attempt resolution of the differences between contending parties. It demonstrates the insistence of the local employer associations that collective bargaining concepts be adapted to conform with traditional premises of local governmental home rule. It also helps us understand the pressures that caused the legislature to veer away from a comprehensive policy statement regarding public employer-employee relations.

Proposals for a comprehensive plan had bogged down when, late in the legislative session, the local government associations and the major local employee organizations reached a limited, fragile agreement. The Assembly and Senate committees primarily involved with the legislation agreed on a joint strategy that gave the appearance of bipartisan, two-house sponsorship. A bill previously adopted by the Senate was amended to carry the new package plan.[12] The Assembly approved it by a roll call count of 62 to 1, and the Senate accepted the Assembly amendments by a 23 to 13 vote on a mixed partisan split.[13] A parliamentary device seldom used in the California legislature was employed to place in the record, as a statement of legislative intent, a legislative counsel opinion and letters exchanged between two of the sponsoring legislators. The legislative counsel advised that the bill did not authorize a public employer to grant an employee organization exclusive representation privileges. This placated the employer associations. He also specified that the only type of organization a public employer could refuse to recognize was one that had none of the agency's employees on its roster or that did not have representation of members as its primary purpose. The two legislative letters said that the sponsoring committee intended to preserve the patterns of employee representation long established in this state and did not intend to authorize exclusive representation.[14] The writers sought thereby to reassure the employee associations as well as the employers.

The basic purpose of the MMB, as it became popularly known, was to get local government-employers and their employees to negotiate procedures by which to meet-and-confer on employment matters. Those drafting the statute were intent on using new language in an effort to emphasize the notion that public employment is unique, although legal analysts point out that several passages were similar to those used in the National Labor Relations Act governing private sector relations.[15] The crux of the matter was that differences between the major contending interest groups were great and that the legislature, rather than attempting to resolve them, in effect incorporated them into the statute.[16] Some attorneys and administrators have lamented the vagueness of the legislative language, but the broad phrases were pleasing to many elected officials because they provided opportunity for informal negotiation and compromise in a variety of specific situations. The prevailing view was that there would be adequate time to amend the statute if consensus developed on any of the major points concerning relationships.

Much of the statute also contained permissive language, apparently because a number of city attorneys serving general-law cities had questioned whether a city council could formally adopt employer-employee relations policies unless specifically authorized to do so. Many local officers also were not yet willing to accept state policy direction.

Local governing bodies and administrators were mandated, however, to meet-and-confer in good faith with employee representatives and to give full consideration to their presentations. After consultation, governing bodies could promulgate rules to govern such matters as procedures for resolving disputes, access by organization representatives to official work spaces, and the sharing of nonconfidential information with the organizations. The local governing bodies' formal authority to decide policies remained unchanged.

Employer recognition of organizations representing small numbers of employees in large work forces proved to be an immediate problem. Some employers adopted the differential recognition procedure developed by Los Angeles County, modeled on the plan promulgated for the federal civil service by the Kennedy Executive Order of 1962, which gave small organizations fewer privileges than those representing a large percentage of the employees. The legislature responded to the problem in 1971 by amending the MMB to authorize, but not to require, recognition of exclusive representatives chosen by a vote of the employees. This was a partial reversal of the legislative intent announced three years previously. Recognition of the right of an individual employee to represent himself was retained.

When disputes arose over the appropriateness of units of representation, the legislature directed that, in the absence of local procedures, they be submitted to the state division of conciliation. Another amendment in 1972 directed that the same action be taken in disputes over the allocation of professional employees to representational units.

Many large local government-employers developed their own procedures and boards in consultation with the organizations operating in their work forces.[17] Los Angeles County was the first and its model was copied by several other jurisdictions. It created by ordinance its own employee relations board whose membership is selected by the county governing board from a panel to which the employee organizations nominate candidates.[18] Santa Clara County chose a second model in which the personnel board was assigned responsibility to determine representation units, assisted by an experienced arbitrator acting as a hearing officer to examine proposals from management and employee organizations. Some other governing bodies chose to make selection of representation units themselves and to submit persistent disagreements to arbitration. Others, particularly those in which a general association had existed for many years, chose to recognize a single organization as the appropriate representative for the entire work force. The choice of procedures depended on the degree of activity and influence displayed by the employee organizations.

Most critics of the Meyers-Milias-Brown Act have decried the lack of a state administrative body possessing authority to act in disputes concerning representational units and recognition of exclusive representatives, and to enforce standards of fair employment practices on both the government-employers and the employee organizations. The absence of a state agency has induced several employee organizations to turn to the courts. This move has caused the trial courts to act as arbitrators. Despite the contention of some critics that the judges were less prepared than labor relations practitioners to develop a new system of public employer-employee relations, most observers have acknowledged that the courts actively supported the legislature's stated intent to encourage communication between employers and employees and to seek peaceful settlement of disputes.[19] After a time appeals have reached the court of appeals and the state Supreme Court, contributing to the case law interpreting the statute.[20]

Some court of appeals decisions have left a question concerning the basis of judgment, but the practical results have been sound and reasonable. Two examples illustrate the point. Fire Fighters Local 1014 sued to force the city of Monrovia to recognize it as the representative of the city firemen. The city recognized the general association as the representative of all its employees. The court ruled the IAFF was entitled to represent the ten firemen who were its members, but left unclear the status of an eleventh person who was not a union member. Moreover, it gave no indication of what it found wrong with the city's policy.[21] In the second case, the Madera County requirement that an organization sign fifty-one percent of the classified positions as members to win recognition as the exclusive representative was challenged by the engineers' union. The court said the requirement was unreasonable, inasmuch as it resulted in recognition of either a single organization or none.[22] Neither case produced a general ruling applicable to other jurisdictions.

Some other decisions have made significant contributions, however. One interpreted the MMB and provisions of the Los Angeles County Ordinance pertaining to scope of representation. The social workers' union contended that the subject of size of worker's case load was negotiable, but the county argued it was not, because the issue involved the level of service to be per-

formed in a function mandated by state law. The court said in the introduction to its opinion that it proposed to give broad scope to the objectives
of the MMB and to permit as much flexibility in employee-government
agency relations as a voluntary system would allow. Ruling that the subject
was bargainable, it said:

The duty to negotiate is not, by itself, a discretionary act under the circumstances.
Negotiation does not mean agreement; neither the state law nor the local ordinance
equates negotiations with compulsory collective bargaining.[23]

The state Supreme Court showed the same flexible attitude. Its first case
interpreting the MMB came in April, 1974, in a dispute between the social
workers' union and Alameda County over the union's right to represent
workers being interviewed by their supervisors regarding use of official
vehicles. County vehicles had been observed parked at the county administrative offices at the time social workers had picketed the building. The
county said the interviews were preparatory to amending the rules governing use of official cars. The union argued that disciplinary action might
result from the interviews. Hence the employees were entitled to union representation. The court cited several precedents from the National Labor
Relations Act, indicating some disinclination to accept the view that the
MMB created a new policy applicable exclusively to public employment.
The ultimate decision, however, rested on the rather narrow set of facts
involved. It found that the interviews were unusual in nature and that a
potential danger of intimidation existed, therefore it ruled in favor of the
union claim. It carefully explained that it found nothing to limit the county's right to adopt a rule against use of county vehicles for non-business
purposes.[24]

More complex issues involved arbitration of unresolved disputes, but the
city administration contended that the subjects at issue related to the necessity of functions performed by the city. The court sought guidance in preceding cases decided under the NLRA. It acknowledged that differences
existed between the public and private sector in labor relations, but observed that employers in both sectors sought to protect managerial decisions from encroachment. It observed that public policy towards the private sector in this state favored peaceful resolution of employment disputes
by arbitration, and that the city charter declared arbitration to be the most
appropriate means to resolve public employee disputes. It found that the
city charter prohibited strikes but gave city employees arbitration as a quid
pro quo. Therefore, it ruled that the four subjects at issue were arbitrable,
but some were subject to certain conditions.[25]

A third decision had even more sweeping application to local govern-

ments. It ruled that an agreement made in accordance with MMB procedures and approved by the governing board is binding on both parties.[26]
The dispute arose over procedure for interpreting data from a salary survey
which the city had agreed to conduct. The memorandum of agreement approved by the council called for payment of salaries that were above the
average computed by a survey of cities customarily used for the purpose.
When the city manager moved to implement the agreement, he computed
salaries on a class-by-class basis, with the result that some classes received
less than the average of all salaries surveyed. The employee association contended that an arithmetical average should be used, but the city rejoined
that all it had agreed to do was conduct a survey. It contended that management had a unilateral right to interpret the agreement. The Supreme
Court, with one justice dissenting, said:

We deal here with a mutually agreed covenant, a labor management contract. We
know of no case that holds that one party can impose his own interpretation upon a
two-party labor-management contract.

The majority took the position that once the council had adopted the negotiated memorandum of agreement, the remaining steps were ministerial in
nature. Justice Mosk, in his dissent, argued that the court was legislating,
not simply interpreting a contract. It seems clear from these decisions that
the court, by using private sector labor law as its guide, has moved the public sector toward similarity with the private sector model. The legislative
history of the Meyers-Milias-Brown Act indicates that the legislature had a
different intention, but it produced a vaguely worded statute, thereby in-
viting interpretation through negotiated agreements and litigation. This is
a disjointed, incremental method of determining policy.

THE MERIT SYSTEM AND COLLECTIVE BARGAINING

The relationship between the merit system of employment policy making
and collective bargaining remains unclear in the mid-1970's. Each statute
concerned with employer-employee relations, beginning with the George
Brown Act in 1961, has expressed a legislative intent to retain civil service
and merit system policies and procedures unimpaired. Neither the advocates nor the opponents of collective bargaining in the legislative skirmishes
have discussed publicly their expectations, whether the merit system is to
be retained or bargained away over time. The nonaffiliated associations,
historic supporters of the merit system civil service, appear to assume that
the procedures will be retained and collective bargaining added as a means

to negotiate compensation and working conditions. The State Employees Association has advocated the retention of the civil service section of the state constitution, but has also sought a method of negotiating with the governor and legislature on compensation. The California School Employees Association points to its historic support of the merit system for classified school workers, but vigorously seeks to expand the scope of bargaining in the Rodda Act to encompass almost all personnel matters. The state federation of labor and the union-affiliated public employee organizations, formerly concerned with civil service legislation, no longer discuss the subject in their annual legislative agenda conferences. In specific instances, they demand retention of local civil service procedures at the same time that they work to establish collective bargaining arrangements. This suggests the conclusion that they hope to retain any procedure so long as it provides them with a useful approach.

The lack of open discussion permits contending groups to avoid the political risks involved in a replacement-reform proposal. To seek outright repeal of the state constitutional article governing civil service, for example, is to run the risk of stirring the concerted opposition of those who associate this drastic reform with the return of patronage and cronyism to the public work force. Many public employees would be disturbed by this prospect and by the potential loss of the job protections associated with the existing system.

Dissatisfaction with merit system civil service administration among organized employees has arisen mainly from transactions that involve interface between the personnel staff and management or supervisors. Administrative officers have been critical of merit system insistence on broad competition, equal opportunity to compete, and conformity in decision-making with procedural rules instead of ad hoc actions. They have contended that personnel administration should be an integral part of the management apparatus. As organized employees have become more aggressive in their demands on management, the administrators have demanded greater authority to make decisions untrammeled by a third party. The strategies and claims have taken on the appearance of a political power struggle. It becomes evident that events are pushing the personnel decision-making process away from the tripartite situation, which involved interchange between employees, the personnel commissions, and public management, and toward a two party model composed of employee organizations and public management. To the extent that action is occurring, policy-making is moving from a process in which policy is expressed by rules having systemwide application to one in which it is made for sub-units within the system by two-party negotiations.

Continuance of the merit system alongside a collective bargaining system in chartered cities and counties depends in the short run on local political leaders' attitudes toward the merit system. Most city and county charters allocate specific duties to a civil service commission or a personnel board, and these cannot be altered unless the local electorate approves charter amendments. Sacramento County, for example, amended its charter language sufficiently to enable the personnel commission to delegate the classification function to management, subject to the commission's general policy review.

The experiences of Los Angeles County and the city of Los Angeles offer different examples of how the relationship between the merit system personnel administration and the collective bargaining system may develop. Both governments have operated under charters that create quasi-independent civil service commissions and both have adopted limited collective bargaining procedures by ordinance. Both have extensive histories of informal relationships between management, the civil service commission, and employee organizations. Differences in government structure and in attitudes of elected officials tend to explain their divergent experiences.

The county is governed by a five-member board, each member of which is elected from a district populated by more than a million persons. Each exercises general authority over several departments, but the board as a whole votes the compensation, benefits, and hours for the eighty-thousand employees.[27] The board is assisted by a chief administrative officer (CAO) whose staff prepares the county budget for board consideration. Employee organizations deal actively with board members and participate heavily in supervisorial elections. The three-member Civil Service Commission, appointed by the board for six-year overlapping terms, is required by the charter to hear appeals and to establish rules governing examinations, classification, and performance evaluations.

The first step toward revision of the county personnel program began in 1964 when the central management staff persuaded the board to appoint a large Citizens Economy and Efficiency Commission (CEEC) to advise county management and to provide a blue ribbon body to lend support for voter education regarding charter revision.

A strike by the county social workers in 1966, the first in the county's history, suddenly focused attention on the personnel decision processes. The board agreed to meet-and-confer with the union and put the agreement in writing. A two track attack on the employer-employee relations situation began to develop. One was an endeavor to pull the personnel program into the central management orbit; the other sought to relieve the pressure on the board members for decisions on employee relations. These efforts were combined in a proposal by the CEEC that gained the supervisors' support.

Changes in board membership had already reduced supervisorial support of the merit system from the level shown for many years. Opposition to the proposal was not organized and the voters approved it. All county personnel functions were combined in a new department of personnel, to be headed by a personnel officer (PO) appointed by the Civil Service Commission, but to report both to the board and to the commission. Compensation analysis and classification administration were combined under the PO, who was instructed to present pay recommendations directly to the board rather than via the CAO. The commission retained rule making and appeals hearing functions, but delegated responsibility for other personnel activities to the PO. The incumbent personnel officer was highly trusted by the board members because he had been the executive officer for the Board of Supervisors prior to this appointment. Previous heads of the civil service program had been career professionals in personnel administration and had not been closely associated with the elected board members.

A proposed employee relations ordinance drafted by the CAO and PO aimed to keep the decision-making authority in administrative hands, but the board, under employee organization pressure, rejected it. The board then appointed a committee of three labor relations attorneys, experienced with National Labor Relations Board procedures, to draft an ordinance. The committee proposed that a County Employee Relations Committee (ERCOM) be created to determine representation units and to adjudicate charges of unfair labor practices. The board adopted this plan in September, 1968, substantially without changes. The SEIU and AFSCME strongly supported the plan, the craft unions supported it without enthusiasm, but the County Employees Association opposed it and filed suit alleging that the ordinance conflicted with the Meyers-Milias-Brown Act. The trial court sustained the ordinance.

The county's personnel program was restructured further when the supervisors designated the personnel officer as the county employee relations officer and established an employee relations unit within the personnel department. In practice, the PO consults with the supervisors and the CAO informally before negotiating with employee representatives for the large number of bargaining units created.[28] The ERCOM certified forty units, and in the first year twenty-one memorandums of agreement were signed, covering thirty-four units and thirty-one thousand employees. Fifty units were certified by July, 1975, to represent seventy-six thousand employees or ninety-three percent of the work force. Nineteen organizations represented one or more units.[29]

The new plan centralized the management structure and changed the role of the department heads. These officers had long enjoyed considerable authority, and several had negotiated informally with employee organizations. Many routinely sought to outmaneuver the CAO on budget and organization matters by appealing to board members. Most had sought to wrest as much control of personnel decisions from the Civil Service Commission and its staff as possible, despite an explicitly worded charter section on civil service. Under the new plan, the county personnel officer became the focal point of decision-making on classification, compensation, and employee relations. Department heads were to be consulted prior to negotiations but were not to be direct participants in that decision process. The changes also caused the CAO to share pre-eminence in the administrative hierarchy with the personnel officer. When the personnel officer retired, however, the board of supervisors appointed the CAO the titular head of the personnel office. A broader reorganization, proposed by an independent citizen panel sponsored by the Los Angeles County Bar Association but defeated in 1976, would have created an elected county executive to head the county administration.[30] This plan would have diminished still further the bureaucratic power of the department heads, the chief administrative officer, and the personnel officer.

Relationships between the civil service and employee relations systems became tense in 1971, when the ERCOM directed the county engineer to reevaluate an employee to whom he had given a low promotion rating because of union activity. The charter assigned performance evaluation and promotion procedures to the personnel officer and the Civil Service Commission, but ERCOM concluded that the issue in this case involved an unfair labor practice. The county management prevailed in its refusal to abide by the ERCOM order because the commission had neither enforcement power nor authority to sue for compliance. Two ERCOM members resigned in protest.[31] This dispute highlighted the fact that the 1967 charter revision had transformed the civil service from a quasi-independent system into a management-directed program. The dispute largely concerned the definition of management rights, although the top management officers chose to portray their position as being protective of the Civil Service Commission's rule-making authority. Four additional ERCOM orders, resisted by county management between 1971 and 1974, even more clearly involved the definition of management rights, a term recognized but not fully defined in the ordinance. County management complied voluntarily in one instance and moved in two others only after employee organizations won a court ruling.[32]

The Board of Supervisors turned to the CEEC for a recommendation, and that body responded with a complex plan for a charter amendment to combine the functions of ERCOM and CSC under a new five-member commission whose members were to be experienced in employee relations. This commission was to be given two staffs, one for employee relations, and one to implement personnel's authority for rule-making and to monitor county management's conformity with the merit principle. The personnel officer would be the agent of the Board of Supervisors and would be relieved of responsibilities with the Civil Service Commission. The task force that produced the plan was pessimistic about giving the CSC and ERCOM concurrent jurisdiction over matters in which their interests overlapped. It chose to give the merit system little more than lip service when it proposed to place the program in an agency to be headed by a board composed entirely of persons having backgrounds in labor relations rather than in merit system operations. This overly complex structural change was not approved. Amendments to the employee relations ordinance have strengthened the ERCOM somewhat, and the parties are adjusting to the relationships involved.

The experience of the city of Los Angeles is dissimilar to that of the county. Its structure is different and the relationships within the structure have developed other patterns. The city is governed by a mayor elected at large and by a council composed of fifteen members elected by districts. A series of citizen commissions, appointed by the mayor for fixed terms, exercises some degree of supervisory authority over most departments. They formerly selected department heads, but a series of charter amendments reduced the authority of most commissions and gave the mayor authority to appoint the chief officers. The water and power, airport, and harbor departments, which manage huge proprietary undertakings, set the salaries for their classified personnel until 1977, when the authority was transferred to the mayor and council.

The chief administrative office, which has evolved from a bureau of efficiency created by the charter in 1924, serves both the mayor and council on budget and management matters. The CAO has specific charter authority and responsibilities that give the office considerable independence. Moreover, incumbents have held office for long periods of time and have established a considerable bureaucratic power base. The personnel committee of the council, composed of three members, is responsive to employee demands, and for many years has exercised significant influence over salaries and employment conditions in the council-controlled departments. It has consistently shown a willingness to implement the charter directive that the city pay at least the prevailing rate of pay to all classes of jobs that can be compared with private employment.

The five-member Civil Service Commission, appointed by the mayor and confirmed by the council, exercises rule-making authority over examinations, classification, appeals, and several other matters, and selects the manager of the personnel department, who enjoys considerable charter-granted authority. Reforms that followed a serious scandal in several city departments, including civil service, in the 1930's intensified support for professional personnel administration consistent with the civil service pattern and this tradition has continued into the 1970's. Three institutions, therefore, hold relatively strong positions. The personnel department carries out its charter assigned functions, the CAO prepares salary and budget recommendations, and the personnel committee provides the main channel for employee organization input regarding wages, hours, and conditions of employment.

Passage of the county's employee relations ordinance and the state's Meyers-Milias-Brown Act in 1968 triggered the first revision of the city program. The CAO prepared and the council accepted a plan to recognize employee organizations informally and to consult them regarding a formal employee relations policy that could be established by ordinance. After lengthy discussions with seventeen organizations, the CAO proposed in November, 1969, an ordinance which provided procedures for determining bargaining units, established a meet-and-confer policy, authorized written memorandums of understanding, created a five-member Employee Relations Board (ERB), and permitted the city's management representative to agree with employee organizations on a choice of impasse procedures. The CAO was to represent the management. The council considered the proposal for more than a year and made two changes, requiring binding arbitration of grievances and certification of an organization as a bargaining representative by simple majority of those voting at a unit election, before adopting it in January, 1971.[33] Most functions performed by the personnel department were exempted from the meet-and-confer procedure.

During the first three years employee relations continued to be determined informally, often through council channels. Most employee organizations were content to work through the personnel committee rather than to negotiate with the CAO, which was inclined to protect the city budget. Mayor Yorty did not exhibit strong interest in employee relations or in the merit system. The first bargaining unit elections were not decided until August, 1972, and no memorandums of understanding were negotiated until after the mayoral election was concluded the following year.

The new mayor, Tom Bradley, who had received substantial city employee organization support, showed an active interest in employee relations. The ordinance was amended to bring all wage-setting departments except water and power under the central negotiation system. The mayor issued an executive order directing the city administration to sign only one memorandum with an employee organization, eliminating the practice in which department heads negotiated some subjects independent of the CAO. He later appointed a citizens' labor-management advisory committee to assist in implementing the ordinance, signalling his desire to push the negotiation process. This desire was assisted when Governor Reagan appointed to a judgeship Councilman Billy Mills, the active and influential chairman of the council's personnel committee, thereby removing him from the city personnel policy system. Mills' replacement as chairman, Robert J. Stevenson, had been recently re-elected with heavy employee organization support and favored putting the ordinance into effect. A management team, composed of the mayor, the CAO and, the chairmen of the council personnel and finance committees met regularly thereafter to determine guidelines for management's negotiations with employee organizations. By July, 1974, the ERB had certified twenty-six bargaining units to represent approximately eighty percent of the city employees, and shortly after that the first memorandum of understanding was presented to the council and ratified. The number of bargaining units was expanded to forty by July, 1976.

When Mayor Bradley had taken office, he followed the precedent of the previous thirty-five years and called for the resignation of all incumbent city commissioners. He appointed four new civil service commissioners after verifying their willingness to support the merit system. Although the mayor frequently has transmitted his views on personnel policy matters to the commissioners, he has shown no disposition to weaken the personnel department. The department and commission continue their authority over classification, examinations, promotions, and discipline as allocated them by the city charter. The employee relations ordinance authorizes the manager of the personnel department to advise the ERB on matters concerning unit determination, a subject closely related to classification, to advise the employee relations staffs of the salary-setting departments, and to conduct training in employee relations in the various departments. Thus far, the city of Los Angeles appears to be an example of compatible cooperation between the traditional merit and civil service systems and a limited collective bargaining system operating within the framework of the Meyers-Milias-Brown Act.

The experience of the school districts and their classified employees with the development of the Rodda Act (SB 160) illustrates some of the problems encountered in adjusting merit system administration and collective bargaining in governments operating under general state law, although several aspects of the bill's history are unique to the schools. Senator Rodda had relied for his support base on an interest group mainly concerned with certificated school employees. Those groups had been most aggressive politically and in employer-employee relations. The classified employees were accustomed, however, to policies and practices more closely comparable with those in city, county, or state governments. Those in approximately one hundred districts, including many of the larger units, were governed by a merit system defined in the Education Code and administered by quasi-independent commissions. A few other districts had established a classified merit system program, but had not elected to bring themselves under the Education Code provisions. Others had combined the administration of programs for classified and certificated employees in a single office that reported to the district superintendent. In many small districts, the board of education had determined all personnel policies with a minimum of administrative assistance.

During the discussion stage of developing the Rodda act, the newly formed California School Personnel Commissioners Association sought to clarify the role intended for merit system administrations. Although the Senator was supportive of the merit system concept, he professed difficulty in fitting that program into a bill cast largely to meet conditions pertaining to certificated employees. He attempted to provide continuance of the merit system for classified employees by inserting the following language:

Nothing contained herein shall be deemed to supersede other provisions of the Education Code and the rules and regulations of public school employers which establish and regulate tenure or a merit or civil service system or which provide for other methods of administering employer-employee relations, so long as the rules and regulations or other methods of the public school employer *do not conflict with* lawful collective agreements [emphasis added].[34]

The language used appears to preserve the merit system and to confine the collective negotiations to prescribed subject areas, but the proviso regarding conflict with lawful collective agreements opens a door to uncharted interpretation by the Educational Employee Relations Board and the courts. Section 3543.2 of the act limits the scope of representation by recognized employee organizations to matters of wages, hours, and other terms and conditions of employment, which are defined to include leave and transfer policies, safety conditions of employment, procedures for evaluating employees, organization security, and grievance procedures. The statute appears to affect three subjects for which the personnel commissions in merit system districts have been assigned responsibility: salary studies and recommendations, procedures for evaluating employees, and pro-

cedures governing leaves. The commissions had previously collected and
analyzed salary data and had recommended pay formulas to the district
boards. The latter had final authority to determine pay but could not alter
the salary relationships between classes of employees established by the
commissions. Procedures for evaluating classified employees' performance
and granting leaves of absence had been subject to commission rules.

The principal tests of the continuance of the merit system administration coequally with collective negotiation appear to rest on the decisions of
the Educational Employee Relations Board regarding complaints of unfair
labor practice filed by employee organizations against districts' management. They will also rest on future action by the legislature, under pressure
from employee organizations to expand the scope of representation. The
previous experience of the first EERB members appeared to indicate that
the board would act vigorously to assure the pre-eminence of the bargaining process. The chairman, a labor relations law specialist and former
member of the Los Angeles County ERCOM, had written strong protests
against decisions giving the Civil Service Commission jurisdiction over matters sought by ERCOM. The second member came from the field staff of
the National Labor Relations Board, and the third was a former legislator
and instructor. Moreover, Governor Brown had repeatedly indicated his
strong support of collective bargaining and his reserve toward the merit
system.

Portents of future legislative efforts began to appear almost simultaneously with the inauguration of the Rodda Act. Rumors circulated that
school boards would attempt to overload and financially embarrass the
EERB by refusing to recognize employee organizations and by calling for
representation elections. It was said that many would challenge employees'
claims to bargain on subjects not clearly specified in the statute, thereby
forcing the organizations to go to court. The CSEA responded by sponsoring AB 3003, which was introduced by Julian Dixon of Los Angeles, the
majority caucus chairman and floor manager for SB 160 in the 1975 session, to expand the scope of bargaining to include any subject on which the
district board and an employee organization might reach agreement. The
CSEA maximized its lobbying effort by convening its annual membership
meeting in Sacramento during the week the Assembly considered the bill.
The bill received an overwhelming vote in the lower house but was defeated in the Senate Industrial Relations Committee due mainly to Senator
Rodda's opposition, aided by the School Personnel Commissioners Association, the Association of School Administrators, and independent classified
school employee groups working independently and not as a coalition. The
CSEA continued to express great discontent with the Rodda Act and re-

turned to the 1977 legislative session with a revised bill which failed passage.

Employer-employee relations in the state government have developed in a context in which the quasi-independent personnel board has occupied a central position in personnel matters, aided by its status as a constitutional agency. Its responsibilities for recommending salary rates to the governor and legislature have rested on legislation, however. The Meyers-Milias-Brown Act exempted the state civil service from its provisions, leaving the original Brown Act of 1961 as the base for state policy toward employee relations. Anticipating further legislation, an Assembly resolution requested the personnel board and the governing bodies of the two university systems to recommend plans.[35]

The board, a majority of whose members were appointees of the retiring governor, Pat Brown, presented a two-part plan after conducting hearings attended by representatives of eleven employee organizations, a taxpayers' association, and the state administration.[36] It concluded that no single management office or agency in state government was constitutionally capable of making an agreement with employee representatives on such matters as salaries, benefits, or hours of work. The board, the governor, and the legislature each had responsibilities for these matters. Final decisions were made through the legislative process. The board suggested, therefore, that the three institutions continue to receive proposals from all fifty recognized employee organizations. It proposed, however, that the appointing authority in each agency and a representative of a majority of the employees negotiate on such matters as work environment conditions, tours of duty, shift assignments, vacation schedules, health and safety practices, transfer policies, rest periods, and service to employee organizations. It concluded that neither it nor the Department of Industrial Relations could perform adequately the tasks required to develop and enforce employment relations among the departments. Therefore it proposed that a three-member state Employment Relations Commission be created and given authority to establish negotiating units in any department when petitioned by an employee organization.

In the meantime, Reagan succeeded Brown in the governorship and he indicated he wished to experiment with policy through an executive order. He felt this procedure permitted greater flexibility than legislation. He designated the Secretary of the Agriculture and Services Agency, a member of the cabinet, to be his representative in conferring formally with employee organization agents concerning salaries and benefits.[37] He emphasized, however, that he did not intend to alter the relationship on salary-setting between the personnel board and the employee organizations, or between the governor and the legislature. He directed his representative to meet-

and-confer in good faith with employee representatives to reach a mutual understanding regarding the need for and amount of general salary adjustment, the total amount of special inequity salary adjustments, and general employee benefits. He instructed him not to discuss merit and related matters, the state's mission, methods and number of employees required to conduct state programs, or working conditions. The SPB criteria for recognizing employee organizations was to be used. If the secretary and an organization reached agreement, a memorandum of understanding was to be prepared, but the governor's representative must await cabinet approval before affixing his signature. Employee representatives were to provide assurance that their organization's members accepted the terms. If agreement were not reached, the secretary was to prepare a memorandum summarizing the areas of disagreement and make it available to all interested parties and individuals.

A test of the administration's policy and procedures developed in the autumn of 1971 when hydroelectric and maintenance employees of the Department of Water Resources began meeting with the department management on several grievances. The subject of pay was discussed but not resolved. In April, the workers voted to strike. After further discussion, the governor's representative, the department director, and the CSEA general manager signed a memorandum expressing their dissatisfaction with the executive order as it then existed and their desire to change it. The state agreed that the Department of Finance would inform the CSEA in advance of public announcement the amount of funds available for these workers' salary adjustments, and the governor would urge the SPB to recognize the urgency of the adjustments. This was the first memorandum of understanding produced in this state's employer-employee relations.[38]

The employees became greatly disturbed, however, when the SPB told them two weeks later it could make no decision on salaries prior to a public hearing set for June 14, and that the governor had not requested them to consider the water resources workers separately from other state employees. Determined to force action, the CSEA called a strike, the state government's first, to begin May 22. The water employees remained out five days, the maximum absence permitted by state rules without incurring dismissal for unauthorized absence. The department, in an effort to prevent repetition of the strike after one day back at work, sought to extract written promises that the workers would not strike again. The CSEA contacted the governor's representative and the department head who developed and signed a second memorandum in which the department agreed to desist from reprisals. A third memorandum outlined a procedure for meeting-and-conferring on matters within the department's jurisdiction. Further discussions were postponed until after the election, in which the CSEA was presenting an initiative constitutional amendment to revise the state's salary-setting procedures.

The governor made a change in representatives shortly after the election and announced a new meet-and-confer policy applicable to department relations. The results of meet-and-confer sessions were no longer to be issued as a signed memorandum. They were to be put in writing and issued as departmental policy directives. Each director was to inform the governor's representative of the subject under consideration prior to the meeting and also before a directive was issued.[39] The water resources department moved to conform, but the CSEA filed suit, contending that the new policy violated the agreement signed in May. The state's rejoinder was: (1) the strike was illegal, (2) the state cannot be bound by a labor agreement, and (3) it can adopt a change of policy unilaterally. The compensation dispute was settled in fact, however, by action of the State Personnel Department and the Board of Control in adjusting the wage rates of the water employees.[40]

The dispute motivated state employees to push harder for collective bargaining legislation, although the administration expressed strong opposition to the principal comprehensive bill insofar as it applied to state employees.[41] The bill expired in the Senate Finance Committee.

During the next legislative session a new compensation concept, known as total equivalent compensation, was adopted after intensive discussions between the governor's representatives, CSEA, and eleven other organizations.[42] This plan was based on the principle that salaries and benefits paid by the state would be equivalent to those paid by private employers and other public jurisdictions. Benefits were to be calculated and added to wages to provide a sum of total compensation.

Efforts to produce legislation giving state employees' collective bargaining rights continued without results. The SPB, a majority of whose members were now Reagan appointees, contributed an interesting set of recommendations. It urged that merit employment, standards of service, organization, work technology, and staffing levels be excluded from bargaining. Furthermore, it asked that protections to preclude "subtle erosion of the merit principle be built into any statute adopted." It recommended that the legislature prescribe five occupational bargaining units composed of (1) office, (2) patient care and institutional, (3) mechanical and trades, (4) professional and technical, and (5) safety, and two composed of blue and white collar supervisors respectively. Managerial and confidential employees would not be granted bargaining rights. It made no recommendation concerning the right to strike or to go to arbitration.[43] Governor Brown, the incoming governor, gave employee relations a high priority on his administration's agenda. He appointed a special assistant to work on the subject and took a direct part in trying to develop a consensus in support of the comprehensive plan set forth in SB 275. Legislative negotiations collapsed toward the end of the summer. In October, the governor issued an executive order creating an Office of Employee Relations in his staff and assigned it duties similar to those Governor Reagan had given a cabinet officer. He chose a former administrative officer of the CSEA as head of the unit. In the executive order, however, the governor indicated he did not intend to modify the role of the personnel board in reporting to the governor and legislature.

The party in opposition to the governor speculated that Brown might establish some form of collective bargaining by executive order, since legislation had failed, and they began to put up roadblocks against this possibility. Senator John Stull requested an opinion from the legislative counsel as to whether the governor could order exclusive recognition of employee organizations, agency shop provisions, and bargaining procedures differing from those authorized in existing legislation. Counsel advised that the George Brown Act of 1961 governed state policy on the subject until new legislation was adopted. The Republican minority leader asked the legislative analyst to comment on the potential costs of a bill that proposed to give state employees collective bargaining. The latter replied that the significant costs of collective bargaining, in his judgment, were not the dollars spent in administration of the system but the less tangible costs which resulted from the transfer of authority from the legislature, where it then resided, to the executive branch. He cited the recent police strike in San Francisco, in which the mayor had assumed authority to make an agreement with the employee representatives. The analyst, a professional economist who had served the legislature for twenty-six years, expressed a preference for the existing policy, in which the state strove to maintain parity with the total compensation paid for similar work in the private sector.[44] The legislature, apparently mindful of adverse public reaction to the San Francisco police strike, took no action on collective bargaining proposals in the 1976 session.

At the close of its 1977 meeting, the legislature adopted a State Employer-Employee Relations Act which provides a limited form of collective bargaining for state employees, to become effective in 1978.[45] Coverage of university employees had been dropped earlier because of continuing opposition in that area. Changes in wording relative to maintenance of membership and units of representation brought support from the state labor federation. The CSEA had been a principal supporter throughout. The plan adopted is similar in many respects to the MMB and Rodda Acts. It limits the scope of bargaining to wages, hours, and conditions of employment, and it recognizes the governor as the state's representative in meet-and-confer sessions with employee agents. Negotiations are to be completed before the legislature adopts the annual budget. Agreements are to be put in writing and submitted to the legislature for consideration. A section that surely will require interpretation says that negotiated agreements supersede statutory sections with which they conflict, although legislative action is required to amend legislation formally. Appropriations to implement any agreement depend on legislative action on the budget.

The act expands to five the membership of the EERB created by the Rodda Act for school affairs, reconstitutes it as a Public Employment Relations Board, and extends its authority to state employee relations. The PERB is authorized to establish procedures for granting exclusive recognition to employee organizations, to determine appropriate units for representation, subject to limited judicial review, and to appoint mediators. It is also to hear charges of unfair labor practices and to issue cease and desist orders. When an exclusive representative is chosen, the personnel board's responsibility to recommend salary ranges for employees in that unit ceases. The SPB is also relieved of responsibility to recommend annually to the legislature the total compensation of civil servants. An exclusive representative may negotiate a plan for maintenance of membership. Earlier drafts of a plan were dropped in favor of negotiated arrangements. Supervisory employees are authorized to be represented in their own unit of representation. Law enforcement employees may join organizations of their choice, but are limited to those composed of like employees.

Several institutional arrangements were considered during the course of legislative deliberations but were discarded or modified. At one point, the State Personnel Board was to be assigned responsibility to enact rules governing employer-employee relations after meeting-and-conferring with employee organizations. The State Conciliation Service was to mediate disputes over appropriateness of representation units. These arrangements were dropped in favor of reconstitution of the two-year old EERB. The SPB is to retain its role of administering the merit system of personnel administration specified in the state constitution. Also at one point, the bill declared a memorandum of agreement to be determinative without further legislative action. This was modified to reassert legislative prerogatives to pass upon changes in legislation, a significant point for the theory of separation of powers in state government.

Each of the several statutes pertaining to employer-employee relations recognizes exclusive representation of employees, in units of common interest, by organizations chosen by the employees concerned. The scope of bargaining remains limited largely to compensation, hours, and conditions of employment within the work units. Legislative bodies retain their basic authority to determine appropriations and thereby decide the distribution of budget funds between compensation of personnel, public works, equipment, and services to the public. The state act is the first to express the expectation that negotiations be completed within the time frame set by the annual budgeting process established by the state constitution.

The state's policy with respect to employee relations, as it has emerged over a sixteen-year period, both reflects and produces a politicization of the entire public employment policy-making process. During the era in which the merit civil service system provided the dominant policy-making process, employment policy was determined mainly within the bureaucracy. Neither the general public nor interest groups outside the bureaucracy were much aware of the transactions. They took little part. Extensive efforts were made during that era to develop and administer formulas to compute employee compensation. Dissatisfaction on the part of some categories of employees with the results of these formulas, plus friction arising from reactions to supervisor and management attitudes and decisions, produced increasingly aggressive strategies by employee organizations. The public was made aware of the unrest by a variety of events. Stepped up election and lobby action by employee organizations made employer-employee relations a very visible issue in local and state politics at a time when group competition for public funds was made more volatile by inflation and slowed economic growth throughout the state and nation. The politicization also coincided with increased concern about expenditures in support of candidates and ballot measures for the purpose of influencing decisions by legislative and executive officers. Some organized public employees have achieved recognition as major actors in a political scene in which, historically, their kind has played minor roles or no part at all. Like most new arrivals to prominence in the political arena, they will be challenged repeatedly by others accustomed to prominence or by others desiring to achieve it. Moreover, numerous groups will continue to compete vigorously to represent clusters of civil servants who have separate values and goals with reference to public employment issues. Organized civil servants do not constitute a unitary force.

NOTES

I: INTRODUCTION

1. New York, Governor's Commission on Public Employee Relations, *Final Report,* 1966. The statute adopted, known as the Taylor Act, followed closely the terms of the report. It was opposed by the AFL-CIO. See AFL-CIO, *Proceedings of the Seventh Constitutional Convention,* vol. 1 (1967), pp. 609-612.

2. James G. March and Herbert A. Simon, *Organizations* (New York: John Wiley & Sons, 1963). This was a particularly influential treatment of the theory of administrative organizations. An extensive literature has been developed since its publication.

3. David Easton, *A Systems Analysis of Political Life* (New York: John Wiley & Sons, 1965).

4. V. O. Key, Jr., *Southern Politics in State and Nation* (New York: Alfred A. Knopf, 1949); V. O. Key, Jr., *American State Politics: an Introduction* (New York: Alfred A. Knopf, 1956). Key's studies strongly influenced the study of American politics, particularly states' politics, for several years.

5. Three examples of literature illustrating this approach are: Thomas R. Dye, *Politics, Economics, and the Public: Policy Outcomes in the American States* (Chicago: Rand McNally & Co., 1966); Herbert Jacob and Kenneth N. Vines, eds., *Politics in the American States* (Boston: Little, Brown & Co., 1971); Thad Beyle and J. Oliver Williams, eds., *The American Governor in Behavioral Perspective* (New York: Harper & Row, 1972).

6. Ira Sharkansky, *Spending in the American States* (Chicago: Rand McNally, 1968); Ira Sharkansky, *Regionalism in American Politics* (Indianapolis: Bobbs-Merrill, 1970); Thomas R. Dye, *Politics, Economics, and the Public.*

7. Nicholas A. Masters, Robert H. Salisbury, and Thomas H. Eliot, *State Politics and the Public Schools* (New York: Alfred A. Knopf, 1964).

8. When the Brookings Institution, with the support of a Ford Foundation grant, studied the impact of collective bargaining on local governments, it divided the project into segments and assigned each segment to a small group of research specialists. Each group published the results of its studies. Legal aspects were reported by Harry H. Wellington and Ralph K. Winter, Jr., *The Unions and the Cities* (Washington, D.C.: The Brookings Institution, 1971). Unionism and employee organizations were studied by Jack Stieber, *Public Employee Unionism: Structure, Growth, Policy* (Washington, D.C.: Brookings Institution, 1973). Management aspects were examined by a sampling process and reported by David T. Stanley, *Managing Local Government under Union Pressure* (Washington, D.C.: Brookings Institution, 1972).

Selected examples of case studies in the subject of public employer-employee relations that focus on one city or a facet of experience in one state are: Raymond D. Horton, *Municipal Labor Relations in New York City: Lessons of the Lindsay-Wagner Years* (New York: Praeger, 1973); Sterling D. Spero and John W. Capozzola, *The Urban Community and its Unionized Bureaucracies: Pressure Politics in Local Government Labor Relations* (New York: Dunellen Press, 1973); Emma Schweppe, *The Firemen's and Patrolmen's Unions in the City of New York* (New York: King's Crown Press, 1948); Byron Yaffe and Howard Goldblatt, *Factfinding and Public Employment Disputes in New York State* (Ithaca: New York State School of Industrial and Labor Relations, 1971).

9. Duane Lockard, *The Politics of State and Local Government* (New York: Macmillan Co., 1969).

10. U.S. Department of Commerce, Bureau of the Census, "Compendium of Public Employment," *1972 Census of Governments, Public Employment,* vol. 3, no. 2, p. 22.

11. *Ibid.*

12. International City Management Association, Urban Data Service, *Reports* (July 1971), p. 2.

13. Charles A. Lindblom, "The Science of 'Muddling Through,'" *Public Administration Review,* vol. 19, no. 2 (Spring 1959), pp. 79-88; David Braybrooke and Charles E. Lindblom, *A Strategy of Decision: Policy Evaluation as a Social Process* (New York: Free Press of Glencoe, 1963).

14. Braybrooke and Lindblom, *A Strategy of Decision.*

15. *Ibid.*

16. *Ibid.,* p. 108

17. *Ibid.,* p. 73.

18. *Ibid.,* p. 78.

19. Frederick C. Mosher, *Democracy and the Public Service* (New York: Oxford University Press, 1968). Paul P. Van Riper also discusses this theme in chapter 17 of his *History of the United States Civil Service* (White Plains and Evanston: Row, Peterson and Co., 1958).

II: PUBLIC EMPLOYEE ORGANIZATIONS — THE ASSOCIATIONS

1. A questionnaire sent out by the Bureau of Governmental Research, University of California, Los Angeles, 1961. Not published. See also California, Department of Industrial Relations, Division of Labor Statistics and Research, *Independent State and Local Public Employee Associations in California* (1963).

2. U.S. Department of Labor, Bureau of Labor Statistics Regional Office and California Human Resources Agency, Division of Labor Statistics and Research, *Independent State and Local Public Employee Associations in California* (1968).

3. Data drawn from a questionnaire circulated to council-manager cities by the International City Managers Association in 1966. Information from this questionnaire appeared in Winston W. Crouch, *Employer-Employee Relations in Council-Manager Cities* (Chicago: International City Managers Association, 1968).

4. Grace M. E. Kenilworth, in *Los Angeles County Employee,* October 1941, p. 5. This paper is published by the Los Angeles County Employees Association.

5. *Los Angeles County Employee,* June 1939, p. 4.

6. Prior to 1944, the Los Angeles County Civil Service Commission did not isolate

the figures for full-time employees from those of part-time and seasonal workers. Since the full-time, permanent employees were the primary base of LACEA membership, a meaningful percentage figure could be computed only for the years in which data on full-time employees was available.

7. *Los Angeles County Employee,* November 1952, p. 12.

8. Walker v. County of Los Angeles, 55 C2d 626; 361 P2d 247 (1961). For a review of the prevailing rate of wage development see, Town Hall, *Pay Policies for Public Personnel: A Report of the Municipal and County Government Section* (Los Angeles: 1961).

9. *California Public Employee Relations (CPER),* no. 1 (February 1969), pp. A-20, B-1.

10. *CPER,* no. 2 (August 1969), pp. 24-26.

11. *Ibid.,* no. 9 (June 1971), pp. 30, 65-67.

12. *Los Angeles Times,* 13 September 1971.

13. *Los Angeles County Employee,* 1 August 1974.

14. California Department of Industrial Relations, *op. cit.* (1963).

15. *CPER,* no. 16 (March 1973), pp. 28-29, 34.

16. Bureau of National Affairs, Inc., *Government Employee Relations Report* (GERR), no. 491 (18 February 1973), p. B-15.

17. *GERR,* no. 496 (26 March 1973), p. B-17.

18. *CPER,* no. 5 (May 1970), p. 47.

19. *Ibid.,* no. 2 (August 1969), p. 33.

20. *Ibid.,* no. 3 (November 1969), p. 53.

21. *All-City Employees Association Handbook* (Los Angeles: 1957).

22. Bill Boyarsky, *Los Angeles Times,* 31 January 1971, Section B.

23. Sanders v. City of Los Angeles, 252 CA2d 488, 60 Cal. Rptr. 539 (1967). Sanders v. City of Los Angeles, 3 C3d 252, 475 P2d 201 (1970). *CPER,* no. 9 (June 1971), pp. 11-15.

24. *El Pueblo* (ACEA Magazine), May 1965, September 1966.

25. Robert Rawitch, *Los Angeles Times,* 15 January 1972.

26. *CPER,* no. 16 (March 1973), p. 33.

27. *Los Angeles Times,* 7 August, 8 August, 18 September 1971.

28. *CPER,* no. 16 (March 1973), p. 33.

29. California Legislature, Assembly Interim Committee on Industrial Relations, *Collective Bargaining for Public Employees* (1960); U.S. Department of Labor, *op. cit.* (1968).

30. Interview between Richard Harris, Research Assistant, Bureau of Governmental Research, UCLA, and Granville DeMerritt, Executive Secretary of the Civil Service Association of San Francisco.

31. *CPER,* no. 8 (March 1971), pp. 30-31.

32. *Ibid.,* no. 15 (November 1972), p. 36.

33. Harris-DeMerritt interview cited previously.

34. California Department of Industrial Relations, *Independent State and Local Associations of Public Employees in California* (1963), p. 10.

35. U.S. Department of Labor, Bureau of Labor Statistics, *op. cit.,* p. 10.

36. *CPER,* no. 3 (November 1969), p. 30.

37. *Ibid.,* no. 5 (May 1970), pp. 39-40.

38. *Ibid.,* no. 19 (December 1973), p. 40.

39. *Ibid.,* no. 2 (August 1969), p. 24.

40. League of California Cities, Los Angeles County Division, *Annual Survey of Salaries and Wage Supplements for Benchmark Positions* (1973).

41. *Los Angeles County Employee,* 1 August 1974. Los Angeles County Employees Association Local 660, SEIU. An affiliation agreement had been approved by the board of both the CLOCEA and LACEA-660.

42. California Department of Industrial Relations, *op. cit.* (1963), p. 10.

43. Richard R. Nelson, "The Assembly of Governmental Employees Stresses Professionalism," *Monthly Labor Review* (November 1973), pp. 56-57.

44. Survey of California cities and employee organizations conducted by the author through the Bureau of Governmental Research, UCLA, in 1962.

45. The California Highway Patrol retirement plan was extended by AB 1333 (Foran), which became *Cal. Stats.* 1968, *ch.* 960.

46. AB 245 (Ketchum et al.), which became *Cal. Stats.* 1970, *ch.* 1600.

47. Harry Bernstein, "Highway Patrolmen Vote Against Strike in Pay Hike Fight," *Los Angeles Times,* 17 July 1971. The association pointed out that patrol salaries are financed by motor vehicle tax funds, not by the state general fund.

48. Eugene J. Devine, *Analysis of Manpower Shortages: Case Studies of Nurses, Policemen, and Teachers* (New York: Praeger, 1970), pp. 66-97.

49. *Los Angeles Times,* 5 November 1963. IAFF Local 748 requested the attorney general to investigate the league's political activities. It also denounced a proposed pay increase for police lieutenants as being discriminatory. Moreover, it alleged that one reason the mayor advocated enactment of a municipal lobbyist control ordinance was to limit the league's political activity.

50. *GERR,* no. 482 (11 December 1972), pp. B-7-9.

51. Bill Boyarsky, "City Workers Make Their Power Felt at the Polls," *Los Angeles Times,* 31 January 1971.

52. *Los Angeles Times,* 21 May, 25 August, 30 August, 1 December 1969.

53. Erwin Baker, "Fire and Police League Demands 11% Pay Hike," *Los Angeles Times,* 30 August 1969.

54. *Los Angeles Times,* 17 June 1969.

55. *Ibid.,* 9 September 1969.

56. Los Angeles Fire and Police Protective League v. City of Los Angeles, 23 CA3d67, 99 Cal. Rptr. 908 (1972).

57. *Los Angeles Times,* 16 July, 17 July, 20 July, 4 August, 1 October 1971.

58. *Ibid.,* 30 June 1973.

59. *Ibid.,* 28 July, 3 November 1969; *CPER* no. 5 (May 1970), pp. 42-43.

60. *Los Angeles Times,* 30 December 1969.

61. Constitution of the Peace Officers Research Association.

62. John P. Kenney, *The California Police* (Springfield, Illinois: Charles C. Thomas, 1964), p. 128.

63. California Department of Industrial Relations, *Independent State and Local Public Employee Associations in California* (1963), p. 10.

64. *CPER,* no. 3 (November 1969), pp. 33-34.

65. *Los Angeles Times,* 6 November 1968.

66. Some of the larger and more militant police associations had threatened to form a state-wide police union if PORAC did not adopt a more aggressive program than it had supported previously. *CPER,* no. 2 (August 1969), pp. 23-24.

67. *CPER,* no. 6 (August 1970), pp. 28-29; *ibid.,* no. 7 (November 1970), p. 33.

68. *Ibid.,* no. 17 (June 1973), p. 49; Lehane v. San Francisco 30 CA3d 105, 106

Cal. Rptr. 918 (1972). Both the state and federal Supreme Courts declined to review the appellate court's decision.

69. *Los Angeles Times*, 1 June 1971. A letter by the president of PORAC gives the association's point of view and the legislative history of SB 333.

70. Joseph Krislov, "The Independent Public Employee Association: Characteristics and Functions," *Industrial and Labor Relations Review* (July 1962), pp. 510-520; Jerry Lelchook, "A Study of State Civil Service Employee Associations," *CPER*, no. 22 (September 1974), pp. 2-16.

71. Lelchook, "State Civil Service Employee Associations."

72. *California State Employee* (CSEA publication), 26 August 1966.

73. *Ibid.*, January-February 1950, pp. 21-25.

74. *CPER*, no. 15 (November 1972), p. 38.

75. California Department of Industrial Relations, Division of Labor Statistics and Research, *Independent State and Local Employee Associations in California, 1963* (Sacramento: 1965).

76. The California State Employees' Association, *Position Statement on Collective Negotiation* (Sacramento: 1967); *California State Employee*, 10 June 1966; *ibid.*, 13 January 1967. Each item reported that renewed support was being given the California Plan by the multi-member federation, the Association of California Employees.

77. *California State Employee*, 25 October 1968.

78. California State Personnel Board, *Report in Response to House Resolution 530* (24 January 1969).

79. *California State Employee*, 31 January 1969.

80. *CPER*, no. 9 (June 1971), pp. 49-52. Executive Order no. R-25-71 was issued February 23, 1971.

81. *Los Angeles Times*, 14 November 1960.

82. *Ibid.*, 11 November, 13 November 1967.

83. *California State Employee*, 15 November 1968.

84. *Ibid.*, 17 October 1969.

85. *GERR*, no. 335 (9 February 1970), p. B-10.

86. *Los Angeles Times*, 8 July 1971.

87. *Ibid.*, 11 July 1971.

88. *CTA Journal* (May 1967), pp. 8-10.

89. *Ibid.*

90. CTA-Section relationships were commented upon extensively in a doctoral dissertation written by Robert Gillingham, who was southern section president in 1945, member of the CTA board of directors 1947-1956, chairman of the committee on organization 1946-1949, president of the board, 1953-1956, and a member of the National Education Association board 1949-1953.

91. David J. Bowan and M. W. Aussieker Jr., "Teacher Negotiations in a Changing Environment," *CPER*, no. 11 (November 1971), p. 6; Lyn R. Clancy Jr., "The History of the American Federation of Teachers in Los Angeles: 1919-1969." (Ed.D. dissertation, UCLA, 1971).

92. Bowan and Aussieker, *op. cit.*

93. *Los Angeles Times*, 7 May 1965.

94. *CPER*, no. 8 (March 1971), p. 42 (Madera Unified School District); *ibid.*, no. 16 (March 1973), pp. 45-46.

95. *Los Angeles Times*, 7 November 1963.

96. The strike and sanction adopted against the Lawndale District in Los Angeles County is a prime example. *CPER*, no. 3 (November 1969), pp. 41-43.

97. *Ibid.*, p. 40. An example is the action of the Association of Richmond Educators.

98. *CPER*, no. 8 (March 1971), pp. 40-42.

99. *Los Angeles Times*, 16 May, 24 May 1965; Clancy, "History of American Federation of Teachers."

100. *CPER*, no. 4 (January 1970), pp. 14-15.

101. The vote was later disputed, but Judge Stratton of the Los Angeles superior court ruled approval had been given. *CPER*, no. 7 (November 1970), pp. 49-57.

102. California Teachers Association, *CTA Action*, 28 April 1972; *CPER*, no. 14 (August 1972), p. 52.

103. *CPER*, no. 14 (August 1972).

104. Suzanne Emery, "CTA Terminology for You or, Understanding the Bureaucracy Title," *CTA Action*, 9 November 1973.

105. Bryan Stevens, "How Unification Pact was Reached," *CTA Action*, 11 January 1974.

106. Max D. Kossoris, "The San Francisco Bay Area 1966 Nurses' Negotiations," *Monthly Labor Review* (June 1967), pp. 8-12.

107. Walter J. Gershenfeld, "Organizing and Bargaining in Hospitals," *Monthly Labor Review* (July 1968), pp. 51-52.

108. *California Nurse* (March 1973).

109. Eugene J. Devine, *Analysis of Manpower Shortages in Local Government: Case Studies of Nurses, Policemen, and Teachers* (New York: Praeger, 1970), pp. 56-58; Kossoris, "San Francisco Nurses' Negotiations."

110. *New York Times*, 12 July, 30 July 1966; Kossoris, *op. cit.; Los Angeles Times*, 11 July, 15 July 1966.

111. Santa Cruz: *Los Angeles Times*, 24 August, 21 September 1966; Imperial: *Los Angeles Times*, 26 September 1966; *Imperial Valley News Press*, 24 September, 16 October 1966; San Luis Obispo: *Los Angeles Times*, 29 May, 7 June, 13 June, 16 June 1967; *San Luis Obispo Telegram-Tribune*, 29 May, 20 June 1967.

112. *Los Angeles Times*, 21 June, 22 June, 23 June, 26 June, 27 June 1967; *Fresno Bee*, 20 June, 26 June 1967.

113. *Los Angeles Times*, 22 August 1966; *New York Times*, 30 August 1966.

114. *New York Times*, 23 August 1966; *Los Angeles Times*, 23 August 1966.

115. *California Nurses Association Bulletin* (November 1968).

116. Harry Bernstein, *Los Angeles Times*, 5 December 1969.

117. Harry Bernstein, "Union Label Dodges; Growth of Nurses Assn. Reflects New Militancy," *Los Angeles Times*, 14 June 1967.

118. *California Nurse* (January 1973).

III: PUBLIC EMPLOYEE ORGANIZATIONS — THE UNIONS

1. David Ziskind, *One Thousand Strikes of Public Employees* (New York: Columbia University Press, 1940).

2. Leo Kramer, *Labor's Paradox* (New York: John Wiley and Sons, 1962), pp. 1-4, 21-23; Richard N. Billings and John Greenya, *Power to the Public Worker* (Washington and New York: Robert B. Luce, 1974).

3. *Monthly Labor Review* (August 1972), p. 38. Jerry Wurf is quoted, saying, "There is jurisdictional chaos in the labor movement. . . . We spend more resources fighting each other than fighting the bosses."

4. Kramer, *Labor's Paradox,* pp. 14-23.

5. *Ibid.,* pp. 49-50.

6. California State Federation of Labor, *Reports of Officers to the Affiliates* (1944), p. 46.

7. *Ibid.* (1945), p. 47.

8. *Ibid.* (1945), pp. 58-59.

9. California Industrial Union Council, *Proceedings of the 8th Annual Convention* (1957); J. Raymond Walsh, *C.I.O.: Industrial Unionism in Action* (New York: W. W. Norton & Co., 1937), pp. 154-158.

10. California Labor Federation, AFL-CIO, *Proceedings of the 3rd Constitutional Convention,* vol. 3 (1960), pp. 369-370.

11. AFL-CIO, *Proceedings,* vol. 2 (1963), pp. 58-59.

12. *Ibid.,* vol. 1 (1963), p. 552.

13. *Ibid.,* vol. 1 (1965), pp. 352, 353-356, 365.

14. *Ibid.,* vol. 1 (1967), p. 588.

15. *Ibid.,* vol. 1 (1965), pp. 339-340.

16. U.S. Bureau of Labor Statistics, *Directory of National Unions and Associations* (Washington, D. C.: Government Printing Office, 1971), pp. 6-7.

17. *Ibid.,* p. 13.

18. Bureau of National Affairs, Inc., *Government Employee Relations Report* (*GERR*), no. 567, 12 August 1974, p. B-9.

19. Kramer, *Labor's Paradox.*

20. *Ibid.,* pp. 27-38.

21. *Public Employee,* July 1960, pp. 10-11 (AFSCME newspaper).

22. *Ibid.*

23. International Chiefs of Police, *Police Unions,* rev. ed. (Washington, D. C.: 1958), p. 12; California State Federation of Labor, *Proceedings,* vol. 14 (1946), p. 113.

24. International Chiefs of Police, *Police Unions,* p. 12.

25. *East Bay Labor Journal,* 9 March 1956.

26. Perez v. Police Commissioners, 78 CA 2d 638, 178 P2d 537 (1947); California State Federation of Labor, *Proceedings* (1949).

27. *Public Employee,* April 1960, p. 6; *ibid.,* July 1960, p. 11.

28. Kramer, *Labor's Paradox,* pp. 103-154.

29. AFL-CIO, *Proceedings,* vol. 1 (1967), pp. 609-611.

30. Donald C. Kay, "State, County and Municipal Employees' Biennial Convention," *Monthly Labor Review* (July 1966), pp. 736-738.

31. John H. Chase, "State, County, and Municipal Employees Convention, 1972," *Monthly Labor Review* (August 1972), p. 39.

32. *Sacramento Valley Union Labor Bulletin,* 20 January 1967.

33. *Ibid.*

34. *Ibid.,* 27 January 1967.

35. *Sacramento Valley Union Labor Bulletin,* 27 January 1967; *California AFL-CIO News,* 17 March 1967.

36. *Los Angeles Citizen,* 28 April 1967.

37. "A Special Report on Sacramento County," *CPER,* no. 10 (August 1971), pp. 8-14.

38. *California AFL-CIO News,* 29 July 1966.

39. *East Bay Labor Journal,* 23 July 1966.

40. *Eureka Times-Herald,* 10 August, 11 August 1966.

41. *CPER,* no. 2 (August 1969), p. 27.

42. *Ibid.,* no. 3 (November 1969), p. 38.

43. *Ibid.,* no. 10 (August 1971), p. 33; *ibid.,* no. 11 (November 1971), p. 40; *ibid.,* no. 16 (March 1973), p. 33.

44. *Ibid.,* no. 2 (August 1969), p. 33; *ibid.,* no. 5 (May 1970), p. 45.

45. *Ibid.,* no. 20 (March 1974), pp. 76-77.

46. *New York Times,* 1 June 1972.

47. Jack Stieber, *Public Employee Unionism: Structure, Growth, Policy* (Washington, D.C.: The Brookings Institution, 1973), p. 3.

48. SEIU Constitution and By-Laws, Article 3, Section 1.

49. *East Bay Labor Journal,* 26 March 1971; *SEIU Public Service News,* May 1971.

50. *GERR,* no. 498 (9 April 1973), p. B-17.

51. Stieber, *Public Employee Unionism,* p. 38.

52. *CPER,* no. 3, pp. 29, 53; *ibid.,* no. 5, p. 43; *ibid.,* no. 18, p. 37.

53. Data drawn originally from a survey of California public employee organizations in 1962, supplemented by field observations at later dates and by figures published in the SEIU proceedings of quadrennial meetings.

54. SEIU, *Proceedings, Fourteenth Quadrennial Convention* (1968), p. 150.

55. *San Francisco Chronicle,* 12 May 1974.

56. SEIU, *Proceedings* (1968), p. 150.

57. *Ibid.,* p. 188.

58. *CPER,* no. 12 (March 1972), p. 39.

59. *GERR,* no. 498 (9 April 1973), p. B-17.

60. *CPER,* no. 17 (June 1973), pp. 44 45.

61. *Ibid.,* no. 12 (March 1972), p. 39.

62. *Ibid.,* no. 18 (August 1973), p. 45.

63. *Ibid.*

64. American Federation of Teachers, Commission on Educational Reconstruction, *Organizing the Teaching Profession* (Glencoe, Illinois: Free Press, 1955), pp. 27-28, 265-267.

65. Resolutions at the 1971 convention dealt with teacher rights, tenure, academic freedom, performance contracting, the voucher system permitting students to choose schools, civil rights, child care centers, drug abuse, racial balance in schools, and women's rights.

66. American Federation of Teachers, *Convention Proceedings* (1971), p. 137.

67. Robert J. Braun, *Teachers and Power* (New York: Simon and Schuster, 1972), pp. 36-39, 49-56.

68. The International Association of Fire Fighters initially organized firemen in private as well as public employment, although the personnel of city fire departments constituted the bulk of its members. When the Griffen-Landrum Act placed restrictions on labor organizations representing private sector employees, the IAFF chose to limit its members to public employees.

69. Leon E. Lunden, "International Association of Fire Fighters Convention," *Monthly Labor Review* (October 1972), p. 53.

70. William Howard McClennan of Boston replaced William Buck, who was given the status of president emeritus. Per capita dues were raised to one dollar.

71. Lunden, "Fire Fighters Convention."

72. Charles Hillinger, "Volunteer Firemen: They Outnumber, Outdo the Pros," *Los Angeles Times,* 20 July 1974.

73. California Federation of Labor, *Proceedings* (1939).

74. Data obtained from a questionnaire distributed to city administrative officers by the Bureau of Governmental Research, University of California, Los Angeles in 1962.

75. California Federation of Labor, *Proceedings* (1972), pp. 283-285.

76. Los Angeles County Fire Fighters Local 1014 AFL-CIO v. City of Monrovia, 24 CA 3d 289, 101 Cal. Rptr. 78 (1972).

77. The City of Claremont proposed to create a public safety department in 1967. Local 1014 campaigned against the proposal. The local represented members in the Santa Monica Fire Department in the police-fire wage parity dispute in 1963.

78. Melendez v. City of Los Angeles, Superior Court of Los Angeles, case C6702. Los Angeles Fire and Police Protective League v. City of Los Angeles, 40 CA 3d 718 (1974).

79. Pasadena Fire Fighters Association v. Board of Directors, 36 CA 3d 901 (1974).

80. "Two Case Studies: Facts and Issues; Police and Firefighters' Strike in San Francisco," *CPER,* no. 27 (December 1975), pp. 19-25.

81. *Los Angeles Citizen,* 14 July 1967. The *Citizen* was published by the Central Labor Council.

82. Lunden, "Fire Fighters Convention." The AFL-CIO and the California Federation of Labor have supported this IAFF policy.

83. George E. Bean and Howard McCalla, "Waste in the Fire House," *Public Management* (October 1963), pp. 218-221.

84. George E. Bean was a nationally recognized city manager, having been president of the International City Managers Association prior to his tenure in San Diego.

85. Gordon W. Bertram, *Consolidated Bargaining in California Construction* (Los Angeles: Institute of Industrial Relations, UCLA, 1966), pp. 34-38.

86. *East Bay Labor Journal,* 7 January 1972.

87. Harry Bernstein, "Government Unions not New Phenomena in L.A.," *Los Angeles Times,* 25 July 1968; Richard Baisden, "Labor Unions in Los Angeles Politics" (Ph.D. dissertation, University of Chicago, 1951).

88. Bill Boyarsky, "City Workers Make their Power Felt at Polls," *Los Angeles Times,* 31 January 1971.

89. *GERR,* no. 369 (5 October 1970), p. B-7.

90. League of California Cities, Los Angeles County Division, *Annual Survey of Salaries and Wages for Benchmark Positions* (Los Angeles: 1973).

91. *CPER,* no. 18 (August 1973), p. 40.

92. *Ibid.,* no. 8 (March 1971), pp. 31-32.

93. Bertram, *Consolidated Bargaining,* pp. 26-28; Garth L. Mangum, *The Operating Engineers* (Cambridge: Harvard University Press, 1964), pp. 147-149.

94. *CPER,* no. 19 (December 1973), p. 41.

95. *Ibid.*

96. *Ibid.,* no. 16 (March 1973), p. 35; *ibid.,* no. 18 (August 1973), pp. 34-35.

97. *Ibid.,* no. 18 (August 1973), pp. 34-35.

98. *Northern California Teamster,* 14 March 1966; *Los Angeles Times,* 2 March 1966.

99. *CPER,* no. 18 (August 1973), pp. 34-35; *ibid.,* no. 15, p. 37; League of California Cities, *Annual Survey of Salaries* (Los Angeles: 1973).

100. Stieber, *Public Employee Unionism,* pp. 4-5.

101. *CPER,* no. 7 (November 1969), pp. 38-39.

102. U.S. Department of Labor, Bureau of Labor Statistics, *Directory of National and International Unions in the U.S.,* Bulletin no. 1665 (1969).

103. *GERR,* no. 366 (14 September 1970), p. B-17.

104. *Ibid.,* no. 388 (15 February 1971), p. B-19.

105. *Ibid.,* no. 476 (30 October 1972), p. B-19.

106. *CPER,* no. 10 (August 1971), p. 35.

107. California Labor Federation, *Proceedings* (1972), pp. 277-306.

108. *California AFL-CIO News,* 9 August 1968.

109. California Labor Federation, *Proceedings* (1972), p. 212.

IV: THE CALIFORNIA POLITICAL SYSTEM

1. Joseph A. Schlesinger, "The Politics of the Executive," in *Politics in the American States,* ed. Herbert Jacobs and Kenneth L. Vines, 2nd ed. (Boston: Little, Brown & Co., 1971), p. 232.

2. Chief Justice Earl Warren, *The Memoirs of Earl Warren* (Garden City, N.Y.: Doubleday & Co., 1977), p. 232.

3. *Ibid.,* pp. 170-171.

4. 312,404 signatures were required between 1975 and 1978.

5. 499,846 signatures were required between 1975 and 1978.

6. Pasadena v. Charleville, 215 C 384, 10 P2d 745 (1932).

7. International Association of Fire Fighters v. City of Palo Alto, 60 C2d 295, 384 P2d (1963); Professional Fire Fighters v. City of Los Angeles, 60 C2d 276, 384 P2d 158 (1963).

8. State of California, 43 *Attorney General's Opinions* 236 (1964).

9. *California AFL-CIO News,* 3 March 1967; California Federation of Labor, *Proceedings* (1968), p. 266.

10. Luther Gulick and L. Urwick, eds., *Papers on the Science of Administration* (New York: Institute of Public Administration, 1937); Louis Brownlow, *A Passion for Politics: The Autobiography of Louis Brownlow* (Chicago: University of Chicago Press, 1955); U.S. President's Committee on Administrative Management, *Report* (Washington, D.C.: Government Printing Office, 1937).

11. Frederick W. Taylor, *The Principles of Scientific Management* (New York: Harper & Row, 1911).

12. U.S. Commission on Organization of the Executive Branch, *The Hoover Commission Report* (New York: McGraw-Hill, 1949).

13. The International City Management Association, *The Municipal Year Book* (Washington, D.C.: ICMA, 1973), pp. 296-299, 327.

14. John P. Kenney, *The California Police* (Springfield, Illinois: Charles C. Thomas, 1964); David J. Bordua and Albert J. Reiss Jr., "Law Enforcement," in *The Uses of Sociology,* eds. Paul F. Lazarsfeld, William H. Sewell, and Harold L. Wilensky (New York: Basic Books, 1967), pp. 275-303; Frederick C. Mosher,

Democracy and the Public Service (New York: Oxford University Press, 1968), chap. 4.

15. *Public Management* (Washington, D.C.: International City Management Association, June 1977), p. 5.

16. Winston W. Crouch, *Guide for Modern Personnel Commissions* (Chicago: International Personnel Management Association, 1973).

17. Wallace S. Sayre, "The Triumph of Techniques Over Purpose," *Public Administration Review,* vol. 8 (Spring 1948), pp. 134-137.

18. U.S. Commission on Civil Rights, *For All the People . . . By All the People: A Report on Equal Opportunity in State and Local Government Employment* (Washington, D.C.: Government Printing Office, 1969).

V: THE POLITICAL RIGHTS OF GOVERNMENT EMPLOYEES

1. William L. Riordon, *Plunkitt of Tammany Hall* (New York: McClure, Phillips & Co., 1905), p. 88.

2. Paul P. Van Riper, *History of the United States Civil Service* (New York: Harper & Row, 1958); Frederick C. Mosher, *Democracy and the Public Service* (New York: Oxford University Press, 1968).

3. This concept was expressed by the city manager and council of South Pasadena in 1952 when they said, "by voluntarily accepting employment with the City of South Pasadena, they (the city employees) assumed the obligation incident to such employment implied agreed to accept same under the conditions as they existed." (*Pasadena Star-News,* 8 January 1952). The Texas Supreme Court used similar wording in CIO v. City of Dallas, "by voluntarily accepting employment; (the appellants) implied agreed to accept same under the conditions as they existed; agreed to accept the employment and compensation under the conditions as they existed; agreed to accept employment and compensation therefore as regulated and controlled by existing . . . (198 SW 143, 146 [1946])." It also appears to be the conclusion President Franklin D. Roosevelt reached in his much quoted letter to the National Federation of Federal Employees, dated August 16, 1937, quoted by David Fellman in *The Constitutional Right of Association* (Chicago: University of Chicago Press, 1963), pp. 52-53, and by Paul P. Van Riper, *op. cit.,* pp. 350-351. The concept is discussed further in Pamela S. Ford, *Political Activities and the Public Service: A Continuing Problem* (Berkeley: Institute of Governmental Studies, UC, 1963), pp. 7-9.

4. The federal Lloyd-La Follette Act, adopted in 1912, is an example. See Van Riper, *op. cit.,* pp. 217, 174-275. Basically, the activities approved by this conception of 'proper' political action are included in the historic citizen's right of petition for redress of grievances.

5. This idea is discussed by Harry H. Wellington and Ralph K. Winter Jr., *The Unions and the Cities* (Washington, D.C.: Brookings Institution, 1972), pp. 24-32. It is also considered, though less directly, by David T. Stanley, *Managing Local Government Under Union Pressure* (Washington, D.C.: Brookings Institution, 1972), pp. 136-152. See also Michael H. Moskow, J. Joseph Loewenberg, and Edward C. Koziara, *Collective Bargaining in Public Employment* (New York: Random House, 1970), pp. 263-271; James A. Belasco, "Municipal Bargaining and Political Power," in J. Joseph Loewenberg and Michael M. Moskow, eds., *Collec-*

tive Bargaining in Government: Readings and Cases (Englewood Cliffs: Prentice-Hall, 1972), pp. 235-250. A prediction that the acquisition of the right to bargain with the employer-government would eliminate the need for public employee organizations to engage in local political activities was expressed (in interviews) by several employee association managers in 1963.

6. Van Riper, *op. cit.,* p. 551; Harry H. Wellington and Ralph K. Winter Jr., *op. cit.,* pp. 69-82; Letter from California Attorney General U. Webb to Honorable John C. Corbett, dated October 24, 1935, reproduced in full in Ford, *op. cit.,* pp. 135-136; Chief Justice Phil Gibson writing for the California Supreme Court in Fort v. Civil Service Commission of Alameda County, 61 C2d 331 (1964); U.S. Government, Commission on Political Activity of Governmental Personnel, *Findings and Recommendations,* vol. 1 (Washington, D.C.: Government Printing Office, 1967), pp. 3-6, 15.

7. Robert A. Dahl, *A Preface to Democratic Theory* (Chicago: University of Chicago Press, 1956), pp. 137-138.

8. A view often expressed by local governmental managers in the 1970's is that because public employees enjoy job tenure under civil service and also possess considerable group political influence, any charter or statute requiring interest disputes to be resolved by arbitration gives employees power disproportionate to that held by management. An example is the city representative's statement in the Vallejo city fire fighters' arbitration award in 1972. See *California Public Employee Relations,* no. 13 (June 1972), pp. 36-40.

9. McAuliffe v. Mayor of New Bedford, 155 Mass. 216, 29 NE 517 (1892); Arch Dotson, "Emerging Doctrine of Privilege in Public Employment," 15 *Public Administration Review* 77-88 (Spring 1955); Arch Dotson, "A General Theory of Public Employment," 16 *Public Administration Review* 197-211 (Summer 1956).

10. *California Statutes* (1899), p. 241; *ibid.,* art. 13 (Civil Service), pp. 350-354; *ibid.,* art. 16, sec. 32 (Political Activity), pp. 363-364.

11. *Cal. Stats.* (1901), p. 832 (City of Fresno); *ibid.* (1907), p. 1277 (City of Riverside).

12. *Ibid.* (1903), p. 599 (City of Salinas); *ibid.* (1903), p. 647 (City of Watsonville).

13. *Ibid.* (1903), p. 555 (City of Los Angeles); *ibid.* (1909), p. 1240 (City of Berkeley); *ibid.* (1907), p. 1176 (City of Long Beach).

14. *Ibid.* (1913), ch. 5, p. 1384 (County of Los Angeles); *ibid.* (1913), art. 9, Civil Service, secs. 41-44.

15. George E. Mowry, *The California Progressives* (Chicago: Quadrangle Books, 1951); Franklin Hichborn, *Story of the California Legislature* (San Francisco: James H. Barry Co.). Separate volumes for the sessions of 1909, 1911, 1913, 1915, and 1921; V. O. Key Jr. and Winston W. Crouch, *The Initiative and the Referendum in California* (Berkeley: University of California Press, 1938).

16. San Francisco, Records of the Registrar of Voters; Los Angeles, Records of the City Clerk.

17. *Pasadena Star-News,* 1 November, 7 November 1926.

18. San Diego, Records of the City Clerk.

19. Scott v. City of Los Angeles, 85 C2d 327, 193 P2d 26 (1948).

20. Spencer v. City of Alhambra, 44 CA 2d 75, 111 P2d 910 (1941); Collins v. City and County of San Francisco, 112 CA 2d 719, 247 P2d 362 (1951).

21. Richard N. Baisden, "Labor Unions in Los Angeles Politics" (Ph.D. disserta-

tion, University of Chicago, 1951). Adolph Spreckels of San Francisco and Dr. John R. Haynes of Los Angeles were particularly prominent advocates of municipal ownership in their respective cities. Franklin K. Lane, a San Francisco Progressive who was Secretary of the Interior in Woodrow Wilson's cabinet, was influential in assisting the Los Angeles water program and the East Bay Municipal Utility District project at Hetch Hetchy through departmental policies on use of water resources originating in national park lands.

22. Baisden, *op. cit.*

23. *Cal. Stats.* (1935), ch. 48. The bill, AB 1970, was processed in accordance with the constitutional provision authorizing emergency legislation. This procedure required approval of two-thirds of the members of each house. The Assembly approved the bill 65-2 and the Senate recorded a 32-0 tally.

24. *Cal. Stats.* (1943), ch. 515. The provision became Government Code, sects. 45030-45031.

25. *Western City* (July, August 1955).

26. Mitchell v. Walker, 140 CA 2d 239, 295 P2d 90 (1956); California, 21 *Attorney General's Opinions* 76 (1958). The decision arose from Monrovia where the voters adopted an initiative ordinance establishing a police and fire salary plan which tied municipal salaries to those paid by Los Angeles County for comparable ranks. The opinion related to a Montebello initiative ordinance which gave police and firemen automatic annual salary adjustments based upon an index figure published by the Bureau of Labor Statistics. The Walker case was often cited as controlling the use of initiative petitions on employment matters in general-law cities. The state Supreme Court declined to hear the appeal. Kugler v. Yocum, a Supreme Court decision written in 1968, rejected the reasoning employed in the Mitchell case on both issues, however. It ruled that an initiative petition circulated by Alhambra city firemen proposing an ordinance containing a formula for setting firemen's salaries at parity with those paid by the County of Los Angeles was a valid proposition to be voted upon by city electors. This case was not decided on the basis of special language in the charter, as was the earlier litigation, Spenser v. City of Alhambra. The fact that the Alhambra voters rejected the firemen's proposal does not alter the statement of law and policy, however.

27. California Legislature, Senate, *Journal,* 18 January 1937, pp. 174-182.

28. The statute was a committee substitute for a bill introduced in the Assembly and was approved on the penultimate day of the 1913 session. Opposition was heaviest in the Senate, where the bill passed 25 to 10, contrasting with a 65 to 6 split in the Assembly. An amendment requiring incumbents to pass examinations was defeated narrowly in the Senate. See Hichborn, *Story of the California Legislature of 1913,* pp. 352-353.

29. California Legislature, Senate, "Report of State Civil Service Commission," *Journal,* 23 February 1933.

30. Robert E. Burke, *Olson's New Deal in California* (Berkeley: University of California Press, 1953), p. 37. The State, County and Municipal Workers of America (CIO) organized SRA employees in some parts of the state. It was alleged that this organization and its members encouraged relief recipients to join the Workers' Alliance.

31. *Cal. Stats.* (1940), ch. 12; California, *Attorney General's Opinions,* 1-NS 2741 (30 October 1941).

32. *U.S. Code,* title 5, sec. 1501-1508.

33. *Ibid.*

34. Between 1939 and 1975, state and local work forces labored under two sets of rules which often proved divergent and unsettling. In California, employees whose salaries were funded by federal grants were more restricted than those paid from state or local sources, although often the two classes worked side by side in the same administrative unit. Instances occurred, for example, in which an administrative analyst in Contra Costa County, employed on a federally funded project, was dismissed for violation of the Hatch Act. An Alameda County employee doing the same type of work and engaging in the same type of after-hours political action, but paid from county funds, was restored to duty by the state court. (Fishkin v. U.S. Civil Service Commission, 309 F Supp. 40 [1969] in Contra Costa, and Rossenfield v. Malcolm, 65 C2d 559 [1966] in Alameda.) This troublesome dichotomy of policy was brought to a close when Congress substantially revised the Hatch Act, effective 1 January 1975. (Federal Election Campaign Act Amendments of 1974, PL 93-443.)

35. *Cal. Stats.* (1947), ch. 424, p. 1251 et seq.

36. *California State Employee* (February 1934), pp. 9-10; *ibid.* (July 1934), pp. 5, 12.

37. *Ibid.* (November 1934).

38. *Ibid.*

39. Burke, *op. cit.*, p. 37.

40. Letter from Attorney General Webb to John C. Corbett, Board of Equalization, 24 October 1935. Cited in Ford, *Political Activities and Public Services* (1963).

41. *Attorney General's Opinions,* NS 1225 (October 1938).

42. *California Government Code,* sect. 19251, based on *Cal. Stats.* (1937), ch. 753, revised by *Cal. Stats.* (1945), ch. 123. Present wording was adopted by *Cal. Stats.* (1949), ch. 174.

43. 19 *Attorney General's Opinions* 150 (1952).

44. *Government Code,* sect. 19251.

45. 34 *Attorney General's Opinions* 244 (1959).

46. 19 *Attorney General's Opinions* 150 (1952).

47. *Ibid.*

48. *Cal. Stats.* (1935), ch. 618; *California Education Code,* sects. 13752-13754. The statute was written by John Steven, who became the director of the district's classified employee personnel system by appointment of the personnel commission created pursuant to the statute.

49. *CTA Journal* (March 1954), p. 9.

50. *Cal. Stats.* (1955), ch. 1112; added sect. 13004 to the *Education Code.* This was AB 203, introduced by Assemblyman Edward E. Elliott (D.) of Los Angeles.

51. *CTA Journal* (January 1955), p. 5. The board order included in the proscribed activities the endorsing of candidates, distribution of literature, solicitation of votes, and solicitation of funds. Any violation of the order was declared to be insubordination punishable by dismissal.

52. *California Constitution,* art. XX, sect. 19.

53. *Cal. Stats.* (1953), ch. 1250; added sects. 1367-1369 to the *Government Code* and made other changes respecting oaths of office.

54. Legislation prohibiting any public agency in California from hiring non-citizens had been adopted in 1915. The Criminal Syndicalism Law, enacted in 1919,

had forbidden any person to advocate or teach the use of violence to accomplish a change in industrial ownership or to effect any political change. *Cal. Stats.* (1919), ch. 188, pp. 281-282; Woodrow C. Whitten, *Criminal Syndicalism and the Law in California:* 1919-1927 (Philadelphia: American Philosophical Society, 1969).

55. The Commission on Political Activity of Government Personnel, *Hearings,* vol. 3 (Washington, D.C.: Government Printing Office, 1968). *Ibid.,* pp. 113-124, 662-670.

56. Testimony of Willard W. Shea, Legal Adviser, League of County Employee Associations to the Commission on Political Activity of Government Personnel, *Commission Report,* vol. 3 (1968), pp. 613-629. See also letter dated August 19, 1952, from County Counsel Harold W. Kennedy to D. F. Cooper: "In oral opinions, we have said that the charter prohibits political activity during county office hours, outside office and while on leave of absence. An employee engages in such political activities only after resigning and severing all connection with the county." See also California State Federation of Labor, *Proceedings,* vol. 54 (1956), p. 427; *ibid.,* vol. 55 (1957), p. 390.

57. Survey of California city and county employment practices conducted in 1963 by the Bureau of Governmental Research, University of California, Los Angeles.

58. Humboldt County, for example, required any appointive county officer or employee to take leave of absence while running for any public office. The attorney general advised that this regulation was overly broad and would probably be overturned if challenged in court. 36 *Attorney General's Opinions* 261 (1960).

59. California Legislature, Assembly, *Journal* (11 June 1963), p. 5135.

60. *Cal. Stats.* (1963), ch. 2000; *Government Code,* sects. 3201-3205. The prohibition upon employees participating in recall election campaigns was stricken by the California Supreme Court in Bagley v. Washington Township Hospital District.

61. 43 *Attorney General's Opinions* 236 (1964).

62. California Federation of Labor, *Proceedings* (1964), pp. 270-280.

63. *El Pueblo.* (Newspaper published by the Los Angeles All-City Employees' Association.)

64. California Legislature, Assembly, *Journal* (16 February 1965), pp. 651; *ibid.* (3 March 1965), p. 917; Senate, *Journal* (2 March 1965), pp. 597-598.

65. Fort v. Civil Service Commission of Alameda County, 61 C2d 331, 392 P2d 385 (1964).

66. Kinnear v. City and County of San Francisco, 61 C2d 341, 392 P2d 391 (1964). Although the Los Angeles County charter was not in contention in either case, it was generally agreed that inasmuch as the sections on political activity in both the Los Angeles and Alameda County charters were similar, the Fort case rendered the Los Angeles law invalid.

67. Bagley v. Washington Township Hospital District, 65 C2d 499, 421 P2d 409 (1966).

68. Rosenfield v. Malcolm, 65 C2d 559, 421 P2d 697 (1967).

69. Los Angeles Teachers Union v. Los Angeles City Board of Education, 455 P2d 827 (1969).

70. Belshaw v. City of Berkeley, 246 Cal. App. 2d 493 (1966).

71. Pranger v. Break, 186 CA 2d 551.

72. The 3rd District Court of Appeal upheld the contention of teachers' associations in Yuba City and San Juan that the Winton Act required district school

boards to meet-and-confer with teacher representatives on district financial policies. The Rodda Act, adopted in 1975, accepts educational policy as a legitimate subject within the scope of bargaining between teacher organizations and school boards.

VI: THE RIGHT TO ORGANIZE

1. *Cal. Stats.* (1959), ch. 723; California, *Labor Code,* secs. 1960-1965 (Firemen); *Cal. Stats.* (1961), ch. 1964; California, *Government Code,* sec. 3500 et seq. (George Act); *Cal. Stats.* (1965), ch. 2041; California, *Education Code,* sec. 13080 et seq. (Winton Act); *Cal. Stats.* (1971), ch. 254; *Government Code,* sec. 3525 et seq. (State Employees).

2. *Nutter* v. *City of Santa Monica,* 74 CA2d 292, 168 P2d 741 (1946).

3. *Santa Monica Evening Outlook,* 8 May, 14 May, 17 May, 27 May, 27 June 1946. The new charter proposed to substitute a manager-council form of government for the commission type then in use. The attorney who drafted the new document was Louis H. Burke, consultant to numerous city councils, later to be the legal advisor to the League of California Cities, and ultimately to be an associate justice of the California Supreme Court. The legislature approved the charter, *Cal. Stats.* (1947), ch. 8. See (Fair Employment Practice), and (The Right of Association and Petition), charter sec. 1101.

4. Survey conducted in 1962 by the Bureau of Governmental Research, University of California, Los Angeles.

5. See Renken v. Compton City School District, 207 CA2d 106, 24 Cal. Rptr. 347 (1962).

6. *San Francisco Municipal Record,* 11 December 1919. Twenty-four years later, however, a new generation of San Francisco firemen voted to affiliate and were chartered by the IAFF as Local 798. *Fire Fighters,* July 1968 (Los Angeles Fire Fighters Union newspaper).

7. San Francisco, *Municipal Record,* 28 October 1920; *ibid.,* 10 November 1920.

8. Richard N. Baisden, "Labor Unions in Los Angeles Politics" (Ph.D. dissertation, University of Chicago, 1958).

9. *Los Angeles Times,* 11 October 1919.

10. Baisden, *op. cit.*

11. *Pasadena Star-News,* 2 January 1952.

12. *Ibid.,* 4 January 1952.

13. *Ibid.,* 8 January 1952.

14. *Ibid.,* 24 January 1952. The local's charter was withdrawn by the IAFF.

15. *Cal. Stats.* 1959, ch. 723, *California Labor Code,* Sects. 1960-1965.

16. International Association of Fire Fighters v. County of Merced, 204 CA2d 387, 722 CaR 270 (1962).

17. Professional Fire Fighters, Inc. v. City of Los Angeles, 60 C2d 276, 384 P2d 158 (1963); International Association of Fire Fighters v. City of Palo Alto, 60 C2d 295, 384 P2d 170 (1963).

18. David Ziskind, *One Thousand Strikes of Government Employees* (New York: Columbia University Press, 1940), p. 41.

19. *The Survey* (10 May 1919), vol. 42, p. 248.

20. *Current History* (October 1919), vol. 11, pp. 54-56.

21. Ziskind, *op. cit.*

22. *American City* (October 1919), vol. 21, pp. 315-316.

23. *Los Angeles Times,* 2 September 1919; Louis B. Perry and Richard S. Perry, *A History of the Los Angeles Labor Movement,* 1911-1941 (Berkeley: University of California Press, 1963), pp. 158-160.

24. *Los Angeles Times,* 2 September 1919.

25. *Ibid.,* 12 October 1919.

26. *Ibid.,* 18 October 1919.

27. *Ibid.,* 2 November 1922.

28. International Chiefs of Police, *Police Unions,* rev. ed. (1958), p. 12; California State Federation of Labor, *Proceedings,* vol. 14 (1946), p. 113.

29. *Los Angeles Times,* 22 March 1947. Local 556, composed of L.A. County Sheriff's Department Employees, was chartered in 1943. California State Federation of Labor, *Reports of Officers* (San Francisco: 1943), p. 68.

30. California Legislature, Assembly, "Report of Subcommittee on Law and Order of the Assembly Committee on Governmental Efficiency and Economy," *Assembly Journal* (18 February 1946), pp. 836-837; S.B. 949 (Williams, Tulare County), 1947 sess., passed by Senate, 28-7; died in Assembly Committee on Industrial Relations.

31. The ordinance included dues check-off privileges for the IAFF local as well as several associations.

32. *Los Angeles Daily News,* 13 March 1946; *Los Angeles Times,* 13 March, 14 March 1946.

33. Perez v. Police Commissioners 78 CA2d 638, 178 P2d 537 (1947). The court cited CIO v. City of Dallas, 198 SW 143, 146 (1946), with approval. In that opinion the Texas Supreme Court had said, "Appellants' main contention seems to be that the ordinance in question is unconstitutional and void because it would deprive them of certain freedoms, rights and privileges granted by both the Federal and State constitutions. We do not think so; these rights and privileges are purely personal and may be waived. Appellants overlook the fact that by voluntarily accepting employment; implied agreement to accept same under the conditions as they existed; agreed to accept the employment and compensation therefore as regulated and controlled by existing laws; especially did they obligate themselves not to organize a labor union or affiliate with one. These employees of the city may assert their constitutional rights and privileges if they choose to do so, but it is quite clear that to assert them under the circumstances would be inconsistent with their duty as employees of the city, and subject them to discharge from the service."

34. *Los Angeles Times,* 22 March 1947 (note editorial page). Local 665 surrendered its charter in 1948. California State Federation of Labor, *Proceedings* (1949).

35. *East Bay Labor Journal,* 9 March 1956.

36. *Ibid.*

37. International Chiefs of Police, *Police Unions* (1958).

38. California Legislature, *Assembly Journal* (1961), pp. 3364. Also see the discussion of this amendment in the preceding pages relative to the right of police to organize.

39. *Ibid.,* p. 4682.

40. California Legislature, Senate, *Journal* (1961), p. 4424.

41. A survey of employer-employee relations in council-manager cities con-

ducted by the International City Managers' Association in 1966. Some of the data from this survey was used in Winston W. Crouch, *Employer-Employee Relations in Council-Manager Cities* (Chicago: International City Managers Association, 1967).

42. 39 *Opinions of the Attorney General* 182 (1962).

43. Tolman v. Underhill, 39 Cal. App. 2d 708, 249 P2d 280 (1952).

44. California School Employees' Association v. Willits Unified School District, 243 Cal. App. 2d 776 (1966).

45. 45 *Opinions of the Attorney General* 74 (1965).

46. 55 *Opinions of the Attorney General* 269 (1972).

47. 45 *Opinions of the Attorney General* 138 (1965).

48. AB 1697 by Carroll (D) of Los Angeles County was kept by the Municipal and County Government Committee. Senator Cobey (D) of Merced County introduced a bill in the Senate, but it was retained by the Governmental Efficiency Committee. Four bills proposing to amend the Brown Act substantially were considered in detail. Two were approved by the Assembly with no dissenting vote, but were left to expire in the Senate's Committee on Governmental Efficiency. Another was recommended for interim study by the Committee on Civil Service and State Personnel, but the Rules Committee declined to take action.

49. *Los Angeles Times,* 24 March, 25 March, 26 March 1965.

50. California Legislature, Assembly, *Journal* (1965), pp. 1467, 1586; California Legislature, Senate, *Journal* (1965), p. 1774. Those opposing the amended bill in the Assembly were almost entirely liberal Democrats.

51. *Los Angeles Times,* 6 March 1970.

52. *Ibid.,* 20 March 1970. A federal court had struck down as overly broad a state statute that forbade firemen or police to belong to labor unions. Atkins v. City of Charlotte, 296 Fed. Supp. 1068 (1969). In 1971, another federal court reached a similar conclusion regarding a statute that forbade local police to form or join unions. Melton v. City of Atlanta, 324 Fed. Supp. 315 (1971).

53. *Los Angeles Times,* 6 May 1965.

54. Ball v. The City Council of the City of Coachella, 252 CA2d 142 (1967).

55. Bagley v. Washington Township Hospital District, 65 C2d 499, 421 P2d 409 (1966). Rosenfield v. Malcolm, 65 C2d 559, 421 P2d 697 (1967).

56. 49 *Opinions of the Attorney General* 1 (1967).

VII: POLITICAL ACTION BY ORGANIZED EMPLOYEES

1. Political scientists differ both in acceptance and in definition of the concept of political culture. Some reject the concept because it cannot be defined or researched in quantitative terms. Others find it useful when studying political attitudes and beliefs of a nation, as did Gabriel Almond and Sydney Verba in their book, *The Civic Culture* (Princeton: Princeton University Press, 1963). Others have used it to analyze political actions and attitudes exhibited in sets of states (regional differences), or within a larger state where there are observable, continuing sectional differences in voter reactions. Daniel Judah Elazar illustrates the latter approach in his book, *American Federalism: A View from the States* (New York: Crowell, 1966). The concept is used here to refer to the predominant attitudes within the state's political system about who may participate in the system and about what participation methods are approved.

2. Information concerning who lobbies in state government and whom they represent has been available for several years. The state legislature required persons paid to represent interested parties before it or its committees to register and file reports, which were published in the appendices to the legislative journals. The Legislative Reform Act, an initiative statute adopted in 1974, supersedes this. It established a Fair Political Practices Commission which has made a number of restrictions on expenditures for lobbying. Reports must be made to this commission. The first was issued in 1977. Fair Political Practices Commission, *$40 Million to Influence California Government: A Report on Lobbying 1975-1976* (Sacramento 1977).

3. Chris Wahle, "California's Most Influential Lobbyists," *California Journal* (September 1974), pp. 293-296.

4. Hearings on AB 1194 (1963) before the Assembly Interim Committee on Industrial Relations and the Assembly Committee on Municipal and County Government.

5. *Cal. Stats.* (1891), ch. 49, p. 47 (police); *Cal. Stats.* (1895), ch. 84, p. 75 (firemen); interpreted by Styring V. City of Santa Ana, 64 CA 2d 12, 147 P 29 689 (1944).

6. Los Angeles City Clerk, "Quarterly Report to the Council for October-December 1972," 29 March 1973. Organizations whose representatives filed in 1967 were: All-City Employees Association; AFSCME; Local 18 of the IBEW; Fire and Police Protective League; Engineers and Architects Association; and Professional Fire Fighters Local 748.

7. Orange County Clerk's Office.

8. Procedures of several public employee associations and unions have been discussed in chapters 2 and 3.

9. Statement filed with the Secretary of State, November 1972.

10. *Los Angeles Times,* 7 September 1973.

11. *CTA Action,* 14 November 1969.

12. Statements filed with the Secretary of State, 25 May 1970.

13. Serrano v. Priest, 5 Cal. 3rd 584; 487 P 2d 1241 (1971).

14. Thomas E. Stanton, "Historical Sketch of Your Association," *The California State Employee* (February 1941), pp. 9-11; *ibid.* (February 1932), pp. 2-3.

15. *Ibid.* (February 1932), pp. 2-3. The law was changed later to provide for election of employee representatives to the PERS board of system members, instead of appointment by the governor.

16. *Ibid.* (17 September 1971).

17. *Ibid.* A plurality of those polled also thought state employees were comparatively well paid.

18. *Ibid.* (22 October 1971).

19. *Ibid.* (24 December 1971).

20. *Ibid.* (14 January 1973).

21. *Ibid.* (14 January 1972); *ibid.* (7 April 1972).

22. *California Public Employee Relations (CPER)*, no. 12 (March 1972), pp. 61-62.

23. *California AFL-CIO News,* 20 October 1972, pp. 1-3.

24. Marion Ross, "State Employer-Employee Relations Initiative Measure," *CPER,* no. 13 (June 1972), pp. 7-11.

25. Statement filed with the Secretary of State.

26. Statement signed by Walter W. Taylor, executive director of CSEA, filed with the Secretary of State.

27. *Los Angeles Times,* 21 November 1972.

28. *Santa Monica Outlook,* 1, 2, 3, 5 November 1938.

29. Kugler v. Yocum, 69 C 2d 371, 445 P 2d 303. (1 October 1968). Justice Tobriner wrote the opinion of the court and was joined by Chief Justice Traynor and Justices Peters, Mosk, and Sullivan. Justice Burke wrote a sharply worded dissent in which Justice McComb joined. The dissenters argued that the ordinance delegated discretionary power to bodies in other jurisdictions, that the council could not delegate such power and, therefore, neither could the voters through use of the initiative. Burke also disagreed with the implementing procedure, saying that he could approve the ordinance only if it required the city administration to take the average of salaries paid firemen in all cities in Los Angeles County, rather than that paid by one or two jurisdictions.

30. *Alhambra Post Advocate,* 11 December 1968.

31. Proposition F on the general election ballot, November 1963.

32. Adopted 7 May 1963 and approved as *Cal. Stats.* (1963), ch. 124.

33. California Federation of Labor, *Proceedings* (1957), p. 47. *East Bay Labor Journal,* 8 January 1961; *ibid.,* 16 March 1961.

34. *Los Angeles Times,* 6 November 1960.

35. Los Angeles City Clerk Records.

36. *Ibid.;* Bill Boyarsky, *Los Angeles Times,* sect. B, 31 January 1971.

37. *Los Angeles Times,* 5 May 1971; *ibid.,* 22 October 1971.

38. Los Angeles City Clerk Records.

39. Report submitted by Don H. Meyer, President of ACEA, filed with Los Angeles City Clerk, Election Division.

40. Contained in documents filed with Los Angeles City Clerk, Election Division.

41. *CPER,* no. 2 (August 1969), pp. 22-23.

42. *Ibid.,* no. 3 (November 1969), pp. 35-36; *ibid.,* no. 5 (May 1970), p. 44.

43. *Ibid.,* no. 6 (August 1970), pp. 33-34. The charter was Proposition E and the arbitration section was Proposition G on the municipal ballot, 2 June 1970. Both were approved by the legislature, *Cal. Stats.* (1970), p. 3771.

44. Sacramento, City Clerk Records, Municipal Election, 1971.

45. *PPA Personnel News* (Chicago: December 1971), p. 90.

46. Oakland Police and Fire Fighters Arbitration Committee (Yes on Measure One) Report on file in Oakland City Clerk's office.

47. The proposal was Measure One on the ballot at the election held 17 April 1973. It was approved by the voters 64,969 to 33,855 and was presented to the state legislature as SCR 54 in the 1973 session. See also *CPER,* no. 17 (June 1973), p. 32.

48. *CTA Action,* 10 September 1971.

49. *Ibid.,* 23 March 1974.

50. *Ibid.,* 8 November 1974.

51. *California State Employee,* 20 September 1974; *ibid.,* 18 October 1974.

52. Tom Goff, "Brown Gets Backing of 2nd Law Group, Hits Reagan Policies," *Los Angeles Times,* 29 September 1974.

53. Bill Hazlett, "Police League Members Step Up Recall Drive," *ibid.,* 3 November 1974.

54. Statement by Capt. Alfred K. Whitehead, president of the local, in *Los Angeles Fire Fighters* (July 1971).

55. *Ibid.*
56. *Los Angeles County Employee,* 15 May 1973; *ibid.,* 15 June 1973.
57. *Ibid.,* 15 May 1974; *ibid.,* 15 October 1974.
58. Bill Boyarsky and Harry Bernstein, *Los Angeles Times,* 25 April 1973.
59. Frank P. Sherwood and Beatrice Markey, *The Mayor and the Fire Chief* (Inter-university case program, no. 43, University of Alabama Press, 1959); California State Federation of Labor, *Proceedings* (1956), pp. 209-210, 271, 274, 299.
60. Gerald Faris, *Los Angeles Times,* part XI, 26 August 1973.
61. City-County of San Francisco, Registrar of Voters, Records. The Transport Workers' Union was listed for two contributions, one of $5,000 and another of $6,000. The combined sum was the second largest amount received by Alioto from union sources, although the Laborers Union No. 261, the Seafarers Union, and the Teamsters Joint Council No. 7 each gave $5,000.
62. The statement of receipts filed by Mayor Yorty with the City Clerk listed $190,320.75. The Fire and Police Protective League, Police Chapter, was listed for $2,000; the Los Angeles Water and Power Defense League for $1,200; and United Fire Fighters of L.A., L.A. City Employees Local 347, and the Architects and Engineers Association for unspecified amounts.

The statement of receipts filed by Councilman Bradley with the City Clerk totaled $263,660. Bill Boyarsky, political writer for the *Los Angeles Times,* writing about the mayoralty primary said, "The campaign reports that the Los Angeles Fire and Police Protective League, traditional source of police and fire personnel's political strength in the city, donated $4,000 to Yorty. This is one of the first indications of political activity on behalf of the mayor by the league, which in the past always had insisted it did not back individual candidates for election, just matters like ballot measures that improved their wages and working conditions. The political situation is complicated in the police and fire field. Firemen, affiliated with the AFL-CIO, have endorsed Bradley," *Los Angeles Times,* 14 May 1973.

63. Statements filed with the San Diego City Clerk's office.
64. Sacramento City Clerk Records.
65. The Los Angeles County Registrar of Voters Records.
66. Doug Shuit, "Union Backs Edelman with Funds, Workers," *Los Angeles Times,* 29 October 1974; Shuit, "Ferraro Gets $500,000 and Edelman $350,000," *ibid.,* 2 November 1974.
67. Louise Ma, "The New Disclosure Law: Charting the Complex Flow of Campaign Contributions," *California Journal* (September 1974), pp. 297-300; Nancy Boyarsky, "Proposition 9: The Local-Government Loopholes," *ibid.,* pp. 301-303.

The Waxman-Dymally Campaign Disclosure Act (*Cal. Stats.* [1963], ch. 1186; *California Election Code,* sects. 11500 et seq.) tightened considerably the requirements for reporting state campaign contributions and expenditures, provided for auditing of returns, and strengthened enforcement. The Political Reform Act of 1974, presented to the voters by initiative petition and adopted by a large vote, restated some of the Waxman-Dymally provisions for reporting, placed limitations on amounts spent for state-wide candidates and ballot measures, and established a Fair Political Practices Commission to provide assistance in enforcing provisions of the act. The act adds title 9 to the *Government Code.*

68. Statements filed with the County Registrar of Voters in each county.
69. Statements filed with the Secretary of State, 1974; California, Fair Political Practices Commission, *Campaign Contribution and Spending Report,* November 2, 1976 *General Election* (1977).

70. Abood v. Detroit Board of Education, Supreme Court of the United States, case no. 75-1153 (23 May 1977). The opinion of the Court and three concurring opinions are reprinted verbatim in *CPER,* no. 34 (September 1977), pp. 63-77. The subject is noted in Bonnie G. Cebulski, "The Agency Shop: California Perspectives on a Landmark Decision," *CPER,* no. 34, pp. 2-8.

71. "Project: Collective Bargaining and Politics in Public Employment," 19 *UCLA Law Review* 1041 (August 1972).

72. Harry H. Wellington and Ralph K. Winter Jr., *The Unions and the Cities* (Washington, D.C.: The Brookings Institution, 1971), pp. 29-32; Robert Dubin, *Working Union-Management Relations: The Sociology of Industrial Relations* (Englewood Cliffs: Prentice-Hall, 1958), pp. 153-163.

73. The Legislature amended the Brown Act to permit governing bodies to meet in executive session for purposes of instructing its representative on bargaining matters. The Rodda Act considers the problem more forthrightly. It requires employee organizations and governing boards alike to state their bargaining proposals in a public session prior to bargaining, which may then be conducted in secret. Employer approval of a negotiated agreement must be adopted by the governing body in a public session.

VIII: POLICY CONCERNING PUBLIC EMPLOYEE STRIKES

1. Bonnie G. Cebulski, "An Analysis of 22 Illegal Strikes and California Law," *California Public Employee Report (CPER),* no. 18 (August 1973), pp. 2-17.

2. Bonnie G. Cebulski, "A Five-Year Study of California Public Employee Strikes," *CPER,* no. 25 (June 1975), pp. 2-5.

3. Nutter v. City of Santa Monica, 72 Cal. App. 2d 292, 168 P2s 741 (1939). The state Supreme Court declined to accept an appeal.

4. City of Los Angeles v. Los Angeles Building and Construction Trades Council, 94 Cal. App. 2d 36, 41; 210 P2d 303 (1949).

5. State v. Brotherhood of Railway Trainmen, 27 Cal. 2d 412; 232 P2d 857 (1951). California v. Taylor et al., 353 U.S. 553 (1957).

6. Los Angeles Metropolitan Transit Authority v. Brotherhood of Railway Trainmen, 54 Cal. 2d 684; 355 P2d 905 (1960). Justice Schauer dissented.

7. An edited version of the memorandum opinion in case no. 312056, County of San Diego, appears in *CPER,* no. 2 (August 1969), pp. 51-54.

8. City of San Diego v. AFSCME Local 127, 8 Cal. App. 3d 308, 87 Cal. Rptr. 258 (1970). The state Supreme Court declined to hear an appeal, three justices dissenting from this action.

9. Almond v. County of Sacramento, 276 Cal. App. 2d 32; 80 Cal. Rptr. 518 (1969). The state Supreme Court declined to hear an appeal, three justices dissenting from this action.

10. Los Angeles Unified School District v. United Teachers: Los Angeles, 24 Cal. App. 3d 142 (1972).

11. Grasko v. Los Angeles City Board of Education, 31 Cal. App. 3d 290 (1973).

12. City and County of San Francisco et al. v. Cooper, S.F. 23210, filed 4 April 1975. An edited text appears in *CPER,* no. 25 (June 1975), pp. 49-56.

13. SB 949, 1941 Session. Senator J. H. Williams, author.

14. The Meyers-Milias-Brown Act (1968). *California Government Code,* secs. 3500-3511.

15. Assembly Advisory Council on Public Employee Relations, *Report and Proposed Statute* (Sacramento, 1973), pp. 228-229.

16. *New York Times,* 25 September 1975.

17. The principal example cited by those who hold this view is the Condon-Wadlin Act of New York state which required public jurisdictions to dismiss striking workers and required that wage increases be withheld for three years from any employee rehired after being thus dismissed. Local officials generally ignored the provisions as being unworkable. The act was replaced by the Taylor Act in 1968.

18. The League of California Cities, at its 1975 convention, adopted a resolution opposing compulsory arbitration.

19. Almond v. County of Sacramento, 276 Cal. App. 2d 32; 80 Cal. Rptr. 318 (1969).

20. East Bay Municipal Employees Union v. Alameda County, 3 Cal. App. 3d 578; 83 Cal. Rptr. 503 (1970).

21. Social Workers Union 535 v. Los Angeles County, 270 Cal. App. 2d 65; 75 Cal. Rptr. 566 (1969).

22. *Sacramento Valley Union Labor Bulletin* (3 February 1967).

23. *Ibid.* (19 February 1967).

24. *Sacramento Bee,* 25 January 1967.

25. *Ibid.,* 26 January 1967.

26. *Ibid.,* 27 January 1967.

27. *Ibid.,* 30 January 1967.

28. *Ibid.,* 1 February 1967.

29. *Ibid.,* 2 February 1967.

30. *Ibid.,* 7 February 1967.

31. *Ibid.,* 2 March 1967.

32. Almond v. County of Sacramento, *op. cit.*

33. In re Barry, 68 Cal. App. 2d 137, 436 P2d 273 (1968).

34. Information drawn from an unpublished memorandum dated 14 October 1975 by the chief city negotiator; news stories in the *San Francisco Chronicle* and *San Francisco Examiner* during the strike and the mayoral election, and "Police and Firefighters' Strike in San Francisco," *CPER,* no. 27 (December 1975), pp. 19-25.

35. California, 53 *Attorney General's Opinions* 423, no. 70-147 (1970).

36. California State Assembly, Veto Message, Assembly bill no. 378; *Assembly Journal* (9 July 1971), p. 6727. The vote in the Assembly was 55-0; that in the Senate was 29-0. No motion to override the veto was offered.

37. California State Legislature, Legislative Counsel opinion no. 17525 (10 September 1974). Full text given in *CPER,* no. 23 (December 1974), pp. 110-111.

38. Bonnie G. Cebulski and Clara Stern, "A Five-Year Study of California Public Employee Strikes," *CPER,* no. 25 (August 1975), p. 5.

39. Donald Wollett, "Mutual Anxiety: A California Proposal." 96 *Monthly Labor Review* 51-52 (September 1973); Merton C. Bernstein, "Alternatives to the Strike in Public Labor Relations," 85 *Harvard Law Review* 459 (1971).

40. J. Joseph Loewenberg and Michael H. Moskow, *Collective Bargaining in Government: Readings and Cases* (Englewood Cliffs, N.J.: Prentice-Hall, 1972), pp. 145-202.

41. Lee Austin, "Landmark Ruling OKs Suit Over Teacher Walkout," *Los Angeles Times,* 11 August 1977.

IX: AN EMERGING POLICY

1. David A. Braybrooke and Charles A. Lindblom, *A Strategy of Decision: Policy Evaluation as a Social Process* (New York: Free Press of Glencoe, 1963), pp. 73-75. Lindblom also discusses a similar theme in *The Policymaking Process* (Englewood Cliffs, N.J.: Prentice-Hall, 1968); and "The Science of 'Muddling Through,'" *Public Administration Review* (Spring 1959), pp. 59-88.

2. Remarks by Gordon H. Winton, Jr. at a conference on employment relations legislation in Los Angeles, 30 March 1971.

3. Berkeley Teachers Association v. Berkeley Federation of Teachers, 254 Cal. App. 2d 660, 62 Cal. Rptr. 515 (1967).

4. West Valley Federation of Teachers, Local 1953 v. Campbell Union High School District, 24 Cal. App. 3d 297, 101 Cal. Rptr. 83 (1972).

5. "Preserve California's Winton Act," *California School Boards* (March 1973), pp. 10-13; testimony of CSBA President Bob Stafford before the Assembly Advisory Council on Public Employer-Employee Relations on 28 July 1972.

6. "Preserve California's Winton Act," p. 12.

7. The California School Board Association plan is discussed in 5 *Pacific Law Journal* 718.

8. *Sacramento Bee,* 11 September 1973.

9. William Barton, "SB 160: Its Evolution," *California School Boards* (November 1975), p. 4.

10. AB 4114 (Vasconcellos) became ch. 1154 of *Cal. Stats.* (1974). This bill passed the Assembly 46 to 7 and the Senate by a tally of 21 to 10.

11. This strategy has been discussed by Senator Rodda and John Bukey in speeches to groups interested in the implementation of the acts.

12. Statement by George Milias at a conference sponsored by the UCLA Institute of Industrial Relations in August 1970. The Democrats organized the Assembly in 1968 but Speaker Unruh appointed Milias, a Republican, to a committee chairmanship. The Democratic and Republican strength was evenly split in the Senate. The name Meyers-Milias-Brown Act, was intended to allocate credit. Assemblyman Charles Meyers, a San Francisco Democrat, had introduced numerous bills for employee organizations. Milias was the chairman of the committee handling this bill, and George Brown, a former Democratic Assemblyman, was the author of the first legislation on employee relations.

13. California Senate *Journal,* 1 August 1968.

14. California Assembly *Journal* (1968), pp. 7080-7084.

15. Joseph R. Grodin, "Public Employee Bargaining in California: The Meyers-Milias-Brown Act in the Courts." *CPER,* no. 12 (March 1972), pp. 2-24. Justice Tobriner noted that such terms as "wages, hours, and other terms and conditions of employment" in the MMBA were taken directly from the NLRA, and justified the use of precedents interpreting the latter to guide the state Supreme Court in its decision in the Vallejo arbitration case. (IAFF v. City of Vallejo, 12 C. 3d 608 [1974]).

16. Grodin, *op. cit.*

17. Marion Ross, "Implementation of the Meyers-Milias-Brown Act by California's Counties and Larger Cities," *CPER,* no. 8 (March 1971), p. 6.

18. See Reginald H. Alleyne, Jr., "The Administering Agency in California Public Employee Relations: Purposes and Structure," *CPER,* no. 14 (August 1972), pp. 2-10.

19. Grodin, *op. cit.*

20. Joseph R. Grodin, "California Public Employee Bargaining Revisited: The MMB Act in the Appellate Courts," *CPER,* no. 21 (June 1974), pp. 2-20.

21. Los Angeles County Firefighters Local 1014 v. City of Monrovia, 24 Cal. App. 3d 289, 101 Cal. Rptr. 78 (1972).

22. Operating Engineers Local Union no. 3 v. Madera County, reproduced in *CPER,* no. 16 (March 1973), pp. 57-59.

23. LACEA Local 660 v. County of Los Angeles, 33 Cal. App. 3d 1, 108 Cal. Rptr. 625 (1973).

24. Social Workers Union, Local 535 v. Alameda County Welfare Department, 11 Cal. 3d 382 (1974). Also reported in *CPER,* no. 21 (June 1974), pp. 64-66.

25. Firefighters Local 1186 v. City of Vallejo, 12 C 3d 608, 116 Cal Rptr. 507 (1974). Reproduced in *CPER,* no. 23 (December 1974), pp. 95-100. The court membership was unanimous in this case.

26. Glendale City Employees Association v. City of Glendale, 15 C. 3d 328, 124 Cal. Rptr. 513 (1975).

27. Los Angeles County, Personnel Department, *Employee Relations Basic Data,* 5th ed. (1975-76).

28. David Lewin, "Local Government Labor Relations in Transition: The Case of Los Angeles," 17 *Labor History* 191-213 (Spring 1976).

29. Data drawn from Personnel Department Report, *op. cit.*

30. The Public Commission on Los Angeles County Government, *To Serve Seven Million* (Los Angeles: 1976).

31. Los Angeles County Citizens Economy and Efficiency Commission, Civil Service-Employee Relations Task Force, *Civil Service and Collective Bargaining in Los Angeles County Government* (Los Angeles: 1973), pp. 78-81.

32. Los Angeles County v. LACEA-SEIU 660; *CPER,* no. 18 (August 1973), pp. 47-49; Los Angeles County Citizens Commission on Efficiency and Economy, *op. cit.,* pp. 81-87.

33. Los Angeles City Ordinance no. 141, 527, adopted 29 January 1971 and amended in February and April 1973.

34. Similar language was used to assure members of community college senates' faculty councils that those bodies could continue to advise district administrations on academic policies, if the advice did not conflict with collective agreements.

35. House Resolution 530, 1968 sess. Adopted 30 July 1968.

36. California State Personnel Board, *Report on Employee Relations in Civil Service* (24 January 1969). Reprinted in *GERR,* no. 285 (24 February 1969).

37. Executive Order no. R-25-71. Reprinted in *CPER,* no. 9 (June 1971), p. 49.

38. *CPER,* no. 14 (August 1972), pp. 19-22.

39. Memorandum issued by James G. Stearns to all agency secretaries and department directors, 1 December 1972.

40. *CPER,* no. 16 (March 1973), pp. 47-48.

41. *CPER,* no. 18 (August 1973), pp. 29-30. An administration representative indicated, however, that SB 32 by Senator Ralph Dills, pertaining to local government employment, was acceptable.

42. *Cal. Stats.* (1974), ch. 374. SB 1764 became the Berryhill Total Compensation Act.

43. *CPER,* no. 24 (March 1975), pp. 70-71.

44. *CPER,* no. 27 (December 1975), pp. 69-70.

45. SB 839 (1977), Senator Ralph Dills (D) of Los Angeles County, author.

INDEX